Stochastic Network Calculus

Yuming Jiang · Yong Liu

Stochastic Network Calculus

 Springer

Yuming Jiang, BSc, MEng, PhD
Department of Telematics
Norwegian University of Science
    and Technology
Trondheim
Norway

Yong Liu, BEng, MEng, PhD
Optical Networks Lab
Department of Electrical and Computer
    Engineering
National University of Singapore
Singapore

ISBN: 978-1-84996-732-7   e-ISBN: 978-1-84800-127-5
DOI: 10.1007/978-1-84800-127-5

British Library Cataloguing in Publication Data
A catalogue record for this book is available from the British Library

Printed on acid-free paper

Springer Science+Business Media
springer.com

To our families

Preface

Network calculus is a theory dealing with queuing systems found in computer networks. Its focus is on performance guarantees. Central to the theory is the use of alternate algebras such as the min-plus algebra to transform complex network systems into analytically tractable systems. To simplify the analysis, another idea is to characterize traffic and service processes using various bounds. Since its introduction in the early 1990s, network calculus has developed along two tracks—deterministic and stochastic. This book is devoted to summarizing results for stochastic network calculus that can be employed in the design of computer networks to provide stochastic service guarantees.

Overview and Goal

Like conventional queuing theory, stochastic network calculus is based on properly defined traffic models and service models. However, while in conventional queuing theory an arrival process is typically characterized by the inter-arrival times of customers and a service process by the service times of customers, the arrival process and the service process are modeled in network calculus respectively by some arrival curve that (maybe probabilistically) upper-bounds the cumulative arrival and by some service curve that (maybe probabilistically) lower-bounds the cumulative service. The idea of using bounds to characterize traffic and service was initially introduced for deterministic network calculus. It has also been extended to stochastic network calculus by exploiting the stochastic nature of arrival and service processes. While stochastic network calculus can be considered as generalized from deterministic network calculus, this generalization is not straightforward. Deterministic network calculus is based on a worst-case analysis that usually does not need to worry about the stochastic behavior of traffic and service. On the other hand, stochastic network calculus must take into consideration in the analysis the stochastic characteristics of traffic and service processes to better make use of their statistical multiplexing gains. For example, while independent case analysis is not considered in deterministic network calculus, it is critical in stochastic network calculus since it can usually provide much better results.

The main goal of this book is to summarize results for stochastic service guarantee analysis using the theory of stochastic network calculus. Since many networks (such as wireless networks) provide only stochastic service guarantees, and many applications (such as multimedia applications) perform well with stochastic service guarantees, the results in this book will be useful for analysis and provision of service guarantees in such network scenarios.

Structure

This book is structured as follows. Chapter 1 gives an introduction to the basic properties required from a theory for tractable performance analysis of computer networks. Also in this chapter, the background knowledge useful for helping understand the rest of the book is presented. Chapter 2 reviews fundamental concepts and results of deterministic network calculus. They include the arrival curve traffic model, the service curve server model, and the basic properties supported by deterministic network calculus. From Chapter 3 to Chapter 9, we focus on introducing important concepts and results in the context of stochastic network calculus. Specifically, Chapter 3 introduces various stochastic traffic models and their relationships with each other as well as with some well-known traffic models such as the effective bandwidth model. Chapter 4 defines stochastic server models for stochastic network calculus and introduces their relationships with each other. Chapter 5 summarizes the basic properties of stochastic network calculus under different combinations of traffic and server models introduced in Chapters 3 and 4, that are obtained without considering the possible independence of arrival and service processes. Chapter 6 focuses on independent case analysis, under which the basic properties of stochastic network calculus under different combinations of traffic and server models are presented. In Chapter 7, the analysis is on stochastic service guarantees under different scheduling disciplines. Also in this chapter, an application using the analysis results in admission control is presented. In Chapter 8, stochastic network calculus is extended and applied to study to the extent to which a flow becomes non-conformant with respect to its initial traffic characterization after it passes through a network. Finally, in Chapter 9, the theory of stochastic network calculus is applied to study generalized processor sharing systems with long-range dependent traffic inputs. In order to provide a more complete picture of the field, an appendix is presented that summarizes the book and discusses open research challenges in the area of stochastic network calculus.

Use of the Book

This book presents an overall picture of the state of the art of stochastic service guarantee analysis and a comprehensive treatment of this active research area. The content of the book can be divided into two parts. The first part, consisting of Chapters 1 to 6, provides the main set of results. The second part, Chapters 7 to 9, extends the first part with more results and example applications of stochastic network calculus. In the appendix, a comprehensive discussion of open research challenges in the area of stochastic network calculus is provided. The book can be used in advanced undergraduate or graduate courses on performance evaluation of computer networks. Such a course should cover the full first part of the book, which provides a first course on stochastic network calculus. The second part can be used flexibly, where each chapter is self-contained. In addition, researchers in the area of performance evaluation of computer networks and provision and analysis of service guarantees in computer networks can also benefit from the comprehensive discussion of stochastic service guarantee issues in this book.

Notes and Acknowledgments

Part of content of this book has been lectured by the first author in two graduate courses related to traffic analysis of communication networks at the Norwegian University of Science and Technology since 2006. Many results in the book are based on works authored or co-authored by the two authors. We would like to thank other people who have contributed to these works. They include Dr. Peder J. Emstad, Dr. Markus Fidler, Dr. Shengming Jiang, Ms. Anne Nevin, Dr. Victor F. Nicola, Dr. Chunming Qiao, Dr. Chen-Khong Tham, Dr. Ian L.-J. Thng, Dr. Qinghe Yin, and Dr. Xiang Yu. In addition, we would like to thank the publisher and Ms. Catherine Brett and Mr. Wayne Wheeler there for their patience, support, and help.

Trondheim, April 2008   *Yuming Jiang*
Singapore, April 2008   *Yong Liu*

Contents

List of Figures

List of Tables

1

Introduction

Network calculus is a theory dealing with queuing systems found in computer networks. Specifically, network calculus is a theory for delay and other service guarantee analysis of computer networks. Its essential idea is to use alternate algebras, particularly the min-plus algebra and max-plus algebra, [6] to transform complex non-linear network systems into analytically tractable linear systems. Since its introduction in the early 1990s [28][29][138], network calculus has developed along two tracks—deterministic and stochastic. Deterministic network calculus has been employed in the design of computer networks to provide deterministic service guarantees for regulated flows. Excellent books summarizing results for deterministic network calculus are available [18][92]. However, service guarantees are typically required by multimedia flows in the network [42][43], which often can tolerate some amount of loss or (excess) delay. For such flows, the provision of stochastic service guarantees is more important because stochastic service guarantees can make better use of the multiplexing gain in the network. This is where stochastic network calculus makes an appearance. In addition, many networks, such as wireless networks and multi-access networks, may only provide stochastic service guarantees. In wireless networks, the capacity of a wireless channel varies over time in a random manner due to channel impairment, contention, and other causes. In multi-access networks such as CSMA (carrier sense multiple access) networks, the server capacity seen by a user is highly dependent on the traffic characteristics of other users. For the analysis and provision of service guarantees in such networks, stochastic network calculus becomes even more important.

This book is devoted to summarizing results for stochastic network calculus and organized as follows. The first chapter gives an introduction to service guarantee analysis, the basic properties required from a theory for tractable analysis of computer networks, and the mathematical background used in the book. The second chapter introduces fundamental concepts and results of deterministic network calculus. The concepts include arrival curve, service curve, and strict service curve. The results include the basic properties supported by deterministic network calculus. Starting in Chapter 3, we

Y. Jiang, Y. Liu, *Stochastic Network Calculus*,
DOI: 10.1007/978-1-84800-127-5_1,

introduce fundamental concepts and results for stochastic network calculus. Specifically, Chapter 3 introduces traffic models for stochastic network calculus and their relations with each other as well as with some well-known traffic models such as the effective bandwidth model. Chapter 4 defines server models for stochastic network calculus and introduces their relations with each other. Chapter 5 summarizes results related to the basic properties for stochastic network calculus under different combinations of traffic and server models introduced in Chapters 2 to 4. These results are presented without considering the possible independence of flows and servers. Similar to Chapter 5, Chapter 6 also presents results under various combinations of traffic and server models. The key difference between these two chapters is that Chapter 6 is devoted to independent case analysis, where flows and service processes are independent. From Chapter 7 to Chapter 9, several extensions and/or applications of stochastic network calculus are presented under different network cases. The appendix summarizes the book and discusses open research challenges in the area.

1.1 Quality of Service Guarantees

With the development and deployment of multimedia and network technologies, multimedia has become an indispensable feature on the Internet. Multimedia applications such as Internet telephony and Internet video make diverse requirements on the services provided by the network. Quality of Service (QoS) refers to the nature of the packet delivery service provided by the network and is the collective effect of service performances determining the degree of satisfaction of a user of the service.

A quality of service guarantee, or service guarantee for short, is either deterministic or stochastic.[1] A *deterministic service guarantee* guarantees that all packets of a flow arrive at the destination within its required performance measures such as throughput, delay, and loss bounds. While such deterministic service provides the highest QoS level, its most important drawback is that it must reserve network resources based on the worst-case scenario and hence leaves a significant portion of network resources unused on average. A *stochastic service guarantee* allows the QoS objectives specified by a flow to be guaranteed with a probability smaller than one. By allowing some packets to violate the required QoS measures, stochastic service guarantees can better exploit the statistical multiplexing gain at network links and hence improve network utilization.

A deterministic service guarantee may be modeled such that the experienced service must never be worse than the desired service, which may be expressed in the following form:

---

[1] The literature also uses *statistical service guarantee* or *probabilistic service guarantee* rather than the stochastic service guarantee in this book.

$$\text{Pr}\left\{\text{Experienced service is not worse than desired service}\right\} = 1. \qquad (1.1)$$

Many methods have been proposed in the literature to derive the worst-case bounds. The works, including [28][29][15][18][19] on deterministic QoS guarantee analysis, have been developed into an elegant theory under the name of network calculus [92], which will be referred to as *deterministic network calculus* in this book.

Similarly, a stochastic service guarantee may be expressed as

$$\text{Pr}\left\{\text{Experienced service is worse than desired service}\right\} \leq \varepsilon, \qquad (1.2)$$

where ε is the permissible probability that a packet violates the desired performance [42][43]. It can be seen that the deterministic service guarantee is a special case of the stochastic service guarantee with $\varepsilon = 0$ in (1.2). The focus of this book is on stochastic service guarantee analysis.

1.2 Basic Properties for Network Analysis

A computer network consists of data flows and network elements. Correspondingly, a theory for network analysis is typically built on two fundamental concepts: *traffic model* and *server model*. A traffic model characterizes the traffic behavior of a flow, and a server model characterizes the service behavior of a network element.

In order to easily apply a theory to network analysis, its traffic models and server models should satisfy some basic properties. The requirement of these basic properties is illustrated in the following example.

Consider a simple network domain consisting of three network nodes $S1$—$S3$ and three flows $F1$—$F3$, as shown in Figure 1.1. Assume $F1$ and $F2$ belong to the same traffic class and share the same edge-to-edge path crossing the network domain. At the second node $S2$, there is a crossing flow $F3$ that shares the server capacity of $S2$ with $F1$ and $F2$. Suppose we are interested in and want to analyze the edge-to-edge delay performance of the path on which $F1$ and $F2$ cross the network. While there can be many approaches to the analysis, the following is an intuitively simple one.

First, a certain traffic model $\mathcal{AM}$ and a certain server model $\mathcal{SM}$ should be properly chosen to represent flows and nodes, so that single-node analysis can be conducted to obtain the delay performance of a flow crossing the node. In addition, the single-node analysis should also give the characterization of the output, which can be represented with the same traffic model $\mathcal{AM}$, so that the single-node delay analysis can be repeatedly extended to a sequence of nodes. Given these, third in the simple approach, since $F1$ and $F2$ belong to the same traffic class and share the same path, an immediate idea is to use an aggregate flow $F1, 2$ to represent the two flows before entering the first node $S1$. This implicitly requires that the aggregate flow $F1, 2$ be represented using characteristics of both $F1$ and $F2$. With the first point in mind, the aggregate

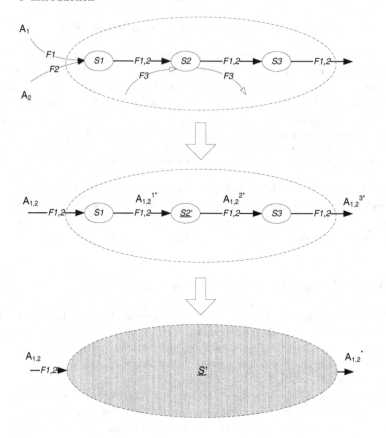

Fig. 1.1. Analysis of a simple network

flow $F1,2$ should be represented using the same traffic model $\mathcal{AM}$ as $F1$ and $F2$. Fourth, at the second node, the aggregate flow $F1,2$ is competing for service capacity with the crossing flow $F3$. A simple way for analysis is to find an equivalent server $S2'$ for the aggregate flow $F1,2$. Under this equivalent server, the aggregate flow is the only input and there is no crossing traffic. Again with the first point in mind, the equivalent server should be represented using the same server model $\mathcal{SM}$ as $S2$ and other nodes. Now, as shown by the middle figure of Figure 1.1, the network is simplified to a sequence of (possibly equivalent) servers on which the node-by-node analysis can be conducted to obtain the delay performance at each node on the path. Then, the edge-to-edge delay performance can be easily derived from the delay performance at each node. However, this is not the end since, as will be shown later (e.g., see Chapter 2), the results from node-by-node analysis can often be significantly improved if the so-called concatenation property exists. This property tells us that the concatenation of nodes can be treated as an equivalent node. As shown by the lower figure of Figure 1.1, with the concatenation property, based on the middle figure, the network can be treated as a single black box node. By applying single-node analysis to the black-box, the desired edge-to-edge delay result is derived, which can be much better than the result obtained from the node-by-node analysis.

In summary, as discussed in the above example, a theory should ideally have the following five basic properties (P.1)—(P.5) to ease tractable network analysis.

- (P.1) – *Service Guarantees*
  Under a chosen traffic model and a chosen server model, single-node stochastic service guarantees such as backlog and delay guarantees can be derived.
- (P.2) – *Output Characterization*
  The output of a flow from a server can be represented using the same traffic model as for the input flow.
- (P.3) – *Concatenation Property*
  The concatenation of servers can be represented using the same server model.
- (P.4) – *Leftover Service*
  The service available to a flow at a server with competing flows can be represented using the same server model.
- (P.5) – *Superposition Property*:
  The superposition of flows can be represented using the same traffic model.

In traditional queuing theory, many models have been proposed to characterize arrival and service. Examples are Poisson arrival processes and service processes with negative exponentially distributed service times for $M/M/1$ systems. Also, a lot of results for single-node systems are available, which correspond to (P.1). Many results are also available from traditional queuing theory that corresponding to (P.5), particularly when sources are independent. For example, the aggregate of two Poisson arrival processes, if they are independent, results in a new Poisson arrival process. Under certain conditions, the output of an $M/M/1$ system can be considered to have a Poisson arrival process, which corresponds to (P.2). However, it is generally hard to conclude that the output can be represented using the same arrival process as the input in traditional queuing theory. In addition, very few results have so far been derived for (P.3) and (P.4) in traditional queuing theory. This partly explains why it is difficult to apply traditional queuing theory to network analysis.

Throughout the rest of this book, we will see that with the five basic properties (P.1)—(P.5), network service guarantee analysis can be conducted. Unless specially highlighted, the networks considered in this book are *feedforward networks* where there are no feedback flows.

1.3 Notation and Mathematical Background

In this book, we consider a discrete time domain with a unit discretization step. We adopt the convention that a packet is considered to be received by a network element when and only when its last bit has arrived at the network element, and a packet is considered out of a network element when and only when its last bit has been transmitted by the network element. A packet can be served only when its last bit has arrived. All queues are assumed to be empty at time 0. Packets within a flow are served in first-in-first-out (FIFO) order.

1.3.1 Notation

We use various processes to model a network that is assumed to be lossless. A process is defined to be a function of time $t(\geq 0)$. It could count the (cumulative) amount of traffic (in number of bits) arriving at some network element, the amount of traffic (in number of bits) departing from the network element, the amount of service (in number of bits) provided by the network element, or the amount of service (in number of bits) that failed to be provided by the network element due to some impairment to it. In this case, we call the process (cumulative) *arrival process,* denoted by $A(t)$, (cumulative) *departure process,* denoted by $A^*(t)$, (cumulative) *service process,* $S(t)$, or (cumulative) *impairment process,* $I(t)$, respectively. We assume all such processes are defined on $t \geq 0$ and by convention have zero value at $t = 0$. We also assume these functions are left-continuous.[2]

Wherever necessary, we use subscripts to distinguish different flows and superscripts to distinguish different network elements. Specifically, A_i^h and A_i^{h*} represent the arrival and departure processes of flow i from network element h, respectively, S_i^h the service process provided to flow i by the network element, and I^h the impairment process suffered by the network element.

For any $0 \leq s \leq t$, we denote $A(s,t) \equiv A(t) - A(s)$, $A^*(s,t) \equiv A^*(t) - A^*(s)$, $S(s,t) \equiv S(t) - S(s)$, and $I(s,t) \equiv I(t) - I(s)$.

In this book, the following function sets are often used. Specifically, we denote by $\mathcal{F}$ the set of non-negative wide-sense increasing functions, where for each function $a(\cdot)$ there holds

$$\mathcal{F} = \{a(\cdot) : \forall 0 \leq x \leq y, 0 \leq a(x) \leq a(y)\}$$

and for any function $a \in \mathcal{F}$ we set $a(x) = 0$ for $\forall x < 0$.

We denote by $\bar{\mathcal{F}}$ the set of non-negative wide-sense decreasing functions where for each function $a(\cdot)$ there holds

---

[2] Whether the functions are left-continuous or right-continuous does not make any difference to the results in this book (e.g., see Chapter 1.1 of [92] for the discussion).

$$\bar{\mathcal{F}} = \{a(\cdot) : \forall 0 \leq x \leq y, 0 \leq a(y) \leq a(x)\}$$

and for any function $a \in \bar{\mathcal{F}}$ we also set $a(x) = 1$ for $\forall x < 0$.

We denote by $\bar{\mathcal{G}}$ the set of functions in $\bar{\mathcal{F}}$ where for each function $a(\cdot) \in \bar{\mathcal{G}}$ its nth-fold integration, denoted by $f^{(n)}(x) \equiv (\int_x^\infty dy)^n f(y)$, is bounded for any $x \geq 0$ and still belongs to $\bar{\mathcal{G}}$ for any $n \geq 0$, or

$$\bar{\mathcal{G}} = \{a(\cdot) : \forall n \geq 0, \left(\int_x^\infty dy\right)^n a(y) \in \bar{\mathcal{G}}\}.$$

A function a is said to be additive if and only if, for all x, y $a(x + y) = a(x) + a(y)$. The function is said to be sub-additive if and only if $a(x + y) \leq a(x) + a(y)$ for all x and y.

For any non-negative functions a, b, the following inequalities hold trivially:

$$\sup_{0 \leq y \leq x} [a(y) + b(y)] \leq \sup_{0 \leq y \leq x} a(y) + \sup_{0 \leq y \leq x} b(y), \tag{1.3}$$

$$\inf_{0 \leq y \leq x} [a(y) - b(y)] \geq \inf_{0 \leq y \leq x} a(y) - \sup_{0 \leq y \leq x} b(y). \tag{1.4}$$

By definition, $A(t)$, $A^*(t)$, $S(t)$, and $I(t)$ belong to $\mathcal{F}$. In addition, it can be shown that all the exponentially decaying functions and functions exhibiting sub-exponential decay belong to $\bar{\mathcal{G}}$.

For any random variable X, its cumulative distribution function (CDF), denoted by $F_X(x) \equiv P\{X \leq x\}$, belongs to $\mathcal{F}$ and its complementary cumulative distribution function (CCDF), denoted by $\bar{F}_X \equiv P\{X > x\}$, belongs to $\bar{\mathcal{F}}$.

The *conventional convolution* of two functions a, b is defined as

$$(a \circledast b)(x) = \int_{-\infty}^\infty a(x - y)b(y)dy,$$

and the *Stieltjes convolution* of two functions a, b is defined as

$$(a * b)(x) = \int_{-\infty}^\infty a(x - y)db(y).$$

We use $[\cdot]^+$ to express the maximum of 0 and a given number, or $[x]^+ \equiv \max\{x, 0\}$. We shall also use $[\cdot]_1$ to denote the minimum of 1 and the given number, i.e., $[x]_1 \equiv \min\{x, 1\}$.

For service guarantee analysis of a system, which could be a network element or a network of elements, we are mainly interested in the *backlog* and *delay*, which are defined as follows [30][18][92]:

Definition 1.1. *Let $A(t)$ and $A^*(t)$ respectively be the arrival process and departure process of a lossless system. The backlog $B(t)$ in the system at time $t \geq 0$ is defined as*

$$B(t) = A(t) - A^*(t).$$

Assuming first-in-first-out (FIFO) ordering, the delay $D(t)$ at time $t \geq 0$ is defined as

$$D(t) = \inf\{d \geq 0 : A(t) \leq A^*(t + d)\}.$$

1.3.2 Min-Plus Algebra Basics

In conventional algebra, addition + and multiplication × are the two most common operations on elements of $\mathcal{R} = (-\infty, +\infty)$. These two operations have a number of properties, such as the closure property, associativity, commutativity, and distributivity, which make the algebraic structure $(\mathcal{R}, +, \times)$ a commutative field.

In min-plus algebra, an algebra structure of interest is $(\mathcal{R} \cup \{+\infty\}, \wedge, +)$. Here, the "addition" operation is $\wedge$ and the "multiplication" operation is $+$, where $\wedge$ denotes the *infimum* or, when it exists, the *minimum*. It can be verified that $(\mathcal{R} \cup \{+\infty\}, \wedge, +)$ has the following properties, and it is called a commutative dioid with zero element $\bar{e} = +\infty$ and identity element $\mathbf{e} = 0$:

- Closure property: $\forall a, b \in (\mathcal{R} \cup \{+\infty\})$, $a \wedge b \in (\mathcal{R} \cup \{+\infty\})$; $a + b \in (\mathcal{R} \cup \{+\infty\})$.
- Associativity: $\forall a, b \in (\mathcal{R} \cup \{+\infty\})$, $(a \wedge b) \wedge c = a \wedge (b \wedge c)$; $(a + b) + c = a + (b + c)$.
- Commutativity: $\forall a, b \in (\mathcal{R} \cup \{+\infty\})$, $a \wedge b = b \wedge a$; $a + b = b + a$.
- Distributivity: $\forall a, b, c \in (\mathcal{R} \cup \{+\infty\})$, $(a \wedge b) + c = (a + b) \wedge (b + c)$.
- Zero element: $\forall a \in (\mathcal{R} \cup \{+\infty\})$, $a \wedge \bar{e} = a$.
- Absorbing zero element: $\forall a \in (\mathcal{R} \cup \{+\infty\})$, $a + \bar{e} = \bar{e} + a = \bar{e}$.
- Identity element: $\forall a \in (\mathcal{R} \cup \{+\infty\})$, $a + \mathbf{e} = \mathbf{e} + a = a$.
- Idempotency of addition: $\forall a \in (\mathcal{R} \cup \{+\infty\})$, $a \wedge a = a$.

For functions in min-plus algebra, the following operations are often used.

The *pointwise infimum*, or *pointwise minimum* if it exists, of functions a and b is

$$(a \wedge b)(x) = \inf[a(x), b(x)].$$

The *pointwise supremum*, or *pointwise maximum* if it exists, of functions a and b is

$$(a \vee b)(x) = \sup[a(x), b(x)].$$

The *min-plus convolution* of functions a and b is

$$(a \otimes b)(x) = \inf_{0 \leq y \leq x} [a(y) + b(x - y)],$$

where, when it applies, "infimum" should be interpreted as "minimum".

The *min-plus deconvolution* of functions a and b is

$$(a \oslash b)(x) = \sup_{y \geq 0} [a(x + y) - b(y)],$$

where, when it applies, "supremum" should be interpreted as "maximum".

It can be verified that $(\mathcal{F}, \wedge, \otimes)$ also has the following properties and is a commutative dioid with zero element $\bar{e}$ and identity element $\mathbf{e}$, where $\bar{e}(x) = +\infty$ for all $x \geq 0$ and $\mathbf{e}(x) = 0$ if $x = 0$ and otherwise $+\infty$ [6][19][92]:

- Closure property: $\forall a, b \in \mathcal{F}$, $a \wedge b \in \mathcal{F}$; $a \otimes b \in \mathcal{F}$.
- Associativity: $\forall a, b \in \mathcal{F}$, $(a \wedge b) \wedge c = a \wedge (b \wedge c)$; $(a \otimes b) \otimes c = a \otimes (b \otimes c)$.
- Commutativity: $\forall a, b \in \mathcal{F}$, $a \wedge b = b \wedge a$; $a \otimes b = b \otimes a$.
- Distributivity: $\forall a, b, c \in \mathcal{F}$, $(a \wedge b) \otimes c = (a \otimes b) \wedge (b \otimes c)$.
- Zero element: $\forall a \in \mathcal{F}$, $a \wedge \bar{\epsilon} = a$.
- Absorbing zero element: $\forall a \in \mathcal{F}$, $a \otimes \bar{\epsilon} = \bar{\epsilon} \otimes a = \bar{\epsilon}$.
- Identity element: $\forall a \in \mathcal{F}$, $a \otimes \mathbf{e} = \mathbf{e} \otimes a = a$.
- Idempotency of addition: $\forall a \in \mathcal{F}$, $a \wedge a = a$.

The following properties also hold for $(\mathcal{F}, \wedge, \otimes)$:

- Comparison: For $\forall a_1, a_2, b_1, b_2 \in \mathcal{F}$, $a_1 \otimes a_2 \leq a_1 \wedge a_2 \leq a_1 \vee a_2$.
- Monotonicity: For $\forall a_1, a_2, b_1, b_2 \in \mathcal{F}$, if $a_1 \leq b_1$ and $a_2 \leq b_2$, then $a_1 \otimes a_2 \leq b_1 \otimes b_2$; $a_1 \wedge a_2 \leq b_1 \wedge b_2$; $a_1 \vee a_2 \leq b_1 \vee b_2$.

Similarly, it can be shown that $(\bar{\mathcal{F}}, \wedge, \otimes)$ is a commutative dioid, but with zero element $\bar{\epsilon}$ and identity element $\bar{e}$, where $\bar{\epsilon}(x) = +\infty$ for all $x \geq 0$ and $\bar{e}(x) = 0$ for all $x \geq 0$. Specifically, $(\bar{\mathcal{F}}, \wedge, \otimes)$ has the following properties:

- Closure property: $\forall a, b \in \bar{\mathcal{F}}$, $a \wedge b \in \bar{\mathcal{F}}$; $a \otimes b \in \bar{\mathcal{F}}$.
- Associativity: $\forall a, b, c \in \bar{\mathcal{F}}$, $(a \wedge b) \wedge c = a \wedge (b \wedge c)$; $(a \otimes b) \otimes c = a \otimes (b \otimes c)$.
- Commutativity: $\forall a, b \in \bar{\mathcal{F}}$, $a \wedge b = b \wedge a$; $a \otimes b = b \otimes a$.
- Distributivity: $\forall a, b, c \in \bar{\mathcal{F}}$, $(a \wedge b) \otimes c = (a \otimes b) \wedge (b \otimes c)$.
- Zero element: $\forall a \in \bar{\mathcal{F}}$, $a \wedge \bar{\epsilon} = a$.
- Absorbing zero element: $\forall a \in \bar{\mathcal{F}}$, $a \otimes \bar{\epsilon} = \bar{\epsilon} \otimes a = \bar{\epsilon}$.
- Identity element: $\forall a \in \bar{\mathcal{F}}$, $a \otimes \bar{e} = \bar{e} \otimes a = a$.
- Idempotency of addition: $\forall a \in \bar{\mathcal{F}}$, $a \wedge a = a$.
- Comparison: $a_1 \wedge a_2 \leq a_1 \vee a_2 \leq a_1 \otimes a_2$.
- Monotonicity: If $a_1 \leq b_1$ and $a_2 \leq b_2$, then $a_1 \otimes a_2 \leq b_1 \otimes b_2$; $a_1 \wedge a_2 \leq b_1 \wedge b_2$; $a_1 \vee a_2 \leq b_1 \vee b_2$.

Besides the various properties summarized above, the min-plus convolution $\otimes$ implies the following [92].

Lemma 1.2. *If a is left-continuous and b is continuous, then for any t there exists some t_0 such that*

$$a \otimes b(t) \equiv a(t - t_0) + b(t_0). \tag{1.5}$$

Additionally, it can be verified that for any functions α and β, there holds

$$(\alpha + c) \otimes \beta = \alpha \otimes \beta + c, \tag{1.6}$$

where c is any constant.

If α and β are sub-additive and $\alpha(0) = \beta(0) = 0$, there hold

$$\alpha \otimes \alpha = \alpha, \tag{1.7}$$

$$\alpha \otimes \beta = \alpha \text{ if } \alpha \leq \beta, \tag{1.8}$$

where c is any constant.

Furthermore, if functions α and β are sub-additive, so are $\alpha \otimes \beta$, $\alpha \wedge \beta$, and $\alpha \oslash \beta$.

1.3.3 Maximum Horizontal Distance and Maximum Vertical Distance

For ease of exposition of results, we adopt the following definitions [31] [92], which will be used throughout the rest of the book.

Definition 1.3. *Consider two functions $\alpha(t)$ and $\beta(t)$. The maximum horizontal distance between them, denoted by $h(\alpha, \beta)$, is defined as*

$$h(\alpha, \beta) = \sup_{s \geq 0} \{\inf \{\tau \geq 0 : \alpha(s) \leq \beta(s + \tau)\}\},$$

and the maximum vertical distance between them, denoted by $v(\alpha, \beta)$, is defined as

$$v(\alpha, \beta) = \sup_{s \geq 0} \{\alpha(s) - \beta(s)\} \equiv \alpha \oslash \beta(0).$$

Figure 1.2 illustrates these two concepts using functions $\alpha(t)$ and $\beta(t)$.

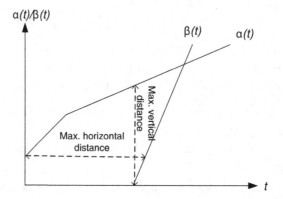

Fig. 1.2. Maximum horizontal and vertical distances between two functions

1.4 Random Variable and Stochastic Process Basics

1.4.1 Random Variables

A *random variable* X is characterized by its *cumulative distribution function* (CDF) $F_X(x)$, defined as

$$F_X(x) = P\{X \leq x\}, -\infty < x < \infty.$$

$F_X(x)$ is a non-negative, never decreasing function of x and belongs to $\mathcal{F}$. In addition, $F(-\infty) = 0$ and $F(\infty) = 1$. The *complementary cumulative distribution function* (CCDF) of the random variable X, denoted by $\bar{F}_X$, is defined as

$$\bar{F}_X = P\{X > x\}, -\infty < x < \infty.$$

It is trivial that $F_X(x) + \bar{F}_X(x) = 1$ for any x. In addition, $\bar{F}_X$ is non-negative and non-increasing, belonging to $\bar{\mathcal{F}}$. Furthermore, $\bar{F}(-\infty) = 1$ and $\bar{F}(\infty) = 0$.

The *probability density function* (pdf) of a random variable X, denoted by $f_X(x)$, is defined as

$$f_X(x) \equiv \frac{dF_X(x)}{dx}.$$

Given the probability density function of a random variable X, its cumulative distribution function is found as

$$F_X(x) = \int_{-\infty}^{x} f_X(y)dy.$$

The *moment generating function* (MGF) of a random variable X, denoted by $M_X(\theta)$, is defined as

$$M_X(\theta) \equiv E[e^{\theta X}]$$
$$= \int_{-\infty}^{\infty} e^{\theta x} f_X(x)dx,$$

where θ is a real variable.

The following inequality, known as the Chernoff bound, gives an upper bound on the CCDF of a random variable X:

$$P\{X \geq x\} \leq e^{-\theta x} E[e^{\theta X}]$$

for all $\theta \geq 0$.

Lemma 1.4. *Consider a random variable X. For any $x \geq 0$, $P\{(X)^+ > x\} = P\{X > x\}$.*

In this book, we are often concerned about the sum of a collection of random variables $\{X_i\}$, namely

$$Z = \sum_{i=1}^{n} X_i.$$

For $Z\, (= \sum_{i=1}^{n} X_i)$, if $X_1, X_2, \ldots, X_n$ are independent, it is known that

$$f_Z(z) = f_{X_1} \circledast f_{X_2} \circledast \cdots \circledast f_{X_n}(z), \tag{1.9}$$

where the convolution is commutative. In addition,

$$M_Z(\theta) = M_{X_1}(\theta) \cdot M_{X_2}(\theta) \cdots \cdots M_{X_n}(\theta). \tag{1.10}$$

In this book, corresponding to (1.9), if $X_1, X_2, \ldots, X_n$ are independent, we often use Stieltjes convolution for F_Z,

$$F_Z(z) = F_{X_1} * F_{X_2} * \cdots * F_{X_n}(z), \tag{1.11}$$

where the Stieltjes convolution is also commutative.

In addition, if $X_1, X_2, \ldots, X_n$ are possibly dependent, the following result is important.

Lemma 1.5. *For the sum of a collection of random variables $Z = \sum_{i=1}^{n} X_i$, no matter whether they are independent or not, there holds for the CCDF of Z*

$$\bar{F}_Z(z) \le \bar{F}_{X_1} \otimes \cdots \otimes \bar{F}_{X_n}(z). \tag{1.12}$$

Proof. We only prove for the sum of two random variables X_1 and X_2, and the proof can be easily extended to $n > 2$.

For any $z \ge x \ge 0$, $\{X_1 + X_2 > z\} \cap \{X_1 \le x\} \cap \{X_2 \le z - x\} = \phi$, where ϕ denotes the null set. We then have

$$\{X_1 + X_2 > z\} \subset \{X_1 > x\} \cup \{X_2 > z - x\}$$

and hence

$$P\{X_1 + X_2 > z\} \le P\{X_1 > x\} + P\{X_2 > z - x\}.$$

Since the above inequality holds for all x, $(0 \le x \le z)$, we get

$$P\{X_1 + X_2 > z\} \le \inf_{0 \le x \le z} [P\{X_1 > x\} + P\{X_2 > z - x\}]$$

or

$$\bar{F}_{X_1 + X_2}(z) \le \bar{F}_{X_1} \otimes \bar{F}_{X_2}(z).$$

While we shall mainly use forms similar to (1.12) to ease expressing results related to the sum of random variables, there are other inequalities that can be used to find upper bounds on the CCDF of Z. These inequalities can indeed be applied to all corresponding results in this book concerning the sum of multiple random variables. One of these inequalities is as follows.

Lemma 1.6. *For the sum of a collection of random variables $Z = \sum_{i=1}^{n} X_i$, no matter whether they are independent or not, there holds for the CCDF of Z*

$$\bar{F}_Z(z) \le \inf_{p_1 + \cdots + p_n = 1} \{\bar{F}_{X_1}(p_1 z) + \cdots + \bar{F}_{X_n}(p_n z)\} \tag{1.13}$$

for any $1 > p_i > 0$, $i = 1, \ldots, n$, satisfying $\sum_{i=1}^{n} p_i = 1$.

1.4.2 Stochastic Processes

A *stochastic process* $X(t)$ is a collection of random variables $\{X(t), t \in T\}$ defined for each t in the index set T. The stochastic process is similarly characterized by its *cumulative distribution function* (CDF) $F_X(x, t)$, defined as for any (allowed) t,

$$F_X(x, t) = P\{X(t) \leq x\}, -\infty < x < \infty.$$

For any t, $F_X(x, t)$ is also non-negative, never decreasing on x, and belongs to $\mathcal{F}$. In addition, $F(-\infty, t) = 0$ and $F(\infty, t) = 1$.

The *complementary cumulative distribution function* (CCDF) of the stochastic process $X(t)$ is defined as

$$\bar{F}_X(X, t) = P\{X(t) > x\}, -\infty < x < \infty.$$

For any t, $\bar{F}_X(x, t)$ is non-negative and non-increasing and belongs to $\bar{\mathcal{F}}$. In addition, $\bar{F}(-\infty, t) = 1$ and $\bar{F}(\infty, t) = 0$. Furthermore, $F_X(x, t) + \bar{F}_X(x, t) = 1$ for all x and any t.

The *probability density function* (pdf) and the *moment generating function* of a stochastic process $X(t)$ are respectively defined as

$$f_X(x, t) \equiv \frac{dF_X(x, t)}{dx}$$

and

$$M_X(\theta(t), t) \equiv E[e^{\theta(t)X(t)}]$$
$$= \int_{-\infty}^{\infty} e^{\theta(t)x} f_X(x, t) dx,$$

where $\theta(t)$ is a real variable possibly dependent on t.

A stochastic process $X(t)$ is said to be *stationary* if $F_X(x, t)$ remains unchanged when t shifts, that is, for any given constant τ, there holds

$$F_X(x, t + \tau) = F_X(x, t).$$

In the stationary case, for ease of expression, we often simply use $F_X(x)$ and $\bar{F}_X(x)$ to represent the CDF and CCDF, respectively.

1.4.3 Stochastic Ordering

For any two random variables X and Y, if $\bar{F}_X(x) \leq \bar{F}_Y(x)$ for all x, or in other words,

$$P\{X > x\} \leq P\{Y > x\} \text{ for all } x,$$

we then say X is stochastically smaller than Y [130][118], written as

$$X \leq_{st} Y.$$

The same notation applies when X and Y are random vectors.

Similarly, for any two stochastic processes $X(t)$ and $Y(t)$, we say $X(t)$ is stochastically smaller than $Y(t)$, written $X(t) \leq_{st} Y(t)$, if, for any t and all x, $P\{X(t) > x\} \leq P\{Y(t) > x\}$.

For two random variables X and Y, the following result holds [130]:

Lemma 1.7. *If $X \leq_{st} Y$, then $f(X) \leq_{st} f(Y)$ for any increasing function f.*

For the same mapping function of random variables, if these random variables are independent, the following result holds (see, e.g., Theorem 2.2.3 in [130]).

Lemma 1.8. *Let $X_1, \ldots, X_n$ be independent and $Y_1, \ldots, Y_n$ be independent. If $X_i \leq_{st} Y_i$, then for any wide-sense increasing function $\Phi(z_1, \ldots, z_n)$ on z_i $(i = 1, \ldots, n)$, there holds*

$$\Phi(X_1, \ldots, X_n) \leq_{st} \Phi(Y_1, \ldots, Y_n).$$

Example 1.9. As an example of Lemma 1.8, letting $\Phi(z_1, \ldots, z_n) = \sum_{i=1}^{n} z_i$, if $X_1, \ldots, X_n$ and $Y_1, \ldots, Y_n$ are independent and $X_i \leq_{st} Y_i$ for all $i = 1, \ldots, n$, we get $\sum_{i=1}^{n} X_i \leq_{st} \sum_{i=1}^{n} Y_i$.

Example 1.10. Let $\Phi(z_1, \ldots, z_n) = \max\{z_1, \ldots, z_n\}$, which can be verified to be wide-sense increasing on z_i. Then, from Lemma 1.8, if $X_1, \ldots, X_n$ and $Y_1, \ldots, Y_n$ are independent and $X_i \leq_{st} Y_i$ for all $i = 1, \ldots, n$, we can conclude that $\max\{X_1, \ldots, X_n\} \leq_{st} \max\{Y_1, \ldots, Y_n\}$. The conclusion holds also for mapping $\Phi(z_1, \ldots, z_n) = \min\{z_1, \ldots, z_n\}$.

For the same mapping function of random variables that are unknown if they are independent, if certain conditions hold, we have the following result (see, e.g., Theorem 2.2.4 in [130] or Theorem 4.3.3 in [108]).

Lemma 1.11. *Suppose that for random variables $\{X_1, \ldots, X_n\}$ and $\{Y_1, \ldots, Y_n\}$, there holds $\{X_1, \ldots, X_n\} \leq_{st} \{Y_1, \ldots, Y_n\}$. Then, for the mapping $Z(t) = \Phi(z_1, \ldots, z_n)$, if it is nondecreasing in $\{z_1, \ldots, z_n\}$, one has $Z'(t) \leq_{st} Z''(t)$, where $Z'(t) = \Phi(X_1, \ldots, X_n)$ and $Z'' = \Phi(Y_1, \ldots, Y_n)$.*

Example 1.12. For the mappings in Examples 1.9 and 1.10, if $\{X_1, \ldots, X_n\} \leq_{st} \{Y_1, \ldots, Y_n\}$, then, based on Lemma 1.11, the same stochastic ordering conclusions hold: i.e., $\sum_{i=1}^{n} X_i \leq_{st} \sum_{i=1}^{n} Y_i$, $\max\{X_1, \ldots, X_n\} \leq_{st} \max\{X_1, \ldots, X_n\}$, and $\min\{X_1, \ldots, X_n\} \leq_{st} \min\{X_1, \ldots, X_n\}$.

1.5 Min-Plus Linearity of Queuing Systems

Consider a lossless network queuing system with arrival process $A(t)$, service process $S(t)$, and departure process $A^*(t)$. In this system, the input is $A(t)$ and the output is $A^*(t)$.

By the definition of backlog in the system, the following relationship holds:

$$A^*(t) = A(t) - B(t). \tag{1.14}$$

The Lindley equation can be used to derive $B(t)$, which is

$$B(t) = \max\{0, B(t-1) + A(t-1,t) - S(t-1,t)\}. \tag{1.15}$$

Equation (1.15) is intuitively clear and says that the amount of traffic backlogged in the system at time t equals the amount of traffic backlogged at time $t-1$ plus the amount of traffic that arrived between $t-1$ and t minus the amount of traffic serviced between $t-1$ and t. By applying (1.15) iteratively to its right-hand side, it becomes

$$B(t) = \sup_{0 \le s \le t} \{A(s,t) - S(s,t)\}. \tag{1.16}$$

Applying (1.16) to (1.14) results in

$$A^*(t) = \inf_{0 \le s \le t} \{A(s) + S(s,t)\} = A \otimes S(t). \tag{1.17}$$

Equation (1.17) establishes the relationship between the output and the input of the queuing system considered.

Relationship (1.17) is very similar to a relationship commonly found for conventional linear communication systems where there holds

$$A^*(t) = A \circledast S(t) \tag{1.18}$$

with $S(t)$ being the impulse response of the system. For such a system, suppose $A(t) = a_1 \times A_1(t) + a_2 \times A_2(t)$ and denote by $A_i^*(t)$ the output of the system when there is only $A_i(t)$ as the input, $i = 1, 2$. The following linearity property holds: For any non-negative constants a_1 and a_2,

$$\begin{aligned} A^*(t) &= [a_1 \times A_1(t) + a_2 \times A_2(t)] \circledast S(t) \\ &= a_1 \times A_1 \circledast S(t) + a_2 \times A_2 \circledast S(t) \\ &= a_1 \times A_1^*(t) + a_2 \times A_2^*(t). \end{aligned} \tag{1.19}$$

Relationship (1.17), however, implies that the queuing system considered is non-linear in the conventional sense with the algebra structure $(\mathcal{R}, +, \times)$.

Suppose now that the input process is the min-plus addition of two processes $A_1(t)$ and $A_2(t)$ in the form

$$A(t) = (a_1 + A_1(t)) \wedge (a_2 + A_2(t)), \tag{1.20}$$

where a_1 and a_2 are any two non-negative constants. Similarly, let us denote by $A_i^*(t)$ the output of the system when there is only $A_i(t)$ as the input, $i = 1, 2$.

Then, from (1.17) and the properties of $\wedge$, $+$ and $\otimes$, we obtain the output from the system as

$$
\begin{aligned}
A^*(t) &= [(a_1 + A_1(t)) \wedge (a_2 + A_2(t))] \otimes S(t) \\
&= [(a_1 + A_1(t)) \otimes S(t)] \wedge [(a_2 + A_2(t)) \otimes S(t)] \\
&= [a_1 + A_1 \otimes S(t)] \wedge [a_2 + A_2 \otimes S(t)] \\
&= [a_1 + A_1^*(t)] \wedge [a_2 + A_2^*(t)].
\end{aligned}
\tag{1.21}
$$

Relationship (1.21) implies that the queuing system considered is linear with the min-plus algebra structure $(\mathcal{R} \cup \{+\infty\}, \wedge, +)$.

1.6 Summary and Bibliographic Comments

This chapter gives a brief introduction to network service guarantee analysis. The five basic properties needed by a theory for systematic network analysis are discussed. To help understand the analysis in the subsequent chapters, some useful notations and mathematical background are introduced that include min-plus algebra, random variable, and stochastic process basics.

The need for the five basic properties has been extensively discussed in the literature. For deterministic network calculus, a complete study of these properties can be found in [18] [92]. For stochastic network calculus, they have also been studied in the literature, although in most cases separately. For example, the superposition property, the output characterization property, and the service guarantee property were studied in [87] [138] [15]. The leftover service property was addressed in [99] [115]. The need for the concatenation property was independently discussed in [73] [24]. The initial effort of addressing the five basic properties together was made by Jiang and Emstad [73]. Jiang [69] proved for the first time all the five basic properties for both the general case and independent case under some specific traffic and server models to be introduced in Chapters 2 and 3.

The notation $(\int_x^\infty dy)^n f(y)$ and the special function set $\bar{\mathcal{G}}$ were initially introduced by Starobinski and Sidi [128] to stochastic service guarantee analysis. The requirement that functions belong to $\bar{\mathcal{G}}$ comes from relations that will be shown in Chapter 5, between the output and the input of a network element, between the delay and backlog performances and the input and the service of the network element, as well as between the service of a concatenation of network elements and the service of each network element. In this book, we often require for any order n that the multiple integral $(\int_x^\infty dy)^n f(y)$ be bounded. However, if the size of the network is known a priori, this requirement can be correspondingly relaxed for n.

Problems

1.1. Prove the properties of $(\mathcal{F}, \wedge, \otimes)$.

1.2. Prove the properties of $(\bar{\mathcal{F}}, \wedge, \otimes)$.

1.3. Prove the commutativity property of the conventional convolution operation $\circledast$.

1.4. Prove the commutativity property of the Stieltjes convolution operation $*$ when the two functions are cumulative distribution functions.

1.5. Prove Lemma 1.2.

1.6. Show the maximum horizontal and vertical distances for $\alpha(t)$ and $\beta(t)$ as shown in Figure 1.2.

1.7. Let $\alpha(t) = \min\{M + C \cdot t, \rho t + \sigma\}$ and $\beta(t) = r \cdot t + \theta$ with $r \geq \rho > 0$ and $C > \rho > 0$. Show the maximum horizontal and vertical distances for $\alpha(t)$ and $\beta(t)$.

1.8. Prove Lemma 1.4.

1.9. Prove Lemma 1.6.

1.10. Prove Lemma 1.7.

1.11. Prove Lemma 1.8.

2

Deterministic Network Calculus

This chapter introduces the basic concepts and results of deterministic network calculus. The concepts include the (deterministic) *arrival curve*, (deterministic) *service curve*, and *strict service curve*. The results include the basic properties (P.1)–(P.5) supported by deterministic network calculus using min-plus algebra.

2.1 Traffic Models

In the context of network calculus, a flow is characterized by its (cumulative) arrival process. In this section, we start with the (σ, ρ) traffic characterization initially proposed by Cruz [28] and then introduce the concept of an arrival curve that is a generalization of the (σ, ρ) traffic model.

2.1.1 (σ, ρ) Traffic Characterization

Consider a flow that generates traffic at rate $a(t)$, which is the amount of traffic generated by the flow in $(t - 1, t]$. Then, the cumulative amount of traffic during $(s, t]$ is $A(s, t) = \sum_{\tau=s+1}^{t} a(\tau)$. Here we adopt the convention that $\sum_{j=m}^{n} a(j) = 0$ if $m < n$.

For such an arrival process, Cruz's (σ, ρ) traffic characterization is defined as follows [28].

Definition 2.1. *A flow is said to be (σ, ρ)-upper constrained, denoted by $A \sim (\sigma, \rho)$, if for all $0 \le s \le t$, there holds*

$$A(s, t) \le \rho \cdot (t - s) + \sigma. \tag{2.1}$$

In Definition 2.1, σ is called the *burstiness parameter* and ρ an upper bound on the long-term average rate of the traffic flow.

Y. Jiang, Y. Liu, *Stochastic Network Calculus*,
DOI: 10.1007/978-1-84800-127-5_2,
© Springer-Verlag London Limited 2008

Example 2.2. In real networks, the traffic generating rate of a flow is always limited by the capacity of the link on which the flow is transmitted. Let C denote the link capacity. We have for all $t \geq 0$, $a(t) \leq C$. Suppose the flow has a maximum packet size L. Then, it can be verified that the flow is (L, C) upper constrained.

To generate (σ, ρ)-constrained traffic, a traffic shaper or traffic regulator may be used. A popular implementation of such a regulator is a *token bucket*.

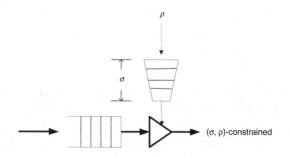

Fig. 2.1. Token bucket regulator

A token bucket is a control mechanism that decides when traffic can be transmitted. Specifically, as depicted in Figure 2.1, the token bucket with token generation rate ρ and token bucket depth σ works as follows:

(i)   The bucket can hold σ tokens and is initially full of tokens.
(ii) A token is added to the bucket every $\frac{1}{\rho}$ seconds. When a token arrives and the bucket is full, the token is discarded.
(iii) When a packet of length l bits arrives, if the number of tokens in the bucket is not smaller than l, then l tokens are removed from the bucket and the packet is immediately sent out of the token bucket.
(iv) When the packet arrives, if there are fewer than l tokens in the bucket, then the packet may either be dropped or queued until there are enough tokens in the bucket, in which case step (iii) will be repeated.

2.1.2 Arrival Curve

In order to deterministically guarantee a certain level of QoS for a flow, the traffic sent by the flow must be limited. In deterministic network calculus, this is represented by using the concept of the (deterministic) arrival curve, defined as follows [92].

Definition 2.3 (Arrival Curve). *A flow is said to have a (deterministic) arrival curve $\alpha \in \mathcal{F}$ if its arrival process $A(t)$ satisfies, for all $0 \leq s \leq t$,*

$$A(t) - A(s) \leq \alpha(t - s) \tag{2.2}$$

or equivalently $A(s,t) \leq \alpha(t - s)$.

The arrival curve model has the following *triplicity principle* [69].

Lemma 2.4 (Triplicity Principle of Arrival Curve). *The following statements are equivalent:*

(i) $\forall 0 \leq s \leq t$, $A(s,t) \leq \alpha(t - s) + x$ *for all* $x \geq 0$;
(ii) $\forall t \geq 0$, $\sup_{0 \leq s \leq t}[A(s,t) - \alpha(t - s)] \leq x$ *for all* $x \geq 0$;
(iii) $\forall t \geq 0$, $\sup_{0 \leq s \leq t} \sup_{0 \leq u \leq s}[A(u,s) - \alpha(s - u)] \leq x$ *for all* $x \geq 0$,

where $\alpha \in \mathcal{F}$.

Proof. It is trivially true that $A(s,t) - \alpha(t - s) \leq \sup_{0 \leq s \leq t}[A(s,t) - \alpha(t - s)]$, from which (ii) implies (i). In addition,

$$\sup_{0 \leq s \leq t} [A(s,t) - \alpha(t - s)]$$
$$\leq \sup_{0 \leq s \leq t} \sup_{s \leq v \leq t} [A(s,v) - \alpha(v - s)]$$
$$= \sup_{0 \leq v \leq t} \sup_{0 \leq s \leq v} [A(s,v) - \alpha(v - s)]$$
$$= \sup_{0 \leq s \leq t} \sup_{0 \leq u \leq s} [A(u,s) - \alpha(s - u)],$$

with which (iii) implies (ii).

For (i) → (ii), it holds since $A(s,t) - \alpha(t - s) \leq x$ for all $0 \leq s \leq t$. For (ii) → (iii), $\sup_{0 \leq s \leq t} \sup_{0 \leq u \leq s}[A(u,s) - \alpha(s - u)] \leq \sup_{0 \leq s \leq t}[x] = x$.

Hence (i), (ii), and (iii) are equivalent. □

By the definition of arrival curve, the right-hand side of $A(s,t) \leq \alpha(t - s) + x$ in Lemma 2.4 (i) defines an arrival curve $\alpha(t - s) + x$, or the traffic amount $A(s,t)$ is upper-bounded by $\alpha(t - s) + x$. In addition, let us construct a virtual single-server queue system that is initially empty, fed with the same traffic A, and has service curve α making $A^*(t) \geq A \otimes \alpha(t)$. Then, the backlog in the virtual system is upper-bounded by $A(t) - A^*(t) \leq \sup_{0 \leq s \leq t}[A(s,t) - \alpha(t - s)] \leq x$, and the maximum backlog up-to-date in the virtual system is upper-bounded by $\sup_{0 \leq s \leq t}[A(s) - A^*(s)] \leq \sup_{0 \leq s \leq t} \sup_{0 \leq u \leq s}[A(u,s) - \alpha(s - u)] \leq x$. Calling Lemma 2.4 (i) the *traffic amount property* of the arrival curve, Lemma 2.4 (ii) its *virtual backlog property*, and Lemma 2.4.(iii) its *maximum virtual backlog property*, Lemma 2.4 states that the three properties of deterministic arrival curve are equivalent. It is in this sense that we call Lemma 2.4 the *triplicity principle* of the arrival curve.

In addition, the definition of arrival curve is equivalent to enforcing that for all $t \geq 0$ there holds

$$A(t) \leq A \otimes \alpha(t) = \inf_{0 \leq s \leq t} \{A(s) + \alpha(t - s)\}. \tag{2.3}$$

Example 2.5. Under the Integrated Services (IntServ) framework of the Internet [12], a 4-tuple (p, M, r, b) is used to specify traffic, where M represents the maximum packet size, p the peak rate, r the token rate, and b the token depth. With such a traffic specification, the flow is constrained by a dual-token bucket and has an arrival curve as illustrated in Figure 2.2:

$$\alpha(t) = (pt + M) \wedge (rt + b) \equiv \min\{pt + M, rt + b\}.$$

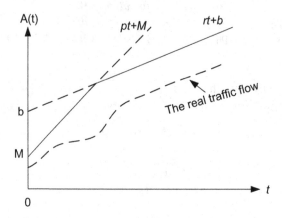

Fig. 2.2. Dual-token bucket constrained traffic

Example 2.6. In the previous example, a dual-token bucket has been considered. Along the same line, the (σ, ρ) model can be extended to the $(\overrightarrow{\sigma}, \overrightarrow{\rho})$ model that maintains (σ, ρ) pairs. More specifically, if there are n such pairs (σ_i, ρ_i), $i = 1, \ldots, n$, the traffic is constrained by $A(s, t) \leq \wedge_{i=1}^{n}\{\rho_i \cdot (t - s) + \sigma_i\} \equiv \min_{1 \leq i \leq n}\{\rho_i \cdot (t - s) + \sigma_i\}$. It is clear that if a flow is constrained by $(\overrightarrow{\sigma}, \overrightarrow{\rho})$, it has an arrival curve

$$\alpha(t) = \min_{1 \leq i \leq n} \{\rho_i \cdot t + \sigma_i\}.$$

It is worth highlighting that for a given flow, its arrival curves are not unique since they are just upper bounds. In the dual-token bucket example, both $pt + M$ and $rt + b$ satisfy the definition of arrival curve and hence are also arrival curves of the dual-token bucket constrained flow. Another example is that, supposing $\alpha(t)$ is an arrival curve of a flow, then for any $k \geq 1$, $k \cdot \alpha(t)$ is also an arrival curve of the flow.

2.1.3 Envelope Process

In the context of deterministic network calculus, another concept is often used interchangeably with arrival curve, which is traffic *envelope process*, defined as follows [15].

Definition 2.7. *A flow is said to have an envelope process $\hat{A}$ on its traffic if its arrival process $A(t)$ satisfies, for all $s, t \geq 0$,*

$$A(s, s+t) \leq \hat{A}(t). \tag{2.4}$$

In this chapter, we shall interpret $\hat{A}(t)$ as a process satisfying (2.4) to *deterministically* bound the arrival process. In this sense, the envelope process model is the same as the arrival curve model. Later, in Chapter 3, we shall interpret $\hat{A}(t)$ as a *possibly stochastic* process. In this way, statistical properties of $\hat{A}(t)$ may be further explored in stochastic network calculus.

Similar to the arrival curve, a flow's envelope process is not unique. Nevertheless, the flow has a *minimum envelope process* (MEP),

$$\hat{A}^{MEP}(t) = \sup_{s \geq 0} A(s, s+t). \tag{2.5}$$

It is clear that $0 \leq \hat{A}^{MEP}(t) \leq \hat{A}^{MEP}(t+\tau)$ for any $\tau \geq 0$ and hence the MEP is wide-sense increasing and belongs to $\mathcal{F}$. In addition, the MEP is sub-additive, which is

$$\hat{A}^{MEP}(t_1 + t_2) \leq \hat{A}^{MEP}(t_1) + \hat{A}^{MEP}(t_2)$$

since there holds

$$
\begin{aligned}
\hat{A}^{MEP}(t_1 + t_2) &= \sup_{s \geq 0} A(s, s + t_1 + t_2) \\
&= \sup_{s \geq 0} [A(s, s+t_1) + A(s+t_1, s+t_1+t_2)] \\
&\leq \sup_{s \geq 0} A(s, s+t_1) + \sup_{s \geq 0} A(s+t_1, s+t_1+t_2) \\
&= \sup_{s \geq 0} A(s, s+t_1) + \sup_{\tau \geq t_1} A(\tau, \tau+t_2) \\
&\leq \hat{A}^{MEP}(t_1) + \hat{A}^{MEP}(t_2).
\end{aligned}
$$

2.2 Server Models

For the provision and analysis of deterministic service guarantees, many server models have been proposed, which include the *latency rate* (LR) server model [129] and the *guaranteed rate* (GR) server model [53]. These server models can often be abstracted or mapped to the general *service curve* server model.

2.2.1 Service Curve

Essentially, a service curve defines a lower bound on the service provided by a server. Formally, the service curve model is defined as follows [92].

Definition 2.8 (Service Curve). *Consider a system S with input process $A(t)$ and output process $A^*(t)$. The system is said to provide to the input a (deterministic) service curve $\beta(t) \in \mathcal{F}$ if for all $t \geq 0$*

$$A^*(t) \geq A \otimes \beta(t). \tag{2.6}$$

The service curve model has the following *duality principle* [69][73].

Lemma 2.9 (Duality Principle of Service Curve). *For any $x \geq 0$, $A \otimes \beta(t) - A^*(t) \leq x$ for all $t \geq 0$ if and only if $\sup_{0 \leq s \leq t}[A \otimes \beta(s) - A^*(s)] \leq x$ for all $t \geq 0$, where $\beta \in \mathcal{F}$.*

Proof. For the "if" part, it holds trivially since $A \otimes \beta(t) - A^*(t) \leq \sup_{0 \leq s \leq t}[A \otimes \beta(s) - A^*(s)]$. For the "only if" part, since $A \otimes \beta(t) - A^*(t) \leq x$ for all $t \geq 0$, $\sup_{0 \leq s \leq t}[A \otimes \beta(s) - A^*(s)] \leq \sup_{0 \leq s \leq t}[x] = x$. □

By the definition of service curve, it is clear that the first part of Lemma 2.9 defines a service curve $\beta(t) - x$. Lemma 2.9 states that if a server provides a service curve $\beta(t) - x$, then there holds $\sup_{0 \leq s \leq t}[A \otimes \beta(s) - A^*(s)] \leq x$ and vice versa. In this sense, we call Lemma 2.9 the *duality principle* of the service curve.

When β is continuous, the service curve property (2.6) is equivalent to saying that for all $t \geq 0$ there exists some $0 \leq t_0 \leq t$ such that [92]

$$A^*(t) \geq A(t_0) + \beta(t - t_0). \tag{2.7}$$

Throughout the rest of this book, the function β is assumed to be continuous on t as used in [92].

For a constant rate FIFO server, t_0 in (2.7) is the beginning of the busy period corresponding to t. In the case where the service curve is latency-rate type (i.e., $\beta(t) = R \cdot t - T$), t_0 may be loosely interpreted as the start of the *burst period* in which traffic from the input considered arrives with rate greater than or equal to R, or $A(t_0, t) \geq R \cdot (t - t^0)$ [68][129].

It is also worth highlighting that the service curves of a system are not unique either since they are just lower bounds. With the monotonicity property of $\otimes$, it is easy to show that if $\beta(t)$ is a service curve, then any function $\beta'(t) \leq \beta(t)$ is also a service curve.

2.2.2 Network Elements Offering Service Curves

This subsection introduces three important types of network elements offering service curves.

A widely used service curve type is the *latency-rate service curve* type, where the service curve is represented using a linear function $\beta(t) = R \cdot t + T$ with R as the rate term and T the latency term. Under the LR and GR models, the literature has proved similar terms for many well-known schedulers,

Table 2.1. Latency and rate terms of some schedulers

Scheduler	Latency	Rate
GPS	0	$\frac{\phi_i}{\sum_i \phi_i} C$
FIFO	$L^{\max}/C$	C
SP	$L^{\max}/C$	C
PGPS/WFQ	$L^{\max}/r + L^{\max}/C$	$\frac{\phi_i}{\sum_i \phi_i} C$
SFQ	$L^{\max}/r + \sum_{m \neq f} L^{\max}/C$	$\frac{\phi_i}{\sum_i \phi_i} C$
DRR	$\left(3 \sum_i Q_i - 2Q_i\right)/C$	$\frac{Q_i}{\sum_i Q_i} C$

such as first-in-first-out (FIFO), strict priority (SP), (ideal) general processor sharing (GPS) [84], packetized general processor sharing (PGPS) [112] or weighted fair queuing (WFQ) [33] [112], virtual clock [142], start-time fair queuing (SFQ), and deficit round robin (DRR) [126] [134]. In [68], the following relationship between LR, GR and service curve has been proved.

Lemma 2.10. *If a scheduler is a latency-rate server (respectively guaranteed-rate server) with rate R and latency T (respectively error term E) to a flow, then the scheduler offers the flow a latency-rate service curve with rate R and latency T (respectively $E + \frac{L^{max}}{R}$, where L^{max} denotes the maximum packet size of the flow).*

With Lemma 2.10, the rate and latency terms can be found for many schedulers under the service curve model. Table 2.1 presents the rate and latency terms for some of them, where C denotes the capacity of the scheduler. For SP, the two terms are for the traffic class at the highest priority level; for GPS, PGPS/WFQ and SFQ, ϕ_i is the weight parameter for the input considered and for DRR, Q_i denotes the quantum size allocated to the input considered. For other schedulers, their rate and latency terms may be found from the literature (e.g., [68] [129] [53] [71]).

Another important type of network element that offers service curves is the *greedy shaper*. A greedy shaper is a shaper that outputs as soon as possible, but delays the input bits in a buffer whenever sending a bit would violate the shaping curve [70] [92]. A greedy shaper has the following property [70] [92].

Lemma 2.11. *For a greedy shaper with shaping curve α, if the shaper buffer is large enough to ensure no loss and is empty at time 0, then its output and input have the following relation:*

$$A^*(t) = A \otimes \alpha(t). \tag{2.8}$$

Equation (2.8) has two implications. One is that the greedy shaper offers a service curve α to the input. Another is that the output is constrained by arrival curve α.

The following result introduces the third type of network element that offers service curves, which is the delay element.

Lemma 2.12. *If a system guarantees a bounded delay T to the input flow, then it offers a service curve $\delta_T(t)$ to the flow,*

$$A^*(t) \geq A \otimes \delta_T(t),\qquad(2.9)$$

where $\delta_T(t)$, called the network calculus impulse function, *is defined as $\delta_T(t) = 0$ for $0 \leq t \leq T$ and $\delta_T(t) = \infty$ for $t > T$.*

2.2.3 Strict Service Curve

An important concept, called the *strict service curve* has often been used to find the service curve of a system and is defined as follows.

Definition 2.13 (Strict Service Curve). *A system S is said to offer a strict service curve β to a flow A if, during any backlogged period $(s, s + t]$ of the flow, the output satisfies $A^*(s, s + t) \geq \beta(t)$.*

It is easy to verify that Definition 2.13 implies Definition 2.8, or, in other words, the following.

Lemma 2.14. *If a system offers a strict service curve β to a flow, then it also offers a service curve β to the flow.*

2.2.4 Service Envelope Process

We define in the following a concept related to the service curve, which is called the *service envelope process*.

Definition 2.15 (Service Envelope Process). *A system is said to provide a service envelope process $\hat{S}(t)$ to the input if for any $t \geq 0$ there holds*

$$A^*(t) \geq A \otimes \hat{S}(t).\qquad(2.10)$$

Just like what has been discussed for the arrival curve and envelope process, the difference in definitions between service curve and service envelope process is also subtle. Later, however, we shall interpret the envelope process as a random process with statistical properties that may be explored in stochastic network calculus and consider the (deterministic) service curve as a deterministic service envelope process.

When a service envelope process makes (2.10) an equality, we call it the maximum service envelope process, defined as follows.

Definition 2.16 (Maximum Service Envelope Process). *The maximum service envelope process of a system, denoted by $\hat{S}^{MSP}(t)$, is a process with which, for any $t \geq 0$, the following equality holds:*

$$A^*(t) = A \otimes \hat{S}^{MSP}(t).\qquad(2.11)$$

Similarly, a concept related to the strict service curve is the *strict service envelope process*, defined as follows:

Definition 2.17 (Strict Service Envelope Process). *A system is said to provide a strict service envelope (SSE) process $\hat{S}(t)$ if the amount of service $S(s, s+t)$ provided by the system in $(s, s+t]$ satisfies, for any $t \geq 0$ and all $s \geq 0$,*

$$S(s, s+t) \geq \hat{S}^{SSE}(t). \tag{2.12}$$

The difference in definitions between strict service curve and strict service envelope process is also subtle. While the former is defined on a backlogged period, the latter describes the behavior of the system in general. Particularly, the following relation is straightforward.

Lemma 2.18. *If a system has a strict service envelope process $\hat{S}(t)$, it provides a strict service curve $\beta(t) = \hat{S}(t)$.*

Another difference in definitions between strict service curve and strict service envelope process is that, later in this book, we shall interpret the envelope process as a random process with statistical properties that may be explored in stochastic network calculus and consider the (deterministic) strict service curve as a deterministic service envelope process.

It is clear that the strict service envelope process definition is stronger than the service envelope process definition. In other words, if a system has a strict service envelope process $\hat{S}(t)$, it also has a service envelope process $\hat{S}(t)$.

In addition, it can be noticed from Definition 2.15 that the definition of a service envelope process is dependent on the arrival process $A(t)$. However, Definition 2.17 generally describes the behavior of the system independent of the arrival.

Similar to envelope process, a system's service envelope process or strict service envelop process is not unique either. Nevertheless, the system has a *maximum strict service envelope process* (MSS)

$$\hat{S}^{MSS}(t) = \inf_{s \geq 0} S(s, s+t).$$

It is clear that $0 \leq \hat{S}^{MSS}(t) \leq \hat{S}^{MSS}(t+\tau)$ for any $\tau \geq 0$ since we always have $S(s, s+t) \leq S(s, s+t+\tau)$ for all $s \geq 0$, and hence the MSS is wide-sense increasing and belongs to $\mathcal{F}$.

2.3 Basic Results

This section presents basic results of deterministic network calculus that correspond to the five basic properties (P.1)–(P.5) for network analysis discussed in Chapter 1. These results are based on the concepts of the arrival curve for the traffic model and the service curve for the server model.

2.3.1 Service Guarantees

The service guarantee property means that the QoS performance bounds such as the delay bound and backlog bound can be derived under the given traffic model and server model. For deterministic network calculus, if the input flow to a system has an arrival curve and the system provides a service curve to the flow, Theorem 2.19 and Theorem 2.21 respectively present the delay bound and backlog bound of the flow at the system.

Theorem 2.19 (Delay Bound). *Consider a system offering a (deterministic) service curve β to the input flow A. Suppose A has a (deterministic) arrival curve α. Then, the delay $D(t)$ of the flow at time t is bounded by*

$$D(t) \leq h(\alpha, \beta).$$

Proof. For the delay, by definition,

$$D(t) = \inf\{\tau \geq 0 : A(t) \leq A^*(t+\tau)\},$$

with which the theorem is equivalent to proving that for any $0 \leq \tau \leq D(t)$ there holds

$$\tau \leq h(\alpha, \beta).$$

In the following, we consider any $(0 \leq)\tau < D(t)$. The delay definition implies that

$$A(t) > A^*(t+\tau),$$

since otherwise if there were be $A(t) \leq A^*(t+\tau)$ we would have $D(t) \leq \tau$, which contradicts the condition $D(t) > \tau$.

Since the system offers a service curve β, according to (2.7) there exists a certain t_0 such that

$$A^*(t+\tau) > A(\tau_0) + \beta(t+\tau-\tau_0).$$

We hence have, with this τ_0,

$$A(t) > A(\tau_0) + \beta(t+\tau-\tau_0).$$

Since the input A has an arrival curve α,

$$\alpha(t-\tau_0) \geq A(t) - A(\tau_0) > \beta(t-\tau_0+\tau),$$

which implies

$$\tau \leq d_{\alpha,\beta}(t-\tau_0),$$

where

$$d_{\alpha,\beta}(t-\tau_0) \equiv \inf\{\tau \geq 0 : \alpha(t-\tau_0) \leq A^*(t-\tau_0+\tau)\}.$$

It is trivial that

$$d_{\alpha,\beta}(t - \tau_0) \leq \sup_{t-\tau_0 \geq 0} \{\inf\{\tau \geq 0 : \alpha(t - \tau_0) \leq A^*(t - \tau_0 + \tau)\}\}$$

$$= \sup_{s \geq 0}\{\inf\{\tau \geq 0 : \alpha(s) \leq A^*(s + \tau)\}\} = h(\alpha, \beta),$$

and hence $\tau \leq h(\alpha, \beta)$, which concludes the proof. $\square$

Example 2.20. Consider that a network element offers a latency-rate service curve $\beta(t) = r \cdot (t - T)^+$ to the input flow that is constrained by a token bucket with token generation rate ρ and bucket size σ. For this input flow, it has an arrival curve $\alpha(t) = \rho \cdot t + \sigma$. From Theorem 2.19, it is clear that, if $\rho \leq r$, the flow experiences a delay bounded by

$$D(t) \leq h\left(\rho \cdot t + \sigma, r \cdot (t - T)^+\right) \leq \frac{\sigma}{r} + T.$$

Theorem 2.21 (Backlog Bound). *Consider a system offering a (deterministic) service curve β to the input flow A. Suppose A has a (deterministic) arrival curve α. Then, the backlog $B(t)$ of the flow at time t is bounded by*

$$B(t) \leq \alpha \oslash \beta(0),$$

where $\alpha \oslash \beta(0) = \sup_{s \geq 0}\{\alpha(s) - \beta(s)\}$.

Proof. According to the definition of deterministic service curve, we have, for all $t \geq 0$,

$$A^*(t) \geq A \otimes \beta(t).$$

Then, for all $t \geq 0$,

$$\begin{aligned}
B(t) &= A(t) - A^*(t) \\
&\leq A(t) - A \otimes \beta(t) \\
&= A(t) - \inf_{0 \leq s \leq t}\{A(t - s) + \beta(s)\} \\
&\leq \sup_{0 \leq s \leq t}\{A(t) - A(t - s) - \beta(s)\} \\
&\leq \sup_{s \geq 0}\{\alpha(s) - \beta(s)\}.
\end{aligned}$$

$\square$

Example 2.22. Consider the same network element as in the previous example, which offers a latency-rate service curve $\beta(t) = r \cdot (t - T)^+$ to the input flow that is constrained by a token bucket with token generation rate ρ and bucket size σ. The input flow has an arrival curve $\alpha(t) = \rho \cdot t + \sigma$. From Theorem 2.21, it is clear that, if $\rho \leq r$, the backlog of the flow in the node is bounded by

$$B(t) \leq \sup_{t \geq 0}\left\{(\rho \cdot t + \sigma) - (r \cdot (t - T)^+)\right\} = \sigma + \rho T.$$

2.3.2 Output Characterization

The output characterization property means that the output of a flow from a system can be represented using the same traffic model as the input flow. This property facilitates the QoS analysis at subsequent nodes. For deterministic network calculus, the property is shown by the following theorem.

Theorem 2.23 (Output Characterization). *Consider a system offering a (deterministic) service curve β to the input flow A. Suppose A has a (deterministic) arrival curve α. Then, the output A^* is also bounded, for all $s, t \geq 0$, by a (deterministic) arrival curve $\alpha^*(t) = \alpha \oslash \beta(t)$ as*

$$A^*(s, s+t) \leq \alpha \oslash \beta(t).$$

Proof. According to the definition of deterministic service curve, we have for all $0 \leq s \leq t$ that there exists a certain $s_0 (\leq t - s)$ such that $A^*(t - s) \geq A(t - s - s_0) + \beta(s_0)$.

Then,

$$
\begin{aligned}
A^*(t) - A^*(t - s) &\leq A^*(t) - A(t - s - s_0) - \beta(s_0) \\
&\leq A(t) - A(t - s - s_0) - \beta(s_0) \\
&\leq \alpha(s + s_0) - \beta(s_0) \\
&\leq \alpha \oslash \beta(s).
\end{aligned}
$$

Hence, we have

$$\alpha^*(t) = \alpha \oslash \beta(t).$$

$\square$

With the service guarantee property (P.1) and the output characterization property (P.2), the end-to-end QoS performance of a sequence of nodes in tandem can be investigated using the so-called *node-by-node analysis* approach. With this approach, the QoS performance at the first node is derived. So is the output characterization from the first node, with which is further applied to the second node to derive the QoS performance at the second node and the output characterization of the second node. This process is repeated until the QoS performance at all the nodes is derived, with which, the end-to-end QoS performance is obtained. To demonstrate this node-by-node network analysis approach, we consider an example below.

Example 2.24. Consider a network of $H(\geq 1)$ nodes in tandem, where the propagation delay is not taken into account. The input flow to the network is constrained by a token bucket with token rate ρ and bucket size σ before entering the network. In other words, the flow has an arrival curve $\alpha^1 = \rho \cdot t + \sigma$ to the first node. In addition, we assume each node h offers to the flow a latency-rate service curve $\beta^h = r \cdot (t - T)^+$, where $r \geq \rho$ and $T \geq 0$. We want to derive a bound on the end-to-end delay of the flow in the network.

At the first node, the delay bound and the output can be derived from Theorem 2.19 and Theorem 2.23 respectively as follows:

$$D^1(t) \leq h(\alpha^1, \beta^1\} = \frac{\sigma}{r} + T,$$

$$\alpha^{1*}(t) = \alpha^1 \oslash \beta^1(t) = \rho \cdot t + \sigma + r \cdot T.$$

Since in the network nodes are placed in tandem, the output from the first node is the input to the second node, which has an arrival curve $\alpha^2 = \alpha^{1*}$. With this and Theorems 2.19 and 2.23, we can further get the delay bound and the output characterization at the second node. This can be repeatedly applied to the network. In general, we have, for $h \geq 1$,

$$D^h(t) \leq \frac{\sigma}{r} + h \cdot T; \tag{2.13}$$

$$\alpha^{h*} = \rho \cdot t + \sigma + h \cdot r \cdot T. \tag{2.14}$$

Based on the node delay bounds, an end-to-end delay bound is derived as

$$D(t) = \sum_{h=1}^{H} D^h(t)$$

$$\leq H \cdot \frac{\sigma}{r} + H \cdot T + \frac{H(H-1)}{2} T. \tag{2.15}$$

2.3.3 Concatenation Property

The concatenation property means that the concatenation of a series of servers in tandem can be considered as one single server and represented using the same server model. Like the output characterization property, the concatenation property can also facilitate the end-to-end QoS performance analysis and improve results obtained from the node-by-node analysis.

Theorem 2.25 (Concatenation Property). *Consider a flow passing through systems S^h, $h = 1, \ldots, H$, in sequence. Suppose each system S^h provides a deterministic service curve $\beta^h \in \mathcal{F}$ to the flow. Then the concatenation of these systems offers a deterministic network service curve β to the flow, which is given by*

$$\beta = \beta^1 \otimes \beta^2 \cdots \otimes \beta^H. \tag{2.16}$$

Proof. We shall only consider the two-system case, from which the proof can be easily extended to the H-system case. Let A^h and A^{h*} be the arrival process and departure process of the hth system, respectively, and A and A^* the arrival process and departure process of the concatenated system, respectively. Then, we have $A = A^1$ and $A^* = A^{2*}$.

Since the departure of the first system is the arrival at the second system, we get $A^{1*} = A^2$. According to the definition of deterministic service curve, we have

$$A^{2*} \geq A^2 \otimes \beta^2$$
$$= A^{1*} \otimes \beta^2$$
$$\geq \left(A^1 \otimes \beta^1(t)\right) \otimes \beta^2$$
$$= A \otimes \left(\beta^1 \otimes \beta^2\right),$$

with which we can conclude that the concatenated system provides a service curve $\beta^1 \otimes \beta^2$ to the flow.   □

The concatenation property is an important result of deterministic network calculus. With the network service curve, the edge-to-edge QoS bounds can be obtained by applying the single- system analysis, and we call this network analysis approach the *edge-to-edge analysis* approach. In addition, the edge-to-edge analysis approach can result in much improved results over the node-by-node analysis. To demonstrate, the same network is considered as for the node-by-node analysis approach.

Example 2.26. Consider the same network as in the example for the node-by-node analysis. With Theorem 2.25, it is known that the network provides a service curve to the flow as

$$\beta = \beta^1 \otimes \beta^2 \cdots \otimes \beta^H$$
$$= r \cdot (t - H \cdot T).$$

With the network service curve β and Theorem 2.19, the end-to-end delay is bounded by

$$D \leq \frac{\sigma}{r} + H \cdot T. \tag{2.17}$$

Comparing (2.17) with (2.15), it is clear that the edge-to-edge analysis gives a much better bound on the end-to-end delay than the node-by-node approach. This improvement comes from two parts. First, the initial burstiness σ is counted only once in (2.17), whereas (2.15) it is counted H times. Second, the term $\frac{H(H-1)}{2} \cdot \theta$ in (2.15) does not appear in (2.17) due to a burstiness increase after passing through nodes . Because of these, facts the literature calls (2.17) the "pay-bursts-only-once" phenomenon [92]. To illustrate the difference between (2.17) and (2.15), Figure 2.3 is presented, where $\sigma = 3$, $r = 10$, and $T = 2$.

Recently, the scaling of end-to-end performance bounds has attracted research attention in the field of network calculus [24]. According to the analysis in Examples 2.24 and 2.26 above, when considering the case with H nodes in tandem, we can see that the end-to-end delay bound obtained from the node-by-node analysis approach scales in $\mathcal{O}\left(H^2\right)$. However, with the concatenation property of the service curve, the end-to-end delay bound obtained scales in $\mathcal{O}(H)$, which gives a much tighter bound.

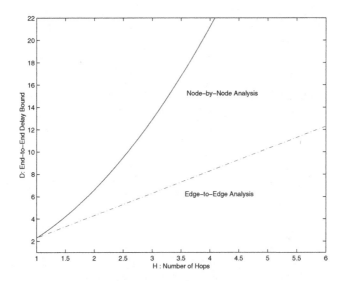

Fig. 2.3. Comparison of node-by-node analysis and edge-to-edge analysis

2.3.4 Leftover Service

In order to provide QoS in a scalable manner, aggregate scheduling has been studied as an important approach. For example, in Differentiated Services (DiffServ) networks [10], service guarantees are provided to aggregates and aggregate scheduling is used instead of per-flow scheduling. For such networks, to derive per-flow QoS bounds, it is desirable to study the per-flow service received by each flow in an aggregate, which is sometimes called *per-flow service under aggregation* [100] and often also called *leftover service* given to a flow by a system where there are more flows competing for the service.

The leftover service property means that the service received by a flow in an aggregate can be represented using the same server model. This property enables the analysis of per-flow QoS under aggregate scheduling. For deterministic network calculus, the leftover service property is presented below.

Theorem 2.27 (Leftover Service). *Consider a system serving an aggregate of two (possibly aggregate) flows A_1 and A_2. Assume the system offers a service curve β to the aggregate, and A_2 has an arrival curve α_2. Then, the system offers to the flow A_1 such that, for any $t \geq 0$,*

$$A_1^*(t) \geq A_1 \otimes (\beta - \alpha_2)^+(t), \tag{2.18}$$

and if $(\beta - \alpha_2)^+ \in \mathcal{F}$, it is a service curve to flow A_1.

Proof. Let A be the aggregate. Then, $A(t) = A_1(t) + A_2(t)$. In addition, $A^* = A_1^*(t) + A_2^*(t)$, from which, together with $A_2^*(t) \leq A^2(t)$, $A_1^*(t) \geq 0$, and $A_1(0) = 0$, we get

$$A_1^* = A^* - A_2^*(t)$$
$$\geq (A \otimes \beta(t) - A_2(t))^+$$
$$= \left(\inf_{0 \leq s \leq t} \{A_1(s) + \beta(t-s) - [A_2(t) - A_2(s)]\} \right)^+$$
$$\geq \left(\inf_{0 \leq s \leq t} \{A_1(s) + (\beta - \alpha)(t-s)\} \right)^+$$
$$= \inf_{0 \leq s \leq t} \{A_1(s) + (\beta - \alpha)^+(t-s)\}$$
$$= A_1 \otimes (\beta - \alpha_2)^+(t).$$

□

2.3.5 Superposition

The superposition property means that the superposition of flows can be represented using the same traffic model. With this property, the aggregate of (possibly many) individual flows can be considered as a single aggregate flow, so that the QoS performance for the aggregate can be derived in the same way as for a single flow.

Consider two flows A_1 and A_2. Suppose A_1 has an arrival curve $\alpha_1(t)$ and A_2 an arrival curve $\alpha_2(t)$, and $A(= A_1 + A_2)$ is the aggregate flow. Then, for the aggregate A, we have, for any $0 \leq s \leq t$, $A(s,t) = A_1(s,t) + A_2(s,t) \leq \alpha_1(t-s) + \alpha_2(t-s)$. In other words, the aggregate flow has an arrival curve $\alpha_1 + \alpha_2$. The analysis can be easily extended to cases where the aggregate is formed by more than two flows. The result is as follows.

Theorem 2.28 (Superposition). *Consider the superposition of n flows A_i, $i = 1, \ldots, n$. If each flow A_i has an arrival curve $\alpha_i \in \mathcal{F}$, the aggregate flow $A = \sum_{i=1}^n A_i$ has an arrival curve $\alpha(t) = \sum_{i=1}^n \alpha_i(t)$.*

2.3.6 Example: Analysis of a Network of Arbitrary Topology

To further demonstrate the use of the deterministic network calculus results, let us consider an aggregate scheduling network of arbitrary topology. We assume each flow has a latency-rate arrival curve $\alpha_i(t) = \rho \cdot t + \sigma$ when entering the network. Flows are aggregated in the FIFO manner in the network. Each node in the network provides a latency-rate service curve $\beta^h(t) = r \cdot (t - T)$ to the aggregate input. The maximum hop count used by any flow is bounded by $H(\geq 1)$. Define $u^h = \frac{n^h \rho}{r}$, where n^h denotes the number of flows sharing the same output link as flow A_i and u^h the utilization level of the link. In the following, we derive the nodal delay bound, the delay bound for the network, and the buffer required to size ensure no loss.

Consider any node in the network. The maximum delay for any flow A_i to arrive at the node is bounded by $(H-1) \cdot d$. Then, the path up to the node for the flow can be considered as a delay element with service curve $\delta_{(H-1) \cdot d}$. With Theorem 2.23, it is clear that the output of the flow from this delay element has an arrival curve $\alpha_i \oslash \delta_{(H-1) \cdot d} = \rho \cdot t + \sigma + \rho(H-1)d$. When $n^h \rho \leq r$, we have

$$d \leq h\left(\alpha^h, \beta^h\right)$$
$$= \frac{n^h \sigma + n^h \rho(H-1)d}{r} + T$$
$$= u^h (H-1)d + \frac{n^h \sigma}{r} + T,$$

from which, when $u^h < \frac{1}{H-1}$, we obtain the delay bound on node h

$$d \leq \frac{1}{1 - u^h(H-1)} \left(\frac{n^h \sigma}{r} + T\right)$$
$$\leq \frac{1}{1 - u^h(H-1)} \left(\frac{1}{H-1}\frac{\sigma}{\rho} + T\right), \tag{2.19}$$

where we have used $u^h \equiv \frac{n^h \rho}{r} < \frac{1}{H-1}$. Let u be the maximum link utilization level in the network, or $u = \max\{u^h\}$, for every node h in the network. Then, there follows immediately from (2.19) the nodal delay bound.

$$d \leq \frac{1}{1 - u(H-1)} \left(\frac{1}{H-1}\frac{\sigma}{\rho} + T\right), \tag{2.20}$$

and the corresponding condition becomes

$$u < \frac{1}{H-1}. \tag{2.21}$$

In addition, we have as a delay bound for the network

$$D \leq \frac{H}{1 - u(H-1)} \left(\frac{1}{H-1}\frac{\sigma}{\rho} + T\right). \tag{2.22}$$

For any node h, we know that the buffer size satisfies

$$B^h(t) \leq v\left(\alpha^h, \beta^h\right).$$

Using an approach similar to that deriving the nodal delay bound (2.20), we obtain that, under condition (2.21), for any node h,

$$B^h(t) \leq \frac{r}{1 - u(H-1)} \left(\frac{1}{H-1}\frac{\sigma}{\rho} + \theta\right). \tag{2.23}$$

The right-hand side of (2.23) gives the buffer size required to ensure no loss.

Comparing this with the tandem network considered in Examples 2.24 and 2.26, it can be found that the pay-bursts-only-once phenomenon does not hold from (2.22) for the network of arbitrary topology where loops may exist. Inequality (2.22) and condition (2.21) imply that, for the network of arbitrary topology, the network delay may not be bounded if condition (2.21) does not hold. This additionally implies that fixing a certain node utilization level may lead to condition (2.21) being unsatisfied and consequently no bounded delay concluded, when H increases. In other words, the scaling on the number of hops may not hold when the node utilization level is fixed. This is contrary to the tandem network case. On the other hand, keeping $u(H-1)$ unchanged, the delay bound given by (2.20) scales in $\mathcal{O}(H)$.

2.4 Summary and Bibliographic Comments

This chapter introduces the basic results of deterministic network calculus. Some important concepts, such as the arrival curve, service curve, and strict service curve have been discussed. Based on these concepts, worst-case backlog, delay and output bounds, and other results corresponding to the five basic properties are also presented under the min-plus algebra.

The (σ, ρ) model was initially addressed by Cruz in [28][29], and its idea of using a curve to upper-bound the cumulative arrival process has greatly simplified and indeed enabled the network case analysis. A generalized form of the (σ, ρ) model was also found in [28], which is called the arrival curve or envelope process in this book.

The latency rate (LR) server model was initially defined by Stiliadis and Varma in [129]. The guaranteed rate (GR) server model was defined by Goyal, Lam, and Vin in [52] and later generalized in [54]. The idea of GR is to capture the deadline guarantee with regard to a virtual time function, which was initially used by Xie and Lam in [135]. The relationship between LR and GR was studied by Jiang in [68]. The idea of using a curve or envelope to lower-bound the service was first considered by Parekh and Gallager [112], Cruz [30], and Sariowan [122]. This idea was later further explored by Chang [17], Le Boudec [90], and Cruz, et al. [2] to study service guarantees. The strict service curve concept was referred to as the strong service curve in Cruz's work [32]. A review of various deterministic server models was made by Jiang [68], where the relationships between these models were also investigated.

The study of deterministic QoS performance bounds was pioneered by Cruz with the concept of (σ, ρ) traffic characterization on burstiness constraints for single-node and multiple-node cases in [28][29]. Some subsequent works [15][30][112][113][122][17][90][2] investigated various deterministic performance bounds under more general traffic models and server models. The works in this direction was later systematically summarized by Chang [18] and Le Boudec and Thiran [92] into an elegant theory deterministic network calculus, mainly by using the concepts of the arrival curve and service curve or their equivalents with the application of min-plus or max-plus algebra [6].

The analysis of the arbitrary topology network was initially made by Charny and Le Boudec in [20]. The analysis was extended by Jiang [67] to consider packetization effects and link capacity constraints.

In recent years, another deterministic server model, called packet scale rate guarantee (PSRG), has been used to define Expedited Forwarding behavior for DiffServ [10] networks. This PSRG concept was defined by Bennett et al. [8] initially for per-hop behavior and later extended to per-domain behavior by Jiang [71]. The single-hop definition of PSRG is indeed equivalent to the *adaptive service curve* server model that was initially introduced in [110] and published in [2]. Some more results for PSRG can be found in [92] and [70].

Problems

2.1. Prove Lemma 2.11.

2.2. Prove Lemma 2.12.

2.3. We were given a token bucket constrained input traffic $A \sim (\sigma, \rho)$ and a rate-guaranteed scheduler providing a service curve in the form of

$$\beta(t) = R(t - T)^{+}.$$

The buffer size for the scheduler is B.

(i)   What is the minimum value of B to guarantee no packet loss in the system?
(ii) What is the minimum rate R guaranteeing that the maximum delay experienced by any packet in the system is less than D?
(iii) What happens if $R < \rho$?

2.4. Consider a system with a rate-guaranteed scheduler providing a service curve in the form of

$$\beta(t) = R(t - T)^{+}.$$

There are N token bucket constrained input flows to this system, each shaped by a token bucket shaper with the same parameters (σ, ρ). The buffer size is B.

(i) How many such flows can be admitted into the system if no packet loss is allowed?
(ii) How many such flows can be admitted into the system if the maximum delay experienced by any packet in this system is required to be less than D?

2.5. Consider a constant-rate server with link capacity C fed with an input traffic flow with maximum packet size M.

(i)   What is the arrival curve for the output process of the constant-rate server?
(ii) Suppose the input traffic is also token bucket constrained with token generation rate r and token bucket size b. What is the arrival curve for the output process of the constant-rate server?
(iii) Following the same condition as in (ii), if the output traffic of the constant rate server is fed into a rate-guaranteed scheduler providing a service curve in the form of

$$\beta(t) = R(t - T)^+,$$

what is the buffer size that guarantees that there is no packet loss in the system? What is the maximum delay a packet may have in the system? What is the arrival curve of the departure process?

2.6. Consider a system with two rate-guaranteed servers in tandem serving two flows A_1 and A_2 that are FIFO-aggregated as shown in Figure 2.4. Assume flow $A_i \sim (\sigma^i, \rho^i)$, $i = 1, 2$. Assume that each server guarantees a service curve $\beta_k = R_k(t - T_k)^+$, $k = 1, 2$ to the aggregate of the two flows.

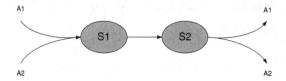

Fig. 2.4. Two servers in tandem

(i)   What are the buffer sizes needed for the first server and the second server, respectively, to guarantee that there is no packet loss in the system?
(ii) There are two approaches to analyzing the QoS experienced by packets from A_1 in the system. The first one is to derive the leftover service curve received by A_1 at each server. After that, the network service curve received for A_1 can be obtained by concatenation. Then, what is the maximum delay a packet may have in the system using this approach?
(iii) The second approach is to derive the network service curve for the aggregate flow using the concatenation property. After that, the leftover service curve for A_1 can be derived under aggregate scheduling. Then, what is the maximum delay a packet may have in the system using this approach?
(iv) Compare and explain the difference between the delay bounds derived from (ii) and (iii).

2.7. In Example 2.3.6, suppose that at the network ingress each flow is constrained by a dual-token bucket with an arrival curve $\alpha(t) = \min\{\rho \cdot t + \sigma, p \cdot t + L\}$. Then, what is the nodal delay bound, what is the network delay bound, what is the buffer size ensuring no loss, and what is the condition for having these finite bounds?

2.8. Consider a system with N servers in tandem providing service to a flow A. Each server is running the WFQ scheduling algorithm with the same capacity C and allocates the same bandwidth to flow A. Assume $A \sim (\sigma, \rho)$. Derive the end-to-end delay bound. To guarantee a certain end-to-end delay, find the minimum bandwidth that should be allocated at each server.

2.9. Consider a system with two servers in tandem providing service to a flow A. The first server guarantees a bounded delay D. The second server offers a strict service curve β. Find the concatenated service curve for this system.

2.10. For the system described in Problem 2.9, if flow $A \sim (\sigma, \rho)$, find the network delay bound using the node-by-node analysis approach.

2.11. For the system described in Problem 2.9, if flow $A \sim (\sigma, \rho)$, find the network delay bound using the concatenation property.

2.12. For the system described in Problem 2.9, if the flow has an arrival curve $\alpha(t) = \min\{\rho \cdot t + \sigma, p \cdot t + L\}$, find the network delay bound using the concatenation property.

3

Traffic Models for Stochastic Network Calculus

In Chapter 2, we introduced important concepts and results from deterministic network calculus. In this and subsequent chapters, we will focus on stochastic network calculus. Particularly here in Chapter 3 we introduce traffic models that have been proposed for stochastic network calculus. These traffic models include three variations of the stochastic arrival curve and traffic models abstracted from the moment generating function of the arrival process. Examples will be given to demonstrate the use of the traffic models introduced in characterizing well-known traffic processes. In addition, the relationships between these stochastic traffic models will be discussed.

3.1 $(\sigma(\theta), \rho(\theta))$ Traffic Characterization

To better understand the $(\sigma(\theta), \rho(\theta))$ stochastic traffic model, let us start with the moment generating function (MGF) of an arrival process $A(s, s+t)$, $t, s \geq 0$, which is

$$M_{A(s,s+t)}(\theta) = E\left[e^{\theta(A(s+t)-A(s))}\right]. \tag{3.1}$$

An upper bound on $M_{A(s,s+t)}(\theta)$ is $\sup_{s \geq 0} M_{A(s,s+t)}(\theta)$, if it exists, or

$$M_{A(s,s+t)}(\theta) \leq \sup_{s \geq 0} M_{A(s,s+t)}(\theta)$$
$$= \sup_{s \geq 0} E\left[e^{\theta(A(s+t)-A(s))}\right]. \tag{3.2}$$

With simple manipulation, (3.2) becomes

$$\frac{1}{\theta} \log E\left[e^{\theta(A(s+t)-A(s))}\right] \leq \frac{1}{\theta} \sup_{s \geq 0} \log E\left[e^{\theta(A(s+t)-A(s))}\right]. \tag{3.3}$$

Y. Jiang, Y. Liu, *Stochastic Network Calculus*,
DOI: 10.1007/978-1-84800-127-5_3,
© Springer-Verlag London Limited 2008

The right-hand side of (3.3) is called *the minimum envelope process of process A with respect to θ* (*θ-MEP*), denoted by $\mathring{A}^{MEP}(\theta, t)$ or

$$\mathring{A}^{MEP}(\theta, t) = \frac{1}{\theta} \sup_{s \geq 0} \log E\left[e^{\theta(A(s+t) - A(s))}\right], \tag{3.4}$$

for which the minimum envelope rate (MER) of A with respect to θ (*θ-MER*), denoted by $\mathring{a}^{MEP}(\theta)$, is defined to be [15]

$$\mathring{a}^{MEP}(\theta) = \limsup_{t \to \infty} \frac{1}{\theta t} \sup_{s \geq 0} \log E\left[e^{\theta(A(s+t) - A(s))}\right]. \tag{3.5}$$

Suppose $A(t)$ has stationary increments; i.e., for any s, $A(s, s+t)$ has the same distribution as $A(t)$. Then (3.5) becomes

$$\mathring{a}^{MEP}(\theta) = \limsup_{t \to \infty} \frac{1}{\theta t} \log E\left[e^{\theta A(t)}\right], \tag{3.6}$$

which is commonly called the *effective bandwidth* of A [18]. Effective bandwidth [36][81][80], is a widely used stochastic traffic model for stochastic QoS analysis in computer networks. It is used particularly to estimate the minimum bandwidth required to guarantee a certain probabilistic QoS for multiple flows under multiplexing. The effective bandwidth of a flow lies between its mean and peak rates. From (3.6), it is clear that if two flows are independent, then the effective bandwidth of the aggregate of the two flows is simply the sum of the effective bandwidths of each flow. This elegant property leads to many applications of effective bandwidth.

Similar to the (σ, ρ) traffic model, it is interesting to study cases where the right-hand side of (3.3) is upper-bounded by a function $\rho(\theta) \cdot t + \sigma(\theta)$ with respect to a chosen θ. Specifically, the $(\sigma(\theta), \rho(\theta))$ stochastic traffic model is defined as follows [15][18].

Definition 3.1. *A process $A(t)$ is said to be $(\sigma(\theta), \rho(\theta))$ upper constrained (for some $\theta > 0$) if, for all $s, t \geq 0$,*

$$\frac{1}{\theta} \log E\left[e^{\theta A(s, s+t)}\right] \leq \rho(\theta) \cdot t + \sigma(\theta). \tag{3.7}$$

It has been shown that many types of traffic can be represented using this $(\sigma(\theta), \rho(\theta))$ model [15][18], which includes exponential on-off, markov modulated process (MMP), and effective bandwidth.

3.2 t.a.c. Stochastic Arrival Curve

In this and subsequent sections, three variations of the *stochastic arrival curve* are introduced, namely the *traffic-amount-centric (t.a.c.) stochastic arrival curve, virtual-backlog-centric (v.b.c.) stochastic arrival curve,* and *maximum-(virtual)-backlog-centric (m.b.c.) stochastic arrival curve.* These stochastic traffic models play critical role in stochastic network calculus.

The t.a.c. stochastic arrival curve model is defined based on the amount of traffic generated by a flow in a time interval. Intuitively, a deterministic arrival curve α tells us that the amount of traffic generated by the flow in any time interval $(s, t]$ is upper-bounded by $\alpha(t-s)$. This *traffic amount property* of the deterministic arrival curve can be used to find its probabilistic counterpart. Particularly, based on the traffic amount intuition, the t.a.c. stochastic arrival curve is defined as follows.

Definition 3.2 (t.a.c. Stochastic Arrival Curve). *A flow is said to have a traffic-amount-centric (t.a.c.) stochastic arrival curve $\alpha \in \mathcal{F}$ with bounding function $f \in \bar{\mathcal{F}}$, denoted by $A \sim_{ta} \langle f, \alpha \rangle$, if for all $0 \leq s \leq t$ and all $x \geq 0$ there holds*

$$P\{A(s,t) - \alpha(t - s) > x\} \leq f(x). \tag{3.8}$$

Many stochastic traffic models have been proposed in the literature for stochastic service guarantee analysis that can be considered as special cases of Definition 3.2, as demonstrated below.

Example 3.3. In this example, we show that the $(\sigma(\theta), \rho(\theta))$ model can be easily mapped to the t.a.c. stochastic arrival curve. Specifically, suppose the arrival process $A(t)$ of a flow is $(\sigma(\theta), \rho(\theta))$-upper constrained. From the definition, it is known that

$$\frac{1}{\theta} \log E\left[e^{\theta A(s,s+t)}\right] \leq \rho(\theta) \cdot t + \sigma(\theta),$$

or equivalently

$$E\left[e^{\theta A(s,s+t)}\right] \leq e^{\theta[\rho(\theta) \cdot t + \sigma(\theta)]}.$$

Applying the Chernoff bound yields

$$P\{A(s, s + t) - \alpha(t) > x\} \leq e^{-\theta x} E\left[e^{\theta(A(s,s+t) - \alpha(t))}\right]$$
$$\leq e^{-\theta x} e^{\theta[\rho(\theta) \cdot t + \sigma(\theta) - \alpha(t)]}. \tag{3.9}$$

The right-hand side of (3.9) implies that for any function $\alpha(t)$ satisfying $\alpha(t) \geq \rho(\theta) \cdot t + \sigma(\theta)$, it is a t.a.c. stochastic arrival curve of the flow with bounding function $e^{-\theta x}$. To conclude, we have the following result.

Theorem 3.4. *If a flow is $(\sigma(\theta), \rho(\theta))$ upper constrained, then it has a t.a.c. stochastic arrival curve $\alpha(t) = \rho(\theta) \cdot t + \sigma(\theta)$ with bounding function $f(x) = e^{-\theta x}$, or $A \sim_{ta} \langle e^{-\theta x}, \rho(\theta) \cdot t + \sigma(\theta) \rangle$.*

Example 3.5. As a special case of the previous example, we can map the *effective bandwidth* model to the t.a.c. stochastic arrival curve model. Specifically, suppose the flow has an effective bandwidth $\rho(\theta)$, which by definition is

$$\rho(\theta) = \lim_{t \to \infty} \sup \frac{1}{\theta t} \log E \left[e^{\theta A(t)} \right]. \tag{3.10}$$

Suppose $A(t)$ has stationary increments, which is a condition often assumed when deriving the effective bandwidth. We then have for any $s, t \geq 0$,

$$A(s, s + t) =_{st} A(t).$$

Note that the effective bandwidth definition (3.10) implies that for every $\epsilon > 0$ there exists some $t_0 < \infty$ such that

$$\frac{1}{\theta} \log E \left[e^{\theta A(s, s+t)} \right] \leq (\rho(\theta) + \epsilon) t \tag{3.11}$$

for all $t \geq t_0$. For any $t < t_0$, since $A(s, s + t)$ is non-decreasing, we get

$$\frac{1}{\theta} \log E \left[e^{\theta A(s, s+t)} \right] \leq (\rho(\theta) + \epsilon) t_0. \tag{3.12}$$

Combining (3.11) and (3.12), we can conclude that

$$\frac{1}{\theta} \log E \left[e^{\theta A(s, s+t)} \right] \leq \max\{ (\rho(\theta) + \epsilon) t, (\rho(\theta) + \epsilon) t_0 \}$$
$$\leq (\rho(\theta) + \epsilon) t + (\rho(\theta) + \epsilon) t_0.$$

Letting $\sigma_\epsilon(\theta) = (\rho(\theta) + \epsilon) t_0$, we get

$$\frac{1}{\theta} \log E \left[e^{\theta A(s, s+t)} \right] \leq (\rho(\theta) + \epsilon) t + \sigma_\epsilon(\theta)$$

and hence A is $(\sigma_\epsilon(\theta), \rho(\theta) + \epsilon)$ upper constrained. Then, from the previous example, its t.a.c stochastic arrival curve characterization is obtained.

Example 3.6. It is also easy to verify that the (deterministic) arrival curve model is a special case of Definition 3.2 in which $f(x) = 0$ for $x \geq 0$.

Example 3.7. In [138], a stochastic traffic model called exponentially bounded burstiness (EBB), is proposed, which is later extended in [128] to the stochastically bounded burstiness (SBB) model.

A flow is said to have EBB if for all $s, t \geq 0$ and all $x > 0$

$$P\{A(s, s+t) - \rho \cdot t > x\} \leq a e^{-bx}, \tag{3.13}$$

where ρ, a and b are constants.

A flow is said to be stochastically bounded bursty with upper rate ρ and bounding function f if there exists $f \in \bar{\mathcal{G}}$ and for all $s, t \geq 0$ and all $x > 0$ there holds for the arrival process $A(t)$

$$P\{A(s, s+t) - \rho \cdot t > x\} \leq f(x). \tag{3.14}$$

Both EBB and SBB are special cases of Definition 3.2. Particularly, letting $\alpha(t) = \rho \cdot t$ and $f(x) = ae^{-bx}$ in Definition 3.2 where a and b are two nonnegative parameters, it reduces to EBB.

In Definition 3.2 letting $\alpha(t) = \rho \cdot t$ and $f(x)$ the function satisfying some constraint, it reduces to SBB. The constraint on the bounding function $f(x)$ in SBB is $f \in \bar{\mathcal{G}}$, where $\bar{\mathcal{G}}$, as defined in Chapter 1, denotes the function class that contains all the functions defined on $[0, \infty]$ with the following properties: (i) any $f \in \bar{\mathcal{G}}$ is non-negative and non-increasing; and (ii) for $f \in \bar{\mathcal{G}}$, letting $f^{(n)}(x)$ be the n-fold integration of function $f(x)$, (e.g., $f^{(1)}(x) = \int_x^\infty f(u)du$), then $f^{(n)} \in \bar{\mathcal{G}}$ for any order $n \geq 0$.

Example 3.8. In [95], a stochastic traffic model called the *effective envelope* was used to study stochastic service guarantees, which is also a special case of the model defined in Definition 3.2. Specifically, letting $x = 0$ and $f(0) = \epsilon$ in (3.8), Definition 3.2 reduces to the effective envelope model.

Example 3.9. Consider a flow with fixed unit packet size. Suppose its packets arrive according to a Poisson process with mean rate λ. Then, in any time interval $(s, s+t]$, $A(s, s+t)$ satisfies, for any $x \geq 0$,

$$P\{A(s, s+t) - \lambda t > x\} \leq \sum_{k=\lceil x+\lambda t\rceil}^{\infty} \left\{ \frac{e^{-\lambda t}[\lambda t]^k}{k!} \right\},$$

where $\lceil x \rceil$ denotes the minimum integer larger than or equal to x.

Example 3.10. Let $a(t)$ denote the traffic that arrived at $(t-1, t]$. Then $A(s, s+t) = \sum_{u=s}^{s+t} a(u)$. Assume $a(u)$, $u = 1, 2, \ldots$, are independent and identically distributed. Then, from the central limit theory, $A(s, s+t)$ converges to a Gaussian process as $t \to \infty$. Because of this, a Gaussian process is often used to approximate the cumulative arrival process. Suppose $a(t)$ has a mean given by λ and a variance v. Then, from a Gaussian distribution, we get for any $\rho > \lambda$

$$P\{A(s, s+t) - \rho t > x\} \leq \Psi\left(\frac{(\rho - \lambda)t + x}{\sqrt{t^2 v}} \right),$$

where $\Psi(x) \equiv \frac{1}{\sqrt{2\pi}} \int_x^\infty e^{-\frac{u^2}{2}} du$.

3.2.1 Difficulties and Additional Constraints

While promising and intuitively simple, the t.a.c. stochastic arrival curve model has limited use if no additional constraint is enforced. To demonstrate this, let us consider a simple node with constant service rate C and with its input flow A satisfying $A \sim_{ta} \langle f, \rho \cdot t \rangle$, where $\rho \leq C$. Suppose we are interested in the backlog $B(t)$. Then, by definition, $B(t) = A(t) - A^*(t)$. Since the node has constant service rate C, it has a (deterministic) service curve $C \cdot t$. In other words, $A^*(t) \geq \inf_{0 \leq s \leq t} \{A(s) + C \cdot (t - s)\}$. Then, we get

$$B(t) \leq A(t) - \inf_{0 \leq s \leq t} \{A(s) + C \cdot (t - s)\}$$

$$= \sup_{0 \leq s \leq t} \{A(s, t) - C \cdot (t - s)\} \tag{3.15}$$

$$\leq \sup_{0 \leq s \leq t} \{A(s, t) - \rho \cdot (t - s)\}. \tag{3.16}$$

Here, we have difficulty in further deriving results from (3.15) or (3.16) if no additional constraint is added since what we have is $P\{A(s, t) - \rho \cdot (t - s) > x\} \leq f(x)$. A similar difficulty will also be met if other performance metrics need to be investigated. Since a constant-rate node is the simplest network case, we hence believe that without additional constraints on the model, it is difficult to apply the stochastic traffic model defined in Definition 3.2 to perform stochastic service guarantee analysis.

To address the difficulty of using a t.a.c. stochastic arrival curve in service guarantee analysis, additional constraints on the bounding function f are needed. Essentially, these constraints are introduced to allow us to find a bounding function on the complementary cummulative distribution function (CCDF) of the right-hand side of (3.15); i.e., for any $x \geq 0$,

$$P\left\{\sup_{0 \leq s \leq t} [A(s, t) - \rho \cdot (t - s)] > x\right\}$$

$$\leq P\left\{\sup_{0 \leq s \leq t} [A(s, t) - \rho \cdot (t - s)]^+ > x\right\} \tag{3.17}$$

$$\leq \sum_{s=0}^{t} P\{[A(s, t) - \rho \cdot (t - s)]^+ > x\}$$

$$= \sum_{s=0}^{t} P\{[A(s, t) - \rho \cdot (t - s)] > x\}$$

$$\leq \sum_{s=0}^{t} f_{s,t}(x), \tag{3.18}$$

where, as in the definition of a t.a.c. stochastic arrival curve, we suppose

$$P\{[A(s, t) - \rho \cdot (t - s)] > x\} \leq f_{s,t}(x). \tag{3.19}$$

Note that, s and t are both explicitly included in the bounding function $f_{s,t}(x)$. In many cases, such as when $A(t)$ has stationary increments or has a stochastic envelope process as to be discussed in Section 3.5, a bounding function dependent only on $t - s$, denoted by $f_{t-s}(x)$, may be sufficient, which is

$$P\{[A(s, t) - \rho \cdot (t - s)] > x\} \leq f_{t-s}(x). \tag{3.20}$$

We then get

$$P\left\{\sup_{0\leq s\leq t}[A(s,t)-\rho\cdot(t-s)]>x\right\}\leq\sum_{\tau=0}^{t}f_\tau(x),\qquad(3.21)$$

which is meaningful only when its right-hand side is upper-bounded by one. For this reason, one constraint is to assume $\sum_{\tau=0}^{\infty}f_\tau(x)$ exists. Letting $f'(x)=\sum_{\tau=0}^{\infty}f_\tau(x)$, this constraint implies there is some $f'(x)$ that makes $P\{\sup_{0\leq s\leq t}[A(s,t)-\rho\cdot(t-s)]>x\}\leq f'(x)$ hold, from which a bound on the CCDF of backlog is easily derived from (3.16). This idea has been used to develop new variations of the stochastic arrival curve, such as the generalized stochastically bounded bursty (gSBB) traffic model [140], the v.b.c. stochastic arrival curve model that is generalized from gSBB, and the m.b.c. stochastic arrival curve model. They will be introduced and discussed in detail in the subsequent sections.

Another constraint that will also often be used in this book is to assume that the bounding function $f(x)$ in (3.8), (3.19), or (3.21) is in $\bar{\mathcal{G}}$; i.e., $f\in\bar{\mathcal{G}}$, as for the SBB model. Here, the subscript has been removed from $f_{s,t}(x)$ or $f_\tau(x)$ to implicitly show that this $f(x)$ is no longer dependent on time. With this constraint, since one can get from (3.15)

$$B(t)\leq\sup_{0\leq s\leq t}\{A(s,t)-\rho\cdot(t-s)-(C-\rho)\cdot(t-s)\},$$

the analysis becomes to find a bound on the CCDF of the right hand side of the inequality above. This is achieved using an analysis similar to that above,

$$P\left\{\sup_{0\leq s\leq t}\{A(s,t)-\rho\cdot(t-s)-(C-\rho)\cdot(t-s)\}>x\right\}$$

$$\leq\sum_{s=0}^{t}P\{[A(s,t)-\rho\cdot(t-s)]>x+(C-\rho)\cdot(t-s)\}$$

$$\leq\sum_{\tau=0}^{t}f(x+(C-\rho)\cdot\tau)\qquad(3.22)$$

$$\leq f(x)+\frac{1}{C-\rho}\int_x^\infty f(y)dy,$$

where step (3.22) implies a requirement similar to that for the constraint discussed above for (3.21).

For $(\sigma(\theta),\rho(\theta))$-constrained traffic, its bounding functions under the t.a.c. stochastic arrival curve characterization can be obtained from (3.9). Interestingly, the bounding function shown as the right-hand side of (3.9) satisfies the first constraint, while the simplified bounding function from (3.9) in Theorem 3.4 satisfies the second constraint. Since the latter bounding function is derived from and looser than (3.9), the bound on the CCDF of backlog obtained based on the first constraint is better.

3.3 v.b.c. Stochastic Arrival Curve

The virtual-backlog-centric (v.b.c.) stochastic arrival curve model explores the *virtual backlog property* of the deterministic arrival curve, which is that the queue length of a virtual single-server queue (SSQ) fed with the same flow with a deterministic arrival curve is upper-bounded.

Specifically, for a flow having an arrival curve, we can construct a virtual single-server queue system fed with the flow that has infinite buffer space, and the buffer is initially empty. Then, suppose the virtual SSQ provides a deterministic service curve α to the flow or $A^*(t) = A \otimes \alpha(0, t)$ for all $t \geq 0$. We now have that the unfinished work or backlog in the SSQ system at time t is $B(t) = A(t) - A^*(t) = \sup_{0 \leq s \leq t}\{A(s, t) - \alpha(t - s)\}$. If the flow is constrained by arrival curve $\alpha(t) + x$ for all $t \geq 0$, it is clear that the backlog at the virtual SSQ is also upper-bounded by x. This is indeed Part (ii) of Lemma 2.4.

Based on the virtual backlog property, we define a virtual-backlog-centric (v.b.c.) stochastic arrival curve as follows.

Definition 3.11 (v.b.c. Stochastic Arrival Curve). *A flow is said to have a virtual-backlog-centric (v.b.c.) stochastic arrival curve $\alpha \in \mathcal{F}$ with bounding function $f \in \bar{\mathcal{F}}$, denoted by $A(t) \sim_{vb} \langle f, \alpha \rangle$, if for all $t \geq 0$ and all $x \geq 0$ there holds*

$$P\left\{ \sup_{0 \leq s \leq t} \{A(s, t) - \alpha(t - s)\} > x \right\} \leq f(x). \tag{3.23}$$

As discussed in Section 3.2.1, the v.b.c. stochastic arrival curve model implies the first constraint introduced there, with which the difficulty discussed in Section 3.2.1 for the t.a.c. stochastic arrival curve is addressed.

We now present a principle of the v.b.c stochastic arrival curve similar to that for the deterministic arrival curve model.

Theorem 3.12. *Let X be some non-negative random variable.*

(i) If $\hat{A}(t; \rho) \leq_{st} X$ for all $t \geq 0$, then $A(s, t) - \alpha(t - s) \leq_{st} X$ for all $0 \leq s \leq t$.
(ii) If $A(s, t) - \alpha(t - s) \leq_{st} X$ for all $0 \leq s \leq t$ and particularly $\{A(0, t) - \alpha(t), \ldots, A(t - 1, t) - \alpha(1)\} \leq_{st} \{X, \ldots, X\}$, then $\sup_{0 \leq s \leq t}\{A(s, t) - \alpha(t - s) \leq_{st} X$ for all $t \geq 0$.

Proof. The first part holds trivially since it is always true that $A(s, t) - \rho(t - s) \leq \sup_{s \leq t}\{A(s, t) - \rho(t - s)\} = \hat{A}(t; \rho)$.

For the second part, the proof is based on a known result for stochastic ordering (see, e.g., Theorem 2.2.3 in [130] or Theorem 4.3.3 in [108]), which is introduced as Lemma 1.8 in this book.

Suppose that for random variables $\{X(1), \ldots, X(t)\}$ and $\{Y(1), \ldots, Y(t)\}$, there holds $\{X(1), \ldots, X(t)\} \leq_{st} \{Y(1), \ldots, Y(t)\}$. Then, for the mapping $Z(t) = \Phi(X_1, \ldots, X_t)$, if it is non-decreasing in $\{x_1, \ldots, x_t\}$, one has $Z'(t) \leq_{st} Z''(t)$, where $Z'(t) = \Phi(X(1), \ldots, X(t))$ and $Z'' = \Phi(Y(1), \ldots, Y(t))$.

For the proof of the second part, it is known that $\sup_{0\leq s\leq t}\{A(s,t)-\alpha(t-s)\} = \max(A(0,t)-\alpha(t),\ldots,A(t-1,t)-\alpha(1))^+$. Let the mapping be $Z(t) = \Phi(X_1,\ldots,X_t) = \max(X_t,\ldots,X_1)^+$ which is clearly non-decreasing. With the given condition, we obtain $\sup_{0\leq s\leq t}\{A(s,t)-\alpha(t-s)\} \leq_{st} \max(X,\ldots,X)^+ = X$ and the second part is proved. $\square$

In Theorem 3.12, by letting $f(x) = P\{X > x\}$, the first part (i.e., $A(s,t)-\alpha(t-s) \leq_{st} X$) implies the definition of a t.a.c. stochastic arrival curve, and the second part (i.e., $\sup_{s\leq t}\{A(s,t) - \alpha(t-s)\} \leq_{st} X$) implies the definition of a v.b.c. stochastic arrival curve.

Comparing Lemma 2.4 with Theorem 3.12, we can see that the former is more general than the latter in the sense that less restriction or assumption is needed for establishing the principle of the arrival curve. In addition, while Lemma 2.4 shows that the traffic amount property is equivalent to its virtual backlog property, the duality of the t.a.c. stochastic arrival curve and v.b.c. stochastic arrival curve holds only in the context of stochastic ordering and with some additional requirements on $A(t)$.

The requirements for the second part of Theorem 3.12 to hold seem to be very restrictive. Because of this, Theorem 3.13 establishes a more general relationship between the t.a.c. stochastic arrival curve and v.b.c. stochastic arrival curve. It is worth highlighting that the second part of Theorem 3.13 does not hold in general if the requirement on the bounding function is relaxed to $f \in \bar{\mathcal{F}}$.

Theorem 3.13. *(i) If a flow has a v.b.c. stochastic arrival curve $\alpha \in \mathcal{F}$ with bounding function $f \in \bar{\mathcal{F}}$, then the flow has a t.a.c. stochastic arrival curve $\alpha \in \mathcal{F}$ with bounding function $f \in \bar{\mathcal{F}}$.*

(ii) Conversely, if a flow has a t.a.c. stochastic arrival curve $\alpha \in \mathcal{F}$ with bounding function $f \in \bar{\mathcal{G}}$, it also has a v.b.c. stochastic arrival curve $\alpha_\theta \in \mathcal{F}$ with bounding function $f^\theta \in \bar{\mathcal{G}}$, where

$$\alpha_\theta(t) = \alpha(t) + \theta \cdot t, \tag{3.24}$$

$$f^\theta(x) = \left[f(x) + \frac{1}{\theta} \int_x^\infty f(y)dy \right]_1, \tag{3.25}$$

for any $\theta > 0$.

Proof. The first part follows easily from the fact that for any $0 \leq s \leq t$, $A(s,t) - \alpha(t-s) \leq \sup_{0\leq s\leq t}\{A(s,t) - \alpha(t-s)\}$.

For the second part, there holds

$$\sup_{0\leq s\leq t} \{A(s,t) - \alpha_\theta(t-s)\} \leq_{st} \sup_{0\leq s\leq t} \{A(s,t) - \alpha_\theta(t-s)\}^+.$$

Since, for any $x \geq 0$, $P\{[A(s,t) - \alpha(t-s) - \theta(t-s)]^+ > x\} = P\{A(s,t) - \alpha(t-s) - \theta \cdot (t-s) > x\} \leq f(x + \theta \cdot (t-s))$, we then have

$$P\left\{\sup_{0\leq s\leq t}\{A(s,t)-\alpha_\theta(t-s)\}>x\right\}$$

$$\leq\sum_{s=0}^{t}P\left\{[A(s,t)-\alpha_\theta(t-s)]^+>x\right\}$$

$$\leq\sum_{s=0}^{t}f(x+\theta\cdot(t-s))=\sum_{\tau=0}^{t}f(x+\theta\cdot\tau)$$

$$\leq\sum_{\tau=0}^{\infty}f(x+\theta\cdot\tau)=f(x)+\sum_{\tau=1}^{\infty}f(x+\theta\cdot\tau)$$

$$\leq f(x)+\frac{1}{\theta}\int_x^\infty f(y)dy.$$

The second part follows from the inequality above and the fact that the probability is always not greater than one. □

Example 3.14. It can be verified that a flow has a (deterministic) arrival curve α, if and only if it has a v.b.c. stochastic arrival curve $A\sim_{vb}\langle 0,\alpha\rangle$.

With Theorem 3.13, it is easy to verify that many types of traffic discussed in the previous subsection also have v.b.c. stochastic arrival curves, which include EBB and SBB.

In addition, based on the following Lemma 3.15, many other types of traffic can also be shown to have v.b.c stochastic arrival curves.

Lemma 3.15. *For a flow, if the arrivals $a(t)\equiv A(t-1,t),t=1,2,\ldots$, are independent and identically distributed (i.i.d.), then there holds*

$$W(t)\leq_{st}W(t+1)\leq_{st}W(\infty),\qquad(3.26)$$

where $W(t)=\sup_{0\leq s\leq t}\{A(s,t)-r\cdot(t-s)\}$ and $W(\infty)$ denotes the steady-state of $W(t)$. In addition, if $W(\infty)$ exists, the corresponding flow has a m.b.c stochastic arrival curve $\alpha(t)=r\cdot t$ with bounding function $P\{W(\infty)>x\}$, or $A\sim_{vb}(r\cdot t,P\{W(\infty)>x\})$.

Proof. For any $t(\geq 0)$, consider the mapping function of random variables $X_1,\ldots,X_t$

$$\Phi(X_1,\ldots,X_t)=\sup_{0\leq s\leq t}\left\{\sum_{u=s+1}^{t}X_u-r\cdot(t-s)\right\},\qquad(3.27)$$

which is clearly wide-sense increasing.

Letting $X_1=a(1),\ldots,X_t=a(t)$ and $X_1=a(2),\ldots,X_t=a(t+1)$ in the mapping function provides two mappings $\Phi(a(1),\ldots,a(t))$ and $\Phi(a(2),\ldots,a(t+1))$, respectively. It is easily verified that $\Phi(a(1),\ldots,a(t))=W(t)$ and $\Phi(a(2),\ldots,a(t+1))=\sup_{0\leq s\leq t}\{A(s+1,t+1)-r(t-s)\}$.

Since $a(t), t = 1, 2, \ldots$, are i.i.d., then from Lemma 1.8 it can be concluded that,

$$\Phi(a(1), \ldots, a(t)) =_{st} \Phi(a(2), \ldots, a(t+1))$$

and hence

$$
\begin{aligned}
W(t) &=_{st} \sup_{0 \leq s \leq t} \{A(s+1, t+1) - r(t-s)\} \\
&= \sup_{0 \leq u-1 \leq t} \{A(u, t+1) - r(t+1-u)\} \\
&= \sup_{1 \leq u \leq t+1} \{A(u, t+1) - r(t+1-u)\} \\
&\leq \sup_{0 \leq u \leq t+1} \{A(u, t+1) - r(t+1-u)\} = W(t+1). \quad (3.28)
\end{aligned}
$$

The conclusion is obtained by iteratively applying (3.28) together with the definition of a v.b.c. stochastic arrival curve.   □

The following examples show that under the same condition as Lemma 3.15, many types of traffic can be readily represented using the v.b.c stochastic arrival curve model.

Example 3.16. We begin with Poisson traffic. Suppose all packets of a flow have the same size L and they arrive according to a Poisson process with mean arrival rate λ. Then, based on Fry's state equations for $M/D/1$ [47], it is straightforward to get the steady-state queue length distribution, from which we can conclude that the flow has a v.b.c. stochastic arrival curve $A(t) \sim_{vb} \langle f^{Poisson}, r \cdot t \rangle$ for any $r > \lambda L$, where, with $a = \lambda L / \rho$ and $k = \lceil \frac{x}{L} \rceil$,

$$f^{Poisson}(x) = 1 - (1-a) \sum_{i=0}^{k} \left[\frac{[a(i-k)]^i}{i!} e^{-a(i-k)} \right]. \quad (3.29)$$

Example 3.17. We next consider Gaussian traffic that has a stationary Gaussian arrival process. Let $\hat{r} \cdot t$ and $\hat{v}(t)$ be the mean and variance of the Gaussian arrival process $A(t)$, respectively. Then, available simulation and analytical results in the literature [21] [83] [1] [104] suggest that, for all $r > \hat{r}$, $\exp\left(-\inf_{s \geq 0} \frac{(x+(r-\hat{r})s)^2}{2\hat{v}(s)}\right)$, is likely an upper bound on $P\{\sup_{0 \leq s \leq t}\{A(s,t) - r \cdot (t-s)\} > x\}$. Hence, for Gaussian traffic, it (approximately) has a v.b.c. stochastic arrival curve $A(t) \sim_{vb} \langle f^{Gaussian}, r \cdot t \rangle$ with

$$f^{Gaussian}(x) = \exp\left(-\frac{(x+(r-\hat{r})s)^2}{2\hat{v}^*}\right), \quad (3.30)$$

where $\hat{v}^* \equiv \hat{v}(s^*)$ and s^* is chosen such that $\frac{(x+(r-\hat{r})s)^2}{2\hat{v}(s)}$ reaches its minimum at s^*.

Example 3.18. In Section 3.1, the $(\sigma(\theta), \rho(\theta))$ model called θ-MER (minimum envelope rate with respect to θ) was introduced. The literature has proved that many types of traffic can be represented using this $(\sigma(\theta), \rho(\theta))$ model [15] [18], which include exponential on-off, Markov modulated process (MMP), and effective bandwidth.

In Example 3.3, the t.a.c. stochastic arrival curve representation of the $(\sigma(\theta), \rho(\theta))$ model was presented. Then, using the second part of Theorem 3.13, its v.b.c. stochastic arrival curve representation can also be obtained easily. Alternatively, assume $a(t), t \geq 0$, are i.i.d. as normally implied by the $(\sigma(\theta), \rho(\theta))$ model, and the corresponding $A(t)$ is $(\sigma(\theta), \rho(\theta))$ upper constrained. Then, it can be verified by applying $f_\tau(x) = e^{-\theta x} e^{\theta[\rho(\theta)\tau - r \cdot \tau + \sigma(\theta)]}$ from (3.9) to (3.21) that

$$P\left\{ \sup_{0 \leq s \leq t} \{A(s,t) - r(t-s)\} > x \right\} \leq \frac{e^{\theta\sigma(\theta)}}{1 - e^{\theta(\rho(\theta)-r)}} e^{-\theta x} \tag{3.31}$$

for any $r > \rho(\theta)$.

Inequality (3.31) implies that the traffic has v.b.c. stochastic service curve $A(t) \sim_{vb} \langle f^{MER}, rt \rangle$ with all $r > \rho(\theta)$ and

$$f^{MER}(x) = \beta(\theta)e^{-\theta x}, \tag{3.32}$$

where
$$\beta(\theta) = e^{\theta\sigma(\theta)}(1 - e^{\theta(\rho(\theta)-r)})^{-1}.$$

An immediate implication of this is that *exponential on-off, Markov modulated process (MMP)* and *effective bandwidth* types of traffic can be readily represented using the v.b.c. stochastic arrival curve, and their corresponding bounding functions can be found [15] [18].

Example 3.19. It is worth highlighting that the traffic models discussed in the examples above have bounding functions with exponential forms and/or belonging to the function set $\bar{\mathcal{G}}$ for which any $f \in \bar{\mathcal{G}}$ implies its n-fold integration $f^{(n)}$ also belongs to $\bar{\mathcal{G}}$. However, some traffic models may not have bounding functions in $\bar{\mathcal{G}}$. One example is the α−stable traffic model [78][79].

The α−stable traffic model characterizes the self-similar behavior of traffic [78] [79]. The model is defined by the four parameters (α, H, c_1, c_2). In [78], it is shown that the queue length of a constant-rate server fed with α-stable traffic satisfies $P\{W(t; r) > x\} \leq C_\alpha \left(\frac{r-m}{c_1}\right)^{-\alpha}$, where r denotes the rate of the server, and C_α and m are parameters determined from (α, H, c_1, c_2). Clearly, such α-stable traffic can also be modeled using a v.b.c. stochastic arrival curve with $A(t) \sim_{vb} \langle f^{Alpha}, rt \rangle$, where

$$f^{Alpha}(x) = C_\alpha \left(\frac{r-m}{c_1}\right)^{-\alpha}. \tag{3.33}$$

Example 3.20. A probabilistic burstiness curve (PBC) uses a stationary random process to model real-time multimedia traffic [23]. Particularly, it uses the steady-state queue distribution of a constant rate server fed with a flow to represent the traffic of the flow: $P\{q \geq x|r\}$, where r is the service rate of the server and the random variable q denotes the steady-state queue length. Comparing PBC with the definition of stochastic arrival curve, it follows from Lemma 3.15 that PBC is a special case of the latter. In other words, if a flow has a PBC $P\{q \geq x|r\}$, it also has v.b.c stochastic arrival curve $A(t) \sim_{vb} \langle f^{PBC}, rt \rangle$ where

$$f^{PBC}(x) = P\{q \geq x|r\}. \tag{3.34}$$

3.4 m.b.c. Stochastic Arrival Curve

The maximum (virtual)-backlog-centric (m.b.c.) stochastic arrival curve model explores the *maximum virtual backlog property* of the deterministic arrival curve, which is that the maximum queue length of a virtual single-server queue (SSQ) fed with the same flow with a deterministic arrival curve is upper-bounded.

Similar to the discussion for the v.b.c. stochastic arrival curve, for a flow having an arrival curve, we can construct a virtual SSQ system fed with the flow that has infinite buffer space, and the buffer is initially empty. Then, suppose the virtual SSQ provides a deterministic service curve α to the flow or $A^*(t) = A \otimes \alpha(t)$ for all $t \geq 0$. As discussed for Lemma 2.4, we have the maximum backlog in the SSQ system at time t as $\sup_{0 \leq s \leq t} W(s) = \sup_{0 \leq s \leq t} \sup_{0 \leq u \leq s} \{A(u, s) - \alpha(s - u)\}$. If the flow is constrained by arrival curve $\alpha(t) + x$ for all $t \geq 0$, it is clear that the maximum backlog at the virtual SSQ is also upper-bounded by x.

Based on the maximum virtual backlog property, we define an m.b.c. stochastic arrival curve as follows.

Definition 3.21 (m.b.c. Stochastic Arrival Curve). *A flow is said to have a* maximum (virtual)-backlog-centric (m.b.c.) stochastic arrival curve $\alpha \in \mathcal{F}$ *with bounding function* $f_t \in \bar{\mathcal{F}}$, *denoted by* $A(t) \sim_{mb} \langle f_t, \alpha \rangle$, *if for all* $t \geq 0$ *and all* $x \geq 0$ *there holds*

$$P\left\{ \sup_{0 \leq s \leq t} \sup_{0 \leq u \leq s} \{A(u, s) - \alpha(s - u)\} > x \right\} \leq f_t(x). \tag{3.35}$$

It is worth highlighting that in Definition 3.21 the bounding function f_t has a subscript t that explicitly states that the function may be dependent on time t.

Example 3.22. It can be verified that a flow has a (deterministic) arrival curve α, if and only if it has an m.b.c. stochastic arrival curve $A \sim_{mb} \langle 0, \alpha \rangle$.

Based on the definitions of t.a.c. stochastic arrival curve, v.b.c. stochastic arrival curve, and m.b.c. stochastic arrival curve, since $A(s,t) - \alpha(t - s) \leq \sup_{0 \leq s \leq t}[A(s,t) - \alpha(t-s)] \leq \sup_{0 \leq s \leq t} \sup_{0 \leq u \leq s}[A(u,s) - \alpha(s-u)]$, the following relationship between them is immediately obtained, whose deterministic counterpart is Lemma 2.4.

Lemma 3.23. $A \sim_{mb} \langle f, \alpha \rangle \longrightarrow A \sim_{vb} \langle f, \alpha \rangle \longrightarrow A \sim_{ta} \langle f, \alpha \rangle$, where $X \longrightarrow Y$ means X implies Y.

It is worth highlighting that while for the (deterministic) arrival curve model, both Lemma 2.4 (i) $\rightarrow$ (ii) $\rightarrow$ (iii) and Lemma 2.4 (i) $\leftarrow$ (ii) $\leftarrow$ (iii) hold, for the stochastic arrival curve, we generally do not have $A \sim_{mb} \langle f, \alpha \rangle \leftarrow A \sim_{vb} \langle f, \alpha \rangle \leftarrow A \sim_{ta} \langle f, \alpha \rangle$.

Let us denote by $M(t)$ the maximum up-to-date backlog at time t in an initially empty system with constant service rate r and arrival process $A(t)$, or formally

$$M(t) \equiv \sup_{0 \leq s \leq t} \sup_{0 \leq u \leq s} [A(u,s) - r(s - u)]. \tag{3.36}$$

It can be easily verified that, for $M(t)$, the equation

$$M(t+1) = \max[M(t), W(t+1)] \tag{3.37}$$

holds, where

$$W(t+1) = \sup_{0 \leq s \leq t+1} [A(s, t+1) - r(t+1-s)].$$

With (3.37), it is clear that

$$M(t) \leq M(t+1) \leq \cdots \leq M(\infty). \tag{3.38}$$

Equations (3.36) and (3.38) present a technique for possibly finding the m.b.c. stochastic arrival curve characterization of an arrival process. They imply that if for some r the complementary probability distribution function (CPDF) $P\{M(t) > x\}$ can be found, then the process has $A \sim_{mb} \langle P\{M(t) > x\}, rt \rangle$. In addition, if $P\{M(\infty) > x\}$ exists, then it can also be used as the bounding function and we can conclude that $A \sim_{mb} \langle P\{M(\infty) > x\}, rt \rangle$. However, (3.38) shows that $M(t)$ increases over t, which implies that in general $M(\infty)$ may not be bounded above, and $M(t)$ could not have a limit distribution. Indeed, there are literature results showing how maximum queue length and maximum weighting time, which are similar to the m.b.c. stochastic arrival curve, may grow with time (e.g., see [3][123][119]).

In the following result, we try to relate the m.b.c. stochastic arrival curve with the v.b.c. stochastic arrival curve, which can be used to further relate the m.b.c. stochastic arrival curve with the t.a.c. stochastic arrival curve.

Theorem 3.24. *(i) If a flow A has an m.b.c. stochastic arrival curve α with bounding function $f(x)$ or $A \sim_{mb} \langle f, \alpha \rangle$, then it has a v.b.c. stochastic arrival curve α with the same bounding function $f(x)$.*

(ii) If a flow A has a v.b.c. stochastic arrival curve α with bounding function f or A $\sim_{vb}$ $\langle f, \alpha \rangle$, then it has an m.b.c. stochastic arrival curve α with bounding function f_t^θ, where

$$f_t^\theta(x) = \left[\frac{1}{\theta} \int_{x-\theta t}^{t} f(y) \, dy \right]_1 \tag{3.39}$$

for any $\theta > 0$.

Proof. The first part follows easily from the fact that $\sup_{0 \le s \le t} [A(s,t) - \alpha(t - s)] \le \sup_{0 \le s \le t} \sup_{0 \le u \le s} [A(u,s) - \alpha(s - u)]$.

For the second part, we have

$$\sup_{0 \le s \le t} \sup_{0 \le u \le s} [A(u,s) - \alpha(s - u)] \le \sup_{1 \le s \le t} \{W(s) - \theta \cdot s\}^+ + \theta \cdot t,$$

where $W(s) = \sup_{0 \le u \le s} [A(u,s) - \alpha(s - u)]$, for which it is known that

$$P\left\{ \sup_{1 \le s \le t} \{W(s) - \theta \cdot s\}^+ + \theta \cdot t > x \right\} \le \sum_{s=1}^{t} P\{[W(s) - \theta \cdot s]^+ + \theta \cdot t > x\}.$$

We then conclude that

$$P\left\{ \sup_{0 \le s \le t} \sup_{0 \le u \le s} [A(u,s) - \alpha_\theta(t - s)] > x \right\}$$

$$\le \sum_{s=1}^{t} P\{[W(s) - \theta \cdot s]^+ + \theta \cdot t > x\}$$

$$\le \sum_{s=1}^{t} f(x - \theta \cdot t + \theta \cdot s) \tag{3.40}$$

$$\le \frac{1}{\theta} \int_{x-\theta \cdot t}^{t} f(y) dy.$$

□

With the relationship established in Theorem 3.24, the m.b.c. stochastic arrival curve of the various types of traffic discussed in the previous section for the v.b.c. stochastic arrival curve can be obtained readily. It is interesting to notice that when t becomes large, the right-hand side of (3.39) tends toward 1. This is consistent with (3.38) and the literature results [3][123][119], which is that the maximum virtual backlog $M(t)$ is increasing on t.

Recent literature suggests an idea that may be used to resolve the time-increasing problem, which is to assume the existence of a timescale T enforced on the traffic and service [96]. For example, one could assume the maximum virtual backlog $M(t)$ is limited by

$$M(t) \le \sup_{t-T \le s \le t} \sup_{0 \le u \le s} [A(u,s) - r(s - u)]. \tag{3.41}$$

Or, one might assume there exists a time scale T such that the following would be used to define the m.b.c. stochastic arrival curve:

$$P\left\{ \sup_{t-T\leq s\leq t}\sup_{0\leq u\leq s}[A(u,s)-r(s-u)]>x \right\}\leq f(x). \qquad (3.42)$$

If either (3.41) or (3.42) had been used, the bounding function in (3.39) would have become $(T+1)\cdot f(x)$.

In this book, however we shall not focus on the timescale approach. Instead, we consider a new model that is a variation of the m.b.c. stochastic arrival curve and is introduced in the following subsection, where the time-increasing problem can be avoided.

3.4.1 θ-m.b.c. Stochastic Arrival Curve

Taking into consideration the time-increasing nature of $M(t)$, we modify (3.35). In the following, we introduce a variation of the m.b.c. stochastic arrival curve that tries to make the bounding function possibly independent of time t by explicitly considering the ever-increasing nature of $M(t)$ in formulating the definition.

Definition 3.25 (θ-m.b.c. Stochastic Arrival Curve). *A flow is said to have a θ-m.b.c. stochastic arrival curve $\alpha \in \mathcal{F}$ with respect to θ, with bounding function $f^\theta(x) \in \bar{\mathcal{F}}$, denoted by $A(t) \sim_{\theta-mb} \langle f^\theta, \alpha \rangle$, if for all $t \geq 0$ and all $x \geq 0$, there holds*

$$P\left\{ \sup_{0\leq s\leq t}\left[\sup_{0\leq u\leq s}(A(u,s)-\alpha(s-u))-\theta\cdot(t-s) \right]>x \right\}\leq f^\theta(x), \qquad (3.43)$$

where θ is some non-negative real value.

Definition 3.21 may be considered as a special case of Definition 3.25 by setting $\theta = 0$ in (3.43). Additionally, the following result for the two models can be easily verified.

Theorem 3.26. *If a flow has an m.b.c. stochastic arrival curve α with bounding function f, it provides a θ-stochastic arrival curve α with bounding function $f^\theta = f$ for any $\theta \geq 0$. Conversely, if the flow has a θ-m.b.c. stochastic arrival curve $\alpha \in \mathcal{F}$ with respect to θ, with bounding function $f^\theta(x)$, it has an m.b.c. stochastic arrival curve α with bounding function $f_t = f^\theta(x - \theta \cdot t)$.*

One appealing aspect of the θ-m.b.c. stochastic arrival curve model is that the bounding function is not necessarily dependent on time t, which is often more desirable than a time-dependent bounding function in the analysis.

The following theorem establishes the relationship between the θ-m.b.c. stochastic arrival curve and the v.b.c. stochastic arrival curve.

Theorem 3.27. *(i) If a flow has a θ-m.b.c. stochastic arrival curve $\alpha \in \mathcal{F}$ with bounding function $f^\theta(x) \in \bar{\mathcal{F}}$, it has a v.b.c. stochastic arrival curve α with bounding function $f^\theta(x)$.*

(ii) Conversely, if a flow has a v.b.c. stochastic arrival curve $\alpha(t)$ with bounding function $f(x) \in \bar{\mathcal{G}}$, it has a θ-m.b.c. stochastic arrival curve $\alpha_\theta(t)$ with bounding function $f^\theta(x)$, where

$$f^\theta(x) = \left[f(x) + \frac{1}{\theta} \int_x^\infty f(y) dy \right]_1$$

for any $\theta > 0$.

Proof. The first part follows immediately by setting $s = t$ on the left hand side of (3.43).

For the second part, it is known that

$$\sup_{0 \le s \le t} \left[\sup_{0 \le u \le s} (A(u,s) - \alpha(s-u)) - \theta \cdot (t-s) \right]$$
$$\le \sup_{0 \le s \le t} \{ W(s) - \theta \cdot (t-s) \}^+, \tag{3.44}$$

where $W(s) = \sup_{0 \le u \le s} [A(u,s) - \alpha(s-u)]$.

Since $P\{W(t) > x\} \le f(x)$, there holds for any $x \ge 0$

$$P \left\{ \sup_{0 \le s \le t} [W(s) - \theta \cdot (t-s)]^+ > x \right\}$$
$$\le \sum_{s=0}^t P \{ W(s) - \theta \cdot (t-s) > x \}$$
$$\le \sum_{s=0}^t f(x + \theta \cdot (t-s))$$
$$\le \sum_{u=0}^\infty f(x + \theta \cdot u) \le f(x) + \frac{1}{\theta} \int_x^\infty f(y) dy, \tag{3.45}$$

and with this and (3.44), the second part is easily verified. $\square$

With Theorem 3.27, the θ-m.b.c. stochastic arrival curve model can be further related to the t.a.c. stochastic arrival curve model through Theorem 3.13.

3.5 Stochastic Envelope Process

In the previous sections, the $(\sigma(\theta), \rho(\theta))$ traffic characterization and several variations of stochastic arrival curve have been introduced. In this section, we discuss stochastic envelope processes.

The *stochastic envelope process* of a flow is defined as follows [15].

Definition 3.28 (Stochastic Envelope Process). *A flow is said to have a stochastic envelope process* $\hat{A}$ *if its arrival process* $A(t)$ *satisfies, for all* $s, t \geq 0$,

$$A(s, s+t) \leq \hat{A}(t). \tag{3.46}$$

The difference in definitions between envelope process defined in Definition 2.7 and the stochastic envelope process defined above is subtle. While $\hat{A}$ is non-random in Definition 2.7, it can be stochastic in Definition 3.28. Hence, Definition 2.7 is a special case of Definition 3.28. For ease of exposition, throughout the rest of the book, we shall use envelope process for both.

As discussed in Chapter 2, a flow's envelope process is not unique. We define the *minimum envelope process* (MEP) of the flow as

$$\hat{A}^{MEP}(t) = \sup_{s \geq 0} A(s, s+t). \tag{3.47}$$

It is clear that the MEP is wide-sense increasing, belonging to $\mathcal{F}$, and the MEP is sub-additive, or

$$\hat{A}^{MEP}(t_1 + t_2) \leq \hat{A}^{MEP}(t_1) + \hat{A}^{MEP}(t_2). \tag{3.48}$$

The moment generating function (MGF) of process $A(s, s+t)$ has the following relation with the MGF of its envelope process $\hat{A}(t)$: for any $s, t \geq 0$,

$$M_A(s, s+t) \leq M_{\hat{A}}(t), \tag{3.49}$$

where $M_A(s, s+t) = E\left[e^{\theta A(s, s+t)}\right]$ and $M_{\hat{A}}(t) = E\left[e^{\theta \hat{A}(t)}\right]$.

Let $a(t) = A(t) - A(t-1)$, $t = 1, 2, \ldots$. If $a(t)$ is a sequence of independent random variables, we then have for any $s, t_1, t_2 \geq 0$,

$$A(s, s+t_1+t_2) = A(s, s+t_1) + A(s+t_1, s+t_1+t_2), \tag{3.50}$$

where $A(s, s+t_1)$ and $A(s+t_1, s+t_1+t_2)$ are independent. Consequently, we have

$$\begin{aligned} M_A(s, s+t_1+t_2) &= M_A(s, s+t_1) M_A(s+t_1, s+t_1+t_2) \\ &\leq M_{\hat{A}}(t_1) M_{\hat{A}}(t_2). \end{aligned} \tag{3.51}$$

Since $A(t)$ has stationary increments, we further have, for any $t_1, t_2 \geq 0$,

$$M_A(t_1 + t_2) \leq M_{\hat{A}}(t_1) M_{\hat{A}}(t_2). \tag{3.52}$$

It can be easily verified that a relation similar to (3.52) holds for the minimum envelope process when $a(t)$ is a sequence of independent random variables,

$$M_{\hat{A}^{MEP}}(t_1 + t_2) \leq M_{\hat{A}^{MEP}}(t_1) M_{\hat{A}^{MEP}}(t_2). \tag{3.53}$$

Theorem 3.29. *Consider a flow* $A(t)$. *Suppose its minimum envelope process is* $(\sigma(\theta), \rho(\theta))$-*constrained.*

(i) The flow has a v.b.c. stochastic arrival curve $\alpha(t) = r \cdot t$ with bounding function $f(x) = \left[\frac{e^{\theta \sigma(\theta)}}{1 - e^{\theta(\rho(\theta) - r)}} e^{-\theta x} \right]_1$ for any $r > \rho(\theta)$ and $x \geq 0$.

(ii) The flow has an m.b.c. stochastic arrival curve $\alpha(t) = r \cdot t$ with bounding function $f(x) = \left[\frac{e^{\theta \sigma(\theta)}}{1 - e^{\theta(\rho(\theta) - r)}} e^{-\theta x} \right]_1$ for any $r > \rho(\theta)$ and $x \geq 0$.

Proof. For the first part, the definition of a minimum envelop process, (3.47), implies that

$$\sup_{0 \leq s \leq t} (A(s,t) - \alpha(t-s))$$
$$\leq \sup_{0 \leq s \leq t} (\hat{A}^{MEP}(t-s) - r \cdot (t-s))$$

and hence

$$P \left\{ \sup_{0 \leq s \leq t} (A(s,t) - r \cdot (t-s)) > x \right\}$$
$$\leq \sum_{s=0}^{t} P\{\hat{A}^{MEP}(t-s) - r \cdot (t-s) > x\}$$
$$\leq \sum_{u=0}^{t} e^{-\theta x} E \left[e^{\theta(\hat{A}^{MEP}(u) - r \cdot (u))} \right]$$
$$\leq \sum_{u=0}^{t} e^{-\theta x} e^{\theta[\sigma(\theta) + (\rho(\theta) - r) \cdot u]}$$
$$\leq e^{-\theta x} \frac{e^{\theta \sigma(\theta)}}{1 - e^{\theta(\rho(\theta) - r)}}. \tag{3.54}$$

For the second part, we get

$$\sup_{0 \leq s \leq t} \left[\sup_{0 \leq u \leq s} (A(u,s) - r \cdot (s-u)) \right]$$
$$\leq \sup_{0 \leq s \leq t} \left[\sup_{0 \leq u \leq s} (\hat{A}^{MEP}(s-u) - \alpha(s-u)) \right]$$
$$\leq \sup_{0 \leq s \leq t} \left[\sup_{0 \leq v \leq s} (\hat{A}^{MEP}(v) - \alpha(v)) \right]$$
$$\leq \sup_{0 \leq v \leq t} (\hat{A}^{MEP}(v) - \alpha(v)),$$

and with this and following the same approach as in (3.54), we obtain

$$P \left\{ \sup_{0 \leq s \leq t} \left[\sup_{0 \leq u \leq s} (A(u,s) - \alpha(s-u)) \right] > x \right\} \leq e^{-\theta x} \frac{e^{\theta \sigma(\theta)}}{1 - e^{\theta(\rho(\theta) - r)}}.$$

$\square$

At the beginning of this chapter, the *minimum envelope process with respect to* θ of a flow $A(t)$, denoted by $\mathring{A}^{MEP}(\theta, t)$, is defined by (3.4) or

$$\mathring{A}^{MEP}(\theta, t) = \frac{1}{\theta} \sup_{s>0} \log E[e^{\theta A(s, s+t)}].$$

Similar to inequality (3.53), it is easy to verify that the *minimum envelop process with respect to* θ is sub-additive, or

$$\mathring{A}^{MEP}(\theta, t_1 + t_2) \leq \mathring{A}^{MEP}(\theta, t_1) + \mathring{A}^{MEP}(t_2). \tag{3.55}$$

Because of the arbitrariness of t_1 and t_2 in (3.52), (3.53), and (3.55), the following result is obtained.

Theorem 3.30. *Consider a sequence of independent and identically distributed random variables, $a(t)$, $t = 1, 2, \ldots$.*

(i) *If $\hat{A}(t)$ is an envelope process of the cumulative arrival process $A(t)$, there holds*

$$M_A(t) \leq \inf_{0 \leq s \leq t} \left[M_{\hat{A}}(s) M_{\hat{A}}(t - s) \right]$$

(ii) *For the minimum envelope process $\hat{A}^{MEP}(t)$, there holds*

$$M_{\hat{A}^{MEP}}(t) \leq \inf_{0 \leq s \leq t} \left[M_{\hat{A}^{MEP}}(s) M_{\hat{A}^{MEP}}(t - s) \right].$$

(iii) *For the minimum envelope process with respect to θ, $\hat{A}^{MEP}(\theta, t)$, there holds*

$$\mathring{A}^{MEP}(\theta, t) \leq \mathring{A}^{MEP}(\theta, t) \otimes \mathring{A}^{MEP}(\theta, t),$$

where

$$\mathring{A}^{MEP}(\theta, t) \otimes \mathring{A}^{MEP}(\theta, t) \equiv \inf_{0 \leq s \leq t} \left[\mathring{A}^{MEP}(\theta, s) + \mathring{A}^{MEP}(\theta, t - s) \right].$$

3.6 Summary and Bibliographic Comments

This chapter introduces several traffic models for stochastic network calculus, which include the $(\sigma(\theta), \rho(\theta))$ model, the *traffic-amount-centric (t.a.c.) stochastic arrival curve* model, the *virtual-backlog-centric (v.b.c.) stochastic arrival curve* model, and the *maximum (virtual)-backlog-centric (m.b.c.) stochastic arrival curve* model and its variation the θ-m.b.c. stochastic arrival curve. Their relationships have also been discussed. It is also shown that many well-known traffic models can be characterized by these traffic models for stochastic network calculus.

The $(\sigma(\theta), \rho(\theta))$ model was proposed by Chang in [15] to extend the deterministic (σ, ρ) model, which was initially introduced by Cruz [28][29], to the stochastic case. In [18], Chang summarized how the $(\sigma(\theta), \rho(\theta))$ model can be used to represent various well-known traffic models, such as exponential on-off, Markov modulated processes (MMP), and effective bandwidth. The effective bandwidth model was introduced in [36][81][80].

The exponentially bounded burstiness (EBB) model was another effort to extend the deterministic (σ, ρ) model to the stochastic case, which was made by Yaron and Sidi [138]. Starobinski and Sidi [128] extended EBB to the stochastically bounded burstiness (SBB) model by replacing the exponential function with a generalized function. Also in [128], the function set $\bar{\mathcal{G}}$ was initially introduced. The t.a.c. stochastic arrival curve model can be considered as a generalization of SBB by considering a more general form of the arrival curve function in the definition.

The generalized stochastically bounded burstiness (gSBB) model is the predecessor and a special case of the v.b.c. stochastic arrival curve model, which was initially defined by Yin, Jiang et al. [140]. Jiang et al. further studied the two models in [74][77]. The m.b.c. stochastic arrival curve model was initially introduced by Jiang [69].

The moment generating function (MGF)-based traffic model proposed by Fidler [44] can be considered as a special case of the general stochastic envelope process representation of traffic. A detailed definition and properties of the MGF-based model can be found in [44].

A recent attempt defines a traffic model directly based on the mean characterization of the arrival process [58]. While this attempt is interesting, it is worth highlighting that all the traffic models introduced in this chapter can be easily extended to study such a mean characterization.

The conversions and relationships between t.a.c., v.b.c, θ-m.b.c, and m.b.c. stochastic arrival curve models are shown in Figures 3.1 and 3.2. The required conversions are indicated by the label of each arc. For those arcs without any labels, those bounding functions can be used directly without any conversion. It has also been shown in this chapter that various stochastic traffic models in the literature can be mapped to these stochastic models, which include *effective envelope* [95], exponential on-off, Markov modulated processes (MMP), $(\sigma(\theta), \rho(\theta))$, and effective bandwidth [36][81][80].

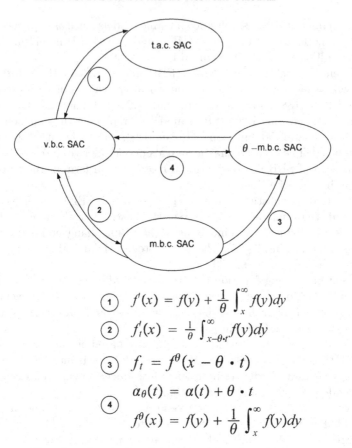

$$\text{①}\quad f'(x) = f(y) + \frac{1}{\theta} \int_x^\infty f(y)dy$$

$$\text{②}\quad f'_t(x) = \frac{1}{\theta} \int_{x-\theta \cdot t}^\infty f(y)dy$$

$$\text{③}\quad f_t = f^\theta(x - \theta \cdot t)$$

$$\text{④}\quad \alpha_\theta(t) = \alpha(t) + \theta \cdot t$$

$$f^\theta(x) = f(y) + \frac{1}{\theta} \int_x^\infty f(y)dy$$

Fig. 3.1. Conversions between stochastic arrival curve models

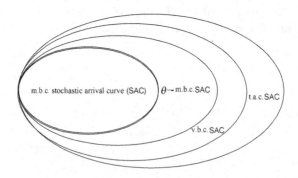

Fig. 3.2. Relationships between stochastic arrival curve models

Problems

3.1. For $(\sigma(\theta), \rho(\theta))$-constrained traffic, the right-hand side of (3.9) provides a bounding functions for its t.a.c. stochastic arrival curve characterization, which satisfies the first constraint discussed in Section 3.2.1. In addition, another bounding function that is derived from (3.9) is provided in Theorem 3.4 and satisfies the second constraint discussed in Section 3.2.1. Derive and compare the bounds on the CCDF of backlog for the system considered in Section 3.2.1 using the methods based on the two constraints in Section 3.2.1.

3.2. Prove the statement in Example 3.14.

3.3. Prove (3.48).

3.4. Prove Lemma 3.23.

3.5. A flow is $(\sigma(\theta), \rho(\theta))$ upper constrained. Find an m.b.c. stochastic arrival curve for this flow.

3.6. Assume that an aggregated flow consists of two flows A_1 and A_2. A_1 has a t.a.c stochastic arrival curve α_1 with bounding function f_1 (i.e. $A_1 \sim_{ta} \langle f_1, \alpha_1 \rangle$), and A_2 is a token bucket constrained traffic with $A_2 \sim (\sigma, \rho)$. Find a t.a.c. stochastic arrival curve of the aggregate traffic flow.

3.7. Assume that an aggregated flow consists of two flows A_1 and A_2. They have t.a.c. stochastic arrival curve α_i with bounding function f_i; i.e., $A_i \sim_{ta} \langle f_i, \alpha_i \rangle$, $i = 1, 2$. Find a t.a.c. stochastic arrival curve of the aggregated flow.

3.8. Assume that an aggregated flow consists of two flows A_1 and A_2. $A_1 \sim_{ta} \langle f_1, \alpha_1 \rangle$, $A_2 \sim_{vb} \langle f_2, \alpha_2 \rangle$. Find a t.a.c. stochastic arrival curve for the aggregated flow.

3.9. Assume that an aggregated flow consists of three flows A_1, A_2, and A_3. $A_1 \sim_{ta} \langle f_1, \alpha_1 \rangle$, $A_2 \sim_{vb} \langle f_2, \alpha_2 \rangle$, and $A_3 \sim_{mb} \langle f_3, \alpha_3 \rangle$. Find a t.a.c. stochastic arrival curve, a v.b.c. stochastic arrival curve, and an m.b.c. stochastic arrival curve for the aggregated flow.

3.10. Assume that a server offers a deterministic service curve β to an input flow. Let $A(t)$ be the input process of the flow with $A(t) \sim_{vb} \langle f, \alpha \rangle$. Let $B(t)$ be the backlog at time t. Let $d(t)$ be the virtual delay at time t. Prove that

$$\Pr\left\{B(t) > B_{\text{sup}}^x\right\} \leq f(x),$$

where $B_{\text{sup}}^x = \sup_{s \geq 0} \{\alpha^x(s) - \beta(s)\}$ and $\alpha^x(s) = \alpha(s) + x$. In addition, prove that

$$\Pr\left\{d(t) > d_{\text{sup}}^x\right\} \leq f(x),$$

where $d_{\text{sup}}^x = h(\alpha^x, \beta) = \sup_{s \geq 0}\{\inf\{\tau \geq 0 : \alpha^x(s) \leq \beta(s+\tau)\}\}$ and $\alpha^x(s) = \alpha(s) + x$. Furthermore, the departure process of the flow from the server has a v.b.c. stochastic arrival curve

$$A^* \sim_{vb} \langle f, \alpha^* \rangle,$$

where

$$\alpha^*(t) = \alpha \oslash \beta(t).$$

3.11. Assume that a server offers a deterministic service curve β to an input flow. Let $A(t)$ be the input process of the flow with $A(t) \sim_{mb} \langle f, \alpha \rangle$. Let $B(t)$ be the backlog at time t. Let $d(t)$ be the virtual delay at time t. Prove that

$$\Pr\{B(t) > B_{\text{sup}}^x\} \leq f(x),$$

where $B_{\text{sup}}^x = \sup_{s \geq 0}\{\alpha^x(s) - \beta(s)\}$ and $\alpha^x(s) = \alpha(s) + x$. In addition,

$$\Pr\{d(t) > d_{\text{sup}}^x\} \leq f(x),$$

where $d_{\text{sup}}^x = h(\alpha^x, \beta) = \sup_{s \geq 0}\{\inf\{\tau \geq 0 : \alpha^x(s) \leq \beta(s+\tau)\}\}$ and $\alpha^x(s) = \alpha(s) + x$. Moreover, the departure process of the flow from the server has an m.b.c. stochastic arrival curve

$$A^* \sim_{mb} \langle f, \alpha^* \rangle,$$

where

$$\alpha^*(t) = \alpha \oslash \beta(t).$$

3.12. Consider a flow that has a t.a.c stochastic arrival curve $\alpha \in \mathcal{F}$ with bounding function $f \in \bar{\mathcal{G}}$. Find its θ-m.b.c. stochastic arrival curve characterization.

3.13. Suppose we are interested in characterizing traffic based on its mean and specifically using the form [58]

$$E[A(s, s+t) - \alpha^\epsilon(t)] \leq \epsilon(t).$$

Find the relationship between this traffic characterization and the t.a.c. (respectively v.b.c., m.b.c. and θ-m.b.c.) stochastic arrival curve characterization.

3.14. Suppose a flow is $(\sigma(\theta), \rho(\theta))$ upper constrained. Find its characterization using the traffic model defined in the proceeding problem.

4

Server Models for Stochastic Network Calculus

In deterministic network calculus, a (deterministic) service curve is used to model the service provided by a system. However, there are many types of systems that may only provide stochastic service. One example is a wireless link in wireless networks. Due to channel impairment, the link is prone to random errors. Consequently, the service provided by the link is stochastic in nature. Even in wired networks, the service provided by a system may also be stochastic. For example, under contention-based multi-access control, such as CSMA/CD in Ethernet, the bandwidth allocated to a host is highly affected by the load from other hosts within the same network. As a result, the service provided by the host to its upper-layer applications is stochastic. In this chapter, several server models for stochastic network calculus will be introduced. In addition, their relationships with each other will also be presented.

4.1 Weak Stochastic Service Curve

In Lemma 2.9, we proved the duality principle of the (deterministic) service curve, which states that for any $x \geq 0$, $A \otimes \beta(t) - A^*(t) \leq x$ for all $t \geq 0$ if and only if $\sup_{0 \leq s \leq t}[A \otimes \beta(s) - A^*(s)] \leq x$ for all $t \geq 0$, where $\beta \in \mathcal{F}$. Based on the former part, we define its probabilistic counterpart as follows.

Definition 4.1 (Weak Stochastic Service Curve). *A system S is said to provide a* weak stochastic service curve $\beta \in \mathcal{F}$ *with bounding function* $g \in \bar{\mathcal{F}}$, *denoted by $S \sim_{ws} \langle g, \beta \rangle$, if for all $t \geq 0$ and all $x \geq 0$ there holds*

$$P\{A \otimes \beta(t) - A^*(t) > x\} \leq g(x). \tag{4.1}$$

The weak stochastic service curve model can be understood in the following way. By the definition of a deterministic service curve, the actual output of a deterministic server $A^*(t)$ is always not less than $A \otimes \beta(t)$. Thus, $A \otimes \beta(t)$ can be considered as the deterministically guaranteed service by the deterministic

Y. Jiang, Y. Liu, *Stochastic Network Calculus*,
DOI: 10.1007/978-1-84800-127-5_4,
© Springer-Verlag London Limited 2008

server without any errors. However, for a stochastic server, such as a wireless link, that is prone to errors, $A \otimes \beta(t)$ cannot be deterministically guaranteed. There is a difference between the ideal service $A \otimes \beta(t)$ provided to the input and the actual output $A^*(t)$. A weak stochastic service curve characterizes this difference x, by introducing a bounding function $g(x)$ for the distribution of the difference x as shown by (4.1).

Comparing Definition 4.1 with the definition of deterministic service curve in Chapter 2, it is clear that the weak stochastic service curve model is an intuitively simple generalization of the deterministic service curve model.

Example 4.2. One can easily verify that if a server has a deterministic service curve β, it has a weak stochastic service curve $S \sim_{ws} \langle 0, \beta \rangle$.

In Chapter 5, we will show that many results can be derived for the single-node case based on the weak stochastic service curve model. However, without additional constraints, it is difficult to prove the concatenation property (P.3) for a weak stochastic service curve.

To address this difficulty, two approaches have been considered. One is to make an additional constraint on the bounding function g. Specifically, the constraint, which will often be used in this book, is that the bounding function be in the function set $\bar{\mathcal{G}}$. Another approach is to introduce a stronger definition. The stochastic service curve model introduced in the following section belongs to the second approach, utilizing the constraint to derive the relationship between the weak stochastic service curve model and the stochastic service curve model, which will also be discussed.

4.2 Stochastic Service Curve

The stochastic service curve model is generalized from the (deterministic) service curve model based on its duality principle. Particularly, it is known from Lemma 2.9 that a system with input $A(t)$ and output $A^*(t)$ has a service curve $\beta(t)$ if and only if for all $t \geq 0$

$$\sup_{0 \leq s \leq t} [A \otimes \beta(s) - A^*(s)] \leq x. \tag{4.2}$$

Inequality (4.2) provides the basis to generalize the (deterministic) service curve model to the stochastic service curve model defined as follows.

Definition 4.3 (Stochastic Service Curve). *A system S is said to provide a stochastic service curve $\beta \in \mathcal{F}$ with bounding function $g_t \in \bar{\mathcal{F}}$, denoted by $S \sim_{sc} \langle g_t, \beta \rangle$, if for all $t \geq 0$ and all $x \geq 0$ there holds*

$$P \left\{ \sup_{0 \leq s \leq t} [A \otimes \beta(s) - A^*(s)] > x \right\} \leq g_t(x). \tag{4.3}$$

It will be shown in Chapter 5 that the stochastic service curve model has the concatenation property. As in the m.b.c. stochastic arrival curve model, an explicit subscript t is used in the bounding function in the stochastic service curve model, highlighting that the bounding function may be dependent on time t.

The following result shows the relationship between the weak stochastic service curve model and the stochastic service curve model.

Theorem 4.4. *(i) If a server S provides to its input A a stochastic service curve $\beta(t)$ with bounding function $g(x)$ or $S \sim_{sc} \langle g, \beta \rangle$, it also provides to the input A a weak stochastic service curve $\beta(t)$ with the same bounding function $g(x)$ or $S \sim_{ws} \langle g, \beta \rangle$.*

(ii) If the server provides to the input a weak stochastic service curve $\beta(t)$ with bounding function $g(x)$ or $S \sim_{ws} \langle g, \beta \rangle$, it provides to the input a stochastic service curve $\beta(t)$ with bounding function $g_t^\theta(x)$ or $S \sim_{sc} \langle g_t^\theta, \beta_{-\theta} \rangle$, where

$$g_t^\theta(x) = \left[\frac{1}{\theta} \int_{x-\theta \cdot t}^{t} g(y) dy \right]_1 \tag{4.4}$$

for any $\theta > 0$.

Proof. The first part follows easily since we always have $A \otimes \beta(t) - A^*(t) \leq \sup_{0 \leq s \leq t} [A \otimes \beta(s) - A^*(s)]$.

For the second part, there holds for any $t \geq s$

$$A \otimes \beta(s) \leq A \otimes \beta(s) - \theta \cdot s + \theta \cdot t$$

and hence

$$P \left\{ \sup_{0 \leq s \leq t} [A \otimes \beta_{-\theta}(s) - A^*(s)] > x \right\}$$

$$\leq P \left\{ \sup_{1 \leq s \leq t} [A \otimes \beta(s) - A^*(s) - \theta \cdot s]^+ > x - \theta \cdot t \right\},$$

for which when $x - \theta \cdot t < 0$, the right hand side is equal to 1. In the following, we assume $x - \theta \cdot t \geq 0$, under which there holds

$$P \left\{ \sup_{0 \leq s \leq t} [A \otimes \beta_{-\theta}(s) - A^*(s)] > x \right\}$$

$$\leq \sum_{s=1}^{t} P \left\{ [A \otimes \beta(s) - A^*(s) - \theta \cdot s] > x - \theta \cdot t \right\}$$

$$\leq \sum_{s=1}^{t} f(x - \theta \cdot t + \theta \cdot s)$$

$$\leq \frac{1}{\theta} \int_{x-\theta \cdot t}^{t} f(y) dy.$$

Combining both cases, the second part is proved. □

With the relationship established in Theorem 4.4, if a weak stochastic service curve of a server is known, the server is shown to also provide a stochastic service curve with bounding function shown by (4.4). It is interesting to notice that when t becomes large, the right-hand side of (4.4) tends toward 1, which may make the bounding function less useful. Recent literature has suggested an idea that may be used to resolve this problem that assumes the existence of a timescale T enforced on the traffic and service [96]. For example, one might assume that the following could hold for all t:

$$\sup_{0 \leq s \leq t} [A \otimes \beta(s) - A^*(s)] \leq \sup_{t-T \leq s \leq t} [A \otimes \beta(s) - A^*(s)]. \qquad (4.5)$$

Or, one could assume there exists a timescale T such that the following would be used to define a stochastic service curve:

$$P\left\{ \sup_{t-T \leq s \leq t} [A \otimes \beta(s) - A^*(s)] > x \right\} \leq g(x). \qquad (4.6)$$

If either (4.5) or (4.6) had been used, the bounding function (4.4) would have become $(T + 1) \cdot g(x)$.

In this book, we shall not focus on the timescale approach. Instead, we consider a new model that is a variation of the stochastic service curve and is introduced in the following subsection, where the time-increasing problem can be avoided.

4.2.1 θ-Stochastic Service Curve

In the following, we introduce a variation of the stochastic service curve in which the bounding function can be independent of time t.

Definition 4.5 (θ-Stochastic Service Curve). *A system S is said to provide a θ-stochastic service curve $\beta \in \mathcal{F}$ with respect to θ, with bounding function $g^\theta \in \bar{\mathcal{F}}$, denoted by $S \sim_{\theta-sc} \langle g^\theta, \beta \rangle$ if, for all $t \geq 0$ and all $x \geq 0$, there holds*

$$P\left\{ \sup_{0 \leq s \leq t} [A \otimes \beta(s) - A^*(s) - \theta \cdot (t - s)] > x \right\} \leq g^\theta(x), \qquad (4.7)$$

where θ is some non-negative real value.

One may view Definition 4.3 as a special case of Definition 4.5 by setting $\theta = 0$ in (4.7). Additionally, the following result for the two models can be easily verified.

Theorem 4.6. *(i) If a system provides a stochastic service curve β with bounding function g, it provides a θ-stochastic service curve β with the same bounding function $g^\theta = g$ for any $\theta \geq 0$.*

(ii) Conversely, if the system provides a θ-stochastic service curve β with respect to θ, with bounding function g^θ, it provides a stochastic service curve β with bounding function $g_t^\theta = g^\theta(x - \theta \cdot t)$.

One appealing aspect of the θ-stochastic service curve model is that its bounding function is not necessarily dependent on time t, which is often more desirable than a time-dependent bounding function in the analysis. In contrast, the stochastic service curve model may generally have a time-dependent bounding function.

The relationship between the weak stochastic service curve model and the θ-stochastic service curve model is as follows.

Theorem 4.7. *(i) If a system provides a θ-stochastic service curve β with respect to θ, with bounding function $g^\theta \in \bar{\mathcal{F}}$, it provides a weak stochastic service curve β with the same bounding function g^θ.*

(ii) Conversely, if the system provides a weak stochastic service curve β with bounding function $g \in \bar{\mathcal{G}}$, it provides a θ-stochastic service curve β with bounding function g^θ for any $\theta > 0$, where

$$g^\theta(x) = \left[g(x) + \frac{1}{\theta} \int_x^\infty g(y)dy \right]_1$$

Proof. The first part follows easily since $A \otimes \beta(t) - A^*(t) \leq \sup_{0 \leq s \leq t} [A \otimes \beta(s) - A^*(s) - \theta \cdot (t - s)]$ by letting $s = t$ on the right-hand side.

For the second part, there holds

$$\sup_{0 \leq s \leq t} [A \otimes \beta(s) - A^*(s) - \theta \cdot (t - s)]$$
$$\leq \sup_{0 \leq s \leq t} [A \otimes \beta(s) - A^*(s) - \theta \cdot (t - s)]^+,$$

and hence, for any $x \geq 0$,

$$P\left\{ \sup_{0 \leq s \leq t} [A \otimes \beta(s) - A^*(s) - \theta \cdot (t - s)] > x \right\}$$
$$\leq \sum_{s=0}^{t} P\{[A \otimes \beta(s) - A^*(s) - \theta \cdot (t - s)] > x\}$$
$$\leq \sum_{u=0}^{t} g(x + \theta \cdot u) \leq g(x) + \sum_{u=1}^{\infty} g(x + \theta \cdot u)$$
$$\leq g(x) + \frac{1}{\theta} \int_x^\infty g(y)dy.$$

$\square$

4.3 Stochastic Strict Service Curve

In deterministic network calculus, several server models can be used to find the service curve of a (deterministic) server, which include the latency rate (LR) server model [129], the guaranteed rate (GR) server model [53], the worst-case service guarantee server model [91], and the strict server model [32]. In order to make use of results developed for the weak stochastic service curve and a stochastic service curve, it is critical to find a such stochastic service curve characterization of a server. In this section, we introduce a *stochastic strict server* to help find the stochastic service curve of a server, which is defined as follows.

Definition 4.8 (Stochastic Strict Service Curve). *A system is said to be a stochastic strict server providing stochastic strict service curve $\beta(t)$ with bounding function $g(x) \in \bar{\mathcal{F}}$ if during any period $(s, t]$ the amount of service $S(s, t)$ provided by the system[1] satisfies*

$$P\{S(s, t) < \beta(t - s) - x\} \leq g(x) \tag{4.8}$$

for any $x \geq 0$.

The stochastic strict server model is the generalization of the strict server model presented in Chapter 2 for deterministic network calculus. The following result establishes its relationship with the weak stochastic service curve model and the stochastic service curve model.

Theorem 4.9. *Consider a system that is a stochastic strict server providing stochastic strict service curve $\beta(t)$ with bounding function $g(x) \in \bar{\mathcal{F}}$.*

(i)   *It provides a weak stochastic service curve $\beta(t)$ with the same bounding function $g(x)$.*

(ii)   *If $g(x) \in \bar{\mathcal{G}}$, it provides a stochastic service curve $\beta_{-\theta}(t) = \beta(t) - \theta \cdot t$ with bounding function $g_t^\theta(x)$,*

$$g_t^\theta(x) = \left[g(x) + \frac{1}{\theta} \int_{x - \theta \cdot t} g(y) dy \right]_1 .$$

(iii) *If $g(x) \in \bar{\mathcal{G}}$, it provides a θ–stochastic service curve $\beta(t)$ with bounding function $g^\theta(x)$:*

$$g^\theta(x) = \left[g(x) + \frac{1}{\theta} \int_x^\infty g(y) dy \right]_1 .$$

Proof. For any time $t \geq 0$, there are two cases. In case 1, t is not within any backlogged period. In this case, there is no backlog in the system at t, which implies that all traffic that arrived up to time t has left the server. Hence, $A^*(t) = A(t)$ and consequently $A \otimes \beta(t) - A^*(t) \leq A(t) + \beta(0) - A^*(t) \leq 0$.

---

[1] If the period $(s, t]$ is a backlogged period for the input flow, $S(s, t)$ is the actual amount of service provided by the system to the input flow within $(s, t]$ or, in other words, $A^*(s, t) = S(s, t)$. Otherwise, $S(s, t)$ denotes the amount of service that the system is capable of providing in this period.

In case 2, t is within a backlogged period. Without loss of generality, assume the backlogged period starts from t_0. Then, $A^*(t_0) = A(t_0)$ and

$$A \otimes \beta(t) - A^*(t)$$
$$\leq A(t_0) + \beta(t - t_0) - A^*(t)$$
$$= \beta(t - t_0) + A^*(t_0) - A^*(t) = \beta(t - t_0) - S(t_0, t).$$

Combining both cases and with (4.8), part (i) is proved. With Part (i) proved, Part (ii) follows from Theorem 4.4 (ii) and Part (iii) from Theorem 4.7 (ii). □

Example 4.10. Consider an exponential server where the input has fixed unit packet size and the service time of each packet has a negative exponential distribution with mean μ^{-1}. Then, during any backlogged period $(s, t]$, it is known that the packets departing from the server have negative-exponentially distributed inter-arrival times with mean μ^{-1}. This is equivalent to saying that the departure has a Poisson process with mean μ^{-1}. In other words, during $(s, t]$, the probability of n packets departing from the server is given by

$$P\{S(s, t) = n\} = \frac{\mu^n (t - s)^n}{n!} e^{-\mu(t-s)},$$

with which we further get, for $\beta(t) = \mu \cdot t$,

$$P\{S(s, t) < \beta(t - s) - x\} \leq \sum_{m=0}^{\lceil \mu(t-s) - x \rceil} \frac{\mu^m (t - s)^m}{m!} e^{-\mu(t-s)}, \qquad (4.9)$$

where $\lceil x \rceil$ denotes the minimum integer larger than or equal to x. So, the server is a stochastic strict server with stochastic strict service curve $\beta(t) = \mu \cdot t$ and bounding function given by (4.9). Then, based on Theorem 4.9, the weak stochastic service curve, the stochastic service curve, and the θ-stochastic service curve characterizations of the server are easily obtained.

4.3.1 Stochastic Strict Server due to Impairment

In this subsection, we introduce an important type of stochastic strict server. In such a stochastic server, the stochastic nature of service is due to some random impairment process.

For example, a wireless channel is a stochastic server, which typically can be considered to operate in two states. If the channel is in "good" condition, data can be sent and received correctly; if the channel is in "bad" condition due to some impairment, no data can be sent or received correctly. Another example is a server shared by multiple flows. In this case, the service provided to a certain flow is affected by the characteristics of the other flows, and we may view these flows together as an impairment process interfering with the service provided by the server to the flow considered.

Based on the discussion above, we may use two processes to characterize the behavior of a stochastic server. These two processes are an *ideal service process* $\hat{S}(t)$ and an *impairment process* $I(t)$. Let $\hat{S}(s,t) \equiv \hat{S}(t) - \hat{S}(s)$ denote the amount of service that the server would have delivered in interval $(s,t]$ if there had been no service impairment in the interval, and $I(s,t)$ the amount of service, called *impaired service*, that cannot be delivered in the interval due to some impairment. Particularly, the service $S(t)$ actually delivered to the input satisfies, for all $t \geq 0$,

$$S(t) = \hat{S}(t) - I(t), \tag{4.10}$$

with $\hat{S}(0) = 0$, $I(0) = 0$ by convention. It is clear that S, $\hat{S}$, and I are in $\mathcal{F}$.

In Definition 4.8, we have defined *stochastic strict server* in the general form. In the following, we define a special type of stochastic strict server.

Definition 4.11. *A system S is said to be a* stochastic strict server *providing* strict service curve *$\hat{\beta} \in \mathcal{F}$ with impairment process I if, during any period $(s,t]$, the actual service $S(s,t)$ provided by the system satisfies*

$$S(s,t) \geq \hat{\beta}(t-s) - I(s,t). \tag{4.11}$$

Note that Definition 4.11 implies $\hat{\beta}(0) = 0$.

Under deterministic network calculus, a similar concept, called *strict service curve*, is defined that states that a strict server is providing strict service curve $\hat{\beta}$ if during any backlogged period $(s,t]$ the service provided or the output $A^*(s,t) \geq \hat{\beta}(t-s)$. From Definition 4.11, it is clear that if there is no impairment or $I(s,t) = 0$ for all $0 \leq s \leq t$, a stochastic strict server due to impairment becomes a (deterministic) strict server providing strict service curve $\hat{\beta}$.

Theorem 4.12 establishes the relationship between Definition 4.11 and Definition 4.8.

Theorem 4.12. *Consider a stochastic strict server S providing strict service curve $\hat{\beta}$ with impairment process I. If the impairment process has a stochastic arrival curve (SAC), or $I \sim_{sac} \langle g, \gamma \rangle$, where $\sim_{sac}$ can be any of $\sim_{ta}$, $\sim_{vb}$, $\sim_{mb}$, or $\sim_{\theta-mb}$, then the server is a stochastic strict server providing stochastic strict service curve β with bounding function g, where $\beta(t) = \hat{\beta}(t) - \gamma(t)$.*

Proof. We shall only prove the theorem when the impairment process has a t.a.c. SAC, i.e., $\sim_{sac}$ is $\sim_{ta}$, since a v.b.c. SAC, m.b.c. SAC, and θ-m.b.c. SAC all imply a t.a.c. SAC.

Consider any backlogged period $(s,t]$. By definition, since $I \sim_{ta} \langle g, \gamma \rangle$, there holds for this period $(s,t]$

$$P\{I(s,t) - \gamma(t-s) > x\} \leq g(x).$$

In addition, since the server is a stochastic strict server providing strict service curve $\hat{\beta}$ with impairment process I, we have for this backlogged period $(s, t]$, by definition,

$$\hat{\beta}(t - s) - S(s, t) - \gamma(t - s) \leq I(s, t) - \gamma(t - s).$$

Hence we get

$$P\{\hat{\beta}(t - s) - S(s, t) > x\} \leq P\{I(s, t) - \gamma(t - s) > x\} \leq g(x),$$

which ends the proof. □

When the stochastic arrival curve characterization of the impairment process is known, Theorem 4.12 can be used together with Theorem 4.9 to find the stochastic service curve characterization of the server. Theorem 4.13 can also be useful.

Theorem 4.13. *Consider a stochastic strict server S providing strict service curve $\hat{\beta}$ with impairment process I.*

(i)   *If the impairment process has a t.a.c. stochastic arrival curve, or $I \sim_{ta} \langle g, \gamma \rangle$, then the server provides a weak stochastic service curve $S \sim_{ws} \langle g, \beta \rangle$ with $\beta(t) = \left[\hat{\beta}(t) - \gamma(t)\right]^{+}$ if $\beta \in \mathcal{F}$.*

(ii)   *If the impairment process has a v.b.c. stochastic arrival curve, or $I \sim_{vb} \langle g, \gamma \rangle$, then the server provides a weak stochastic service curve $S \sim_{ws} \langle g, \beta \rangle$ with $\beta(t) = \left[\hat{\beta}(t) - \gamma(t)\right]^{+}$ if $\beta \in \mathcal{F}$.*

(iii) *If the impairment process has an m.b.c. stochastic arrival curve, or $I \sim_{mb} \langle g_t, \gamma \rangle$, then the server provides a stochastic service curve $S \sim_{sc} \langle g_t, \beta \rangle$ with $\beta(t) = \left[\hat{\beta}(t) - \gamma(t)\right]^{+}$ if $\beta \in \mathcal{F}$.*

(iv)   *If the impairment process has a θ-m.b.c. stochastic arrival curve, or $I \sim_{\theta-mb} \langle g^{\theta}, \gamma \rangle$, then the server provides a θ-stochastic service curve $S \sim_{\theta-sc} \langle g^{\theta}, \beta \rangle$ with $\beta(t) = \hat{\beta}(t) - \gamma(t)$ if $\beta \in \mathcal{F}$.*

Proof. Part (i) follows directly from Theorem 4.12 and Theorem 4.9. While part (ii) can also be proved from Theorem 4.12 and Theorem 4.9, we introduce the following detailed proof that will be used to prove Parts (iii) and (iv).

For any time $s \geq 0$, there are two cases. In case 1, s is not within any backlogged period. In this case, there is no backlog in the server at s, which implies that all traffic that arrived up to time s has left the server. Hence, $A^*(s) = A(s)$ and consequently $A \otimes \beta(s) - A^*(s) \leq A(s) + \beta(0) - A^*(s) \leq 0$. In case 2, s is within a backlogged period. Without loss of generality, assume the backlogged period starts from s_0. Then, $A^*(s_0) = A(s_0)$, and

$$A \otimes \beta(s) - A^*(s)$$
$$\leq A(s_0) + \beta(s - s_0) - A^*(s)$$
$$= \beta(s - s_0) + A^*(s_0) - A^*(s) = \beta(s - s_0) - A^*(s_0, s)$$
$$\leq I(s_0, s) + \beta(s - s_0) - \hat{\beta}(s - s_0)$$
$$= I(s_0, s) - \gamma(s - s_0)$$
$$\leq \sup_{0 \leq u \leq s} [I(u, s) - \gamma(s - u)].$$

Combining both cases, we conclude that, for any $s \geq 0$,

$$A \otimes \beta(s) - A^*(s) \leq \left(\sup_{0 \leq u \leq s} [I(u, s) - \gamma(s - u)] \right)^+, \qquad (4.12)$$

and with this, together with the assumption that the impairment process has a v.b.c. stochastic arrival curve, Part (ii) is proved.

From (4.12), we also have

$$\sup_{0 \leq s \leq t} [A \otimes \beta(s) - A^*(s)] \leq \left(\sup_{0 \leq s \leq t} \sup_{0 \leq u \leq s} [I(u, s) - \gamma(s - u)] \right)^+, \qquad (4.13)$$

and with this, $I \sim_{mb} \langle g_t, \gamma \rangle$, and the definition of a stochastic service curve, Part (iii) is easily proved.

Also from (4.12), we can get

$$\sup_{0 \leq s \leq t} [A \otimes \beta(s) - A^*(s) - \theta \cdot (t - s)]$$
$$\leq \left(\sup_{0 \leq s \leq t} \left[\sup_{0 \leq u \leq s} [I(u, s) - \gamma(s - u)] - \theta \cdot (t - s) \right] \right)^+, \qquad (4.14)$$

and with this, $I \sim_{\theta - mb} \langle g^\theta, \gamma \rangle$, and the definition of a θ–stochastic service curve, Part (iv) is proved. $\square$

Example 4.14. Consider a wireless system consisting of a constant-rate server and a wireless link. The constant-rate server provides a strict service curve $\beta = Ct$. The wireless link is prone to error, which can be modelled by an impairment process I. Then, according to Theorem 4.12, the wireless system can be modelled by a stochastic strict server providing various stochastic strict service curves that can be obtained according to the stochastic model of the impairment process from Theorem 4.13.

4.4 Service Envelope Process

In Section 2.2.4 of Chapter 2, the *service envelope process* and the *strict service envelope process* were defined. Their definitions are repeated below.

Definition 4.15 (Service Envelope Process). *A system is said to provide a service envelope process* $\hat{S}(t)$ *to the input if for any* $t \geq 0$ *there holds*

$$A^*(t) \geq A \otimes \hat{S}(t). \tag{4.15}$$

Definition 4.16 (Strict Service Envelope Process). *A system is said to provide a strict service envelope process* $\hat{S}(t)$ *if the amount of service* $S(s, s+t)$ *provided by the system in* $(s, s+t]$ *satisfies, for any* $t \geq 0$ *and all* $s \geq 0$,

$$S(s, s + t) \geq \hat{S}^{SSE}(t). \tag{4.16}$$

In Section 2.2.4 of Chapter 2, $\hat{S}(t)$ and $\hat{S}^{SSE}(t)$ are interpreted as deterministic curves. In this sense, Definition 3.46 implies a (deterministic) service curve $\hat{S}(t)$ and Definition 2.17 implies a (deterministic) strict service curve $\hat{S}^{SSE}(t)$.

In the rest of this book, we shall treat $\hat{S}(t)$ and $\hat{S}^{SSE}(t)$ as possibly random processes. As discussed in Section 2.2.4 of Chapter 2, the service envelope process $\hat{S}(t)$ describes the behavior of the system in general, which is independent of whether the period $(s, s + t]$ is within a backlogged period of the system. This implies the following result.

Theorem 4.17. *If a system has a strict service envelope process* $\hat{S}^{SSE}(t)$, *it is a stochastic strict server satisfying that during any backlogged period* $(s, t]$, *the service provided by the system satisfies* $S(s, t) \geq \hat{S}(t - s)$.

A system's strict service envelope process is not unique. Its *maximum strict service envelope process* (MSS) is defined as

$$\hat{S}^{MSS}(t) = \inf_{s \geq 0} S(s, s + t). \tag{4.17}$$

It is clear that $0 \leq \hat{S}^{MSS}(t) \leq \hat{S}^{MSS}(t + \tau)$ for any $\tau \geq 0$ since we always have $S(s, s + t) \leq S(s, s + t + \tau)$ for all $s \geq 0$, and hence the MSS process is wide-sense increasing and belongs to $\mathcal{F}$.

Let $\hat{S}(t)$ be a service envelope process of the system. From its moment generating function, we get

$$M_{\hat{S}(t)}(-\theta) = E\left[e^{-\theta \hat{S}(t)}\right]. \tag{4.18}$$

A bound on $M_{\hat{S}(t)}(-\theta)$ is $\sup_{s \geq 0} M_{\hat{S}(t)}(-\theta)$ if it exists, or

$$M_{\hat{S}(t)}(-\theta) \leq \sup_{s \geq 0} M_{\hat{S}(t)}(-\theta) = \sup_{s \geq 0} E\left[e^{-\theta \hat{S}(t)}\right]. \tag{4.19}$$

With simple manipulation, (4.19) becomes

$$-\frac{1}{\theta} \log E\left[e^{-\theta \hat{S}(t)}\right] \geq -\frac{1}{\theta} \sup_{s \geq 0} \log E\left[e^{-\theta \hat{S}(t)}\right]. \tag{4.20}$$

Note that, from the definition, a service envelope process is generally dependent on the arrival process. In the following, we focus on strict service processes to decouple the service process from the arrival process. When $\hat{S}(t)$ in (4.18), (4.19) and (4.20) is a strict service envelope process, we get for any $s, t \geq 0$,

$$M_{S(s,s+t)}(-\theta) \leq M_{\hat{S}^{SSE}(t)}(-\theta) \leq \sup_{s \geq 0} M_{\hat{S}^{SSE}(t)}(-\theta) \quad (4.21)$$

$$-\frac{1}{\theta} \log E\left[e^{-\theta S(s,s+t)}\right] \geq -\frac{1}{\theta} \sup_{s \geq 0} \log E\left[e^{-\theta \hat{S}^{SSE}(t)}\right]. \quad (4.22)$$

From (4.22), the effective service rate (ESR) of $\hat{S}^{SSE}$ with respect to θ, denoted by $\mathring{r}(\theta)$, is defined to be

$$\mathring{r}(\theta) = -\limsup_{t \to \infty} \frac{1}{\theta t} \sup_{s \geq 0} \log E\left[e^{-\theta\left(\hat{S}^{SSE}(t)\right)}\right]. \quad (4.23)$$

Suppose the service process has stationary increments, i.e., $S(s, s+t) =_{st} S(t)$ for all $s, t \geq 0$. Then, replacing $\hat{S}^{SSE}(t)$ with $S(t)$ in (4.23), we get

$$\mathring{r}^{(c)}(\theta) = -\limsup_{t \to \infty} \frac{1}{\theta t} \sup_{s \geq 0} \log E\left[e^{-\theta(S(t))}\right], \quad (4.24)$$

which is often called the *effective capacity* of S in the literature [133]. Since $S(t) \geq \hat{S}^{SSE}(t)$ for all t, an effective service rate is never greater than the effective capacity of the system.

4.4.1 Latency Rate Characterization

Similar to the $(\sigma(\theta), \rho(\theta))$ traffic model, one may be interested in studying cases where the right-hand side of (4.20) is upper-bounded by a latency-rate function $r(\theta) \cdot (t - b(\theta))$ with respect to a chosen θ. For this, we define the $(b(\theta), r(\theta))$-constrained server characterization as follows.

Definition 4.18. *A system is said to be* $(b(\theta), r(\theta))$ *lower constrained for some* $\theta > 0$, *if for all* $s, t \geq 0$,

$$-\frac{1}{\theta} \log E\left[e^{-\theta S(s,s+t)}\right] \geq r(\theta) \cdot (t - b(\theta)). \quad (4.25)$$

Similar to using $(\sigma(\theta), \rho(\theta))$ to characterize traffic, Definition 4.18 uses a latency term and a rate term, with respect to $\theta(> 0)$, to characterize the service. Definition 4.18 may also be considered as an extension of the deterministic latency-rate service curve discussed in Chapter 2 to the stochastic case.

The following result relates the $(b(\theta), r(\theta))$ service characterization to the stochastic strict service curve characterization.

Theorem 4.19. *Consider a system S. If the service provided by the system is $(b(\theta), r(\theta))$ lower constrained, then the system provides a stochastic strict service curve β^θ with bounding function g^θ, where*

$$\beta^\theta(t) = r(\theta) \cdot (t - b(\theta)), \qquad (4.26)$$
$$g^\theta(x) = e^{-\theta x}. \qquad (4.27)$$

Proof. Since the service is $(b(\theta), r(\theta))$ lower constrained, then from the definition it is known that

$$E\left[e^{-\theta S(s, s+t)}\right] \leq e^{-\theta[r(\theta) \cdot (t - b(\theta))]}.$$

Applying the Chernoff bound yields

$$P\{\beta(t) - S(s, s+t) > x\} \leq e^{-\theta x} E\left[e^{\theta(\beta(t) - S(s, s+t))}\right]$$
$$= e^{-\theta x} e^{\theta \beta(t)} E\left[e^{-\theta S(s, s+t)}\right]$$
$$\leq e^{-\theta x} e^{-\theta[r(\theta) \cdot (t - b(\theta)) - \beta(t)]}$$
$$\leq e^{-\theta x}, \qquad (4.28)$$

where the last step holds for any function $\beta(t)$ satisfying $\beta(t) \leq r(\theta) \cdot (t - b(\theta))$.

Since inequality (4.28) holds for all $s, t \geq 0$, it implies that the system provides a stochastic strict service curve $\beta \leq r(\theta) \cdot (t - b(\theta))$ with bounding function $e^{-\theta x}$. □

4.4.2 Relationship with $(\sigma(\theta), \rho(\theta))$ Traffic Characterization

In Section 4.3.1, we introduced an important type of stochastic strict server. In such a stochastic server, the stochastic nature of service is due to some random impairment process. In addition, in Theorems 4.12 and 4.13, the service characterization of the server is related to the traffic characterization of the impairment process. In the following, a similar relationship is established between the $(b(\theta), r(\theta))$ service characterization and the $(\sigma(\theta), \rho(\theta))$ traffic characterization.

Theorem 4.20. *Consider a stochastic strict server S providing strict service curve $\hat{\beta} = C \cdot t$ with impairment process I. If the impairment process is $(\sigma(\theta), \rho(\theta))$–upper constrained, then the server is $(b(\theta), r(\theta))$ lower constrained, where $r(\theta) = C - \rho(\theta)$ and $b(\theta) = \sigma(\theta)/r(\theta)$.*

Proof. Since the impairment process is $(\sigma(\theta), \rho(\theta))$ upper constrained, we have for all $s, t \geq 0$,

$$\frac{1}{\theta} \log E\left[e^{\theta I(s, s+t)}\right] \leq \rho(\theta) \cdot t + \sigma(\theta).$$

Since the server is a stochastic strict server with impairment process I, there holds by definition

$$S(s, s + t) \geq C \cdot t - I(s, s + t),$$

and hence

$$-\frac{1}{\theta} \log E \left[e^{-\theta S(s,s+t)} \right] \geq -\frac{1}{\theta} \log E \left[e^{-\theta(C \cdot t - I(s,s+t))} \right]$$
$$\geq C \cdot t - \rho(\theta) \cdot t - \sigma(\theta)$$
$$= r(\theta) \cdot (t - b(\theta)). \tag{4.29}$$

□

4.5 Summary and Bibliographic Comments

This chapter introduces several extensions of the deterministic service curve characterization to the stochastic case. Particularly, we have defined the weak stochastic service curve model, the stochastic service curve model, and the stochastic strict server model. In addition, one important type of stochastic strict service is defined in which the stochastic nature of the service is characterized with an impairment process. Moreover, we have extended the study of the service envelope process to a larger extent in the sense that the envelop process is treated as a random process. Based on this study, a latency-rate characterization of the stochastic service is defined that is analogous to the $(\sigma(\theta), \rho(\theta))$ model that has been used to characterize traffic.

Comparing this with the development of stochastic traffic models introduced in Chapter 2, alert readers may find that the stochastic server models are developed in an analogous way. As can be seen in Chapter 2, EBB is a direct extension of the deterministic arrival curve model by allowing some traffic arrival violation and characterizing such a violation by an exponential bounding function. EBB is then generalized to SBB. SBB is further generalized to a t.a.c. stochastic arrival curve, which is the basis for other stochastic arrival models. In this chapter, the weak stochastic service curve model is also a direct extension of the deterministic service curve model by allowing service violation and characterizing such a violation by a generalized bounding function. The stochastic service curve model may be viewed as a further development of the weak stochastic service curve model since without additional constraint the latter does not support the concatenation property, as will be shown in the next chapter. While a θ-stochastic service curve is a special case of the stochastic service curve model, it has a critical property different from the general model in that the bounding function under the θ-stochastic service curve model can be independent of time.

The definition of a stochastic strict server allows us to decouple the service from the input, in the sense that the service characterization is not linked to the input process as it is under the weak stochastic service curve model and the stochastic service curve model. The introduction of impairment process to the stochastic strict server further enables us to identify the source causing the random nature of the service. The concepts of stochastic strict server and impairment process can be used to characterize the interdependency between service processes and traffic processes, which will lead to significant improvements on performance bounds, as will be shown later, in Chapter 6.

The weak stochastic service curve model can be considered as a generalization of the (minimum) *effective service curve* model introduced in [96] and the *statistical service curve* model in [24][25]. It was defined and studied under the name of stochastic service curve in Liu, Tham and Jiang [99] and Liu, Tham and Jiang [100].

The stochastic service curve model was initially introduced by Jiang and Emstad in [74] and further investigated by Jiang in [69]. The stochastic strict server model may be traced back to Lee [93]. A related model, called *effective capacity*, was defined by Wu and Negt in [133] to model wireless links. The impairment process concept was initially considered by Jiang and Emstad in [74]. In [69], Jiang further showed that this concept can be used to decouple service processes and traffic processes and hence be applied to independent case analysis, to be introduced in Chapter 6.

The θ-stochastic service curve model and the $(b(\theta), r(\theta))$ service characterization, while newly defined in this chapter, also have a close relation to the existing literature. Particularly, the θ-stochastic service curve model is related to an intermediate model used in [24][25] when the authors studied the concatenation property of their defined statistical service curve model. The $(b(\theta), r(\theta))$ service characterization is analogous to the $(\sigma(\theta), \rho(\theta))$ traffic characterization initially proposed and studied by Chang in [15] [18].

A recent attempt defines a service model based on the mean characterization of the service process [58]. While this attempt is interesting, it is worth highlighting that all the server models introduced in this chapter can be easily extended to study such mean characterizations.

The conversions and relationships among the various stochastic server models are shown in Figures 4.1 and 4.2, respectively. The required conversions are indicated by the label of each arc. For those arcs without any labels, those bounding functions can be used directly without any conversion.

Figures 3.1 and 4.1 show some analogies between the traffic models and the server models introduced here and in the previous chapter. Indeed, more analogies will be found in the following chapters.

Problems

4.1. Assume that a server offers a weak stochastic service curve $S \sim_{ws} \langle g, \beta \rangle$ to a flow with deterministic arrival curve $\alpha(t)$. Let $B(t)$ be the backlog and $d(t)$ the virtual delay at time t.

(i)   Prove that

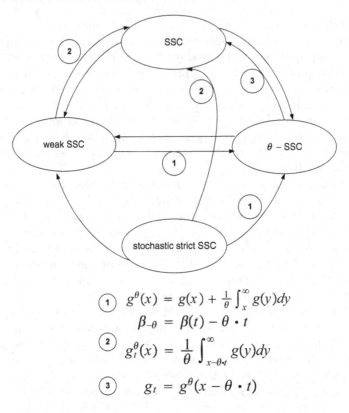

$$\begin{array}{ll} \text{①} & g^\theta(x) \;=\; g(x) + \frac{1}{\theta} \int_x^\infty g(y)dy \\[4pt] & \beta_{-\theta} \;=\; \beta(t) - \theta \cdot t \\[6pt] \text{②} & g_t^\theta(x) \;=\; \frac{1}{\theta} \int_{x-\theta \cdot t}^\infty g(y)dy \\[6pt] \text{③} & g_t \;=\; g^\theta(x - \theta \cdot t) \end{array}$$

Fig. 4.1. Conversions between stochastic service curves

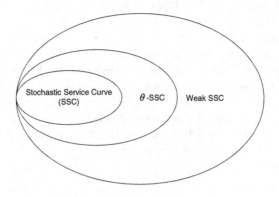

Fig. 4.2. Relationships between stochastic service curves

$$\Pr\left\{B\left(t\right) > B^x_{\max}\right\} \leq g\left(x\right),$$

where $B^x_{\max} = \sup\limits_{s \geq 0}\left\{\alpha^x\left(s\right) - \beta\left(s\right)\right\}$ and $\alpha^x\left(s\right) = \alpha\left(s\right) + x$.

(ii) Prove that

$$\Pr\left\{d\left(t\right) > d^x_{\max}\right\} \leq g\left(x\right),$$

where $d^x_{\max} = h\left(\alpha^x, \beta\right) = \sup_{s \geq 0}\left\{\inf\left\{\tau \geq 0 : \alpha^x\left(s\right) \leq \beta\left(s + \tau\right)\right\}\right\}$ and $\alpha^x\left(s\right) = \alpha\left(s\right) + x$.

(iii) Prove the departure process of the flow from the server has a v.b.c stochastic arrival curve

$$A^* \sim_{vb} \langle g, \alpha^* \rangle,$$

where $\alpha^*(t) = \alpha \oslash \beta(t)$.

4.2. Assume that a server offers a stochastic service curve $S \sim_{sc} \langle g, \beta \rangle$ to a flow with deterministic arrival curve $\alpha\left(t\right)$. Let $B\left(t\right)$ be the backlog and $d\left(t\right)$ the virtual delay at time t.

(i) Prove that

$$\Pr\left\{B\left(t\right) > B^x_{\max}\right\} \leq g\left(x\right),$$

where $B^x_{\max} = \sup\limits_{s \geq 0}\left\{\alpha^x\left(s\right) - \beta\left(s\right)\right\}$ and $\alpha^x\left(s\right) = \alpha\left(s\right) + x$.

ii Prove that

$$\Pr\left\{d\left(t\right) > d^x_{\max}\right\} \leq g\left(x\right),$$

where $d^x_{\max} = h\left(\alpha^x, \beta\right) = \sup_{s \geq 0}\left\{\inf\left\{\tau \geq 0 : \alpha^x\left(s\right) \leq \beta\left(s + \tau\right)\right\}\right\}$ and $\alpha^x\left(s\right) = \alpha\left(s\right) + x$.

iii Prove that the departure process of the flow from the server has an m.b.c. stochastic arrival curve

$$A^* \sim_{mb} \langle g, \alpha^* \rangle,$$

where $\alpha^*(t) = \alpha \oslash \beta(t)$.

4.3. Consider a stochastic strict server providing stochastic strict service curve $\hat{\beta}(t) = \hat{r} \cdot t$ with impairment process I to its input, which has a deterministic arrival curve $\alpha\left(t\right)$. Derive backlog bound, delay bound, and the arrival curve characterization of the departure process.

4.4. Find the weak stochastic service curve, the stochastic service curve, and the θ-stochastic service curve characterizations of the server as shown in Example 4.10.

4.5. Consider a wireless system consisting of a constant rate server and a wireless link. The constant rate server provides a strict service curve $\beta = Ct$. The wireless link is prone to error, which is modeled by an impairment process I that is a Gaussian process with

$$P\{A(s, s + t) - \rho t > x\} \leq \Psi\left(\frac{(\rho - \lambda)t + x}{\sqrt{t^2 v}}\right),$$

where $\Psi(x) \equiv \frac{1}{\sqrt{2\pi}} \int_x^\infty e^{-\frac{u^2}{2}} du$. Find the stochastic model of this wireless system.

4.6. Considering the wireless system as shown in Problem 4.5, there is an input flow with deterministic arrival curve $\alpha(t)$. Let $B(t)$ be the backlog and $d(t)$ the virtual delay at time t. Find the stochastic bounds for $B(t)$ and $d(t)$.

4.7. Prove Theorem 4.9 (ii).

4.8. Prove Theorem 4.9 (iii).

4.9. Prove Theorem 4.13 (i).

4.10. Prove Theorem 4.13 (ii).

4.11. Suppose (4.5) holds. Find the relationship between the weak stochastic service curve and stochastic service curve.

4.12. Suppose (4.6) holds. Find the relationship between the weak stochastic service curve and stochastic service curve.

4.13. Suppose we are interested in charactering service based on its mean and specifically using the form [58]

$$E[A \otimes \beta^\xi(t) - A^*(t)] \le \xi(t).$$

Find the relationship between this service characterizing and the various stochastic arrival curve characterizations.

4.14. Suppose a server provides stochastic strict service that is $(b(\theta), r(\theta))$-lower constrained. Find its characterization using the server model defined in the preceeding problem.

5

Basic Properties of Stochastic Network Calculus

This chapter introduces the basic results of stochastic network calculus under the various traffic models and server models discussed earlier in Chapters 3 and 4. We focus particularly on the five basic properties introduced in Chapter 1 that are essential for network service guarantee analysis.

5.1 Service Guarantees

We start by deriving probabilistic bounds on the backlog and delay under different combinations of traffic and server models.

5.1.1 Backlog Bound

Consider a system with arrival process $A(t)$, service process $S(t)$, and departure process $A^*(t)$. By definition, the backlog in the system at time $t \geq 0$ is

$$B(t) = A(t) - A^*(t), \qquad (5.1)$$

which implies that if both $A(t)$ and $A^*(t)$ were known, $B(t)$ would be derived. However, in most cases, $A^*(t)$ needs to be derived from $B(t)$; i.e., $A^*(t) = A(t) - B(t)$, which causes the chicken–egg problem.

The Lindley equation can be used to derive $B(t)$:

$$B(t) = \max\{0, B(t-1) + A(t-1, t) - S(t-1, t)\}. \qquad (5.2)$$

By applying (5.2) iteratively to its right-hand side, the Lindley equation results in

$$B(t) = \sup_{0 \leq s \leq t} \{A(s, t) - S(s, t)\}, \qquad (5.3)$$

and consequently

$$A^*(t) = A(t) - B(t) = \inf_{0 \leq s \leq t} \{A(s) + S(s, t)\}. \qquad (5.4)$$

Y. Jiang, Y. Liu, *Stochastic Network Calculus*,
DOI: 10.1007/978-1-84800-127-5_5,
© Springer-Verlag London Limited 2008

In the simple case where the system provides a constant service rate c to the input, (5.2) becomes

$$B(t) = \sup_{0 \le s \le t} \{A(s,t) - c \cdot (t - s)\}.$$

Comparing the right-hand side of the equation above with the definitions of the various stochastic traffic models defined in Chapter 3, we find that the probabilistic bound of $B(t)$ is easily derived if the input has a v.b.c. stochastic arrival curve (SAC) or a m.b.c. SAC, or an θ-m.b.c. SAC. However, if the input is known only with its $(\sigma(\theta), \rho(\theta))$ or t.a.c. SAC characterization, additional effort is needed to derive $B(t)$ from such input traffic characterizations.

For the more general case where the system provides stochastic service to the input, the following method can be used to derive $B(t)$. Specifically, (5.1) can be rewritten for any functions $\alpha(t)$ and $\beta(t)$ in $\mathcal{F}$, as

$$\begin{aligned}
B(t) &= A(t) - A^*(t) = [A(t) - A \otimes \beta(t)] + [A \otimes \beta(t) - A^*(t)] \\
&= \sup_{0 \le s \le t} \{A(s,t) - \alpha(t-s) + \alpha(t-s) - \beta(t-s)\} + [A \otimes \beta(t) - A^*(t)] \\
&\le \sup_{0 \le s \le t} \{A(s,t) - \alpha(t-s)\} + \sup_{0 \le s \le t} \{\alpha(s) - \beta(s)\} + [A \otimes \beta(t) - A^*(t)] \\
&\le \sup_{0 \le s \le t} \{A(s,t) - \alpha(t-s)\} + \sup_{t \ge 0}\{\alpha(t) - \beta(t)\} + [A \otimes \beta(t) - A^*(t)]. \quad (5.5)
\end{aligned}$$

The right-hand side of (5.5) implies a sufficient condition to obtain $P\{B(t) > x\}$; that is, $P\{\sup_{0 \le s \le t}\{A(s,t) - \alpha(t-s)\} > x\}$ and $P\{A \otimes \beta(t) - A^*(t) > x\}$ are known and

$$\lim_{t \to \infty} \frac{1}{t}[\alpha(t) - \beta(t)] \le 0. \tag{5.6}$$

In the rest of the book, unless explicitly stated, we shall assume inequality (5.6) holds.

Based on the analysis above, we present results for a probabilistic backlog bound under different combinations of the traffic models and server models introduced in Chapters 3 and 4.

For backlog, if the input has a v.b.c. SAC and the system provides a weak stochastic service curve (SSC), we can conclude immediately from (5.5) that $P\{B(t) > x\} \le f \otimes g(x - \alpha \oslash \beta(0))$. Since both the m.b.c. SAC and θ-m.b.c SAC imply a v.b.c. SAC, and both SSC and θ–SSC imply weak SSC, the conclusion is readily extended to cases where the input has either an m.b.c. SAC or a θ–m.b.c SAC and/or the system provides either an SSC or a θ-SSC. Formally, we have Theorem 5.1 under these combinations.

Theorem 5.1. *Consider a system S with input A. If the input has a v.b.c. (or m.b.c. or θ-m.b.c.) stochastic arrival curve $\alpha \in \mathcal{F}$ with bounding function $f \in \hat{\mathcal{F}}$, (i.e., $A \sim_{sac} \langle f, \alpha \rangle$), where $\sim_{sac}$ is one of either $\sim_{vb}$, $\sim_{mb}$, or $\sim_{\theta-mb}$ and the system provides to the input a weak stochastic service curve (or stochastic* *service curve, or θ–stochastic service curve)* $\beta \in \mathcal{F}$ *with bounding function* $g \in \bar{\mathcal{F}}$, *i.e.* $S \sim_{ssc} \langle g, \beta \rangle$ *where* $\sim_{ssc}$ *is either one of* $\sim_{ws}$, $\sim_{sc}$, $\sim_{\theta-sc}$, *then for all* $t \geq 0$ *and* $x \geq 0$, *the backlog* $B(t)$ *is bounded by*

$$P\{B(t) > x\} \leq f \otimes g(x - \alpha \oslash \beta(0)). \tag{5.7}$$

Based on the relationship between t.a.c SAC and v.b.c SAC in Theorem 3.13 which is also shown in Figure 3.1, the following result is obtained.

Corollary 5.2. *Consider a system S with input A. Suppose the input has a t.a.c stochastic arrival curve $\alpha \in \mathcal{F}$ with bounding function $f \in \bar{\mathcal{F}}$ (i.e., $A \sim_{ta} \langle f, \alpha \rangle$) and the system provides to the input a weak stochastic service curve (or stochastic service curve or θ-stochastic service curve) $\beta \in \mathcal{F}$ with bounding function $g \in \bar{\mathcal{F}}$ (i.e., $S \sim_{ssc} \langle g, \beta \rangle$, where $\sim_{ssc}$ is one of either $\sim_{ws}$, $\sim_{sc}$, or $\sim_{\theta-sc}$). Then, for all $t \geq 0$ and $x \geq 0$, the backlog $B(t)$ is bounded by*

$$P\{B(t) > x\} \leq f^{\theta} \otimes g(x - \alpha \oslash \beta(0)), \tag{5.8}$$

where $f^{\theta}(x) = f(x) + \frac{1}{\theta} \int_x^{\infty} f(y) dy$ *for any* $\theta > 0$.

Actually, Theorems 5.1 and 5.2 show the backlog bounds under all combinations of the various SAC and SSC models defined in Chapters 3 and 4.

Similarly, the following theorem can be derived according to the mapping between the $(\sigma(\theta), \rho(\theta))$ upper constrained traffic characterization and the t.a.c. SAC model shown in Theorem 3.4 and the mapping between the $(b(\theta), r(\theta))$ lower constrained service characterization and the weak SSC model as shown in Theorem 4.19.

Corollary 5.3. *Consider a system S with input A. Suppose the input is $(\sigma(\theta), \rho(\theta))$ upper constrained, and the service provided by the system is $(b(\theta), r(\theta))$ lower constrained. Then, the backlog $B(t)$ is bounded by*

$$P\{B(t) > x\} \leq f^{\theta} \otimes g^{\theta}(x - \alpha \oslash \beta(0)), \tag{5.9}$$

where $f^{\theta}(x) = e^{-\theta x}$, $\alpha(t) = \rho(\theta) \cdot t + \sigma(\theta)$, $\beta(t) = r(\theta) \cdot (t - b(\theta))$, *and* $g^{\theta}(x) = e^{-\theta x}$ *for any* $\theta > 0$.

5.1.2 Delay Bound

Now we discuss the probabilistic delay bounds under different combinations of traffic models and server models. For a delay in the system at time $t \geq 0$, by definition, it is

$$D(t) = \inf\{\tau : A(t) \leq A^*(t + \tau)\}, \tag{5.10}$$

which implies that, for any $x \geq 0$, if $D(t) > x$, there must be $A(t) > A^*(t+x)$ since otherwise if $A(t) \leq A^*(t + x)$ and $D(t) \leq x$, that would contradict the condition $D(t) > x$. In other words, event $\{D(t) > x\}$ implies event $\{A(t) > A^*(t+x)\}$, or

$$\{D(t) > x\} \subset \{A(t) > A^*(t+x)\},$$

and hence

$$P\{D(t) > x\} \leq P\{A(t) > A^*(t+x)\}. \tag{5.11}$$

Following similar steps in (5.5), we can get

$$\begin{aligned}
&A(t) - A^*(t+x) \\
&= \sup_{0 \leq s \leq t+x} [A(t) - A(s) - \alpha(t-s) + \alpha(t-s) - \beta(t+x-s)] \\
&\quad + A \otimes \beta(t+x) - A^*(t+x) \\
&\leq \sup_{0 \leq s \leq t+x} [A(t) - A(s) - \alpha(t-s)] \\
&\quad + A \otimes \beta(t+x) - A^*(t+x) \\
&\quad + \sup_{0 \leq s \leq t+x} [\alpha(t-s) - \beta(t+x-s)] \tag{5.12} \\
&\leq \sup_{0 \leq s \leq t} [A(t) - A(s) - \alpha(t-s)] \\
&\quad + A \otimes \beta(t+x) - A^*(t+x) \\
&\quad + \sup_{0 \leq s \leq t+x} [\alpha(t-s) - \beta(t+x-s)], \tag{5.13}
\end{aligned}$$

where the step from (5.12) to (5.13) holds because by default $A(t) \leq A(t+y)$ for any $y > 0$, $\alpha(y) = 0$ for any $y < 0$.

Under the same sufficient condition as for analyzing the backlog, the complementary cumulative distribution function of the right-hand side of (5.13) is bounded and so are the left-hand side of (5.13) and the delay.

With simple manipulation, we have from (5.13)

$$\begin{aligned}
&A(t) - A^* (t + h(\alpha + y, \beta)) \\
&\leq \sup_{0 \leq s \leq t} [A(t) - A(s) - \alpha(t-s)] \\
&\quad + A \otimes \beta (t + h(\alpha + y, \beta)) - A^* (t + h(\alpha + y, \beta)) - y, \tag{5.14}
\end{aligned}$$

where $h(\alpha + y, \beta)$ is the maximum horizontal distance between functions $\alpha(t) + y$ and $\beta(t)$ for $y \geq 0$. This is obtained by simply replacing $x = h(\alpha + y, \beta)$ in (5.13), and with the definition of maximum horizontal distance function $h(\cdot, \cdot)$, that implies $\alpha(u) + y \leq \beta(u + h(\alpha + y, \beta))$ for any u.

Similar to the backlog, if the input has a v.b.c SAC and the system provides a weak SSC, we immediately conclude from (5.14) and (5.11) that for any $t \geq 0$ and $y \geq 0$, the delay $D(t)$ is bounded by $P\{D(t) > h(\alpha + y, \beta)\} \leq f \otimes g(y)$.

Since both the m.b.c. SAC and θ-m.b.c. SAC imply a v.b.c. SAC, and both the SSC and θ-SSC imply a weak SSC, the conclusion is also readily extended to cases where the input has either an m.b.c. SAC or a θ-m.b.c. SAC, and/or the system provides either an SSC or a θ-SSC. Similar to the backlog analysis, we have the following result for delay.

Theorem 5.4. *Consider a system S with input A. Suppose that the input has a v.b.c. (or m.b.c. or θ-m.b.c.) stochastic arrival curve $\alpha \in \mathcal{F}$ with bounding function $f \in \bar{\mathcal{F}}$ (i.e., $A \sim_{sac} \langle f, \alpha \rangle$ where $\sim_{sac}$ is one of either $\sim_{vb}$, $\sim_{mb}$, or $\sim_{\theta-mb}$) and the system provides to the input a weak stochastic service curve (or stochastic service curve or θ-stochastic service curve) $\beta \in \mathcal{F}$ with bounding function $g \in \bar{\mathcal{F}}$ (i.e., $S \sim_{ssc} \langle g, \beta \rangle$, where $\sim_{ssc}$ is one of either $\sim_{ws}$, $\sim_{sc}$, or $\sim_{\theta-sc}$). Then, for all $t \geq 0$ and $x \geq 0$, the delay $D(t)$ is bounded by*

$$P\{D(t) > h(\alpha + x, \beta)\} \leq f \otimes g(x). \tag{5.15}$$

Based on the relationship between the t.a.c. SAC and v.b.c. SAC in Theorem 3.13, the following result is obtained.

Corollary 5.5. *Consider a system S with input A. Suppose the input has a t.a.c. stochastic arrival curve $\alpha \in \mathcal{F}$ with bounding function $f \in \hat{\mathcal{G}}$ (i.e., $A \sim_{ta} \langle f, \alpha \rangle$) and the system provides to the input a weak stochastic service curve (or stochastic service curve, or θ-stochastic service curve) $\beta \in \mathcal{F}$ with bounding function $g \in \bar{\mathcal{F}}$ (i.e., $S \sim_{ssc} \langle g, \beta \rangle$ where $\sim_{ssc}$ is one of either $\sim_{ws}$, $\sim_{sc}$, or $\sim_{\theta-sc}$). Then, for all $t \geq 0$ and $x \geq 0$, the delay $D(t)$ is bounded by*

$$P\{D(t) > h(\alpha + x, \beta)\} \leq f^{\theta} \otimes g(x), \tag{5.16}$$

where $f^{\theta}(x) = f(x) + \frac{1}{\theta} \int_x^{\infty} f(y)dy$ for any $\theta > 0$.

Actually, Theorems 5.4 and 5.5 show the stochastic delay bounds under all combinations of the various SAC and SSC models defined in Chapters 3 and 4.

Similarly, the following theorem can be derived according to the mapping between the $(\sigma(\theta), \rho(\theta))$ upper constrained traffic characterization and t.a.c. SAC shown in Theorem 3.4 and the mapping between the $(b(\theta), r(\theta))$ lower constrained service characterization and weak SSC as shown in Theorem 4.19.

Corollary 5.6. *Consider a system S with input A. Suppose the input is $(\sigma(\theta), \rho(\theta))$ upper constrained and the service provided by the system is $(b(\theta), r(\theta))$ lower constrained. The delay $D(t)$ is bounded by*

$$P\{D(t) > h(\alpha + x, \beta)\} \leq f^{\theta} \otimes g^{\theta}(x), \tag{5.17}$$

where $f^{\theta}(x) = e^{-\theta x}$, $\alpha(t) = \rho(\theta) \cdot t + \sigma(\theta)$, $\beta(t) = r(\theta) \cdot (t - \sigma(\theta))$, and $g^{\theta}(x) = e^{-\theta x}$ for any $\theta > 0$.

Example 5.7. Consider a server with constant service rate C. If the input is an EBB (exponentially bounded burstiness) process, i.e.

$$P\{A(s,t) - \alpha(t-s) > x\} \leq f(x),$$

where $\alpha = \rho \cdot t$, and $f(x) = ae^{-bx}$. As shown in Chapter 2, EBB is a special case of t.a.c. stochastic arrival curve. In addition, the constant-rate server provides a deterministic service curve $\beta(t) = Ct$, which is a special case of weak stochastic service curve. Then, according to Theorem 5.2, for all $t \geq 0$ and $x \geq 0$, the backlog $B(t)$ of this system is bounded by

$$P\{B(t) > x\} \leq f^\theta \otimes g(x - \alpha \oslash \beta(0))$$
$$= f^\theta(x - \alpha \oslash \beta(0)) = f^\theta(x)$$
$$= ae^{-bx} + \frac{ae^{-bx}}{\theta b}$$

for any $\theta > 0$.

5.2 Output Characterization

This section presents results for characterizing the output traffic. The focus is on using the same traffic model as the input for the characterization.

Equation (5.4) implies the following: for any $t \geq s \geq 0$,

$$A^*(t) - A^*(s) = A(t) - A(s) - (B(t) - B(s)).$$

If the backlog has an upper bound b (i.e., $B(t) \leq b$ for all $t \geq 0$), we immediately get

$$A^*(t) - A^*(s) \leq A(t) - A(s) - b,$$

and in this case it is easy to show that the output has the same characterization as the input. Specifically, we have the following result.

Theorem 5.8. *Consider a system S with input A. Suppose the backlog of A in the system is upper-bounded by b for all times. If the input has a stochastic arrival curve $\alpha(t)$ with bounding function $f(x)$, denoted by $A \sim_{sac} \langle f(x), \alpha(t) \rangle$, where $\sim_{sac}$ can be one of either $\sim_{tac}$, $\sim_{vbc}$, $\sim_{mbc}$ or $\sim_{\theta-mbc}$, then the output also has a stochastic arrival curve $\alpha(t)$ with bounding function $f(x+b)$; i.e., $A^* \sim_{sac} \langle f(x+b), \alpha(t) \rangle$.*

In general, the backlog may not be deterministically upper-bounded. In such cases, to characterize the output traffic requires some effort.

5.2.1 Output t.a.c Stochastic Arrival Curve

First, we focus on characterizing the output traffic with the t.a.c. stochastic arrival curve model. For any $t \geq s \geq 0$ and any functions $\alpha, \beta \in \mathcal{F}$, there holds

$$A^*(t) - A^*(s) \leq A(t) - A \otimes \beta(s) + [A \otimes \beta(s) - A^*(s)]$$
$$= \sup_{0 \leq u \leq s} \{A(u,t) - \alpha(t-u) + \alpha(t-u) - \beta(s-u)\} + [A \otimes \beta(s) - A^*(s)]$$
$$\leq \sup_{0 \leq u \leq t} \{A(u,t) - \alpha(t-u)\} + \sup_{0 \leq v \leq s} \{\alpha(t-s+v) - \beta(v)\}$$
$$+[A \otimes \beta(t) - A^*(t)] \tag{5.18}$$
$$\leq \sup_{0 \leq u \leq t} \{A(u,t) - \alpha(t-u)\} + \alpha \oslash \beta(t-s) + [A \otimes \beta(s) - A^*(s)], \tag{5.19}$$

where $\alpha \oslash \beta(t) = \sup_{u \geq 0}\{\alpha(t+u) - \beta(u)\}$.

Rewriting (5.19), we get

$$A^*(s,t) - \alpha \oslash \beta(t-s)$$
$$\leq \sup_{0 \leq u \leq t} \{A(u,t) - \alpha(t-u)\} + [A \otimes \beta(s) - A^*(s)], \tag{5.20}$$

which implies that if the input m.b.c SAC and the system's weak SSC are known, the output t.a.c SAC characterization is easily derived.

Since the m.b.c. SAC and θ-m.b.c. SAC imply the v.b.c. SAC and the SSC and θ-SSC imply the weak SSC, we have the following theorem.

Theorem 5.9. *Consider a system S with input A. If the input has a v.b.c. (or m.b.c or θ-m.b.c.) stochastic arrival curve $\alpha \in \mathcal{F}$ with bounding function $f \in \bar{\mathcal{F}}$ (i.e., $A \sim_{sac} \langle f, \alpha \rangle$ where $\sim_{sac}$ is one of either $\sim_{vb}$, $\sim_{mb}$, or $\sim_{\theta-mb}$) and the system provides to the input a weak stochastic service curve (or stochastic service curve or θ-stochastic service curve) $\beta \in \mathcal{F}$ with bounding function $g \in \bar{\mathcal{F}}$ (i.e., $S \sim_{ssc} \langle g, \beta \rangle$ where $\sim_{ssc}$ is one of either $\sim_{ws}$, $\sim_{sc}$, or $\sim_{\theta-sc}$) then the output has a t.a.c. stochastic arrival curve $\alpha \oslash \beta$ with bounding function $f \otimes g$; i.e., $A^* \sim_{ta} \langle f \otimes g, \alpha \oslash \beta \rangle$.*

Based on the relationship between the t.a.c. SAC and v.b.c. SAC as shown in Theorem 3.13, the following result is obtained.

Corollary 5.10. *Consider a system S with input A. If the input has a t.a.c. stochastic arrival curve $\alpha \in \mathcal{F}$ with bounding function $f \in \bar{\mathcal{G}}$ (i.e., $A \sim_{ta} \langle f, \alpha \rangle$) and the system provides to the input a weak stochastic service curve (or stochastic service curve or θ-stochastic service curve) $\beta \in \mathcal{F}$ with bounding function $g \in \bar{\mathcal{F}}$ (i.e., $S \sim_{ssc} \langle g, \beta \rangle$ where $\sim_{ssc}$ is one of either $\sim_{ws}$, $\sim_{sc}$, or $\sim_{\theta-sc}$), then the output has a t.a.c. stochastic arrival curve $\alpha_\theta \oslash \beta$ with bounding function $f \otimes g^\theta$, i.e., $A^* \sim_{ta} \langle f^\theta \otimes g, \alpha_\theta \oslash \beta \rangle$, where $\alpha_\theta(t) = \alpha(t) + \theta \cdot t$ and $f^\theta(x) = f(x) + \frac{1}{\theta} \int_x^\infty f(x)$ for any $\theta > 0$.*

In addition, the following theorem follows from Theorem 5.9, the mapping between the $(\sigma(\theta), \rho(\theta))$ upper constrained traffic characterization and v.b.c. SAC shown in Example 3.18, and the mapping between $(b(\theta), r(\theta))$–lower constrained service characterization and weak SSC shown in Theorem 4.19.

Corollary 5.11. *Consider a system S with input A. Suppose the input is $(\sigma(\theta), \rho(\theta))$ upper constrained, $a(t) \equiv A(t-1,t), t = 1, 2, \ldots,$ are i.i.d., and the service provided by the system is $(b(\theta), r(\theta))$ lower constrained. Then, the output has a t.a.c stochastic arrival curve $\alpha \oslash \beta$ with bounding function $f \otimes g$; i.e., $A^* \sim_{ta} \langle f \otimes g, \alpha \oslash \beta \rangle$, where $f(x) = \frac{e^{\theta \sigma(\theta)}}{1 - e^{\theta(\rho(\theta) - r)}} e^{-\theta x}$, $\alpha(t) = r \cdot t$, $\beta(t) = r(\theta) \cdot (t - b(\theta))$, and $g(x) = e^{-\theta x}$ for any $\theta > 0, r < \rho(\theta)$.*

5.2.2 Output v.b.c. Stochastic Arrival Curve

We now characterize the output traffic with the v.b.c. stochastic arrival curve model.

Based on (5.20), we can get

$$\sup_{0 \le s \le t} \{A^*(s,t) - \alpha \oslash \beta(t-s)\}$$

$$\le \sup_{0 \le u \le t} \{A(u,t) - \alpha(t-u)\} + \sup_{0 \le s \le t} \{A \otimes \beta(s) - A^*(s)\}, \qquad (5.21)$$

from this and the fact that the m.b.c. SAC and θ-m.b.c. SAC imply a v.b.c. SAC, the following theorem can be easily verified.

Theorem 5.12. *Consider a system S with input A. If the input has a v.b.c. (or m.b.c. or θ-m.b.c.) stochastic arrival curve $\alpha \in \mathcal{F}$ with bounding function $f \in \bar{\mathcal{F}}$ (i.e., $A \sim_{sac} \langle f, \alpha \rangle$, where $\sim_{sac}$ is either one of $\sim_{vb}$, $\sim_{mb}$, or $\sim_{\theta-mb}$) and the system provides to the input a stochastic service curve $\beta \in \mathcal{F}$ with bounding function $g \in \bar{\mathcal{F}}$ (i.e., $S \sim_{sc} \langle g, \beta \rangle$), then the output has a v.b.c. stochastic arrival curve $\alpha \oslash \beta$ with bounding function $f \otimes g$, i.e. $A^* \sim_{vb} \langle f \otimes g, \alpha \oslash \beta \rangle$.*

Based on the relationship between the stochastic service curve and θ-stochastic service curve shown in Theorem 4.6, the following result is obtained.

Corollary 5.13. *Consider a system S with input A. If the input has a v.b.c. (or m.b.c. or θ-m.b.c.) stochastic arrival curve $\alpha \in \mathcal{F}$ with bounding function $f \in \bar{\mathcal{F}}$ (i.e., $A \sim_{sac} \langle f, \alpha \rangle$, where $\sim_{sac}$ is one of either $\sim_{vb}$, $\sim_{mb}$, or $\sim_{\theta-mb}$) and the system provides to the input a θ-stochastic service curve $\beta \in \mathcal{F}$ with bounding function $g^\theta \in \bar{\mathcal{F}}$ (i.e. $S \sim_{\theta-sc} \langle g^\theta, \beta \rangle$), then the output has a v.b.c. stochastic arrival curve $\alpha \oslash \beta$ with bounding function $f \otimes g_t$; i.e., $A^* \sim_{vb} \langle f \otimes g_t, \alpha \oslash \beta \rangle$, where $g_t(x) = g^\theta(x - \theta \cdot t)$.*

In addition, based on the relationship between the stochastic service curve and weak stochastic service curve shown in Theorem 4.4, the following result can be easily verified.

Corollary 5.14. *Consider a system S with input A. If the input has a v.b.c. (or m.b.c. or θ-m.b.c.) stochastic arrival curve $\alpha \in \mathcal{F}$ with bounding function $f \in \bar{\mathcal{F}}$ (i.e., $A \sim_{sac} \langle f, \alpha \rangle$ where $\sim_{sac}$ is one of either $\sim_{vb}$, $\sim_{mb}$, or $\sim_{\theta-mb}$)*

and the system provides to the input a weak stochastic service curve $\beta \in \mathcal{F}$ with bounding function $g \in \bar{\mathcal{G}}$ (i.e., $S \sim_{ws} \langle g, \beta \rangle$), then the output has a v.b.c. stochastic arrival curve $\alpha \oslash \beta_{-\theta}$ with bounding function $f \otimes g_t^\theta$; i.e., $A^* \sim_{vb}$ $\langle f \otimes g_t^\theta, \alpha \oslash \beta_{-\theta} \rangle$, where $\beta_{-\theta}(t) = \beta(t) - \theta \cdot t$ and $g_t^\theta(x) = \left[\frac{1}{\theta} \int_{x-\theta t}^\infty g(y)\, dy \right]_1$.

Corollaries 5.13 and 5.14 are obtained directly from the relationship of a θ-stochastic service curve or weak stochastic service curve with a stochastic service curve. The resulting bounding functions for the output are time-dependent. In the following, we present results for the output characterization where the bounding function does not rely on time.

Let $\alpha_\theta(t) = \alpha(t) + \theta \cdot t$. Similar to (5.19), we get, for any $\theta > 0$,

$$A^*(t) - A^*(s) - \alpha_\theta \oslash \beta(t-s)$$
$$\leq A(t) - A \otimes \beta(s) + A \otimes \beta(s) - A^*(s) - \alpha_\theta \oslash \beta(t-s)$$
$$\leq A(t) - A \otimes \beta(s) - \alpha \oslash \beta(t-s) + A \otimes \beta(s) - A^*(s) - \theta \cdot (t-s)$$

since $\sup_{w \geq 0}[\alpha(t-s+w) + (t-s+w)\theta - \beta(w)] \geq \sup_{w \geq 0}[\alpha(t-s+w) - \beta(w)] + (t-s)\theta$. Then, there holds:

$$\sup_{0 \leq s \leq t} \{A^*(t) - A^*(s) - \alpha_\theta \oslash \beta(t-s)\}$$

$$\leq \sup_{0 \leq s \leq t} [A(t) - A \otimes \beta(s) - \alpha \oslash \beta(t-s)]$$
$$+ \sup_{0 \leq s \leq t} [A \otimes \beta(s) - A^*(s) - \theta \cdot (t-s)] \tag{5.22}$$

$$\leq \sup_{0 \leq s \leq t} \left[\sup_{0 \leq u \leq s} \{A(t) - A(u) - \beta(s-u) - \sup_{w \geq 0}\{\alpha(t-s+w) - \beta(w)\}\} \right]$$
$$+ \sup_{0 \leq s \leq t} [A \otimes \beta(s) - A^*(s) - \theta \cdot (t-s)]$$

$$\leq \sup_{0 \leq s \leq t} \sup_{0 \leq u \leq s} \{A(t) - A(u) - \alpha(t-u)\}$$
$$+ \sup_{0 \leq s \leq t} [A \otimes \beta(s) - A^*(s) - \theta \cdot (t-s)] \tag{5.23}$$

$$= \sup_{0 \leq u \leq t} \{A(t) - A(u) - \alpha(t-u)\} \tag{5.24}$$
$$+ \sup_{0 \leq s \leq t} [A \otimes \beta(s) - A^*(s) - \theta \cdot (t-s)]. \tag{5.25}$$

From (5.24), we can conclude the following theorem.

Theorem 5.15. *Consider a system S with input A. If the input has a v.b.c. (or m.b.c. or θ–m.b.c.) stochastic arrival curve $\alpha \in \mathcal{F}$ with bounding function $f \in \bar{\mathcal{F}}$ (i.e., $A \sim_{sac} \langle f, \alpha \rangle$ where $\sim_{sac}$ is one of either $\sim_{vb}$, $\sim_{mb}$, or $\sim_{\theta-mb}$) and the system provides to the input a θ–stochastic service curve $\beta \in \mathcal{F}$ with bounding function $g^\theta \in \bar{\mathcal{F}}$ (i.e., $S \sim_{\theta-sc} \langle g^\theta, \beta \rangle$), then the output has a v.b.c. stochastic arrival curve $\alpha_\theta \oslash \beta$ with bounding function $f \otimes g^\theta$; i.e., $A^* \sim_{vb}$ $\langle f \otimes g^\theta, \alpha_\theta \oslash \beta \rangle$, where $\alpha_\theta(t) = \alpha(t) + \theta \cdot t$.*

Then, based on the relationship between the θ–stochastic service curve and weak stochastic service curve, the following result is easily verified.

Corollary 5.16. *Consider a system S with input A. If the input has a v.b.c. (or m.b.c. or θ–m.b.c.) stochastic arrival curve $\alpha \in \mathcal{F}$ with bounding function $f \in \bar{\mathcal{F}}$ (i.e., $A \sim_{sac} \langle f, \alpha \rangle$ where $\sim_{sac}$ is one of either $\sim_{vb}$, $\sim_{mb}$, or $\sim_{\theta-mb}$) and the system provides to the input a weak stochastic service curve $\beta \in \mathcal{F}$ with bounding function $g \in \bar{\mathcal{G}}$ (i.e., $S \sim_{ws} \langle g, \beta \rangle$), then the output has a v.b.c. stochastic arrival curve $\alpha_\theta \oslash \beta_{-\theta}$ with bounding function $f \otimes g^\theta$; i.e., $A^* \sim_{vb} \langle f \otimes g^\theta, \alpha_\theta \oslash \beta_{-\theta} \rangle$, where $\alpha_\theta(t) = \alpha(t) + \theta \cdot t$, $\beta_{-\theta}(t) = \beta(t) - \theta \cdot t$, and $g^\theta(x) = g(x) + \frac{1}{\theta} \int_x^\infty g(y) \, dy$ for any $\theta > 0$.*

If the input has a t.a.c. SAC, we can use the relationship between the t.a.c. SAC and v.b.c. SAC to represent the input with a v.b.c. SAC and consequently get the following results under the stochastic service curve, θ-stochastic service curve, and weak stochastic service curve.

Corollary 5.17. *Consider a system S with input A. If the input has a t.a.c. stochastic arrival curve $\alpha \in \mathcal{F}$ with bounding function $f \in \bar{\mathcal{G}}$ (i.e., $A \sim_{ta} \langle f, \alpha \rangle$) and the system provides to the input a stochastic service curve $\beta \in \mathcal{F}$ with bounding function $g \in \bar{\mathcal{F}}$ (i.e., $S \sim_{sc} \langle g, \beta \rangle$), then the output has a v.b.c. stochastic arrival curve $\alpha_\theta \oslash \beta$ with bounding function $f^\theta \otimes g$; i.e., $A^* \sim_{vb} \langle f^\theta \otimes g, \alpha_\theta \oslash \beta \rangle$, where $\alpha_\theta(t) = \alpha(t) + \theta \cdot t$ and $f^\theta(x) = f(x) + \frac{1}{\theta} \int_x^\infty f(y) dy$ for any $\theta > 0$.*

Corollary 5.18. *Consider a system S with input A. If the input has a t.a.c. stochastic arrival curve $\alpha \in \mathcal{F}$ with bounding function $f \in \bar{\mathcal{G}}$ (i.e., $A \sim_{ta} \langle f, \alpha \rangle$) and the system provides to the input a θ-stochastic service curve $\beta \in \mathcal{F}$ with bounding function $g^{\theta_2} \in \bar{\mathcal{F}}$ (i.e. $S \sim_{\theta-sc} \langle g^{\theta_2}, \beta \rangle$), then*

- *the output has a v.b.c. stochastic arrival curve $\alpha \oslash \beta$ with bounding function $f^{\theta_1} \otimes g_t$, (i.e., $A^* \sim_{vb} \langle f^{\theta_1} \otimes g_t, \alpha_{\theta_1} \oslash \beta \rangle$), where $\alpha_{\theta_1}(t) = \alpha(t) + \theta_1 \cdot t$, $f^{\theta_1}(x) = f(x) + \frac{1}{\theta_1} \int_x^\infty f(y) dy$, and $g_t(x) = g^{\theta_2}(x - \theta_2 \cdot t)$ for any $\theta_1, \theta_2 > 0$) or*

- *the output has a v.b.c. stochastic arrival curve $\alpha_\theta \oslash \beta$ with bounding function $f^{\theta_1} \otimes g^{\theta_2}$; i.e., $A^* \sim_{vb} \langle f^{\theta_1} \otimes g^{\theta_2}, \alpha_\theta \oslash \beta \rangle$, where $\alpha_\theta(t) = \alpha(t) + (\theta_1 + \theta_2) \cdot t$ and $f^{\theta_1}(x) = f(x) + \frac{1}{\theta_1} \int_x^\infty f(y) dy$ for any $\theta_1, \theta_2 > 0$.*

Corollary 5.19. *Consider a system S with input A. If the input has a t.a.c. stochastic arrival curve $\alpha \in \mathcal{F}$ with bounding function $f \in \bar{\mathcal{G}}$ (i.e., $A \sim_{ta} \langle f, \alpha \rangle$) and the system provides to the input a weak stochastic service curve $\beta \in \mathcal{F}$ with bounding function $g \in \bar{\mathcal{G}}$ (i.e., $S \sim_{ws} \langle g, \beta \rangle$), then*

- *the output has a v.b.c. stochastic arrival curve $\alpha_{\theta_1} \oslash \beta_{-\theta_2}$ with bounding function $f^{\theta_1} \otimes g_t^{\theta_2}$ (i.e., $A^* \sim_{vb} \langle f^{\theta_1} \otimes g_t^\theta, \alpha_{\theta_1} \oslash \beta_{-\theta_2} \rangle$, where $\alpha_{\theta_1}(t) = \alpha(t) + \theta_1 \cdot t$, $\beta_{-\theta_2}(t) = \beta(t) - \theta_2 \cdot t$, $f^{\theta_1}(x) = f(x) + \frac{1}{\theta_1} \int_x^\infty f(y) dy$ and $g_t^\theta(x) = \frac{1}{\theta_2} \int_{x-\theta_2 t}^\infty g(y) \, dy$, for any $\theta_1, \theta_2 > 0$) or*

- the output has a v.b.c stochastic arrival curve $\alpha_\theta \oslash \beta$ with bounding function $f^{\theta_1} \otimes g^{\theta_2}$, i.e., $A^* \sim_{vb} \langle f^{\theta_1} \otimes g^{\theta_2}, \alpha_\theta \oslash \beta \rangle$, where $\alpha_\theta(t) = \alpha(t) + (\theta_1 + \theta_2) \cdot t$, $f^{\theta_1}(x) = f(x) + \frac{1}{\theta_1} \int_x^\infty f(y) dy$, and $g^{\theta_2}(x) = g(x) + \frac{1}{\theta_2} \int_x^\infty g(y) dy$ for any $\theta_1, \theta_2 > 0$.

As a special case, the following result follows from Corollary 5.16, the mapping between the $(\sigma(\theta), \rho(\theta))$ upper constrained traffic characterization and v.b.c. SAC shown in Example 3.18, and the mapping between the $(b(\theta), r(\theta))$ lower constrained service characterization and weak SSC shown in Theorem 4.19.

Corollary 5.20. *Consider a system S with input A. Suppose the input is $(\sigma(\theta), \rho(\theta))$ upper constrained, $a(t) \equiv A(t-1, t), t = 1, 2, \ldots$, are i.i.d., and the service provided by the system is $(b(\theta), r(\theta))$ lower constrained. Then, the output has a v.b.c. stochastic arrival curve $\alpha_\theta \oslash \beta$ with bounding function $f^\theta \otimes g^\theta$; i.e., $A^* \sim_{vb} \langle f^\theta \otimes g^\theta, \alpha_\theta \oslash \beta \rangle$, where $f(x) = \frac{e^{\theta\sigma(\theta)}}{1 - e^{\theta(\rho(\theta)-r)}} e^{-\theta x}$, $\alpha_\theta(t) = (r+\theta) \cdot t$, and $g^\theta(x) = e^{-\theta x} + \frac{1}{\theta} \int_x^\infty e^{-\theta y} dy$ for any $\theta > 0, r < \rho(\theta)$.*

5.2.3 Output m.b.c Stochastic Arrival Curve

We now characterize the output traffic with the m.b.c. stochastic arrival curve model.

Based on (5.21), the following is obtained:

$$\sup_{0 \le s \le t} \sup_{0 \le u \le s} [A^*(u, s) - \alpha \oslash \beta(s-u)]$$
$$\le \sup_{0 \le s \le t} \sup_{0 \le u \le s} [A(u, s) - \alpha(s-u)] + \sup_{0 \le s \le t} [A \otimes \beta(s) - A^*(s)]. \quad (5.26)$$

Inequality (5.26) implies that the output m.b.c. stochastic arrival curve characterization is easily derived if the input's m.b.c. stochastic arrival curve characterization and the system's stochastic service curve characterization are known. Specifically, we have the following result.

Theorem 5.21. *Consider a system S with input A. If the input has an m.b.c. stochastic arrival curve $\alpha \in \mathcal{F}$ with bounding function $f \in \bar{\mathcal{F}}$ (i.e., $A \sim_{mb} \langle f, \alpha \rangle$) and the system provides to the input a stochastic service curve $\beta \in \mathcal{F}$ with bounding function $g \in \bar{\mathcal{F}}$ (i.e., $S \sim_{sc} \langle g, \beta \rangle$), then the output has an m.b.c. stochastic arrival curve $\alpha \oslash \beta$ with bounding function $f \otimes g$; i.e., $A^* \sim_{mb} \langle f \otimes g, \alpha \oslash \beta \rangle$.*

Based on the relationship between the weak stochastic service curve and stochastic service curve shown in Theorem 4.4, we have the following.

Corollary 5.22. *Consider a system S with input A. If the input has an m.b.c stochastic arrival curve $\alpha \in \mathcal{F}$ with bounding function $f \in \bar{\mathcal{F}}$ (i.e., $A \sim_{mb} \langle f, \alpha \rangle$) and the system provides to the input a weak stochastic service curve*

$\beta \in \mathcal{F}$ with bounding function $g \in \bar{\mathcal{G}}$ (i.e., $S \sim_{ws} \langle g, \beta \rangle$), then the output has an m.b.c. stochastic arrival curve $\alpha \oslash \beta_{-\theta}$ with bounding function $f \otimes g_t^{\theta}$; i.e., $A^* \sim_{mb} \langle f \otimes g_t^{\theta}, \alpha \oslash \beta_{-\theta} \rangle$, where $g_t^{\theta}(x) = \frac{1}{\theta} \int_{x-\theta t}^{\infty} g(y)\, dy$ and $\beta_{-\theta}(t) = \beta(t) - \theta \cdot t$ for any $\theta > 0$.

Based on the relationship between the stochastic service curve and θ-stochastic service curve, we have the following.

Corollary 5.23. *Consider a system S with input A. If the input has an m.b.c. stochastic arrival curve $\alpha \in \mathcal{F}$ with bounding function $f \in \bar{\mathcal{F}}$ (i.e., $A \sim_{mb} \langle f, \alpha \rangle$) and the system provides to the input a θ-stochastic service curve $\beta \in \mathcal{F}$ with bounding function $g^{\theta} \in \bar{\mathcal{F}}$ (i.e., $S \sim_{sc} \langle g^{\theta}, \beta \rangle$), then the output has an m.b.c. stochastic arrival curve $\alpha \oslash \beta$ with bounding function $f \otimes g_t(x)$; i.e., $A^* \sim_{mb} \langle f \otimes g_t, \alpha \oslash \beta \rangle$, where $g_t(x) = g^{\theta}(x - \theta t)$.*

Corresponding to Theorem 5.21, Corollary 5.22 and Corollary 5.23, where the input is modeled with m.b.c stochastic arrival curve, Corollaries 5.24 to Corollary 5.26 have the input modeled with a θ-m.b.c. stochastic arrival curve.

Corollary 5.24. *Consider a system S with input A. If the input has a θ-m.b.c. stochastic arrival curve $\alpha \in \mathcal{F}$ with respect to $\theta(> 0)$ with bounding function $f^{\theta} \in \bar{\mathcal{F}}$ (i.e., $A \sim_{\theta-mb} \langle f^{\theta}, \alpha \rangle$) and the system provides to the input a stochastic service curve $\beta \in \mathcal{F}$ with bounding function $g \in \bar{\mathcal{F}}$ (i.e., $S \sim_{sc} \langle g, \beta \rangle$), then the output has an m.b.c. stochastic arrival curve $\alpha \oslash \beta$ with bounding function $f_t \otimes g(x)$; i.e., $A^* \sim_{mb} \langle f_t \otimes g, \alpha \oslash \beta \rangle$, where $f_t(x) = f^{\theta}(x - \theta t)$ for any $\theta > 0$.*

Corollary 5.25. *Consider a system S with input A. If the input has a θ-m.b.c. stochastic arrival curve $\alpha \in \mathcal{F}$ with bounding function $f^{\theta_1} \in \bar{\mathcal{F}}$ (i.e., $A \sim_{\theta-mb} \langle f^{\theta_1}, \alpha \rangle$) and the system provides to the input a weak stochastic service curve $\beta \in \mathcal{F}$ with bounding function $g \in \bar{\mathcal{G}}$ (i.e., $S \sim_{ws} \langle g, \beta \rangle$), then the output has an m.b.c. stochastic arrival curve $\alpha \oslash \beta$ with bounding function $f_t \otimes g^{\theta_2}$; i.e., $A^* \sim_{mb} \langle f_t \otimes g^{\theta_2}, \alpha \oslash \beta \rangle$, where $f_t(x) = f^{\theta_1}(x - \theta_1 t)$ and $g^{\theta_2}(x) = \frac{1}{\theta_2} \int_{x-\theta t}^{\infty} g(y)\, dy$ for any $\theta_1, \theta_2 > 0$.*

Corollary 5.26. *Consider a system S with input A. If the input has a θ-m.b.c. stochastic arrival curve $\alpha \in \mathcal{F}$ with bounding function $f^{\theta_1} \in \bar{\mathcal{F}}$ (i.e., $A \sim_{\theta-mb} \langle f^{\theta_1}, \alpha \rangle$) and the system provides to the input a θ-stochastic service curve $\beta \in \mathcal{F}$ with bounding function $g^{\theta_2} \in \bar{\mathcal{F}}$ (i.e., $S \sim_{sc} \langle g^{\theta_2}, \beta \rangle$), then the output has an m.b.c. stochastic arrival curve $\alpha \oslash \beta$ with bounding function $f_t \otimes g_t$; i.e., $A^* \sim_{mb} \langle f_t \otimes g_t, \alpha \oslash \beta \rangle$, where $f_t(x) = f^{\theta_1}(x - \theta_1 t)$ and $g_t(x) = g^{\theta_2}(x - \theta_2 t)$ for any $\theta_1, \theta_2 > 0$.*

We now consider that the input is modeled with a v.b.c. stochastic arrival curve. Corresponding to Theorem 5.21, Corollary 5.22 and Corollary 5.23, Corollaries 5.27 to 5.29 are easily obtained based on the relationship between the v.b.c. stochastic arrival curve and m.b.c. stochastic arrival curve shown in Theorem 3.24.

Corollary 5.27. *Consider a system S with input A. If the input has a v.b.c. stochastic arrival curve $\alpha \in \mathcal{G}$ with bounding function $f \in \bar{\mathcal{G}}$ (i.e., $A \sim_{vb} \langle f, \alpha \rangle$) and the system provides to the input a stochastic service curve $\beta \in \mathcal{F}$ with bounding function $g \in \bar{\mathcal{F}}$ (i.e. $S \sim_{sc} \langle g, \beta \rangle$), then the output has an m.b.c. stochastic arrival curve $\alpha \oslash \beta$ with bounding function $f_t \otimes g$; i.e., $A^* \sim_{mb} \langle f_t \otimes g, \alpha \oslash \beta \rangle$, where $f_t(x) = \frac{1}{\theta} \int_{x-\theta t}^{\infty} f(y)\, dy$ for any $\theta > 0$.*

Corollary 5.28. *Consider a system S with input A. If the input has a v.b.c. stochastic arrival curve $\alpha \in \mathcal{F}$ with bounding function $f \in \bar{\mathcal{G}}$ (i.e., $A \sim_{vb} \langle f, \alpha \rangle$) and the system provides to the input a weak stochastic service curve $\beta \in \mathcal{F}$ with bounding function $g \in \bar{\mathcal{G}}$ (i.e., $S \sim_{ws} \langle g, \beta \rangle$), then the output has an m.b.c. stochastic arrival curve $\alpha \oslash \beta_{-\theta_2}$ with bounding function $f_t \otimes g^{\theta_2}$; i.e., $A^* \sim_{mb} \langle f_t \otimes g^{\theta_2}, \alpha \oslash \beta_{-\theta_2} \rangle$, where $f_t = \frac{1}{\theta_1} \int_{x-\theta_1 t}^{\infty} f(y)\, dy$, $g^{\theta_2}(x) = \frac{1}{\theta_2} \int_{x-\theta_2 t}^{\infty} g(y)\, dy$ and $\beta_{-\theta_2}(t) = \beta(t) - \theta_2 \cdot t$ for any $\theta_1, \theta_2 > 0$.*

Corollary 5.29. *Consider a system S with input A. If the input has a v.b.c. stochastic arrival curve $\alpha \in \mathcal{F}$ with bounding function $f \in \bar{\mathcal{G}}$ (i.e., $A \sim_{vb} \langle f, \alpha \rangle$) and the system provides to the input a θ-stochastic service curve $\beta \in \mathcal{F}$ with bounding function $g^{\theta_2} \in \bar{\mathcal{F}}$ (i.e., $S \sim_{\theta-sc} \langle g^{\theta_2}, \beta \rangle$), then the output has a m.b.c stochastic arrival curve $\alpha \oslash \beta$ with bounding function $f_t \otimes g_t^{\theta_2}(x)$; i.e., $A^* \sim_{mb} \langle f_t \otimes g_t^{\theta_2}, \alpha \oslash \beta \rangle$, where $f_t = \frac{1}{\theta_1} \int_{x-\theta_1 t}^{\infty} f(y)\, dy$, and $g_t^{\theta_2}(x) = g^{\theta_2}(x - \theta_2 t)$ for any $\theta_1, \theta_2 > 0$.*

We then consider that the input is initially modeled with a v.b.c. stochastic arrival curve. In this case, we can first convert it into a v.b.c. stochastic arrival curve and then into an m.b.c. stochastic arrival curve. Afterwards, we can apply Theorem 5.21, Corollary 5.22, and Corollary 5.23 and obtain Corollaries 5.30, 5.31, and 5.32, respectively.

Corollary 5.30. *Consider a system S with input A. If the input has a t.a.c. stochastic arrival curve $\alpha \in \mathcal{F}$ with bounding function $f \in \bar{\mathcal{G}}$ (i.e., $A \sim_{ta} \langle f, \alpha \rangle$) and the system provides to the input a stochastic service curve $\beta \in \mathcal{F}$ with the bounding function $g \in \bar{\mathcal{F}}$ (i.e., $S \sim_{sc} \langle g, \beta \rangle$), then the output has an m.b.c. stochastic arrival curve $\alpha_{\theta_1} \oslash \beta$ with bounding function $f_t \otimes g$; i.e., $A^* \sim_{mb} \langle f_t \otimes g, \alpha_{\theta_1} \oslash \beta \rangle$ where $f_t(x) = \frac{1}{\theta_2} \int_{x-\theta_2 t}^{\infty} \hat{f}(y)\, dy$, $\hat{f}(y) = f(y) + \frac{1}{\theta_1} \int_y^{\infty} f(z)\, dz$, and $\alpha_{\theta_1}(t) = \alpha(t) + \theta_1 \cdot t$ for any $\theta_1, \theta_2 > 0$.*

Corollary 5.31. *Consider a system S with input A. If the input has a t.a.c. stochastic arrival curve $\alpha \in \mathcal{F}$ with bounding function $f \in \bar{\mathcal{G}}$ (i.e., $A \sim_{ta} \langle f, \alpha \rangle$) and the system provides to the input a weak stochastic service curve $\beta \in \mathcal{F}$ with bounding function $g \in \bar{\mathcal{F}}$ (i.e., $S \sim_{ws} \langle g, \beta \rangle$), then the output has a m.b.c stochastic arrival curve $\alpha_{\theta_1} \oslash \beta$ with bounding function $f_t \otimes g^{\theta_2}$; i.e., $A^* \sim_{mb} \langle f_t \otimes g^{\theta_2}, \alpha_{\theta_1} \oslash \beta \rangle$, where $f_t(x) = \frac{1}{\theta_3} \int_{x-\theta_3 t}^{\infty} \hat{f}(y)\, dy$ and $\hat{f}(y) = f(y) + \frac{1}{\theta_1} \int_y^{\infty} f(z)\, dz$, $g^{\theta_2}(x) = \frac{1}{\theta_2} \int_{x-\theta_2 t}^{\infty} g(y)\, dy$, and $\alpha_{\theta_1}(t) = \alpha(t) + \theta_1 \cdot t$ for any $\theta_1, \theta_2, \theta_3 > 0$.*

Corollary 5.32. *Consider a system S with input A. If the input has a t.a.c stochastic arrival curve $\alpha \in \mathcal{F}$ with bounding function $f \in \bar{\mathcal{G}}$ (i.e., $A \sim_{ta} \langle f, \alpha \rangle$) and the system provides to the input a θ-stochastic service curve $\beta \in \mathcal{F}$ with bounding function $g^{\theta_2} \in \bar{\mathcal{F}}$ (i.e., $S \sim_{\theta-sc} \langle g^{\theta_2}, \beta \rangle$), then the output has an m.b.c stochastic arrival curve $\alpha_{\theta_1} \oslash \beta$ with bounding function $f_t \otimes g^{\theta_2}$; i.e, $A^* \sim_{mb} \langle f_t \otimes g_t^{\theta_2}, \alpha_{\theta_1} \oslash \beta \rangle$, where $f_t(x) = \frac{1}{\theta_3} \int_{x-\theta_3 t}^{\infty} \hat{f}(y) \, dy$ and $\hat{f}(y) = f(y) + \frac{1}{\theta_1} \int_y^{\infty} f(z) \, dz$, $g_t^{\theta_2}(x) = g^{\theta_2}(x - \theta_2 t)$, and $\alpha_{\theta_1}(t) = \alpha(t) + \theta_1 \cdot t$ for any $\theta_1, \theta_2, \theta_3 > 0$.*

5.2.4 Output θ-m.b.c. Stochastic Arrival Curve

Based on the relationships of the θ-m.b.c. stochastic arrival curve with the m.b.c., v.b.c. and t.a.c. stochastic arrival curves, the output θ-m.b.c. stochastic arrival curve characterization can be readily obtained from results in the previous subsections, when the input is characterized using an m.b.c., v.b.c. or t.a.c. stochastic arrival curve. We leave this to the reader to investigate further.

In addition, when the input is characterized using the θ-m.b.c. stochastic arrival curve model, we easily obtain from (5.21)

$$\sup_{0 \leq s \leq t} \left[\sup_{0 \leq u \leq s} [A^*(u, s) - \alpha \oslash \beta(s - u)] - \theta(t - s) \right]$$

$$\leq \sup_{0 \leq s \leq t} \left[\sup_{0 \leq u \leq s} [A(u, s) - \alpha(s - u)] - \theta(t - s) \right]$$
$$+ \sup_{0 \leq s \leq t} [A \otimes \beta(s) - A^*(s)], \tag{5.27}$$

from which we have the following result.

Theorem 5.33. *Consider a system S with input A. If the input has an m.b.c. or θ-m.b.c. stochastic arrival curve $\alpha \in \mathcal{F}$, with bounding function $f \in \bar{\mathcal{F}}$ (i.e., $A \sim_{sac} \langle f, \alpha \rangle$, where $\sim_{sac}$ can be either $\sim_{mb}$ or $\sim_{\theta-mb}$), and the system provides to the input a stochastic service curve $\beta \in \mathcal{F}$ with bounding function $g \in \bar{\mathcal{F}}$, (i.e. $S \sim_{sc} \langle g, \beta \rangle$), then the output has a θ-m.b.c. stochastic arrival curve $\alpha \oslash \beta$ with bounding function $f \otimes g$, i.e., $A^* \sim_{\theta-mb} \langle f \otimes g, \alpha \oslash \beta \rangle$.*

Then, based on the relationship between the stochastic service curve and θ-stochastic service curve, the following result is obtained.

Corollary 5.34. *Consider a system S with input A. If the input has a θ-m.b.c. or m.b.c. stochastic arrival curve $\alpha \in \mathcal{F}$ with bounding function $f \in \bar{\mathcal{F}}$ (i.e., $A \sim_{sac} \langle f, \alpha \rangle$, where $\sim_{sac}$ can be either $\sim_{\theta-mb}$ or $\sim_{mb}$), and the system provides to the input a θ-stochastic service curve $\beta \in \mathcal{F}$ with bounding function $g^\theta \in \bar{\mathcal{F}}$ (i.e. $S \sim_{\theta-sc} \langle g, \beta \rangle$), then the output has a θ-m.b.c. stochastic arrival curve $\alpha \oslash \beta$ with bounding function $f \otimes g_t^\theta(x)$; i.e., $A^* \sim_{\theta-mb} \langle f \otimes g_t^\theta, \alpha \oslash \beta \rangle$, where $g_t^\theta(x) = g^\theta(x - \theta \cdot t)$.*

The following corollary is based on Theorem 5.33 and the relationship between the stochastic service curve and weak stochastic service curve.

Corollary 5.35. *Consider a system S with input A. If the input has a θ-m.b.c. or m.b.c. stochastic arrival curve $\alpha \in \mathcal{F}$ with bounding function $f \in \bar{\mathcal{F}}$ (i.e., $A \sim_{sac} \langle f, \alpha \rangle$, where $\sim_{sac}$ can be either $\sim_{\theta-mb}$ or $\sim_{mb}$) and the system provides to the input a weak stochastic service curve $\beta \in \mathcal{F}$ with bounding function $g \in \hat{\mathcal{G}}$ (i.e., $S \sim_{ws} \langle g, \beta \rangle$), then the output has a θ-m.b.c. stochastic arrival curve $\alpha \oslash \beta_{-\theta}$ with bounding function $f \otimes g_t^\theta(x)$; i.e., $A^* \sim_{\theta-mb} \langle f \otimes g_t^\theta, \alpha \oslash \beta_{-\theta} \rangle$, where $\beta_{-\theta}(t) = \beta(t) - \theta \cdot t$ and $g_t^\theta(x) = \frac{1}{\theta} \int_{x-\theta \cdot t} g(y) dy$ for any $\theta > 0$.*

5.3 Concatenation Property

This section presents the concatenation property of the stochastic service curve, θ-stochastic service curve, and weak stochastic service curve for stochastic network calculus.

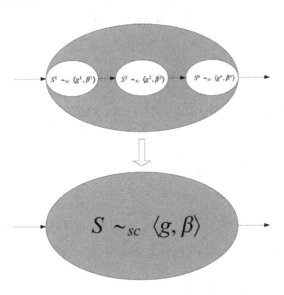

Fig. 5.1. Concatenation property of stochastic service curve

As illustrated in Figure 5.1, it can be proved that multiple systems in tandem, each of which provides a stochastic service curve to the input, can be concatenated and viewed as one system characterized by a stochastic service curve. Particularly, we have the following concatenation property of a stochastic service curve.

Theorem 5.36. *Consider a flow passing through a network of N systems in tandem. If each system $n(= 1, 2, \ldots, N)$ provides a stochastic service curve $S^n \sim_{sc} \langle g^n, \beta^n \rangle$ to its input, then the network guarantees to the flow a stochastic service curve $S \sim_{sc} \langle g, \beta \rangle$ with*

$$\beta(t) = \beta^1 \otimes \beta^2 \otimes \cdots \otimes \beta^N(t) \tag{5.28}$$

$$g(x) = g^1 \otimes g^2 \otimes \cdots \otimes g^N(x). \tag{5.29}$$

Proof. We shall only prove the two-node case, from which the proof can be easily extended to the N-node case. For the two-node case, the departure of the first node is the arrival at the second node, so $A^{1*}(t) = A^2(t)$. In addition, the arrival at the network is the arrival to the first node, or $A(t) = A^1(t)$, and the departure from the network is the departure from the second node, or $A^*(t) = A^{2*}(t)$, where $A(t)$ and $A^*(t)$ denote the arrival process at and departure process from the network, respectively. We then have

$$\sup_{0 \le s \le t} [A \otimes \beta^1 \otimes \beta^2(s) - A^*(s)]$$

$$= \sup_{0 \le s \le t} [(A^1 \otimes \beta^1) \otimes \beta^2(s) - A^{2*}(s)]. \tag{5.30}$$

Now let us consider any s, $(0 \le s \le t)$, for which we get

$$(A^1 \otimes \beta^1) \otimes \beta^2(s) - A^{2*}(s)$$
$$= (A^1 \otimes \beta^1) \otimes \beta^2(s) - A^{2*}(s)$$
$$= \inf_{0 \le u \le s} [A^1 \otimes \beta^1(u) + \beta^2(s - u) - A^{1*}(u) + A^2(u)] - A^{2*}(s)$$
$$\le \sup_{0 \le u \le t} [A^1 \otimes \beta^1(u) - A^{1*}(u)] + \inf_{0 \le u \le s} [A^2(u) + \beta^2(s - u)] - A^{2*}(s)$$
$$= \sup_{0 \le u \le t} [A^1 \otimes \beta^1(u) - A^{1*}(u)] + A^2 \otimes \beta(s) - A^{2*}(s). \tag{5.31}$$

Applying (5.31) to (5.30), we obtain

$$\sup_{0 \le s \le t} [A \otimes \beta^1 \otimes \beta^2(s) - A^*(s)]$$

$$\le \sup_{0 \le u \le t} [A^1 \otimes \beta^1(u) - A^{1*}(u)] + \sup_{0 \le u \le t} [A^2 \otimes \beta^2(u) - A^{2*}(u)], \tag{5.32}$$

and with this, since both nodes provide a stochastic service curve to their input, the theorem follows from Lemma 1.5 and the definition of a stochastic service curve. $\square$

In deriving (5.31), we have proved $[(A^1 \otimes \beta^1) \otimes \beta^2(s) - A^{2*}(s)] \leq \sup_{0 \leq u \leq s}[A^1 \otimes \beta^1(u) - A^{1*}(u)] + \sup_{0 \leq u \leq s}[A^2 \otimes \beta^2(u) - A^{2*}(u)]$ for all $s \geq 0$. However, if we want to prove the concatenation property for a weak stochastic service curve, we need to prove $[(A^1 \otimes \beta^1) \otimes \beta^2(s) - A^{2*}(s)] \leq [A^1 \otimes \beta^1(s) - A^{1*}(s)] + [A^2 \otimes \beta^2(s) - A^{2*}(s)]$ for all $s \geq 0$, which is difficult to obtain and does not hold in general. This explains why a weak stochastic service curve does not have property (P.2) when servers only provide weak stochastic service curves.

Since a stochastic service curve implies a weak stochastic service curve, the following result follows immediately from Theorem 5.36, particularly (5.31).

Corollary 5.37. *Consider a flow passing through a network of N systems in tandem. If each system $n(= 1, 2, \ldots, N - 1)$ provides a stochastic service curve $S^n \sim_{sc} \langle g^n, \beta^n \rangle$, and system N provides a weak stochastic service curve $S^N \sim_{ws} \langle g^N, \beta^N \rangle$ to their input, then the network guarantees to the flow a weak stochastic service curve $S \sim_{ws} \langle g, \beta \rangle$ with*

$$\beta(t) = \beta^1 \otimes \beta^2 \otimes \cdots \otimes \beta^N(t), \qquad (5.33)$$

$$g(x) = g^1 \otimes g^2 \otimes \cdots \otimes g^N(x). \qquad (5.34)$$

In the network of tandem systems, if each system provides a θ-stochastic service curve, the following theorem holds.

Theorem 5.38. *Consider a flow passing through a network of N systems in tandem. If each system $n(= 1, 2, \ldots, N)$ provides a θ-stochastic service curve $S^n \sim_{\theta^n - sc} \langle g^n, \beta^n \rangle$ to its input, then, if $\beta \in \mathcal{F}$, the network guarantees to the flow a weak stochastic service curve $S \sim_{ws} \langle g, \beta \rangle$ with*

$$\beta(t) = \beta^1 \otimes \beta^2_{-\theta} \otimes \cdots \otimes \beta^N_{-(N-1)\theta}(t),$$

$$g(x) = g^1 \otimes g^2 \otimes \cdots \otimes g^N(x),$$

where $\beta^n_{-(n-1)\theta}(t) = \beta^n(t) - (n-1)\theta$, $n = 1, \ldots, N$, for any $\theta > 0$.

Theorem 5.38 is proved by iteratively applying the following result.

Lemma 5.39. *Consider any functions $A(t), A^*(t), b(t), c(t), d(t), e(t)$. The following relationships hold:*

$$A \otimes b \otimes c(t) \leq \sup_{0 \leq s \leq t} [A \otimes b(s) - A^*(s) - \theta \cdot (t - s)] + A^* \otimes c_\theta(t), \quad (5.35)$$

$$[d \otimes e]_\theta (t) = d_\theta \otimes e_\theta(t), \qquad (5.36)$$

$$[d \otimes e]_{-\theta} (t) = d_{-\theta} \otimes e_{-\theta}(t), \qquad (5.37)$$

for any $\theta \geq 0$, where $\alpha_\theta(t) = \alpha(t) + \theta \cdot t$, $\alpha_{-\theta}(t) = \alpha(t) - \theta \cdot t$.

Proof. For (5.35), we have

$$A \otimes b \otimes c(t)$$
$$= \inf_{0 \le s \le t} \{A \otimes b(s) - A^*(s) - \theta \cdot (t - s) + A^*(s) + c(t - s) + \theta \cdot (t - s)\}$$
$$\le \sup_{0 \le s \le t} [A \otimes b(s) - A^*(s) - \theta \cdot (t - s)] + A^* \otimes c_\theta(t).$$

For (5.36), we have

$$[d \otimes e]_\theta (t) = d \otimes e(t) + \theta \cdot (t)$$
$$= \inf_{0 \le s \le t} \{d(s) + \theta \cdot s + e(t - s) + \theta \cdot (t - s)\}$$
$$= \inf_{0 \le s \le t} \{d_\theta(s) + e_\theta(t - s)\} = d_\theta \otimes e_\theta(t)$$

and (5.37) can be verified similarly. □

Lemma 5.39 may be used iteratively. For example, letting $c(t) = d \otimes e(t)$ in (5.35), we immediately obtain from (5.36)

$$A \otimes b \otimes (d \otimes e)(t) \le \sup_{0 \le s \le t} [A \otimes b(s) - A^*(s) - \theta \cdot (t - s)] + A^* \otimes d_\theta \otimes e_\theta(t). \quad (5.38)$$

By iteratively applying Lemma 5.39, we can get

$$A \otimes \beta^1 \otimes \beta^2_{-\theta} \otimes \cdots \otimes \beta^N_{-(N-1)\theta}(t) - A^*(t)$$
$$\le \sup_{0 \le s \le t} [A^1 \otimes \beta^1(s) - A^{1*}(s) - \theta \cdot (t - s)]$$
$$+ \sup_{0 \le s \le t} [A^2 \otimes \beta^2(s) - A^{2*}(s) - \theta \cdot (t - s)] + \cdots +$$
$$+ \sup_{0 \le s \le t} [A^{N-1} \otimes \beta^{N-1}(s) - A^{(N-1)*}(s) - \theta \cdot (t - s)]$$
$$+ A^N \otimes \beta (t) - A^*(t), \quad (5.39)$$

and with this, Theorem 5.38 can be easily verified since $A^N \otimes \beta (t) - A^*(t) \le \sup_{0 \le s \le t} [A^{N-1} \otimes \beta^2(s) - A^{(N-1)*}(s) - \theta \cdot (t - s)]$.

Based on the relationship between the weak stochastic service curve and θ-stochastic service curve shown in Theorem 4.7, the following corollary, which presents the concatenation property for the θ-stochastic service curve model, immediately follows from Theorem 5.38.

Corollary 5.40. *Consider a flow passing through a network of N systems in tandem. If each system $n(= 1, 2, \ldots, N)$ provides a θ-stochastic service curve $S^n \sim_{\theta^n - ss} \langle g^n, \beta^n \rangle$ to its input and $g \in \bar{G}$, then the network guarantees to the flow a θ-stochastic service curve $S \sim_{\theta - sc} \langle g^\theta, \beta \rangle$, where $g^\theta(x) = g(x) + \frac{1}{\theta} g^{(1)}(x)$ and*

$$\beta(t) = \beta^1 \otimes \beta^2_{-\theta} \otimes \cdots \otimes \beta^N_{-(N-1)\theta}(t),$$
$$g(x) = g^1 \otimes g^2 \otimes \cdots \otimes g^N(x),$$

with $\beta^n_{-(n-1)\theta}(t) = \beta^n(t) - (n - 1)\theta$, $n = 1, \ldots, N$.

Also based on the relationship between the weak stochastic service curve and θ-stochastic service curve shown in Theorem 4.7, the following corollary presents the concatenation property for the weak stochastic service curve model, obtained particularly from (5.39).

Corollary 5.41. *Consider a flow passing through a network of N systems in tandem. If each system $n(=1,2,\ldots,N)$ provides weak stochastic service curve $S^n \sim_{ws} \langle g^n, \beta^n \rangle$ to its input and $g \in \bar{\mathcal{G}}$, then the network guarantees to the flow a weak stochastic service curve $S \sim_{ws} \langle g, \beta \rangle$, where*

$$\beta(t) = \beta^1 \otimes \beta^2_{-\theta} \otimes \cdots \otimes \beta^N_{-(N-1)\theta}(t),$$

$$g(x) = g^{1,\theta_1} \otimes g^{2,\theta_2} \otimes \cdots \otimes g^{N,\theta_N}(x),$$

with $\beta^n_{-(n-1)\theta}(t) = \beta^n(t) - (n-1)\theta$ for $n = 1,\ldots,N$, $g^{n,\theta_n}(x) = g(x) + \frac{1}{\theta_n}\int_x^\infty g(y)dy$ for $n=1,\ldots,N-1$, and $g^{N,\theta}(x)=g^N(x)$ for any $\theta,\theta_1,\cdots,\theta_N>0$.

5.4 Leftover Service Characterization

This section presents results for characterizing the leftover service under aggregate scheduling. To ease the expression, we consider the case where there are two flows competing for resources in a system under aggregate scheduling. Consider a system fed with a flow A that is the aggregation of two constituent flows A_1 and A_2. Suppose both the service characterization from the server and traffic characterization from A_2 are given, and we are interested in characterizing the service received by A_1, with which per-flow bounds for A_1 can then be easily obtained using earlier results.

For the output, there holds $A^*(t) = A_1^*(t) + A_2^*(t)$. In addition, we have $A^*(t) \le A(t)$, $A_1^*(t) \le A_1(t)$, and $A_2^*(t) \le A_2(t)$. We now have for any $s \ge 0$

$$A_1 \otimes (\beta - \alpha_2)(s) - A_1^*(s)$$
$$= \inf_{0 \le u \le s}[A(u) + \beta(s-u) - \alpha_2(s-u) - A_2(u)] - A^*(s) + A_2^*(s)$$
$$\le [A \otimes \beta(s) - A^*(s)] + A_2(s) - \inf_{0 \le u \le s}[A_2(u) + \alpha_2(s-u)]$$
$$= [A \otimes \beta(s) - A^*(s)] + \sup_{0 \le u \le s}[A_2(u,s) - \alpha_2(s-u)]. \tag{5.40}$$

5.4.1 Leftover Weak Stochastic Service Curve

From (5.40), together with the fact that both the m.b.c SAC and θ-m.b.c SAC imply v.b.c. SAC and both the SSC and θ-SSC imply a weak SSC, the following theorem can be easily verified.

Theorem 5.42. *Consider a system S with input A that is the aggregation of two constituent flows A_1 and A_2. Suppose A_2 has a v.b.c. (or m.b.c. or θ-m.b.c.) stochastic arrival curve $\alpha \in \mathcal{F}$ with bounding function $f \in \bar{\mathcal{F}}$ (i.e., $A_2 \sim_{sac} \langle f_2, \alpha_2 \rangle$), where $\sim_{sac}$ is one of either $\sim_{vb}$, $\sim_{mb}$, or $\sim_{\theta-mb}$) and the system provides to the input a weak stochastic service curve (or a stochastic service curve or a θ-stochastic service curve) $\beta \in \mathcal{F}$ with bounding function $g \in \bar{\mathcal{F}}$; i.e., $S \sim_{ssc} \langle g, \beta \rangle$ where $\sim_{ssc}$ is one of either $\sim_{ws}$ or $\sim_{sc}$ and $\sim_{\theta-sc}$. Then, if $\beta - \alpha_2 \in \mathcal{F}$, A_1 receives a weak stochastic service curve $\beta - \alpha_2$ with bounding function $f_2 \otimes g(x)$; i.e., $S_1 \sim_{ws} \langle f_2 \otimes g(x), \beta - \alpha_2 \rangle$.*

Based on the relationship between the t.a.c. SAC and v.b.c. SAC, we can obtain the following result from Theorem 5.42.

Corollary 5.43. *Consider a system S with input A that is the aggregation of two constituent flows A_1 and A_2. Suppose A_2 has a t.a.c. stochastic arrival curve $\alpha \in \mathcal{F}$ with bounding function $f \in \bar{\mathcal{G}}$ (i.e., $A_2 \sim_{ta} \langle f_2, \alpha_2 \rangle$) and the system provides to the input a weak stochastic service curve (or a stochastic service curve or a θ-stochastic service curve) $\beta \in \mathcal{F}$ with bounding function $g \in \hat{\mathcal{F}}$; i.e., $S \sim_{ssc} \langle g, \beta \rangle$, where $\sim_{ssc}$ is one of either $\sim_{ws}$ or $\sim_{sc}$ and $\sim_{\theta-sc}$. Then, if $\beta - \alpha_{2,\theta} \in \mathcal{F}$, A_1 receives a weak stochastic service curve $\beta - \alpha_{2,\theta}$ with bounding function $f_2^\theta \otimes g(x)$; i.e., $S_1 \sim_{ws} \langle f_2^\theta \otimes g(x), \beta - \alpha_{2,\theta} \rangle$, where $f_2^\theta = f_2(x) + \frac{1}{\theta} \int_x^\infty f_2(y) dy$ and $\alpha_{2,\theta}(t) = \alpha(t) + \theta \cdot t$ for any $\theta > 0$.*

Since a deterministic service curve is a special case of a stochastic service curve, we have the following result.

Corollary 5.44. *Consider a system S with input A that is the aggregation of two constituent flows A_1 and A_2. Suppose A_2 has a v.b.c. (or m.b.c., or θ-m.b.c.) stochastic arrival curve $\alpha \in \mathcal{F}$ with bounding function $f \in \bar{\mathcal{F}}$ (i.e., $A_2 \sim_{sac} \langle f_2, \alpha_2 \rangle$, where $\sim_{sac}$ is one of either $\sim_{vb}$, $\sim_{mb}$, or $\sim_{\theta-mb}$. In addition, the system provides to the input a deterministic service curve $\beta \in \mathcal{F}$. Then, if $\beta - \alpha_2 \in \mathcal{F}$, A_1 receives a weak stochastic service curve $\beta - \alpha_2$ with bounding function f_2; i.e., $S_1 \sim_{ws} \langle f_2, \beta - \alpha_2 \rangle$.*

Corollary 5.44 can be easily verified since $0 \otimes f_2(x) = \min_{0 \le u \le x} [0 + f_2(u)] \le f_2(x)$. An important implication of this corollary is that a deterministic server with a deterministic service curve can be considered as a stochastic server with weak stochastic service curve for each input flow. This property is very useful for deriving stochastic QoS bounds per-flow under aggregate scheduling since there are many types of servers that provide a deterministic service curve as, introduced in Chapter 2.

5.4.2 Leftover Stochastic Service Curve

From (5.40), we easily get

$$\sup_{0 \le s \le t} [A_1 \otimes (\beta - \alpha_2)(s) - A_1^*(s)]$$

$$= A_1 \otimes (\beta - \alpha_2)(s_0) - A_1^*(s_0)$$

$$\le \sup_{0 \le s \le t} [A \otimes \beta(s) - A^*(s)] + \sup_{0 \le s \le t} \sup_{0 \le u \le s} [A_2(u, s) - \alpha_2(s - u)], \quad (5.41)$$

and with this, the following theorem can be verified.

Theorem 5.45. *Consider a system S with input A that is the aggregation of two constituent flows, A_1 and A_2. Suppose A_2 has an m.b.c stochastic arrival curve $\alpha \in \mathcal{F}$ with bounding function $f \in \bar{\mathcal{F}}$ (i.e., $A_2 \sim_{mb} \langle f_2, \alpha_2 \rangle$) and the system provides to the input a stochastic service curve $\beta \in \mathcal{F}$ with bounding function $g \in \bar{\mathcal{F}}$; (i.e., $S \sim_{sc} \langle g, \beta \rangle$). Then, if $\beta - \alpha_2 \in \mathcal{F}$, A_1 receives a stochastic service curve $\beta - \alpha_2$ with bounding function $f_2 \otimes g$; i.e., $S_1 \sim_{sc} \langle f_2 \otimes g, \beta - \alpha_2 \rangle$.*

With Theorem 5.45 and based on the relationship between the weak stochastic service curve and stochastic service curve, Corollary 5.46 is obtained.

Corollary 5.46. *Consider a system S with input A that is the aggregation of two constituent flows A_1 and A_2. Suppose A_2 has an m.b.c. stochastic arrival curve $\alpha \in \mathcal{F}$ with bounding function $f \in \bar{\mathcal{F}}$ (i.e., $A_2 \sim_{mb} \langle f_2, \alpha_2 \rangle$) and the system provides to the input a weak stochastic service curve $\beta \in \mathcal{F}$ with bounding function $g \in \bar{\mathcal{G}}$ (i.e., $S \sim_{ws} \langle g, \beta \rangle$). Then, if $\beta - \alpha_2 \in \mathcal{F}$, A_1 receives a stochastic service curve $\beta - \alpha_2$ with bounding function $f_2 \otimes g_t^\theta$; (i.e., $S_1 \sim_{sc} \langle f_2 \otimes g_t^\theta, \beta - \alpha_2 \rangle$), where $g_t^\theta = \frac{1}{\theta} \int_{x - \theta t}^\infty g(y) \, dy$ for any $\theta > 0$.*

In addition, based on the relationship between the θ-stochastic service curve and stochastic service curve, the following result is obtained.

Corollary 5.47. *Consider a system S with input A that is the aggregation of two constituent flows A_1 and A_2. Suppose A_2 has an m.b.c. stochastic arrival curve $\alpha \in \mathcal{F}$ with bounding function $f \in \bar{\mathcal{F}}$ (i.e., $A_2 \sim_{mb} \langle f_2, \alpha_2 \rangle$) and the system provides to the input a θ-stochastic service curve $\beta \in \mathcal{F}$ with bounding function $g^\theta \in \bar{\mathcal{F}}$ (i.e., $S \sim_{\theta-sc} \langle g^\theta, \beta \rangle$). Then, if $\beta - \alpha_2 \in \mathcal{F}$, A_1 receives a stochastic service curve $\beta - \alpha_2$ with bounding function $f_2 \otimes g_t^\theta$ (i.e., $S_1 \sim_{sc} \langle f_2 \otimes g_t(x), \beta - \alpha_2 \rangle$), where $g_t^\theta = g^\theta(x - \theta \cdot t)$ for any $\theta > 0$.*

Corresponding to Theorem 5.45, Corollary 5.46, and Corollary 5.47, the following results are obtained based on the relationship between the v.b.c stochastic arrival curve and m.b.c stochastic arrival curve.

Corollary 5.48. *Consider a system S with input A that is the aggregation of two constituent flows A_1 and A_2. Suppose A_2 has a v.b.c. stochastic arrival curve $\alpha \in \mathcal{F}$ with bounding function $f \in \bar{\mathcal{G}}$ (i.e., $A_2 \sim_{vb} \langle f_2, \alpha_2 \rangle$) and the system provides to the input a stochastic service curve $\beta \in \mathcal{F}$ with bounding function $g \in \bar{\mathcal{F}}$ (i.e., $S \sim_{sc} \langle g, \beta \rangle$). Then, if $\beta - \alpha_2 \in \mathcal{F}$, A_1 receives a* *stochastic service curve* $\beta - \alpha_{2,\theta}$ *with bounding function* $f_{2,t}^{\theta} \otimes g(x)$ *(i.e.,* $S_1 \sim_{sc}$ $\langle f_{2,t}^{\theta} \otimes g(x), \beta - \alpha_{2,\theta} \rangle$), *where* $f_{2,t}^{\theta}(x) = \frac{1}{\theta} \int_{x-\theta t}^{\infty} f_2(y)\,dy$, *and* $\alpha_{2,\theta}(t) = \alpha(t) + \theta \cdot t$ *for any* $\theta > 0$.

Corollary 5.49. *Consider a system S with input A that is the aggregation of two constituent flows A_1 and A_2. Suppose A_2 has a v.b.c. stochastic arrival curve $\alpha \in \mathcal{F}$ with bounding function $f \in \bar{\mathcal{G}}$ (i.e., $A_2 \sim_{vb} \langle f_2, \alpha_2 \rangle$) and the system provides to the input a θ-stochastic service curve $\beta \in \mathcal{F}$ with bounding function $g^{\theta} \in \bar{\mathcal{F}}$; i.e., $S \sim_{\theta-sc} \langle g^{\theta}, \beta \rangle$. Then, if $\beta - \alpha_2 \in \mathcal{F}$, A_1 receives a stochastic service curve $\beta - \alpha_{2,\theta}$ with bounding function $f_{2,t}^{\theta} \otimes g_t(x)$; i.e., $S_1 \sim_{sc} \langle f_{2,t}^{\theta} \otimes g_t^{\theta}, \beta - \alpha_2 \rangle$, where $f_{2,t}^{\theta}(x) = \frac{1}{\theta_2} \int_{x-\theta_2 t}^{\infty} f_2(y)\,dy$, $\alpha_{2,\theta}(t) = \alpha(t) + \theta_2 \cdot t$, and $g_t^{\theta} = g^{\theta}(x - \theta_1 \cdot t)$ for any $\theta_1, \theta_2 > 0$.*

Corollary 5.50. *Consider a system S with input A that is the aggregation of two constituent flows A_1 and A_2. Suppose A_2 has a v.b.c. stochastic arrival curve $\alpha \in \mathcal{F}$ with bounding function $f \in \bar{\mathcal{G}}$ (i.e., $A_2 \sim_{vb} \langle f_2, \alpha_2 \rangle$) and the system provides to the input a weak stochastic service curve $\beta \in \mathcal{F}$ with bounding function $g \in \bar{\mathcal{G}}$; i.e., $S \sim_{ws} \langle g, \beta \rangle$. Then, if $\beta - \alpha_2 \in \mathcal{F}$, A_1 receives a stochastic service curve $\beta - \alpha_{2,\theta}$ with bounding function $f_{2,t}^{\theta} \otimes g_t^{\theta}(x)$, i.e. $S_1 \sim_{sc} \langle f_{2,t}^{\theta} \otimes g_t, \beta - \alpha_2 \rangle$, where $f_{2,t}^{\theta}(x) = \frac{1}{\theta_2} \int_{x-\theta_2 t}^{\infty} f_2(y)\,dy$, $\alpha_{2,\theta}(t) = \alpha(t) + \theta_2 \cdot t$, and $g_t^{\theta} = \frac{1}{\theta_1} \int_{x-\theta_1 t}^{\infty} g(y)\,dy$ for any $\theta_1, \theta_2 > 0$.*

Similarly, the following results correspond to Theorem 5.45, Corollaries 5.46 and 5.47 and are obtained based on the relationship between the θ-m.b.c. stochastic arrival curve and m.b.c. stochastic arrival curve.

Corollary 5.51. *Consider a system S with input A that is the aggregation of two constituent flows A_1 and A_2. Suppose A_2 has a θ-m.b.c stochastic arrival curve $\alpha \in \mathcal{F}$ with bounding function $f \in \bar{\mathcal{F}}$ (i.e., $A_2 \sim_{\theta-mb} \langle f_2^{\theta}, \alpha_2 \rangle$) and the system provides to the input a stochastic service curve $\beta \in \mathcal{F}$ with bounding function $g \in \bar{\mathcal{F}}$; i.e., $S \sim_{sc} \langle g, \beta \rangle$. Then, if $\beta - \alpha_2 \in \mathcal{F}$, A_1 receives a stochastic service curve $\beta - \alpha_2$ with bounding function $f_{2,t}^{\theta} \otimes g$; i.e., $S_1 \sim_{sc} \langle f_{2,t}^{\theta} \otimes g, \beta - \alpha_2 \rangle$, where $f_{2,t}^{\theta}(x) = f_2^{\theta}(x - \theta t)$ for any $\theta > 0$.*

Corollary 5.52. *Consider a system S with input A that is the aggregation of two constituent flows A_1 and A_2. Suppose A_2 has a θ-m.b.c. stochastic arrival curve $\alpha \in \mathcal{F}$ with bounding function $f \in \bar{\mathcal{F}}$; (i.e., $A_2 \sim_{\theta-mb} \langle f_2^{\theta}, \alpha_2 \rangle$) and the system provides to the input a θ-stochastic service curve $\beta \in \mathcal{F}$ with bounding function $g^{\theta} \in \bar{\mathcal{F}}$; i.e., $S \sim_{sc} \langle g^{\theta}, \beta \rangle$. Then, if $\beta - \alpha_2 \in \mathcal{F}$, A_1 receives a stochastic service curve $\beta - \alpha_2$ with bounding function $f_{2,t}^{\theta} \otimes g_t^{\theta}$; i.e., $S_1 \sim_{sc} \langle f_{2,t}^{\theta} \otimes g_t^{\theta}, \beta - \alpha_2 \rangle$, where $f_{2,t}^{\theta}(x) = f_2^{\theta_2}(x - \theta_2 t)$ and $g_t^{\theta} = g^{\theta}(x - \theta_1 t)$ for any $\theta_1, \theta_2 > 0$.*

Corollary 5.53. *Consider a system S with input A that is the aggregation of two constituent flows A_1 and A_2. Suppose A_2 has a θ-m.b.c stochastic arrival curve $\alpha \in \mathcal{F}$ with bounding function $f \in \bar{\mathcal{F}}$, i.e. $A_2 \sim_{\theta-mb} \langle f_2^{\theta}, \alpha_2 \rangle$, and* the system provides to the input a weak stochastic service curve $\beta \in \mathcal{F}$ with bounding function $g \in \bar{\mathcal{F}}$, i.e. $S \sim_{ws} \langle g, \beta \rangle$. Then, if $\beta - \alpha_2 \in \mathcal{F}$, A_1 receives a stochastic service curve $\beta - \alpha_2$ with bounding function $f_{2,t}^{\theta} \otimes g_t^{\theta}$, i.e. $S_1 \sim_{sc} \langle f_{2,t}^{\theta} \otimes g_t^{\theta}, \beta - \alpha_2 \rangle$, where $f_{2,t}^{\theta}(x) = f_2^{\theta}(x - \theta_2 t)$ and $g_t^{\theta} = \frac{1}{\theta_1} \int_{x - \theta_1 t}^{\infty} g^{\theta}(y) dy$ for any $\theta_1, \theta_2 > 0$.

Finally, we suppose the input A_2 is characterized using a t.a.c. stochastic arrival curve. The following results correspond to Theorem 5.45, Corollary 5.46, and Corollary 5.47 and are similarly obtained based on the relationship between the t.a.c. stochastic arrival curve and m.b.c. stochastic arrival curve.

Corollary 5.54. *Consider a system S with input A that is the aggregation of two constituent flows A_1 and A_2. Suppose A_2 has a t.a.c stochastic arrival curve $\alpha \in \mathcal{F}$ with bounding function $f \in \bar{\mathcal{G}}$ (i.e., $A_2 \sim_{ta} \langle f_2, \alpha_2 \rangle$) and the system provides to the input a stochastic service curve $\beta \in \mathcal{F}$ with bounding function $g \in \bar{\mathcal{F}}$; i.e., $S \sim_{sc} \langle g, \beta \rangle$. Then, if $\beta - \alpha_2 \in \mathcal{F}$, A_1 receives a stochastic service curve $\beta - \alpha_{2,\theta}$ with bounding function $f_{2,t}^{\theta} \otimes g$; i.e., $S_1 \sim_{sc} \langle f_{2,t}^{\theta} \otimes g, \beta - \alpha_{2,\theta} \rangle$, where $f_{2,t}^{\theta}(x) = \frac{1}{\theta_2} \int_{x - \theta_2 t}^{\infty} \hat{f}_2(y) dy$, $\hat{f}_2(y) = f(y) + \frac{1}{\theta_1} \int_y^{\infty} f(z) dz$, and $\alpha_{2,\theta}(t) = \alpha_2(t) + \theta_1 \cdot t$ for any $\theta_1, \theta_2 > 0$.*

Corollary 5.55. *Consider a system S with input A that is the aggregation of two constituent flows A_1 and A_2. Suppose A_2 has a t.a.c stochastic arrival curve $\alpha \in \mathcal{F}$ with bounding function $f \in \bar{\mathcal{G}}$ (i.e., $A_2 \sim_{ta} \langle f_2, \alpha_2 \rangle$) and the system provides to the input a θ-stochastic service curve $\beta \in \mathcal{F}$ with bounding function $g^{\theta} \in \bar{\mathcal{F}}$; (i.e., $S \sim_{\theta - sc} \langle g^{\theta}, \beta \rangle$). Then, if $\beta - \alpha_2 \in \mathcal{F}$, A_1 receives a stochastic service curve $\beta - \alpha_{2,\theta}$ with bounding function $f_{2,t}^{\theta} \otimes g_t^{\theta}$; (i.e., $S_1 \sim_{sc} \langle f_{2,t}^{\theta} \otimes g_t^{\theta}, \beta - \alpha_{2,\theta} \rangle$), where $f_{2,t}^{\theta}(x) = \frac{1}{\theta_2} \int_{x - \theta_2 t}^{\infty} \hat{f}_2(y) dy$, $\hat{f}_2(y) = f(y) + \frac{1}{\theta_1} \int_y^{\infty} f(z) dz$, $g_t^{\theta} = g^{\theta}(x - \theta_3 t)$, and $\alpha_{2,\theta}(t) = \alpha_2(t) + \theta_1 \cdot t$ for any $\theta_1, \theta_2, \theta_3 > 0$.*

Corollary 5.56. *Consider a system S with input A that is the aggregation of two constituent flows A_1 and A_2. Suppose A_2 has a t.a.c. stochastic arrival curve $\alpha \in \mathcal{F}$ with bounding function $f \in \bar{\mathcal{G}}$ (i.e., $A_2 \sim_{ta} \langle f_2, \alpha_2 \rangle$) and the system provides to the input a weak stochastic service curve $\beta \in \mathcal{F}$ with bounding function $g \in \bar{\mathcal{G}}$ (i.e., $S \sim_{ws} \langle g, \beta \rangle$). Then, if $\beta - \alpha_2 \in \mathcal{F}$, A_1 receives a stochastic service curve $\beta - \alpha_{2,\theta}$ with bounding function $f_{2,t}^{\theta} \otimes g_t^{\theta}$; (i.e., $S_1 \sim_{sc} \langle f_{2,t}^{\theta} \otimes g_t^{\theta}, \beta - \alpha_{2,\theta} \rangle$), where $f_{2,t}^{\theta}(x) = \frac{1}{\theta_2} \int_{x - \theta_2 t}^{\infty} \hat{f}_2(y) dy$, $\hat{f}_2(y) = f(y) + \frac{1}{\theta_1} \int_y^{\infty} f(z) dz$, $g_t^{\theta} = \frac{1}{\theta_3} \int_{x - \theta_3 t}^{\infty} g(y) dy$, and $\alpha_{2,\theta}(t) = \alpha_2(t) + \theta_1 \cdot t$ for any $\theta_1, \theta_2, \theta_3 > 0$.*

5.4.3 Leftover θ-Stochastic Service Curve

From (5.40), we also obtain, for any $\theta_1, \theta_2 > 0$ and $\theta = \theta_1 + \theta_2$,

$$\sup_{0 \leq s \leq t} [A_1 \otimes (\beta - \alpha_2)(s) - A_1^*(s) - \theta(t - s)]$$

$$\leq \sup_{0 \leq s \leq t} [A \otimes \beta(s) - A^*(s) - \theta_1(t - s)]$$

$$+ \sup_{0 \leq s \leq t} \left[\sup_{0 \leq u \leq s} [A_2(u, s) - \alpha_2(s - u)] - \theta_2(t - s) \right] \qquad (5.42)$$

and with this and the relationship between the m.b.c. SAC and θ-m.b.c. SAC and the relationship between the stochastic service curve and θ-stochastic service curve, the following theorem can be easily verified.

Theorem 5.57. *Consider a system S with input A that is the aggregation of two constituent flows A_1 and A_2. Suppose A_2 has an m.b.c. (or θ-m.b.c.) stochastic arrival curve $\alpha \in \mathcal{F}$ with bounding function $f \in \bar{\mathcal{F}}$ (i.e., $A_2 \sim_{mb} \langle f_2, \alpha_2 \rangle$ (or $A_2 \sim_{\theta-mb} \langle f_2, \alpha_2 \rangle$)) and the system provides to the input a stochastic service curve (or θ-stochastic service curve) $\beta \in \mathcal{F}$ with bounding function $g \in \bar{\mathcal{F}}$ (i.e., $S \sim_{sc} \langle g, \beta \rangle$ (or $S \sim_{\theta-sc} \langle g, \beta \rangle$)). Then, if $\beta - \alpha_2 \in \mathcal{F}$, A_1 receives a θ-stochastic service curve $\beta - \alpha_2$ with bounding function $f_2 \otimes g(x)$; i.e., $S_1 \sim_{\theta-sc} \langle f_2 \otimes g(x), \beta - \alpha_2 \rangle$.*

Based on the relationship between the weak stochastic service curve and θ-stochastic service curve, the following corollary is obtained.

Corollary 5.58. *Consider a system S with input A that is the aggregation of two constituent flows A_1 and A_2. Suppose A_2 has an m.b.c. (or θ-m.b.c.) stochastic arrival curve $\alpha \in \mathcal{F}$ with bounding function $f \in \bar{\mathcal{F}}$ (i.e., $A_2 \sim_{mb} \langle f_2, \alpha_2 \rangle$ (or $A_2 \sim_{\theta-mb} \langle f_2, \alpha_2 \rangle$)) and the system provides to the input a weak stochastic service curve $\beta \in \mathcal{F}$ with bounding function $g \in \bar{\mathcal{G}}$, (i.e., $S \sim_{ws} \langle g, \beta \rangle$). Then, if $\beta - \alpha_2 \in \mathcal{F}$, A_1 receives a θ-stochastic service curve $\beta - \alpha_2$ with bounding function $f_2 \otimes g^\theta(x)$; i.e., $S_1 \sim_{\theta-sc} \langle f_2 \otimes g^\theta(x), \beta - \alpha_2 \rangle$, where $g^\theta = g(x) + \frac{1}{\theta} \int_x^\infty g(y) dy$ for any $\theta > 0$.*

Corresponding to Theorem 5.57 and Corollary 5.58, Corollaries 5.59 and 5.60 are obtained based on the relationship between the v.b.c. stochastic arrival curve and θ-m.b.c. stochastic arrival curve.

Corollary 5.59. *Consider a system S with input A that is the aggregation of two constituent flows A_1 and A_2. Suppose A_2 has a v.b.c. stochastic arrival curve $\alpha \in \mathcal{F}$ with bounding function $f \in \bar{\mathcal{G}}$, i.e. $A_2 \sim_{vb} \langle f_2, \alpha_2 \rangle$ and the system provides to the input a stochastic service curve (or θ-stochastic service curve) $\beta \in \mathcal{F}$ with bounding function $g \in \bar{\mathcal{F}}$ (i.e., $S \sim_{sc} \langle g, \beta \rangle$ (or $S \sim_{\theta-sc} \langle g, \beta \rangle$)). Then, if $\beta - \alpha_{2,\theta} \in \mathcal{F}$, A_1 receives a θ-stochastic service curve $\beta - \alpha_{2,\theta}$ with bounding function $f_2^\theta \otimes g$; i.e., $S_1 \sim_{\theta-sc} \langle f_2^\theta \otimes g(x), \beta - \alpha_{2,\theta} \rangle$, where $f_2^\theta = f_2(x) + \frac{1}{\theta} \int_x^\infty f_2(y) dy$ and $\alpha_{2,\theta}(t) = \alpha_2(t) + \theta t$ for any $\theta > 0$.*

Corollary 5.60. *Consider a system S with input A that is the aggregation of two constituent flows A_1 and A_2. Suppose A_2 has a v.b.c. stochastic arrival curve $\alpha \in \mathcal{F}$ with bounding function $f \in \bar{\mathcal{G}}$; (i.e., $A_2 \sim_{vb} \langle f_2, \alpha_2 \rangle$)*

and the system provides to the input a weak stochastic service curve $\beta \in \mathcal{F}$ with bounding function $g \in \bar{\mathcal{G}}$; (i.e., $S \sim_{ws} \langle g, \beta \rangle$). Then, if $\beta - \alpha_{2,\theta} \in \mathcal{F}$, A_1 receives a θ-stochastic service curve $\beta - \alpha_{2,\theta}$ with bounding function $f_2^\theta \otimes g^\theta$; i.e., $S_1 \sim_{\theta-sc} \langle f_2^\theta \otimes g^\theta, \beta - \alpha_{2,\theta} \rangle$, where $f_2^\theta = f_2(x) + \frac{1}{\theta_2} \int_x^\infty f_2(y) dy$, $g^{\theta_1} = g(x) + \frac{1}{\theta_1} \int_x^\infty g(y) dy$, and $\alpha_{2,\theta}(t) = \alpha_2(t) + \theta_2 t$ for any $\theta_1, \theta_2 > 0$.

Finally, based on the relationship between the t.a.c. stochastic arrival curve and θ-m.b.c. stochastic arrival curve, we can have Corollaries 5.61 and 5.62, which correspond to Theorem 5.57 and Corollary 5.58.

Corollary 5.61. *Consider a system S with input A that is the aggregation of two constituent flows A_1 and A_2. Suppose A_2 has a t.a.c stochastic arrival curve $\alpha \in \mathcal{F}$ with bounding function $f \in \bar{\mathcal{G}}$; (i.e., $A_2 \sim_{ta} \langle f_2, \alpha_2 \rangle$) and the system provides to the input a stochastic service curve (or θ-stochastic service curve) $\beta \in \mathcal{F}$ with bounding function $g \in \bar{\mathcal{F}}$; i.e., $S \sim_{sc} \langle g, \beta \rangle$ (or $S \sim_{\theta-sc} \langle g, \beta \rangle$). Then, if $\beta - \alpha_{2,\theta} \in \mathcal{F}$, A_1 receives a θ-stochastic service curve $\beta - \alpha_{2,\theta}$ with bounding function $f_2^\theta \otimes g$, i.e., $S_1 \sim_{\theta-sc} \langle f_2^\theta \otimes g, \beta - \alpha_{2,\theta} \rangle$, where $f_2^\theta = \hat{f}_2(x) + \frac{1}{\theta_2} \int_x^\infty \hat{f}_2(y) dy$, $\hat{f}_2(y) = f(y) + \frac{1}{\theta_1} \int_y^\infty f(z) dz$, and $\alpha_{2,\theta_2}(t) = \alpha_2(t) + \theta_2 t$, for any $\theta_1, \theta_2 > 0$.*

Corollary 5.62. *Consider a system S with input A that is the aggregation of two constituent flows A_1 and A_2. Suppose A_2 has a t.a.c stochastic arrival curve $\alpha \in \mathcal{F}$ with bounding function $f \in \bar{\mathcal{G}}$; (i.e., $A_2 \sim_{ta} \langle f_2, \alpha_2 \rangle$) and the system provides to the input a weak stochastic service curve $\beta \in \mathcal{F}$ with bounding function $g \in \bar{\mathcal{G}}$; i.e., $S \sim_{ws} \langle g, \beta \rangle$. Then, if $\beta - \alpha_{2,\theta} \in \mathcal{F}$, A_1 receives a θ-stochastic service curve $\beta - \alpha_{2,\theta}$ with bounding function $f_2^\theta \otimes g^\theta$; i.e., $S_1 \sim_{\theta-sc} \langle f_2^\theta \otimes g^\theta, \beta - \alpha_{2,\theta} \rangle$, where $f_2^{\theta_2} = \hat{f}_2(x) + \frac{1}{\theta_2} \int_x^\infty \hat{f}_2(y) dy$, $\hat{f}_2(y) = f(y) + \frac{1}{\theta_3} \int_y^\infty f(z) dz$, and $g^{\theta_1} = g(x) + \frac{1}{\theta_1} \int_x^\infty g(y) dy$ and $\alpha_{2,\theta}(t) = \alpha_2(t) + \theta_2 t$ for any $\theta_1, \theta_2, \theta_3 > 0$.*

5.5 Superposition Property

The superposition property means that the superposition of flows can be represented using the same traffic model. With this property, the aggregate of (possibly many) individual flows may be considered as a single aggregate flow, so that the QoS performance for the aggregate can be derived in the same way as for a single flow. This section discusses the superposition property for the various stochastic traffic models introduced in Chapter 2.

Consider N flows with arrival processes $A_i(t)$, $i = 1, \ldots, N$. Let $A(t)$ be the superposition of the N flows. In other words, we have for any $s, t \geq 0$,

$$A(s, s + t) = A_1(s, s + t) + \cdots + A_N(s, s + t).$$

Then, for any functions $\alpha_i(t)$, $i = 1, \ldots, N$, we have

$$A(s, s+t) - [\alpha_1(t) + \cdots + \alpha_N(t)]$$
$$= [A_1(s, s+t) - \alpha_1(t)] + \cdots + [A_N(s, s+t) - \alpha_N(t)]. \qquad (5.43)$$

With (5.43), the superposition property of the t.a.c. stochastic arrival curve can be easily verified.

Theorem 5.63. *Consider N flows with arrival processes $A_i(t)$, $i = 1, \ldots, N$, respectively. Let $A(t)$ denote the aggregate arrival process. If $\forall i, A_i \sim_{ta} \langle f_i, \alpha_i \rangle$, then $A \sim_{ta} \langle f, \alpha \rangle$ with $\alpha(t) = \sum_{i=1}^{N} \alpha_i(t)$ and $f(x) = f_1 \otimes \cdots \otimes f_N(x)$.*

From (5.43), we can also obtain

$$\sup_{0 \leq s \leq t} [A(s, t) - [\alpha_1(t - s) + \cdots + \alpha_N(t - s)]]$$
$$\leq \sup_{0 \leq s \leq t} [A_1(s, t) - \alpha_1(t - s)] + \cdots + \sup_{0 \leq s \leq t} [A_N(s, t) - \alpha_N(t - s)], \qquad (5.44)$$

and with this, the superposition property of the v.b.c. stochastic arrival curve can be derived.

Theorem 5.64. *Consider N flows with arrival processes $A_i(t)$, $i = 1, \ldots, N$, respectively. Let $A(t)$ denote the aggregate arrival process. If $\forall i, A_i \sim_{vb} \langle f_i, \alpha_i \rangle$, then $A \sim_{vb} \langle f, \alpha \rangle$ with $\alpha(t) = \sum_{i=1}^{N} \alpha_i(t)$ and $f(x) = f_1 \otimes \cdots \otimes f_N(x)$.*

Further, from (5.44), we get

$$\sup_{0 \leq s \leq t} \sup_{0 \leq u \leq s} [A(u, s) - [\alpha_1(s - u) + \cdots + \alpha_N(s - u)]]$$
$$\leq \sup_{0 \leq s \leq t} \sup_{0 \leq u \leq s} [A_1(u, s) - \alpha_1(s - u)] + \cdots$$
$$+ \sup_{0 \leq s \leq t} \sup_{0 \leq u \leq s} [A_N(u, s) - \alpha_N(s - u)] \qquad (5.45)$$

with which, the superposition property of the m.b.c. stochastic arrival curve is obtained.

Theorem 5.65. *Consider N flows with arrival processes $A_i(t)$, $i = 1, \ldots, N$, respectively. Let $A(t)$ denote the aggregate arrival process. If $\forall i, A_i \sim_{mb} \langle f_i, \alpha_i \rangle$, then $A \sim_{mb} \langle f, \alpha \rangle$ with $\alpha(t) = \sum_{i=1}^{N} \alpha_i(t)$ and $f(x) = f_1 \otimes \cdots \otimes f_N(x)$.*

Also from (5.44), we get for any $\theta_1, \ldots, \theta_N > 0$ and $\theta = \theta_1 + \cdots + \theta_N$

$$\sup_{0 \leq s \leq t} \left[\sup_{0 \leq u \leq s} \{A(u, s) - [\alpha_1(s - u) + \cdots + \alpha_N(s - u)]\} - \theta \cdot (t - s) \right]$$
$$\leq \sup_{0 \leq s \leq t} \left[\sup_{0 \leq u \leq s} [A_1(u, s) - \alpha_1(s - u)] - \theta_1 \cdot (t - s) \right] + \cdots$$
$$+ \sup_{0 \leq s \leq t} \left[\sup_{0 \leq u \leq s} [A_N(u, s) - \alpha_N(s - u)] - \theta_N \cdot (t - s) \right], \qquad (5.46)$$

and with this, the superposition property of the m.b.c. stochastic arrival curve is obtained.

Theorem 5.66. *Consider N flows with arrival processes $A_i(t)$, $i = 1, \ldots, N$, respectively. Let $A(t)$ denote the aggregate arrival process. If $\forall i, A_i \sim_{\theta-mb} \langle f_i, \alpha_i \rangle$, then $A \sim_{\theta-mb} \langle f^\theta, \alpha \rangle$ with $\alpha(t) = \sum_{i=1}^N \alpha_i(t)$, and $f^\theta(x) = f_1^{\theta_1} \otimes \cdots \otimes f_N^{\theta_N}(x)$ for any $\theta_1, \ldots, \theta_N > 0$ and $\theta = \theta_1 + \cdots + \theta_N$.*

5.6 Scaling of End-to-End Delay Bound

As discussed earlier in Chapter 2, when we consider the deterministic network with n nodes in tandem, we see that the end-to-end delay bound obtained is a scaling in $\mathcal{O}\left(n^2\right)$ from the node-by-node analysis approach. However, with the concatenation property of the service curve, the end-to-end delay bound is a scaling in $\mathcal{O}\left(n\right)$, which gives a much tighter bound. The *scaling property* provides us an important metric for evaluating the tightness and scalability of performance bounds under different approaches.

In this section, we investigate the scaling property of end-to-end delay bounds under a stochastic setting to demonstrate the use of stochastic network calculus results introduced in this chapter.

Consider the scenario shown in Figure 5.2.A. Flow F passes n servers in tandem. Each server is a constant-rate server with capacity C. At each server, a cross-flow joins and leaves. Assume flow F and all cross-flows have the same m.b.c. stochastic arrival curve (SAC) $A \sim_{mb} \langle r, f \rangle$ with $f(x) = ae^{-bx}$. To ensure the stability of the system, we also assume $2r < C$. We are interested in deriving the stochastic end-to-end delay bound for flow F and investigate how the delay bound increases as the number of servers increases.

To facilitate the explanation, we introduce a useful lemma as follows, which can also be found from [24].

Lemma 5.67. *For any positive numbers a_k, b_k, $k = 1, \cdots, K$ and any $x \geq 0$, we have*

$$\inf_{x_1 + \cdots + x_K = x} \sum_{k=1}^K a_k e^{-b_k x_k} = e^{\frac{-x}{w}} \prod_{k=1}^K (a_k b_k w)^{\frac{1}{b_k w}},$$

where $w = \sum_{k=1}^K \frac{1}{b_k}$.

Proof. Let

$$a_k b_k e^{-b_k x_k} = \lambda, \quad k = 1, \cdots, K.$$

Then,

$$\sum_{k=1}^K a_k e^{-b_k x_k} = \sum_{k=1}^K \frac{\lambda}{b_k}. \tag{5.47}$$

Let $w = \sum_{k=1}^K \frac{1}{b_k}$ and $p_k = \frac{1}{b_k w}$. Since $\sum_{i=1}^K p_i = 1$, we have

$$\lambda = \prod_{k=1}^K \lambda^{p_k} = e^{-x/w} \prod_{k=1}^K \left(\frac{a_k}{w p_k} \right)^{p_k}. \tag{5.48}$$

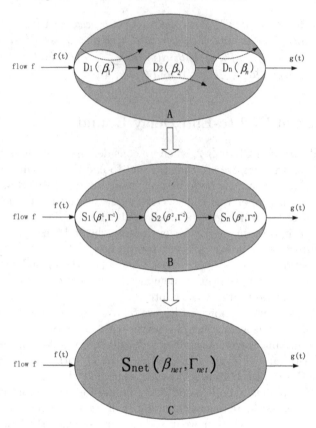

Fig. 5.2. Stochastic servers in tandem

Combining (5.47) and (5.48), this lemma follows.   □

We now derive end-to-end stochastic delay bounds for the flow F. We first base the derivation on the concatenation property and then derive if using the node-by-node analysis approach.

5.6.1 Delay Bound From the Concatenation Property

As shown in Figure 5.2.B, according to Theorem 5.45, each node provides a leftover stochastic service curve

$$S^i \sim_{sc} \langle \beta^i, \Gamma^i \rangle,$$

where

$$\beta_i(t) = (C - r) t$$

and

$$\Gamma^i(x) = f(x).$$

Then, as shown in Figure 5.2 C, according to the concatenation property of the stochastic service curve, we have

$$S_{net} \sim_{sc} (\beta_{net}, \Gamma_{net}),$$

where

$$\beta_{net} = \beta^1 \otimes \cdots \otimes \beta^n = (C - r)t$$

and

$$f_{net} = \Gamma^1 \otimes \cdots \otimes \Gamma^n.$$

In addition, according to Theorem 5.4, we can have the stochastic end-to-end delay bound for flow F

$$P\{D > h(\alpha + x, \beta_{net})\} \le f \otimes \Gamma^1 \otimes \cdots \otimes \Gamma^n(x),$$

and with this and Lemma 5.67, we have

$$P\left\{D > \frac{x}{C - r}\right\} \le e^{-\frac{xb}{n+1}} (a(n + 1)). \tag{5.49}$$

Then, we determine the delay bound d such that $P\{D > d\} \le \varepsilon$, where ε is a small delay bound violation probability.

Let $d = \frac{x}{C-r}$ and set the right side of (5.49) equal to ε. We have for the delay bound d

$$d = \frac{n+1}{(C - r)b} \log \frac{(a(n + 1))}{\varepsilon}. \tag{5.50}$$

It is found from (5.50) that the delay bound derived from the concatenation property scales in $\mathcal{O}(n \log n)$, where n is the number of nodes the flow passes through.

5.6.2 Delay Bound from Node-by-Node Analysis

Now we derive the stochastic end-to-end delay bound by using the node-by-node analysis approach. As shown in Figure 5.2.B, for the first node, according to Theorem 5.4, we can have the following delay bound at the first node

$$P\left\{D_1 > \frac{x}{C - r}\right\} \le f \otimes \Gamma^1(x).$$

For the second node, we need to have the input burstiness of flow F at the second node, which is the output burstiness of flow F at the first node. According to Theorem 5.21, the input of flow F has an m.b.c. SAC $\langle f \otimes \Gamma^1(x), r \rangle$. Then we have the following delay bound at the second node:

$$P\left\{D_2 > \frac{x}{C - r}\right\} \le f \otimes \Gamma^1 \otimes \Gamma^2(x).$$

Similarly, we have the following delay bound at each node i on the path

$$P\left\{D_i > \frac{x}{C-r}\right\} \leq f \otimes \Gamma^1 \otimes \cdots \otimes \Gamma^i,$$

and with this, following the same approach as in getting (5.49), we obtain

$$P\left\{D_i > \frac{x}{C-r}\right\} \leq e^{-\frac{xb}{i+1}}\left(a(i+1)\right). \tag{5.51}$$

Now we consider the distribution of $D_1 + D_2 + \cdots + D_n$. According to Lemma 5.67, we have

$$P\left\{D > \frac{x}{C-r}\right\} \leq e^{-\frac{2xb}{(n+1)(n+3)}}\left(a\frac{(n+1)(n+3)}{2}\right) \tag{5.52}$$

Then, we determine the delay bound d such that $P\{D > d\} \leq \varepsilon$, where ε is a small delay bound violation probability.

Letting $d = \frac{x}{C-r}$ and setting the right side of (5.49) equal to ε, we have

$$d = \frac{(n+1)(n+3)}{2\left(C-r\right)b}\log\frac{\left(a\frac{(n+1)(n+3)}{2}\right)}{\varepsilon}. \tag{5.53}$$

It is found from (5.53) that the delay bound derived through node-by-node analysis scales in $\mathcal{O}\left(n^2\log n\right)$. Comparing this with the stochastic delay bound obtained in (5.50) by using the concatenation property, it is clear that the one in (5.50) is much better than the one obtained in (5.53) through node-by-node analysis.

5.7 Calculus on Traffic and Service Envelope Processes

In Chapters 2 and 3, the traffic envelope process and service envelope process respectively were introduced. This section presents results based on these processes. Theorems 5.68 to 5.73 correspond to the five basic properties. Their proofs follow similarly from their deterministic counterpart theorems and the definitions of stochastic envelope process in Definition 3.28, service envelope process in Definition 4.15, and strict service envelope process in Definition 4.16.

Theorem 5.68 (Delay Bound). *Consider a system that provides a service envelope process $\hat{S}(t)$ to the input flow $A(t)$. Suppose A has a stochastic envelope process $\hat{A}$. Then, the delay $D(t)$ of the flow at time t satisfies*

$$D(t) \leq h\left(\hat{A}(t), \hat{S}(t)\right).$$

Theorem 5.69 (Backlog Bound). *Consider a system that provides a service envelope process $\hat{S}(t)$ to the input flow $A(t)$. Suppose A has a stochastic envelope process $\hat{A}$. Then, the backlog $B(t)$ of the flow at time t satisfies*

$$B(t) \leq \hat{A} \oslash \hat{S}(0).$$

Theorem 5.70 (Output Characterization). *Consider a system that provides a service envelope process $\hat{S}(t)$ to the input flow $A(t)$. Suppose A has a stochastic envelope process $\hat{A}$. Then, the output A^* has a stochastic envelope process $\hat{A}^*$, i.e., for all $s, t \geq 0$, $A^*(s, s+t) \leq \hat{A}^*(t)$, where*

$$\hat{A}^*(t) = \hat{A} \oslash \hat{S}(t).$$

Theorem 5.71 (Concatenation Property). *Consider a flow passing through systems S^h, $h = 1, \ldots, H$, in sequence. Suppose each system S^h provides a service envelope process $\hat{S}^h(t)$ to the input. Then the concatenation of these systems offers a service envelope process $\hat{S}$ to the flow, where*

$$\hat{S}(t) = \hat{S}^1 \otimes \hat{S}^2 \cdots \otimes \hat{S}^H(t). \tag{5.54}$$

Theorem 5.72 (Leftover Service). *Consider a system serving an aggregate of two (possibly aggregate) flows A_1 and A_2. Assume the system provides a service envelope process $\hat{S}$ to the aggregate, and A_2 has a stochastic envelope process $\hat{A}_2$. Then, the system offers to the flow A_1 a service envelope process $\hat{S}_1(t)$, where*

$$\hat{S}_1(t) = (\hat{S} - \hat{A}_2)(t). \tag{5.55}$$

Theorem 5.73 (Superposition). *Consider the superposition of n flows A_i, $i = 1, \ldots, n$. If each flow A_i has a stochastic envelope process $\hat{A}_i(t)$, then the aggregate flow $A = \sum_{i=1}^{n} A_i$ has a stochastic envelope process $\hat{A}(t) = \sum_{i=1}^{n} \hat{A}_i(t)$.*

While looking similar to the corresponding deterministic results, Theorems 5.68 to 5.73 indeed have critical differences from their deterministic counterparts. One is that all envelope processes in Theorems 5.68 to 5.73 are random processes. Due to this, another difference is that in order to use Theorems 5.68 to 5.73 in real network analysis, the statistical properties of the various envelope processes have to be known and explored. The third difference is that to apply Theorems 5.68 to 5.73, strict service envelope process is often needed instead of service envelope process. This is because, as shown by its definition, the service envelope process model is dependent on the input process, which complicates finding the service envelope process. In Chapter 6, moment generating functions of the various envelope processes will be used to derive the five basic properties, where strict service envelope processes are implicitly required and the analysis generally assumes independence between the envelope processes considered.

Table 5.1. Properties provided by a combination of traffic model and server model

	weak SSC	SSC	θ-SSC
t.a.c. SAC	(P.1), (P.5)	(P.1), (P.3), (P.5)	(P.1), (P.3), (P.5)
v.b.c. SAC	(P.1), (P.4), (P.5)	(P.1)–(P.3), (P.5)	(P.1), (P.3), (P.5)
m.b.c. SAC	(P.1), (P.4), (P.5)	(P.1)–(P.5)	(P.1)–(P.5)
θ-m.b.c. SAC	(P.1), (P.4), (P.5)	(P.1), (P.5)	(P.1)–(P.5)

5.8 Summary and Bibliographic Comments

In this chapter, we presented the five basic properties of stochastic network calculus under the various traffic models and server models introduced in Chapters 3 and 4.

Table 5.1 summarizes the properties that are provided by the combination of a traffic model, chosen from t.a.c., v.b.c., m.b.c., and θ-m.b.c. stochastic arrival curve (SAC), and a server model, chosen from weak stochastic service curve, stochastic service curve (SSC), and θ–stochastic service curve, without any additional constraints on the traffic model or the server model, where, as introduced in Chapter 1, (P.1)–(P.5) denote the following properties:

- (P.1) – Service Guarantees
- (P.2) – Output Characterization
- (P.3) – Concatenation Property
- (P.4) – Leftover Service
- (P.5) – Superposition Property

In Chapter 3, we discussed that under the context of network calculus, many (if not most) traffic models used in the literature [138] [31] [128] [140] [14] [95] [98] [5] [74] [73] [24] belong to the t.a.c. and/or v.b.c. stochastic arrival curve. In Chapter 4, many (if not most) server models [93][31][14][95][98][5][24] were shown to belong to the weak stochastic service curve. Table 5.1 shows that, without additional constraints, these works can only support part of the five required properties for stochastic network calculus. In contrast, under the combination of the m.b.c. stochastic arrival curve and stochastic service curve, all five basic properties have been proved in this chapter without additional constraints added to these two models. While appealing, this combination has a potential problem in the bounding function under the m.b.c. stochastic arrival curve or stochastic service curve may be dependent on time.

Note that with some additional constraints on the bounding functions in the models discussed in Table 5.1, one combination may have more properties among (P.1)–(P.5) than those listed in the table. The most frequently used constraint in this book is the bounding function belonging to $\bar{\mathcal{G}}$. This constraint, initially suggested by Starobinski and Sidi [128], is that the bounding function belongs to a specific subset of $\bar{\mathcal{F}}$, denoted by $\bar{\mathcal{G}}$, which consists of all functions in $\bar{\mathcal{F}}$ whose nth-fold integration still belongs to the subset for any $n \geq 1$. Under this constraint, as presented in this chapter, the unlisted properties among (P.1)–(P.5) can be proved for the combination of the t.a.c. or v.b.c. stochastic arrival curve and weak stochastic service curve, and particularly for the combination of a θ-stochastic arrival curve and θ-stochastic service curve. It is worth highlighting that if the bounding functions considered are in $\bar{\mathcal{G}}$, the set of results for the combination of a θ-stochastic arrival curve and θ-stochastic service curve can be used as the basis for deriving the basic properties for all other combinations. Except for combinations where an m.b.c. stochastic arrival curve and/or stochastic service curve is used, the results can have bounding functions independent on time. This makes the θ-stochastic arrival curve and θ-stochastic service curve models attractive.

Another constraint, which was recently proposed by Li, et al. [96], assumes that there is a *timescale* T that bounds the convolution in the definition of a weak stochastic service curve. In [96], Li et al. also discussed network cases where such timescales exist. As an analogy, we may assume the existence of a timescale T that bounds the convolution in the m.b.c. stochastic arrival curve model and stochastic service curve model. Consequently, we conjecture that all results presented in this chapter under combinations where the m.b.c. stochastic arrival curve and/or stochastic service curve are used will be bounded by such timescales, and this solves the possibly time-dependent bounding function problem with the m.b.c. stochastic arrival curve and stochastic service curve.

Also note that Table 5.1 only provides a comparison of the basic properties supported by a combination of the four types of stochastic arrival curves and the three types of stochastic service curves. While we believe they cover a wide range of traffic models and server models proposed and studied in the literature as discussed in Chapters 3 and 4, there are other types of traffic and server models that are not covered by them.

One type uses a sequence of random variables to stochastically bound the arrival process [87] or the service process [115]. Properties similar to (P.1), (P.3), (P.4), and (P.5) have been studied [87][115]. These studies generally need the independence assumption. Under these types of traffic and service models, several problems remain open. One is the concatenation property (P.2), another is the general case analysis, and the third is researching/designing approaches to map known traffic and service characterizations to the required sequences of random variables.

Another type is built upon moments or moment generating functions. This type was initially used for traffic (see e.g. Chang [15] and Knightly [85]) and has also been extended to service (see, e.g., Chang [18], Wu and Negt [133], and Fidler [44]). The independence assumption is generally required between arrival and service processes. Extensive studies have been conducted for deriving the characteristics of a process under this type of model from some known characterization of the process [15][16][18]. The main challenges for this type are the concatenation property and the general case analysis. For these, we have presented results in Section 3.5 in Chapter 3 that allow us to further relate known traffic/service characterizations to the traffic and service models discussed in this book.

Scaling of end-to-end performance bounds has recently attracted research interest in the context of stochastic network calculus. The purpose is to study similar scaling properties found in deterministic network calculus. Essentially the study is related to investigating the concatenation property under stochastic settings. In Section 5.6, it is shown that with the concatenation property, the end-to-end stochastic delay bound obtained scales in $\mathcal{O}(n \log n)$. However, if the node-by-node analysis is used, the bound scales in $\mathcal{O}(n^2 \log n)$. Similar observations were made by Fidler [44] and Ciucu et al. [25]. It should be noted that the scalings from the analysis in Section 5.6 and [25] do not assume the independence between arrival processes and service processes. With the independence assumption, a scaling of $O(n)$ can indeed be obtained for the end-to-end stochastic delay bound as discussed by Fidler [44] and as will also be shown in the next chapter.

All the results in this chapter are proved for the general case where flows and servers could be dependent. In the next chapter, the independent case will be investigated, and the investigation can help improve performance bounds significantly.

Problems

5.1. Consider a server fed with a flow A that is the aggregation of two constituent flows A_1 and A_2. Suppose the server provides a deterministic service curve β to the aggregate flow A. Also suppose flows A_1 and A_2 have v.b.c stochastic arrival curve $A_i \sim_{vb} \langle f_i, \alpha_i \rangle$, $i = 1, 2$. Derive the leftover service curve received by A_1 and stochastic delay bound for A_1.

5.2. Consider a server fed with a flow A that is the aggregation of two constituent flows A_1 and A_2. Suppose that the server provides a deterministic service curve β to the aggregate flow A, and flows A_1 and A_2 have m.b.c. stochastic arrival curve $A_i \sim_{mb} \langle f_i, \alpha_i \rangle$, $i = 1, 2$. Derive the leftover service curve received by A_1.

5.3. Consider a system with three servers S_1, S_2, and S_3 in tandem, where S_1 provides a deterministic service curve β_1, $S_2 \sim_{wc} \langle g_2, \beta_2 \rangle$, and $S_3 \sim_{sc} \langle g_3, \beta_3 \rangle$. Derive an end-to-end service curve for this system.

5.4. Consider a constant-rate server with capacity C fed with a Poisson input flow with average arrival rate λ. The packet size is exponentially distributed with mean value μ but limited by a maximum packet size M.

(i) Derive a probabilistic delay bound for the flow using the methods discussed in this chapter.

(ii) Derive a delay distribution for the flow using queuing theory, and explain the difference with the results obtained in (i).

5.5. A server is called a fluctuation constrained server if [93]

$$\int_a^b C\,(t)\,dt \geq (\mu\,(b-a) - \delta)^+\,,$$

where $C\,(t)$ is the instantaneous output capacity of a server. The server is fed by constant input traffic with rate ρ.

(i) Derive the backlog bound for the system.
(ii) Derive the delay bound for the system.

5.6. A stochastic process A is called an exponentially bounded bursty (EBB) process if for any $x \geq 0$, [138]

$$P\{A\,(t) \geq x\} \leq ae^{-bx}.$$

Consider a system with an EBB input and a constant-rate server with capacity C.

(i) Derive the backlog bound for the system.
(ii) Derive the delay bound for the system.

5.7. Prove Theorem 5.68.

5.8. Prove Theorem 5.69.

5.9. Prove Theorem 5.70.

5.10. Prove Theorem 5.71.

5.11. Prove Theorem 5.72.

5.12. Prove Theorem 5.73.

5.13. Suppose traffic is characterized by

$$E[A(s, s+t) - \alpha^\epsilon(t)] \leq \epsilon(t)$$

and service by [58]

$$E[A \otimes \beta^\xi(t) - A^*(t)] \leq \xi(t).$$

Derive the five basic properties under this combination of traffic model and server model directly from the definitions of these two models, and discuss what additional constraints are needed to allow the derivation.

5.14. Based on the basic properties of the various stochastic arrival curve and stochastic service curve models presented in this chapter, find the five basic properties for the combination of traffic model and server model introduced in the previous problem. Compare them with the results obtained from the previous problem.

6

Independent Case Analysis

In this chapter, we exploit the independence between traffic processes and service processes to improve performance bounds. Two approaches will be introduced. One is based on the concept of a stochastic strict service process due to impairment, introduced in Section 4.3. Another is based on the concepts of traffic and service envelope processes introduced in Section 5.7 and applies moment generating functions (MGF) for the analysis.

In Chapter 5, various results for stochastic network calculus were presented. These results were obtained without considering the dependence condition between flows and servers. In this chapter, we focus on independent case analysis and introduce the five basic properties (P.1)–(P.5) when flows and servers are independent.

6.1 Introduction

We start with a lemma, which is followed by a simple example to demonstrate the importance of independent case analysis.

Lemma 6.1. *Consider non-negative random variables X and Y. Suppose they are independent and $\bar{F}_X(x) \leq f(x)$ and $\bar{F}_Y(x) \leq g(x)$, where $\bar{F}_X(x)$ and $\bar{F}_Y(x)$, respectively, denote their complementary cummulative distribution functions (CCDF), and $f, g \in \bar{\mathcal{F}}$. Then, for all $x \geq 0$, there holds*

$$P\{X + Y > x\} \leq 1 - (\bar{f} * \bar{g})(x), \tag{6.1}$$

where $\bar{f}(x) = 1 - [f(x)]_1$ and $\bar{g}(x) = 1 - [g(x)]_1$.

Proof. For independent random variables X and Y, it is well known that $F_{X+Y} = F_X * F_Y \equiv \int_{-\infty}^{+\infty} F_X(x-y) dF_Y(y)$. Since X and Y are non-negative, $F_X(x) = 0$ and $F_Y(x) = 0$ for all $x < 0$. Hence, $F_{X+Y} = \int_0^x F_X(x-y) dF_Y(y)$. Notice that $F_X, F_Y, \bar{f}$, and $\bar{g}$ are wide-sense increasing, $\bar{f} \leq F_X$ and $\bar{g} \leq F_Y$, and the Stieltjes convolution operation is commutative. Then

Y. Jiang, Y. Liu, *Stochastic Network Calculus*,
DOI: 10.1007/978-1-84800-127-5_6,
© Springer-Verlag London Limited 2008

$$F_X * F_Y(x) = \int_0^x F_X(x-y)dF_Y(y)$$
$$\geq \int_0^x \bar{f}(x-y)dF_Y(y) = \int_0^x F_Y(x-y)d\bar{f}(y)$$
$$\geq \int_0^x \bar{g}(x-y)d\bar{f}(y) = (\bar{f} * \bar{g})(x),$$

and with this and $P\{X+Y > x\} = \bar{F}_{X+Y} = 1 - F_X * F_Y$, the lemma is proved. $\square$

Example 6.2. In Lemma 1.5, it was proved that $P\{X+Y > x\} \leq (f \otimes g)(x)$. If X and Y are independent, we then have two bounds for $P\{X+Y > x\}$, which are (1.12) and (6.1). Suppose $f(x) = g(x) = e^{-x}$. With Lemma 1.5, we obtain

$$P\{X+Y > x\} \leq 2e^{-x/2},$$

and with Lemma 6.1, we get

$$P\{X+Y > x\} \leq (1+x)e^{-x}.$$

These two bounds are plotted in Figure 6.1. The figure clearly shows that the bound obtained from Lemma 6.1 is much better than the bound from Lemma 1.5.

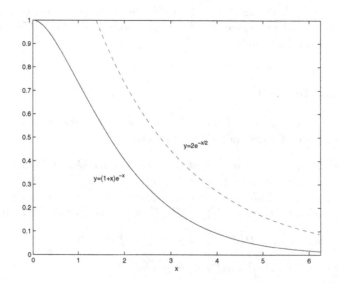

Fig. 6.1. Comparison of Lemmas 6.1 and 1.5

This example implies that by considering the independence condition, significant improvement may be obtained for the result.

From the example above, we expect that when flows and servers are independent in a network, much better results or tighter bounds can be obtained for properties (P.1)–(P.5). However, except for the superposition property (P.5), it is not straightforward to obtain properties (P.1)–(P.4) for the independent case.

The difficulty relates to the dependences implied in the definitions of the various stochastic service curve server models introduced in Chapter 4. For example, the weak stochastic service curve model is defined on the following inequality that duplicates (4.1):

$$P\{A \otimes \beta(t) - A^*(t) > x\} \le g(x). \tag{6.2}$$

The definition of the weak stochastic service curve model implies that a weak stochastic service curve $\beta(t)$ is generally dependent on the arrival process $A(t)$ and the output process $A^*(t)$. Similar dependence can be found in the stochastic service curve model and the θ-the stochastic service curve model, as well as in the stochastic service envelope process definition.

The difficulty also relates to the inherent dependences found in intermediate results obtained by using the analysis approach in the previous chapter. For example, in (5.26), we obtain

$$\sup_{0 \le s \le t} \sup_{0 \le u \le s} [A^*(u, s) - \alpha^*(s - u)]$$

$$\le \sup_{0 \le s \le t} \sup_{0 \le u \le s} [A(u, s) - \alpha(s - u)] + \sup_{0 \le s \le t} [A \otimes \beta(s) - A^*(s)] \tag{6.3}$$

where both $\sup_{0 \le s \le t} \sup_{0 \le u \le s} [A(u, s) - \alpha(s - u)]$ and $\sup_{0 \le s \le t} [A \otimes \beta(s) - A^*(s)]$ are defined to depend on the arrival process A, which further makes them dependent on each other.

In deterministic network calculus, the dependences mentioned above do not cause any difficulties in the analysis since only deterministic worst case scenarios are considered and the dependences need not be taken into account.

In stochastic network calculus, however, the dependences make it difficult to obtain independent case results directly. For example, even when the bounds on the complementary probability distribution functions (CPDF) of the two terms on the right-hand side of (6.3) are given, we cannot apply Lemma 6.1 to (6.3) since these two terms are inherently dependent, as discussed above.

In the following section, the concept of a *stochastic strict server*, which was introduced earlier in Chapter 4, is used to help decouple the dependences discussed above. As a result, a further independent case analysis on properties (P.1)–(P.4) can be conducted.

6.2 Analysis Based on Stochastic Strict Server

In Section 4.3, we introduced the concept of a *stochastic strict server*. In addition, we defined a special type of stochastic strict server. In such a stochastic server, the stochastic nature of service is due to some random impairment processes. Particularly, a system is said to be a *stochastic strict server* providing *strict service curve* $\hat{\beta} \in \mathcal{F}$ with *impairment process* I if, during any period $(s, t]$, the actual service $S(s, t)$ provided by the system satisfies

$$S(s, t) \geq \hat{\beta}(t - s) - I(s, t). \tag{6.4}$$

Note that in defining *stochastic strict server due to impairment* only one impairment process I is used, which can actually be the superposition of multiple constituent processes that cause the system to be unable to deliver the corresponding service to the input considered. Two important types of such processes are worth highlighting. One is the process describing the actually impaired service. For example, due to random errors, a wireless channel fails to deliver the corresponding service to its users. In this case, the error process can be considered an impairment process. Another important type of processes that can be viewed as an impairment processes to the flow considered is due to cross traffic or flows competing service with the flow considered.

Also in Section 4.3, it has been shown that when the stochastic arrival curve characterization of the impairment process is known, the stochastic service curve characterization of the stochastic strict server can be found as shown by Theorems 4.12 and 4.13.

In the rest of this section, we further exploit the concept of a stochastic strict server due to impairment and present results under independent case analysis. The focus is on the five basic properties introduced in Chapter 1.

6.2.1 Backlog and Delay Bounds

We start with the backlog bound and delay bound. We proved in (5.5) that

$$
\begin{aligned}
&B(t) \\
&\leq \sup_{0 \leq s \leq t} \{A(s, t) - \alpha(t - s)\} + \sup_{t \geq 0}\{\alpha(t) - \beta(t)\} + A \otimes \beta(t) - A^*(t). \tag{6.5}
\end{aligned}
$$

In addition, assuming the server is a stochastic strict server providing strict service curve $\hat{\beta}$ with impairment process $I \sim_{ta} \langle g, \gamma \rangle$, we have from (4.12) that

$$A \otimes \beta(t) - A^*(t) \leq \left(\sup_{0 \leq s \leq t} [I(s, t) - \gamma(t - s)] \right)^+, \tag{6.6}$$

where $\beta(t) = \hat{\beta}(t) - \gamma(t)$. Applying (6.6) to (6.5), we get

$$
\begin{aligned}
B(t) &\leq \sup_{0 \leq s \leq t} \{A(s, t) - \alpha(t - s)\} + \left(\sup_{0 \leq s \leq t} [I(s, t) - \gamma(t - s)] \right)^+ \\
&\quad + \alpha \oslash \beta(0). \tag{6.7}
\end{aligned}
$$

If A and I are independent random processes, since α, β, and γ are non-random functions, the first two terms on the right-hand side of (6.7) are also independent. Then, together with the fact the m.b.c. stochastic arrival curve and θ-m.b.c stochastic arrival curve imply a v.b.c. stochastic arrival curve, we have the following theorem.

Theorem 6.3. *Consider a system S with input A. Let $\sim_{sac}$ be either $\sim_{vb}$, $\sim_{mb}$, or $\sim_{\theta-mb}$. Suppose the input has a stochastic arrival curve $\alpha \in \mathcal{F}$ with bounding function $f \in \bar{\mathcal{F}}$; i.e., $A \sim_{sac} \langle f, \alpha \rangle$. Also suppose the server is a stochastic strict server providing strict service curve $\hat{\beta}$ with impairment process $I \sim_{sac} \langle g, \gamma \rangle$. If A and I are independent, the backlog $B(t)$ is guaranteed such that, for all $x \geq 0$,*

$$P\{B(t) > x\} \leq 1 - \bar{f} * \bar{g}\left(x + \inf_{s \geq 0}[\beta(s) - \alpha(s)]\right)$$

where $\beta(t) = \hat{\beta}(t) - \gamma(t)$, $\bar{f}(x) = 1 - [f(x)]_1$, and $\bar{g}(x) = 1 - [g(x)]_1$.

If the input process and/or the impairment process is characterized by a t.a.c. stochastic arrival curve, the corresponding results of Theorem 6.3 easily follow from the relationship between the t.a.c. stochastic arrival curve and v.b.c. stochastic arrival curve introduced in Theorem 3.13.

For the delay $D(t)$, under the same assumption as for (6.6), we proved in (5.13) that

$$
\begin{aligned}
P\{D(t) > x\} &\leq P\{X_1 + X_2 > \inf_{s \geq 0}[\beta(s) - \alpha(s - x)]\} \\
&\leq P\{X_1 + X_3 > \inf_{s \geq 0}[\beta(s) - \alpha(s - x)]\}
\end{aligned}
\tag{6.8}
$$

with

$$
\begin{aligned}
X_1 &= \sup_{0 \leq s \leq t}[A(s, t) - \alpha(t - s)], \\
X_2 &= A \otimes \beta(t + x) - A^*(t + x), \\
X_3 &= \left(\sup_{0 \leq s \leq t + x}[I(s, t + x) - \gamma(t + x - s)]\right)^+,
\end{aligned}
$$

where we have used $X_2 \leq X_3$ based on (4.12).

If A and I are independent, X_1 and X_3 are also independent. Then, together with the fact that the m.b.c. stochastic arrival curve and θ-m.b.c. stochastic arrival curve imply the v.b.c. stochastic arrival curve, we have the following theorem.

Theorem 6.4. *Consider a system S with input A. Let $\sim_{sac}$ be either $\sim_{vb}$, $\sim_{mb}$, or $\sim_{\theta-mb}$. Suppose the input has a stochastic arrival curve $\alpha \in \mathcal{F}$ with bounding function $f \in \bar{\mathcal{F}}$; i.e., $A \sim_{sac} \langle f, \alpha \rangle$. Also suppose the server is a stochastic strict server providing strict service curve $\hat{\beta}$ with impairment process $I \sim_{sac} \langle g, \gamma \rangle$. If A and I are independent, the delay $D(t)$ is guaranteed such that, for all $x \geq 0$,*

$$P\{D(t) > h\,(\alpha + x, \beta)\} \le 1 - \bar{f} * \bar{g}(x),$$

where $\beta(t) = \hat{\beta}(t) - \gamma(t)$, $\bar{f}(x) = 1 - [f(x)]_1$ and $\bar{g}(x) = 1 - [g(x)]_1$.

If the input process and/or the impairment process are characterized by a t.a.c. stochastic arrival curve, the corresponding results of Theorem 6.4 can be obtained from Theorem 6.3 and based on the relationship between the t.a.c. stochastic arrival curve and v.b.c. stochastic arrival curve introduced in Theorem 3.13.

6.2.2 Output Characterization

First, we consider the output t.a.c. stochastic arrival curve characterization. Assuming the server is a stochastic strict server providing strict service curve $\hat{\beta}$ with impairment process $I \sim_{ta} \langle g, \gamma \rangle$, we get from (5.20) and (4.12)

$$A^*(s,t) - \alpha \oslash \beta(t - s)$$
$$\le \sup_{0 \le u \le t} \{A(u,t) - \alpha(t - u)\} + [A \otimes \beta(s) - A^*(s)]$$
$$\le \sup_{0 \le u \le t} \{A(u,t) - \alpha(t - u)\} + \left(\sup_{0 \le u \le s} [I(u,s) - \gamma(s - u)] \right)^+ . \quad (6.9)$$

If A and I are independent, the two terms on the right-hand side of (6.9) are also independent. Then, together with the relationship between the t.a.c. stochastic arrival curve and v.b.c. stochastic arrival curve introduced in Theorem 3.13, we have the following result on output traffic characterization from (6.9).

Theorem 6.5. *Consider a system S with input A. Let $\sim_{sac}$ be either $\sim_{vb}$, $\sim_{mb}$, or $\sim_{\theta-mb}$. Suppose the input has a stochastic arrival curve $\alpha \in \mathcal{F}$ with bounding function $f \in \bar{\mathcal{F}}$; i.e., $A \sim_{sac} \langle f, \alpha \rangle$. Also suppose the server is a stochastic strict server providing strict service curve $\hat{\beta}$ with impairment process $I \sim_{sac} \langle g, \gamma \rangle$. If A and I are independent, the output has a t.a.c. stochastic arrival curve $A^* \sim_{ta} \langle f^*, \alpha^* \rangle$ with*

$$\alpha^*(t) = \alpha \oslash \beta(t),$$
$$f^*(x) = 1 - \bar{f} * \bar{g}(x),$$

where $\beta(t) = \hat{\beta}(t) - \gamma(t)$, $\bar{f}(x) = 1 - [f(x)]_1$, and $\bar{g}(x) = 1 - [g(x)]_1$.

If the input process and/or the impairment process are characterized by a t.a.c. stochastic arrival curve, the output t.a.c. stochastic arrival curve characterization can be derived from Theorem 6.5 based on the relationship between the t.a.c. stochastic arrival curve and v.b.c. stochastic arrival curve introduced in Theorem 3.13.

Let us now consider the output t.a.c. stochastic arrival curve characterization. Under the same conditions as in Theorem 6.5, if $f^* \in \bar{\mathcal{G}}$, the output v.b.c. stochastic arrival curve characterization can also be obtained from Theorem 6.5 based on the relationship between the t.a.c. stochastic arrival curve and v.b.c. stochastic arrival curve. Specifically, we have the following corollary.

Corollary 6.6. *Under the same conditions as Theorem 6.5, if $f^* \in \bar{\mathcal{G}}$, the output has a v.b.c stochastic arrival curve $A^* \sim_{vb} \langle f^{*,\theta}, \alpha_\theta^* \rangle$ with*

$$\alpha_\theta^*(t) = \alpha \oslash \beta(t) + \theta \cdot t,$$
$$f^{*,\theta}(x) = f^*(x) + \frac{1}{\theta} \int_x^\infty f^*(y) dy,$$

where $\beta(t) = \hat{\beta}(t) - \gamma(t)$, $f^*(x) = 1 - \bar{f} * \bar{g}(x)$, $\bar{f}(x) = 1 - [f(x)]_1$ and $\bar{g}(x) = 1 - [g(x)]_1$, for any $\theta > 0$.

Alternatively, for the output v.b.c. stochastic arrival curve characterization, we get from (6.9) that

$$\sup_{0 \le s \le t} \{A^*(s,t) - \alpha \oslash \beta(t-s)\}$$
$$\le \sup_{0 \le s \le t} \{A(s,t) - \alpha(t-s)\}$$
$$+ \left(\sup_{0 \le s \le t} \sup_{0 \le u \le s} [I(u,s) - \gamma(s-u)] \right)^+ \tag{6.10}$$

and

$$\sup_{0 \le s \le t} \{A^*(s,t) - \alpha \oslash \beta(t-s) - \theta \cdot (t-s)\}$$
$$\le \sup_{0 \le s \le t} \{A(s,t) - \alpha(t-s)\}$$
$$+ \sup_{0 \le s \le t} \left[\left(\sup_{0 \le u \le s} [I(u,s) - \gamma(s-u)] \right)^+ - \theta \cdot (t-s) \right], \tag{6.11}$$

and with this we can conclude the following theorem.

Theorem 6.7. *Consider a system S with input A. Suppose the input has a stochastic arrival curve $\alpha \in \mathcal{F}$ with bounding function $f \in \bar{\mathcal{F}}$; i.e., $A \sim_{sac} \langle f, \alpha \rangle$, where $\sim_{sac}$ is either $\sim_{vb}$, $\sim_{mb}$, or $\sim_{\theta-mb}$. Also suppose the server is a stochastic strict server providing strict service curve $\hat{\beta}$ with impairment process I. Assume A and I are independent.*

- *If $I \sim_{mb} \langle g, \gamma \rangle$, the output has a v.b.c stochastic arrival curve $A^* \sim_{vb} \langle f^*, \alpha^* \rangle$ with $\alpha^*(t) = \alpha \oslash \beta(t)$ and $f^*(x) = 1 - \bar{f} * \bar{g}(x)$;*

- If $I \sim_{\theta-mb} \langle g^{\theta}, \gamma \rangle$, the output has a v.b.c stochastic arrival curve $A^* \sim_{vb}$ $\langle f^{*,\theta}, \alpha_{\theta}^* \rangle$ with $\alpha_{\theta}^*(t) = \alpha \oslash \beta(t) + \theta \cdot t$ and $f^{*,\theta}(x) = 1 - \bar{f} * g^{\theta}(x)$, where $\beta(t) = \hat{\beta}(t) - \gamma(t)$, $\bar{f}(x) = 1 - [f(x)]_1$, $\bar{g}(x) = 1 - [g(x)]_1$ and $\bar{g}^{\theta}(x) = 1 - [g^{\theta}(x)]_1$, for any $\theta > 0$.

Under the same conditions as in Theorem 6.5, if the input is characterized by a t.a.c. stochastic arrival curve and/or the impairment process is by other types of stochastic arrival curves, the output v.b.c. stochastic arrival curve characterization can also be obtained from Theorem 6.5 based on its relationship with the v.b.c. stochastic arrival curve for the input, m.b.c. stochastic arrival curve, or θ-m.b.c. stochastic arrival curve for the impairment process.

We now consider the output m.b.c. stochastic arrival curve characterization. Under the same conditions as in Theorem 6.5, if $f^* \in \bar{\mathcal{G}}$, the output m.b.c. stochastic arrival curve characterization can also be obtained from Theorem 6.5 based on the relationship between the m.b.c. stochastic arrival curve and v.b.c. stochastic arrival curve. Specifically, we have the following corollary.

Corollary 6.8. *Under the same conditions as Theorem 6.5, if $f^* \in \bar{\mathcal{G}}$, the output has an m.b.c. stochastic arrival curve $A^* \sim_{mb} \langle f_t^{*,\theta}, \alpha_{\theta}^* \rangle$ with $\alpha_{\theta}^*(t) = \alpha \oslash \beta(t) + \theta \cdot t$ and $f_t^{*,\theta}(x) = \frac{1}{\theta} \int_{x-\theta t}^{\infty} f^*(y) dy$, where $\beta(t) = \hat{\beta}(t) - \gamma(t)$, $f^*(x) = 1 - \bar{f} * \bar{g}(x)$, $\bar{f}(x) = 1 - [f(x)]_1$, and $\bar{g}(x) = 1 - [g(x)]_1$ for any $\theta > 0$.*

Alternatively, from (5.26), it is known that

$$\sup_{0 \le s \le t} \sup_{0 \le u \le s} [A^*(u, s) - \alpha^*(s - u)]$$
$$\le \sup_{0 \le s \le t} \sup_{0 \le u \le s} [A(u, s) - \alpha(s - u)] + \sup_{0 \le s \le t} [A \otimes \beta(s) - A^*(s)]. \quad (6.12)$$

In addition, with the strict stochastic server assumption, it has been shown in (4.13) that

$$\sup_{0 \le s \le t} [A \otimes \beta(s) - A^*(s)] \le \left(\sup_{0 \le s \le t} \sup_{0 \le u \le s} [I(u, s) - \gamma(s - u)] \right)^+. \quad (6.13)$$

Applying (6.13) to (6.12), we get

$$\sup_{0 \le s \le t} \sup_{0 \le u \le s} [A^*(u, s) - \alpha^*(s - u)]$$
$$\le \sup_{0 \le s \le t} \sup_{0 \le u \le s} [A(u, s) - \alpha(s - u)] + \quad (6.14)$$
$$\left(\sup_{0 \le u \le t} \sup_{u \le s \le t} [I(u, s) - \gamma(s - u)] \right)^+. \quad (6.15)$$

Since A and I are independent and so are the first two terms on the right-hand side of (6.14), the following theorem follows easily.

Theorem 6.9. *Consider a system S with input A. Suppose the input has an m.b.c. stochastic arrival curve $\alpha \in \mathcal{F}$ with bounding function $f \in \bar{\mathcal{F}}$; i.e., $A \sim_{mb} \langle f, \alpha \rangle$. Also suppose the server is a stochastic strict server providing strict service curve $\hat{\beta}$ with impairment process I and the impairment process has an m.b.c. stochastic arrival curve $I \sim_{mb} \langle g, \gamma \rangle$. If A and I are independent, the output has an m.b.c. stochastic arrival curve $A^* \sim_{mb} \langle f^*, \alpha^* \rangle$ with $\alpha^*(t) = \alpha \oslash \beta(t)$ and $f^*(x) = 1 - \bar{f} * \bar{g}(x)$, where $\beta(t) = \hat{\beta}(t) - \gamma(t)$, $\bar{f}(x) = 1 - [f(x)]_1$, and $\bar{g}(x) = 1 - [g(x)]_1$.*

Under other types of traffic arrival curves for the input and the impairment process, the corresponding output m.b.c. stochastic arrival curve can be derived from Corollary 6.8 and Theorem 6.9 based on the relationships among the various types of traffic arrival curve characterizations presented in Chapter 3.

Finally, we consider the output θ–m.b.c. stochastic arrival curve characterization. Under the same conditions as in Theorem 6.5, if $f^* \in \bar{\mathcal{G}}$, the output m.b.c. stochastic arrival curve characterization can also be obtained from Theorem 6.5 based on the relationship between the t.a.c. stochastic arrival curve and m.b.c. stochastic arrival curve. Specifically, we have the following corollary.

Corollary 6.10. *Under the same conditions as in Theorem 6.5, if $f^* \in \bar{\mathcal{G}}$, the output has a v.b.c. stochastic arrival curve $A^* \sim_{vb} \langle f^{*,\theta}, \alpha_\theta^* \rangle$ with*

$$\alpha_\theta^*(t) = \alpha \oslash \beta(t) + (\theta_1 + \theta_2) \cdot t,$$

$$f^{*,\theta}(x) = \hat{f}^*(x) + \frac{1}{\theta_2} \int_x^\infty \hat{f}^*(y) dy,$$

where $\beta(t) = \hat{\beta}(t) - \gamma(t)$, $\hat{f}^*(x) = f^*(x) + \frac{1}{\theta_1} \int_x^\infty f^*(y) dy$, $f^*(x) = 1 - \bar{f} * \bar{g}(x)$, $\bar{f}(x) = 1 - [f(x)]_1$, and $\bar{g}(x) = 1 - [g(x)]_1$ for any $\theta_1, \theta_2 > 0$.

Alternatively, from (5.27), it is known that

$$\sup_{0 \le s \le t} \left[\sup_{0 \le u \le s} [A^*(u, s) - \alpha \oslash \beta(s - u)] - \theta(t - s) \right]$$

$$\le \sup_{0 \le s \le t} \left[\sup_{0 \le u \le s} [A(u, s) - \alpha(s - u)] - \theta(t - s) \right]$$
$$+ \sup_{0 \le s \le t} [A \otimes \beta(s) - A^*(s)], \tag{6.16}$$

which, with (6.13) applied, results in

$$\sup_{0 \le s \le t} \left[\sup_{0 \le u \le s} [A^*(u, s) - \alpha \oslash \beta(s - u)] - \theta(t - s) \right]$$

$$\le \sup_{0 \le s \le t} \left[\sup_{0 \le u \le s} [A(u, s) - \alpha(s - u)] - \theta(t - s) \right]$$
$$+ \left(\sup_{0 \le s \le t} \sup_{0 \le u \le s} [I(u, s) - \gamma(s - u)] \right)^+. \tag{6.17}$$

Then, we similarly have the following result.

Theorem 6.11. *Consider a system S with input A. Suppose the input has a θ-m.b.c. stochastic arrival curve $\alpha \in \mathcal{F}$ with bounding function $f \in \bar{\mathcal{F}}$; i.e., $A \sim_{\theta-mb} \langle f, \alpha \rangle$. Also suppose the server is a stochastic strict server providing strict service curve $\hat{\beta}$ with impairment process I, and the impairment process has an m.b.c. stochastic arrival curve $I \sim_{mb} \langle g, \gamma \rangle$. If A and I are independent, the output has a θ-m.b.c stochastic arrival curve $A^* \sim_{mb} \langle f^*, \alpha^* \rangle$ with $\alpha^*(t) = \alpha \oslash \beta(t)$ and $f^*(x) = 1 - \bar{f} * \bar{g}(x)$, where $\beta(t) = \hat{\beta}(t) - \gamma(t)$, $\bar{f}(x) = 1 - [f(x)]_1$ and $\bar{g}(x) = 1 - [g(x)]_1$.*

Under other types of traffic arrival curves for the input and the impairment process, the corresponding output θ-m.b.c stochastic arrival curve can be derived from Corollary 6.10 and Theorem 6.11 based on the relationships among the various types of traffic arrival curve characterizations presented in Chapter 3.

6.2.3 Concatenation Property

Consider two servers in tandem. If each server provides a stochastic service curve β^n, $n = 1, 2$, we have shown in (5.32) that

$$\sup_{0 \leq s \leq t} [A \otimes \beta^1 \otimes \beta^2(s) - A^*(s)]$$

$$\leq \sup_{0 \leq s \leq t} [A^1 \otimes \beta^1(s) - A^{1*}(s)] + \sup_{0 \leq s \leq t} [A^2 \otimes \beta^2(s) - A^{2*}(s)]. \quad (6.18)$$

Assume each server is a stochastic strict server providing strict service curve $\hat{\beta}^n$, $n = 1, 2$, with impairment process $I^n \sim_{mb} \langle g^n, \gamma^n \rangle$. Let $\beta^n(t) = \hat{\beta}^n(t) - \gamma^n(t)$. We then have (6.13), and applying it to (6.18), we obtain

$$\sup_{0 \leq s \leq t} [A \otimes \beta^1 \otimes \beta^2(s) - A^*(s)]$$

$$\leq \left(\sup_{0 \leq s \leq t} \sup_{0 \leq u \leq s} [I^1(u, s) - \gamma^1(s - u)] \right)^+$$

$$+ \left(\sup_{0 \leq s \leq t} \sup_{0 \leq u \leq s} [I^2(u, s) - \gamma^2(s - u)] \right)^+. \quad (6.19)$$

If I^1 and I^2 are independent, so are the two terms of the right-hand side of (6.19). The discussion above can be easily extended to more than two nodes, and the following theorem is obtained that corresponds to the concatenation property of the stochastic service curve.

Theorem 6.12. *Consider a flow passing through a network of N nodes in tandem, and assume each node is a stochastic strict server providing stochastic strict service curve $\hat{\beta}^n$ with impairment process $I^n \sim_{mb} \langle g^n, \gamma^n \rangle$. If I^n are* *independent and* $\beta^n \in \mathcal{F}$, $(n = 1, 2, \ldots, N)$, *then the network guarantees to the flow a stochastic service curve* $S \sim_{sc} \langle g, \beta \rangle$ *with*

$$\beta(t) = \beta^1 \otimes \beta^2 \otimes \cdots \otimes \beta^N(t),$$
$$g(x) = 1 - \bar{g}^1 * \bar{g}^2 * \cdots * \bar{g}^N(x),$$

where $\beta^n(t) = \hat{\beta}^n(t) - \gamma^n(t)$, $\bar{g}^n(x) = 1 - [g^n(x)]_1$, $n = 1, 2, \ldots, N$.

By iteratively applying Lemma 5.39, we have in (5.39) that

$$A \otimes \beta^1 \otimes \beta^2_{-\theta} \otimes \cdots \otimes \beta^N_{-(N-1)\theta}(t) - A^*(t)$$
$$\leq \sup_{0 \leq s \leq t} \left[A^1 \otimes \beta^1(s) - A^{1*}(s) - \theta \cdot (t - s) \right]$$
$$+ \sup_{0 \leq s \leq t} \left[A^2 \otimes \beta^2(s) - A^{2*}(s) - \theta \cdot (t - s) \right] + \cdots +$$
$$+ \sup_{0 \leq s \leq t} \left[A^{N-1} \otimes \beta^{N-1}(s) - A^{(N-1)*}(s) - \theta \cdot (t - s) \right]$$
$$+ A^N \otimes \beta(t) - A^*(t). \tag{6.20}$$

Assume each server is a stochastic strict server providing strict service curve $\hat{\beta}^n$, $n = 1, 2, \ldots, N$, with impairment process $I^n \sim_{\theta-mb} \langle g^n, \gamma^n \rangle$. Let $\beta^n(t) = \hat{\beta}^n(t) - \gamma^n(t)$. We then have (4.14), and applying it to (6.20), we obtain

$$A \otimes \beta^1 \otimes \beta^2_{-\theta} \otimes \cdots \otimes \beta^N_{-(N-1)\theta}(t) - A^*(t)$$
$$\leq \left(\sup_{0 \leq s \leq t} \left[\sup_{0 \leq u \leq s} [I^1(u, s) - \gamma^1(s - u)] - \theta \cdot (t - s) \right] \right)^+$$
$$+ \left(\sup_{0 \leq s \leq t} \left[\sup_{0 \leq u \leq s} [I^2(u, s) - \gamma^2(s - u)] - \theta \cdot (t - s) \right] \right)^+ + \cdots +$$
$$+ \left(\sup_{0 \leq s \leq t} \left[\sup_{0 \leq u \leq s} [I^{N-1}(u, s) - \gamma^{N-1}(s - u)] - \theta \cdot (t - s) \right] \right)^+$$
$$+ \left(\sup_{0 \leq s \leq t} [I^N(s, t) - \gamma^N(t - s)] \right)^+. \tag{6.21}$$

If I^n, $n = 1, 2, \ldots, N$, are independent, so are the terms on the right-hand side of (6.21), and hence the following result is obtained.

Theorem 6.13. *Consider a flow passing through a network of* N *nodes in tandem, and assume each node is a stochastic strict server providing stochastic strict service curve* $\hat{\beta}^n$ *with impairment process* $I^n \sim_{\theta-mb} \langle g^n, \gamma^n \rangle$. *If* I^n *are independent,* $\beta^n_{-(n-1)\theta} \in \mathcal{F}$, *and* $g^n \in \bar{\mathcal{F}}$, $(n = 1, 2, \ldots, N)$, *then the network guarantees to the flow a weak stochastic service curve* $S \sim_{ws} \langle g, \beta \rangle$ *with*

$$\beta(t) = \beta^1 \otimes \beta^2_{-\theta} \otimes \cdots \otimes \beta^N_{-(N-1)\theta}(t), \tag{6.22}$$
$$g(x) = 1 - \bar{g}^1 * \bar{g}^2 * \cdots * \bar{g}^N(x), \tag{6.23}$$

where

$$\beta^n_{-(n-1)\theta}(t) = \hat{\beta}^n(t) - \gamma^n(t) - (n-1)\theta \cdot t, \qquad n = 1, 2, \ldots, N,$$
$$\bar{g}^n(x) = 1 - [g^n(x)]_1, \qquad n = 1, 2, \ldots, N,$$

for any $\theta > 0$.

Based on the relationship between the weak stochastic service curve and θ-stochastic service curve, the following result corresponds to the concatenation property of the θ-stochastic service curve.

Corollary 6.14. *Under the same conditions as in Theorem 6.13, if $g \in \bar{\mathcal{G}}$, the network guarantees to the flow a θ-stochastic service curve $S \sim_{\theta-sc} \langle g^\theta, \beta \rangle$ with $g^\theta(x) = g(x) + \frac{1}{\theta} \int_x^y g(y)dy$, where $\beta(t)$ and $g(x)$ are as shown in (6.22) and (6.23), respectively.*

Based on the relationship between the v.b.c. stochastic arrival curve and θ-m.b.c. stochastic arrival curve, the following result corresponds to the concatenation property of the weak stochastic service curve.

Corollary 6.15. *Consider a flow passing through a network of N nodes in tandem, and assume each node is a stochastic strict server providing stochastic strict service curve $\hat{\beta}^n$ with impairment process $I^n \sim_{vb} \langle g^n, \gamma^n \rangle$. If I^n are independent, $\beta^n_{-(n-1)\theta} \in \mathcal{G}$, and $g^n \in \bar{\mathcal{G}}$, $(n = 1, 2, \ldots, N)$, then the network guarantees to the flow a weak stochastic service curve $S \sim_{ws} \langle g, \beta \rangle$ with*

$$\beta(t) = \beta^1 \otimes \beta^2_{-\theta} \otimes \cdots \otimes \beta^N_{-(N-1)\theta}(t), \tag{6.24}$$
$$g(x) = 1 - \bar{g}^{1,\theta_1} * \bar{g}^{2,\theta_2} * \cdots * \bar{g}^{N,\theta_N}(x), \tag{6.25}$$

where

$$\beta^n_{-(n-1)\theta}(t) = \hat{\beta}^n(t) - \gamma^n(t) - (n-1)\theta \cdot t, \qquad n = 1, 2, \ldots, N,$$
$$\bar{g}^{n,\theta_n}(x) = 1 - \left[g^n(x) + \frac{1}{\theta_n} \int_x^\infty g^n(y)dy\right]_1, \qquad n = 1, 2, \ldots, N-1,$$
$$\bar{g}^{N,\theta_N}(x) = 1 - [g^N(x)]_1,$$

for any $\theta, \theta_1, \ldots, \theta_{N-1} > 0$.

6.2.4 Leftover Service Characterization

Consider a system fed with a flow A that is the aggregation of two constituent flows, A_1 and A_2. For the output, there holds $A^*(t) = A_1^*(t) + A_2^*(t)$. In addition, we have $A^*(t) \leq A(t)$, $A_1^*(t) \leq A_1(t)$, and $A_2^*(t) \leq A_2(t)$. As in (5.40), we have for functions β, α_2 and any $t \geq 0$

$$A_1 \otimes (\beta - \alpha_2)(t) - A_1^*(t)$$
$$\leq [A \otimes \beta(t) - A^*(t)] + \sup_{0 \leq s \leq t} [A_2(s,t) - \alpha_2(t-s)], \tag{6.26}$$

from which we also have as in (5.41) and (5.42),

$$\sup_{0 \leq s \leq t} [A_1 \otimes (\beta - \alpha_2)(s) - A_1^*(s)]$$
$$\leq \sup_{0 \leq s \leq t} [A \otimes \beta(s) - A^*(s)] + \sup_{0 \leq s \leq t} \sup_{0 \leq u \leq s} [A_2(u,s) - \alpha_2(s-u)] \tag{6.27}$$

and

$$\sup_{0 \leq s \leq t} [A_1 \otimes (\beta - \alpha_2)(s) - A_1^*(s) - \theta(t-s)]$$
$$\leq \sup_{0 \leq s \leq t} [A \otimes \beta(s) - A^*(s) - \theta_1(t-s)]$$
$$+ \sup_{0 \leq s \leq t} \left[\sup_{0 \leq u \leq s} [A_2(u,s) - \alpha_2(s-u)] - \theta_2(t-s) \right] \tag{6.28}$$

for any $\theta_1, \theta_2 > 0$ and $\theta = \theta_1 + \theta_2$.

Assume the system is a stochastic strict server providing strict service curve $\hat{\beta}$ with impairment process $I \sim_{sac} \langle g, \gamma \rangle$, where $\sim_{sac}$ may be $\sim_{vb}$, $\sim_{mb}$, or $\sim_{\theta-mb}$. Let $\beta(t) = \hat{\beta}(t) - \gamma(t)$. We then have (4.12), (4.13) and (4.14), and applying them respectively to (6.26), (6.27), and (6.28), we obtain the following theorems.

Theorem 6.16 (Leftover Weak Stochastic Service Curve). *Consider a server fed with a flow A that is the aggregation of two constituent flows A_1 and A_2. Assume the server is a stochastic strict server to the aggregate, providing stochastic strict service curve $\hat{\beta}$ with impairment process $I \sim_{vb} \langle g, \gamma \rangle$.*

(i) The server guarantees that

$$A_1 \otimes (\beta - \alpha_2)(t) - A_1^*(t)$$
$$\leq \left(\sup_{0 \leq s \leq t} [I(s,t) - \gamma(t-s)] \right)^+ + \sup_{0 \leq s \leq t} [A_2(s,t) - \alpha_2(t-s)]. \tag{6.29}$$

(ii) If A_2 and I are independent, $A_2 \sim_{mb} \langle f_2, \alpha_2 \rangle$, and $\beta_1' \in \mathcal{F}$, then the server guarantees to flow A_1 a weak stochastic service curve $S_1 \sim_{ws} \langle g_1', \beta_1' \rangle$, where

$$g_1'(x) = 1 - \bar{g} * \bar{f}_2(x), \quad \beta_1'(t) = \beta(t) - \alpha_2(t),$$

with $\beta(t) = \hat{\beta}(t) - \gamma(t)$, $\bar{g}(x) = 1 - [g(x)]_1$, and $\bar{f}_2(x) = 1 - [f_2(x)]_1$.

Theorem 6.17 (Leftover Stochastic Service Curve). *Consider a server fed with a flow A that is the aggregation of two constituent flows A_1 and A_2. Assume the server is a stochastic strict server to the aggregate, providing stochastic strict service curve $\hat{\beta}$ with impairment process $I \sim_{mb} \langle g, \gamma \rangle$.*

(i) *The server guarantees that*

$$\sup_{0\le s\le t} [A_1 \otimes (\beta - \alpha_2)(s) - A_1^*(s)]$$

$$\le \left(\sup_{0\le s\le t} \sup_{0\le u\le s} [I(u,s) - \gamma(s-u)] \right)^+$$

$$+ \sup_{0\le s\le t} \sup_{0\le u\le s} [A_2(u,s) - \alpha_2(s-u)]. \tag{6.30}$$

(ii) *If A_2 and I are independent, $A_2 \sim_{mb} \langle f_2, \alpha_2 \rangle$, and $\beta_1' \in \mathcal{F}$, then the server guarantees to flow A_1 a stochastic service curve $S_1 \sim_{sc} \langle g_1', \beta_1' \rangle$, where*

$$g_1'(x) = 1 - \bar{g} * \bar{f}_2(x), \quad \beta_1'(t) = \beta(t) - \alpha_2(t),$$

with $\beta(t) = \hat{\beta}(t) - \gamma(t)$, $\bar{g}(x) = 1 - [g(x)]_1$, and $\bar{f}_2(x) = 1 - [f_2(x)]_1$.

Theorem 6.18 (Leftover θ-Stochastic Service Curve). *Consider a server fed with a flow A that is the aggregation of two constituent flows A_1 and A_2. Assume the server is a stochastic strict server to the aggregate, providing stochastic strict service curve $\hat{\beta}$ with impairment process $I \sim_{\theta-mb} \langle g, \gamma \rangle$.*

(i) *The server guarantees that*

$$\sup_{0\le s\le t} [A_1 \otimes (\beta - \alpha_2)(s) - A_1^*(s) - \theta(t-s)]$$

$$\le \left(\sup_{0\le s\le t} \left[\sup_{0\le u\le s} [I(u,s) - \gamma(s-u)] - \theta_1 \cdot (t-s) \right] \right)^+$$

$$+ \sup_{0\le s\le t} \left[\sup_{0\le u\le s} [A_2(u,s) - \alpha_2(s-u)] - \theta_2(t-s) \right] \tag{6.31}$$

for any $\theta_1, \theta_2 > 0$ and $\theta = \theta_1 + \theta_2$.

(ii) *If A_2 and I are independent, $A_2 \sim_{\theta-mb} \langle f_2, \alpha_2 \rangle$, and $\beta_1' \in \mathcal{F}$, then the server guarantees to flow A_1 a θ-stochastic service curve $S_1 \sim_{\theta-sc} \langle g_1', \beta_1' \rangle$, where*

$$g_1'(x) = 1 - \bar{g} * \bar{f}_2(x), \quad \beta_1'(t) = \beta(t) - \alpha_2(t)$$

with $\beta(t) = \hat{\beta}(t) - \gamma(t)$, $\bar{g}(x) = 1 - [g(x)]_1$, and $\bar{f}_2(x) = 1 - [f_2(x)]_1$.

Note that in Theorems 6.16 to 6.18, the first part is an intermediate step for getting the second part. The intention of including the first part is as follows: When the leftover service property is used to derive other results, such as the concatenation property, the first part can be applied to their derivations. Then, if flows and the impairment processes of servers are independent, Lemma 6.1 can be used to derive the corresponding independent case bounds. However, if we were only given the second part, such an independent case analysis could not be applied and the general case (min, +) analysis in Chapter 5 would have to be used. As a result, looser bounds may be obtained.

Also note that from the viewpoint of the service provided to flow A_1, $A_2(t)$ can be considered as an impairment process. In other words, for flow A_1, the server has two independent impairment processes $I(t)$ and $A_2(t)$. From this viewpoint, Theorems 6.16 to 6.18 can also be proved based on the independent case superposition property in the next subsection and the results for the stochastic strict server due to impairment in Section 4.3.1.

Based on the relationships between the stochastic arrival curve models and between the stochastic service curve models, the corresponding results of Section 5.4 can be derived from Theorems 6.16 to 6.18 for the independent case.

6.2.5 Superposition Property

The superposition property means that the superposition of flows can be represented using the same traffic model. With this property, the aggregate of (possibly many) individual flows may be considered as a single aggregate flow, so that the QoS performance for the aggregate can be derived in the same way as for a single flow. This section discusses the superposition property for the various stochastic traffic models introduced in Chapter 2.

Consider N flows with arrival processes $A_i(t)$, $i = 1, \ldots, N$. Let $A(t)$ be the superposition of the N flows. In other words, we have for any $s, t \geq 0$,

$$A(s, s + t) = A_1(s, s + t) + \cdots + A_N(s, s + t).$$

It has been shown in (5.43), (5.44), (5.45), and (5.46) that, for any functions $\alpha_i(t)$, $i = 1, \ldots, N$, we have

$$
\begin{aligned}
& A(s, s + t) - [\alpha_1(t) + \cdots + \alpha_N(t)] \\
&= [A_1(s, s + t) - \alpha_1(t)] + \cdots + [A_N(s, s + t) - \alpha_N(t)],
\end{aligned}
\tag{6.32}
$$

$$
\begin{aligned}
& \sup_{0 \leq s \leq t} [A(s, t) - [\alpha_1(t - s) + \cdots + \alpha_N(t - s)]] \\
&\leq \sup_{0 \leq s \leq t} [A_1(s, t) - \alpha_1(t - s)] + \cdots + \sup_{0 \leq s \leq t} [A_N(s, t) - \alpha_N(t - s)],
\end{aligned}
\tag{6.33}
$$

$$
\begin{aligned}
& \sup_{0 \leq s \leq t} \sup_{0 \leq u \leq s} [A(u, s) - [\alpha_1(s - u) + \cdots + \alpha_N(s - u)]] \\
&\leq \sup_{0 \leq s \leq t} \sup_{0 \leq u \leq s} [A_1(u, s) - \alpha_1(s - u)] + \cdots \\
& \quad + \sup_{0 \leq s \leq t} \sup_{0 \leq u \leq s} [A_N(u, s) - \alpha_N(s - u)]
\end{aligned}
\tag{6.34}
$$

$$\sup_{0 \le s \le t} \left[\sup_{0 \le u \le s} \{ A(u,s) - [\alpha_1(s-u) + \cdots + \alpha_N(s-u)] \} - \theta \cdot (t-s) \right]$$

$$\le \sup_{0 \le s \le t} \left[\sup_{0 \le u \le s} [A_1(u,s) - \alpha_1(s-u)] - \theta_1 \cdot (t-s) \right] + \cdots$$

$$+ \sup_{0 \le s \le t} \left[\sup_{0 \le u \le s} [A_N(u,s) - \alpha_N(s-u)] - \theta_N \cdot (t-s) \right]. \tag{6.35}$$

Assume $A_i(t)$, $i = 1, \ldots, N$, are independent. Then, the independent case superposition properties in Theorems 6.19 to 6.22 follow from (6.32) to (6.35), respectively.

Theorem 6.19. *Consider N flows with arrival processes $A_i(t)$, $i = 1, \ldots, N$. Let $A(t)$ denote the aggregate arrival process. If $A_i(t)$ are independent processes and $\forall i$, $A_i \sim_{ta} \langle f_i, \alpha_i \rangle$, then $A \sim_{ta} \langle f, \alpha \rangle$ with $\alpha(t) = \sum_{i=1}^{N} \alpha_i(t)$ and $f(x) = 1 - \bar{f}_1 * \cdots * \bar{f}_N(x)$, where $\bar{f}_i = 1 - f_i$ and $*$ denotes the Stieltjes convolution.*

Theorem 6.20. *Consider N flows with arrival processes $A_i(t)$, $i = 1, \ldots, N$. Let $A(t)$ denote the aggregate arrival process. If $A_i(t)$ are independent processes and $\forall i$, $A_i \sim_{vb} \langle f_i, \alpha_i \rangle$, then $A \sim_{vb} \langle f, \alpha \rangle$ with $\alpha(t) = \sum_{i=1}^{N} \alpha_i(t)$ and $f(x) = 1 - \bar{f}_1 * \cdots * \bar{f}_N(x)$, where $\bar{f}_i = 1 - f_i$ and $*$ denotes the Stieltjes convolution.*

Theorem 6.21. *Consider N flows with arrival processes $A_i(t)$, $i = 1, \ldots, N$. Let $A(t)$ denote the aggregate arrival process. If $A_i(t)$ are independent processes and $\forall i$, $A_i \sim_{mb} \langle f_i, \alpha_i \rangle$, then $A \sim_{mb} \langle f, \alpha \rangle$ with $\alpha(t) = \sum_{i=1}^{N} \alpha_i(t)$ and $f(x) = 1 - \bar{f}_1 * \cdots * \bar{f}_N(x)$, where $\bar{f}_i = 1 - f_i$ and $*$ denotes the Stieltjes convolution.*

Theorem 6.22. *Consider N flows with arrival processes $A_i(t)$, $i = 1, \ldots, N$. Let $A(t)$ denote the aggregate arrival process. If $A_i(t)$ are independent processes and $\forall i$, $A_i \sim_{\theta-mb} \langle f_i, \alpha_i \rangle$, then $A \sim_{\theta-mb} \langle f^{\theta}, \alpha \rangle$ with $\alpha(t) = \sum_{i=1}^{N} \alpha_i(t)$ and $f^{\theta}(x) = 1 - \bar{f}_1^{\theta_1} * \cdots * \bar{f}_N^{\theta_N}(x)$, where $\bar{f}_i^{\theta} = 1 - f_i^{\theta}$ and $*$ denotes the Stieltjes convolution for any $\theta_1, \ldots, \theta_N > 0$ and $\theta = \theta_1 + \cdots + \theta_N$.*

6.2.6 Scaling of End-to-End Delay Bound

In Section 5.6, it was introduced that the end-to-end delay bound is a scaling in $\mathcal{O}(n^2 \log n)$ from the node-by-node analysis approach and a scaling in $\mathcal{O}(n \log n)$ from the concatenation property of the stochastic service curve. In Section 5.6, the possible independence between flows and servers is not taken into account. To demonstrate the use of independent case analysis results, we consider the same network as studied in Section 5.6 and show that the end-to-end delay bound is a scaling in $\mathcal{O}(n)$ when some independence conditions are satisfied.

Specifically, we consider a network of n servers in tandem through which flow A passes. Each server is a constant-rate server with capacity C. At each server, there is a cross-flow that joins and leaves. Assume the considered flow A and all the cross flows are independent. For ease of expression, we also assume that flow considered and all cross-flows have the same m.b.c. stochastic arrival curve (SAC) $r \cdot t$ with bounding function $f(x) = e^{-x}$ and $2r < C$.

As discussed in Section 4.3.1, each server along the end-to-end path of the flow F considered can be viewed as a stochastic strict server with impairment process. Particularly, it is a stochastic strict server S providing strict service curve $\hat{\beta}(t) = Ct$ with impairment process $I^i \sim_{mb} \langle f, r \rangle$, $i = 1, \ldots, n$. Then, it is known from Theorem 6.12 that the network provides to the flow an end-to-end stochastic service curve $\beta(t)$. More specifically, iteratively applying (6.18) and (6.13), we can obtain

$$\sup_{0 \le s \le t} [A \otimes \beta(t) - A^*(s)]$$

$$\le \left(\sup_{0 \le s \le t} \left[\sup_{0 \le u \le s} [I^1(u, s) - r(s - u)] \right] \right)^+ + \cdots$$

$$+ \left(\sup_{0 \le s \le t} \left[\sup_{0 \le u \le s} [I^n(u, s) - r(s - u)] \right] \right)^+. \tag{6.36}$$

For the end-to-end delay $D(t)$, (6.36) can be applied to Theorem 6.4 and particularly (6.8). Then, one easily obtains

$$P\{D(t) > x\} \le P\{X + Y_1 + \cdots + Y_n > rx\}$$

with

$$X = \sup_{0 \le s \le t} \sup_{0 \le u \le s} [A(u, s) - r(s - u)],$$

$$Y_i = \left(\sup_{0 \le s \le t} \left[\sup_{0 \le u \le s} [I^i(u, s) - r(s - u)] \right] \right)^+, \quad i = 1, \ldots, n.$$

Since A and I^i, $i = 1, \ldots, n$ are independent, so are X and Y_i, $i = 1, \ldots, n$. In addition, we have simply assumed the same bounding function e^{-x} for X and Y_i. So, $X + Y_1 + \cdots + Y_n$ is Gamma-distributed with parameters $\Gamma(n+1, 1)$. Then, we get for the end-to-end delay bound

$$P\{D(t) > x\} \le 1 - \frac{\gamma(n + 1, rx)}{(n + 1)!}, \tag{6.37}$$

where the function $\gamma(n, x)$ is defined as

$$\gamma(n, x) = \int_0^x y^{n-1} e^{-y} dy.$$

While (6.37) provides a good delay bound, it is difficult to see how it scales with respect to the number of servers in the network. In the following, we consider a possibly looser bound, but it is easy to see its scaling. From the Chernoff bound, we get

$$P\{D(t) > x\} \leq e^{-\theta r x} M_{X+Y_1+\cdots+Y_n}(\theta)$$

$$= e^{-\theta r x} [M_X(\theta)]^{n+1} \tag{6.38}$$

$$= \frac{1}{(1-\theta)^{n+1}} e^{-\theta r x}. \tag{6.39}$$

Suppose ϵ is the allowed delay violation probability. Letting the right-hand side of (6.38) equal ϵ, we then have the corresponding delay bound

$$d = \frac{1}{\theta r} \left[\log \frac{1}{\epsilon} + (n+1) \log \frac{1}{(1-\theta)} \right],$$

which clearly scales in $\mathcal{O}(n)$.

Note that the right-hand side of (6.37) is obtained directly from the distribution function of $X + Y_1 + \cdots + Y_n$, while the right-hand side of (6.38) is an upper bound on the distribution function. It can hence be concluded that the end-to-end delay bound under the independent case is a scaling of $\mathcal{O}(n)$.

6.3 Calculus with Moment Generating Functions

This section presents stochastic network calculus results based on moment generating functions (MGFs). In Chapters 3 and 4, respectively we introduced the concepts of the traffic envelope process and service envelope process. In Chapter 5, we showed that the five basic properties can be represented using traffic and service envelope processes. In this section, we further present the corresponding results using the moment generating functions of these processes.

6.3.1 Moment Generating Function Basics

As introduced in Chapter 1, the moment generating function of a random variable X is defined, for any $\theta \geq 0$

$$M_X(\theta) = E e^{\theta X}, \tag{6.40}$$

where E is the expectation of its argument.

Let $M_X(-\theta) = E e^{-\theta X}$. It can be easily verified that

$$M_{\min[X,Y]}(\theta) \leq \min [M_X(\theta), M_Y(\theta)], \tag{6.41}$$

$$M_{\max[X,Y]}(-\theta) \leq \min [M_X(-\theta), M_Y(-\theta)]. \tag{6.42}$$

For two independent variables, it is known that

$$M_{X+Y}(\theta) = M_X(\theta) M_Y(\theta), \tag{6.43}$$
$$M_{X-Y}(\theta) = M_X(\theta) M_Y(-\theta), \tag{6.44}$$

and

$$M_{X+Y}(-\theta) = M_X(-\theta) M_Y(-\theta), \tag{6.45}$$
$$M_{X-Y}(-\theta) = M_X(-\theta) M_Y(\theta). \tag{6.46}$$

Once the MGF is obtained for a random variable X, the complementary cumulative distribution function (CCDF) of X is bounded by the well-known Chernoff bound as follows:

$$P\{X \geq x\} \leq e^{-\theta x} E e^{\theta X} = e^{-\theta x} M_X(\theta). \tag{6.47}$$

Throughout this book, we often deal with min-plus convolutions or deconvolutions of functions or random processes. To deal with them using moment generating functions, we define the operators $\star$ and $\circ$ as

$$X \star Y(t) = \sum_{s=0}^{t} X(s) Y(t-s), \tag{6.48}$$

$$X \circ Y(\tau, t) = \sum_{s=0}^{\tau} X(s+t) Y(s), \tag{6.49}$$

where $X(t)$ and $Y(t)$ are two processes. The operator $\star$ indeed defines the discrete convolution operation. When $\tau \to \infty$ in (6.49), we denote

$$X \circ Y(t) \equiv \sum_{s=0}^{\infty} X(s+t) Y(s).$$

We then have the following result for min-plus convolution $X \otimes Y(t)$.

Lemma 6.23. *Let $X(t)$ and $Y(t)$ be independent random processes. The moment generating function of their min-plus convolution is upper-bounded:*

$$M_{X \otimes Y(t)}(-\theta) \leq [M_X(-\theta) \star M_Y(-\theta)](t).$$

Proof. We have from the definition

$$M_{X \otimes Y(t)}(-\theta) = E e^{-\theta \inf_{0 \leq s \leq t}[X(s)+Y(t-s)]}.$$

An upper bound on $M_{X \otimes Y}(-\theta, t)$ for any $\theta \geq 0$ is

$$M_{X \otimes Y(t)}(-\theta) \leq E \sup_{0 \leq s \leq t} [e^{-\theta[X(s)+Y(t-s)]}]$$

$$\leq E \sum_{s=0}^{t} e^{-\theta[X(s)+Y(s-t)]}$$

$$= \sum_{s=0}^{t} E\left[e^{-\theta X(s)}\right] \cdot E\left[e^{-\theta Y(t-s)}\right].$$

□

An important property of Lemma 6.23 is that it can be easily extended to the min-plus convolution of multiple random processes,

$$M_{X_1 \otimes X_2 \otimes \cdots \otimes X_n(t)}(-\theta) \le [M_{X_1}(-\theta) \star M_{X_2}(-\theta) \star \cdots \star M_{X_n}(-\theta)](t).$$

For ease of expression, we define a generalized version of the min-plus de-convolution as

$$(x \oslash y)(\tau, t) = \sup_{0 \le s \le \tau} [x(s+t) - y(s)],$$

which reduces to the normal min-plus deconvolution definition when $\tau \to \infty$. We now have the following result for the generalized min-plus deconvolution.

Lemma 6.24. *Let $X(t)$ and $Y(t)$ be independent random processes. The moment generating function of their min-plus deconvolution is upper-bounded:*

$$M_{X \oslash Y(\tau, t)}(\theta) \le [M_X(\theta) \circ M_Y(-\theta)](\tau, t).$$

Proof. We have from the definition

$$M_{X \oslash Y(\tau, t)}(\theta) = E e^{\theta \sup_{0 \le s \le \tau}[X(s+t) - Y(s)]}$$

$$\le E \left[\sum_{s0}^{\tau} e^{\theta[X(s+t) - Y(s)]} \right]$$

$$\le \sum_{s=0}^{\tau} E \left[e^{\theta X(s+t)} \right] E \left[e^{-\theta Y(s)} \right].$$

☐

6.3.2 Basic Properties and Performance Bounds

In Section 5.7, the basis network calculus properties have been introduced based on the concepts of the traffic envelope process and service envelope process. In the rest of this section, these results are reproduced by applying the corresponding moment generating functions, Lemma 6.23 and the Chernoff bound. We shall only present in detail the delay analysis using moment generating functions. For other properties, they follow similarly based on the results in Section 5.7.

By definition, the delay in a system at time t is

$$D(t) = \inf\{\tau : A(t) \le A^*(t + \tau)\}.$$

Suppose A has a traffic envelope process $\hat{A}$ and the system provides a service envelope process $\hat{S}(t)$. Then, we have

$$A(t) - A^*(t + \tau)$$

$$= \sup_{0 \le s \le t+\tau} [A(t) - A(s) - \hat{A}(t - s) + \hat{A}(t - s) - \hat{S}(t + \tau - s)]$$

$$+ A \otimes \hat{S}(t + \tau) - A^*(t + \tau)$$

$$\le \sup_{0 \le s \le t+\tau} [A(t) - A(s) - \hat{A}(t - s)] + A \otimes \hat{S}(t + \tau) - A^*(t + \tau)$$

$$+ \sup_{0 \le s \le t+\tau} [\hat{A}(t - s) - \hat{S}(t + \tau - s)]. \tag{6.50}$$

For the first term on the right-hand side of (6.50), when $0 \le s \le t$, $A(t) - A(s) - \hat{A}(t-s) \le 0$ by the definition of a traffic envelope process, and when $t < s \le t+\tau$, we also have $A(t) - A(s) - \hat{A}(t-s) \le 0$ because $\hat{A} \ge 0$ and A is a non-decreasing function. For the second term, we have $A \otimes \hat{S}(t+\tau) - A^*(t+\tau) \le 0$ from the definition of a service envelope process. Applying both to (6.50), we obtain

$$A(t) - A^*(t + \tau) \le \sup_{0 \le s \le t+\tau} [\hat{A}(t - s) - \hat{S}(t + \tau - s)],$$

where we always have $\hat{A}(t - s) - \hat{S}(t + \tau - s) \le 0$ when $t < s \le t + \tau$. It is hence sufficient to consider only $0 \le s \le t$:

$$D(t) \le \inf \left\{ \tau : \sup_{0 \le s \le t} [\hat{A}(s) - \hat{S}(s + \tau)] \le 0 \right\}.$$

In addition, as shown by (5.11) in Section 5.1, we have, for all $x \ge 0$,

$$P\{D(t) > x\} \le P\{A(t) > A^*(t + x)\}.$$

Following the discussion above, we easily get from the Chernoff bound

$$P\{D(t) > x\} \le P \left\{ \sup_{0 \le s \le t} [\hat{A}(s) - \hat{S}(s + x)] > 0 \right\}$$

$$\le E e^{\theta \sup_{0 \le s \le t} [\hat{A}(s) - \hat{S}(s+x)]},$$

and if $A(t)$ and $\hat{S}(t)$ are independent,

$$P\{D(t) > x\} \le \sum_{s=0}^{t} M_{\hat{A}(s)}(\theta) M_{\hat{S}(s+x)}(-\theta)$$

$$= \left[M_{\hat{S}}(-\theta) \circ M_{\hat{A}}(\theta) \right] (t, x)$$

for any $\theta \ge 0$.

Formally, we have derived the following result.

Corollary 6.25 (Delay Bound). *Consider a system that provides a* **strict** *service envelope process $\hat{S}(t)$ to the input flow $A(t)$. Suppose A has a stochastic envelope process $\hat{A}$. Then, the delay $D(t)$ of the flow at time t satisfies*

$$D(t) \leq \inf \left\{ \tau : \sup_{0 \leq s \leq t} [\hat{A}(s) - \hat{S}(s + \tau)] \leq 0 \right\},$$

and if $\hat{A}$ and $\hat{S}(t)$ are independent, there holds

$$P\{D(t) > x\} \leq \left[M_{\hat{S}}(-\theta) \circ M_{\hat{A}}(\theta) \right] (t, x)$$

for any $\theta \geq 0$.

Corollary 6.26 (Backlog Bound). *Consider a system that provides a* **strict** *service envelope process $\hat{S}(t)$ to the input flow $A(t)$. Suppose A has a stochastic envelope process $\hat{A}$. Then the backlog $B(t)$ of the flow at time t satisfies*

$$B(t) \leq \hat{A} \oslash \hat{S}(0),$$

and particularly if $\hat{A}$ and $\hat{S}$ are independent, there holds

$$M_{B(t)}(\theta) \leq \left[M_{\hat{A}}(\theta) \circ M_{\hat{S}}(-\theta) \right] (t, 0)$$

and

$$P\{B(t) > x\} \leq e^{-\theta x} \left[M_{\hat{A}}(\theta) \circ M_{\hat{S}}(-\theta) \right] (t, 0)$$

for any $\theta \geq 0$.

Corollary 6.27 (Output Characterization). *Consider a system that provides a* **strict** *service envelope process $\hat{S}(t)$ to the input flow $A(t)$. Suppose A has a stochastic envelope process $\hat{A}$. Then, the output A^* has a stochastic envelope process*

$$\hat{A} = \hat{A} \oslash \hat{S}(t),$$

and particularly, if $\hat{A}$ and $\hat{S}$ are independent, there holds

$$M_{\hat{A}^*(t)}(\theta) \leq \left[M_{\hat{A}}(\theta) \circ M_{\hat{S}}(-\theta) \right] (t)$$

and, for any $s, t \geq 0$,

$$P\{\hat{A}^*(s, s + t) > x\} \leq e^{-\theta x} \left[M_{\hat{A}}(\theta) \circ M_{\hat{S}}(-\theta) \right] (t)$$

for any $\theta \geq 0$.

Corollary 6.28 (Concatenation Property). *Consider a flow passing through systems S^h, $h = 1, \ldots, H$, in sequence. Suppose each system S^h provides a* **strict** *service envelope process $\hat{S}^h(t)$ to the input, and $\hat{S}^h(t)$, $h = 1, \ldots, H$ are independent. Then, the concatenation of these systems offers to the flow a service envelope process*

$$\hat{S}(t) = \hat{S}^1 \otimes \hat{S}^2 \cdots \otimes \hat{S}^H(t),$$

and particularly, if S^h, $h = 1, \ldots, H$, are independent, there holds

$$M_{\hat{S}(t)}(-\theta) \leq M_{\hat{S}^1(t)}(-\theta) \star \cdots \star M_{\hat{S}^H(t)}(-\theta). \tag{6.51}$$

Corollary 6.29 (Leftover Service). *Consider a system serving an aggregate of two (possibly aggregate) flows A_1 and A_2. Assume the system provides a* **strict** *service envelope process $\hat{S}$ to the aggregate, and A_2 has a stochastic envelope process $\hat{A}_2$. Then, the system offers to the flow A_1 a service envelope process*

$$\hat{S}_1(t) = (\hat{S} - \hat{A}_2)(t),$$

and particularly, if $\hat{S}$ and $\hat{A}_2$ are independent, there holds

$$M_{\hat{S}_1(t)}(\theta) = M_{\hat{S}(t)}(\theta) \cdot M_{\hat{A}_2(t)}(-\theta). \tag{6.52}$$

Corollary 6.30 (Superposition). *Consider the superposition of n flows A_i, $i = 1, \ldots, n$. If each flow A_i has a stochastic envelope process $\hat{A}_i(t)$, then the aggregate flow $A = \sum_{i=1}^{n} A_i$ has a stochastic envelope process*

$$\hat{A}(t) = \sum_{i=1}^{n} \hat{A}_i(t),$$

and particularly, if A_i, $i = 1, \ldots, n$, are independent, there holds

$$M_{\hat{A}(t)}(\theta) = M_{\hat{A}_1(t)} \cdots M_{\hat{A}_n(t)}(\theta).$$

It is worth highlighting that in the results above, strict service envelope processes are required instead of service envelope processes. This is because by definition the service envelope process of a server is coupled with both its arrival process and departure process; i.e., the stochastic envelope process, the arrival process, and the departure process are dependent. If we had only assumed service envelope processes, the independence analysis would not have been applicable.

Note that, based on Corollary 6.25 for delay and Corollary 6.28 for concatenation, it is easily seen that the end-to-end delay in a tandem network satisfies

$$P\{D^{e2e}(t) > x\} \leq \left[\left(M_{\hat{S}^1(t)}(-\theta) \star \cdots \star M_{\hat{S}^H(t)}(-\theta) \right) \circ M_{\hat{A}}(\theta) \right](t, x)$$

for any $\theta \geq 0$.

For the tandem network considered in Sections 5.6 and 6.2.6, if the cross traffic is $(\sigma(\theta), \rho(\theta))$ constrained, it is shown in [44] that the end-to-end delay scales in $\mathcal{O}(n)$, which is consistent with the finding in Section 6.2.6, where a different approach is used for independent case analysis.

6.4 Summary and Bibliographic Comments

We began this chapter with a simple example demonstrating the performance improvement when the independence condition is taken into account. We then introduced two approaches to independent case analysis. One is based on the concept of a stochastic strict server. This approach is the focus of this chapter. We showed that the five basic properties can be proved for the independent case. As an example, we considered the scaling issue of the end-to-end delay bound of a tandem network that was also studied in Chapter 5. It was shown in Section 5.6 that while the end-to-end delay bound obtained from node-by-node analysis scales in $\mathcal{O}\left(n^2 \log n\right)$, it has a scaling in $\mathcal{O}\left(n \log n\right)$ by utilizing the concatenation property. In this chapter, we further showed in Section 6.2.6 that, by exploiting the independence condition, the end-to-end delay bound has a scaling in $\mathcal{O}(n)$.

In Section 6.3, we introduced another approach that can be used for the independent case analysis. In this approach, moment generating functions are applied to the traffic and service envelope processes and the five basic properties based on these processes introduced in Section 5.7. Comparing this with the approach introduced in Section 6.2, the approach based on the moment generating function is perhaps conceptually easier to adopt since the moment generating function is a well-known concept used in analyzing stochastic processes. However, when it comes to deriving closed-form bounds, the approach based on the moment generating function may need some hard work. In addition, the bounds obtained may be looser than those from the approach based on the stochastic strict server.

In the stochastic network calculus literature, independence has long been considered in the analysis. Particularly, independence is often assumed between flows in the vast effective bandwidth literature (e.g., [36] [81] [80]) and early stochastic network calculus works (e.g., [138] [15]). However, these works mainly focused on the superposition property and the single-node deterministic server case. The independent case analysis approach introduced in Section 6.2 was initially proposed by Jiang [69]. The paper [69] provides the first full analysis of the five basic properties for the independent case. The concept of a stochastic strict server due to impairment, an important concept for independent case analysis, was initially proposed by Jiang and Emstad [73]. Applying moment generating functions to the independent case analysis of the full five basic properties was first made by Fidler [44]. Also in [44], it was reported that the end-to-end delay bound for the tandem network as studied in Section 6.2.6 has a scaling in $\mathcal{O}(n)$. While this conclusion comes after some complex analysis in [44], it can be easily obtained from the approach based on the stochastic strict server as shown in Section 6.2.6.

Problems

6.1. Consider a server fed with a flow A that is the aggregation of two constituent independent flows A_f and A_h. Suppose the server provides a deterministic strict service curve β to the aggregate flow A. Flow A_h has m.b.c. stochastic arrival curve $A_h \sim_{mb} \langle f^h, r^h \rangle$ and $\beta^f \in \mathcal{F}$.

(i) Prove that flow A_f receives a stochastic strict service curve β with *impairment process $I = A_h(t) - A_h(t - s)$.*

(ii) Derive the per-flow service curve received by A_f.

6.2. Consider a constant-rate server with link capacity C fed with N input flows with maximum packet size M. All flows are independent of each other and all are $(\sigma(\theta), \rho(\theta))$ upper constrained with the same parameters. The buffer size is B.

(i) How many such flows can be admitted into the system such that the buffer overflow probability is less than P_{loss}?

(ii) How many such flows can be admitted into the system such that the probability that the delay experienced by a packet in this system is greater than D is less than P_{delay}?

6.3. What is the MGF of the service process for a constant-rate server with link capacity C?

6.4. What is the MGF of a Poisson process with mean arrival rate λ and mean packet size μ?

6.5. Consider a constant-rate server with link capacity C fed with a Poisson input flow with arrival rate λ. The packet size is exponentially distributed with mean μ but limited by a maximum packet size M. Analyze the delay distribution using the MGF-based approach and compare it with the results obtained by queuing theory and the approach based on stochastic network calculus.

6.6. Prove Theorem 6.18.

6.7. Prove Corollary 6.26.

6.8. Prove Corollary 6.27.

6.9. Prove Corollary 6.28.

6.10. Prove Corollary 6.29.

7

Analysis on Scheduling Disciplines

In the previous chapters, we have introduced several traffic models and server models and the basic properties for stochastic network calculus. These models are general and so are the results. In this chapter, we consider a special traffic model where the stochastic arrival curve has the (σ, ρ) form. This model is known as the generalized stochastically bounded bursty (gSBB) traffic model [140]. Some interesting properties of the gSBB model are presented in addition to those of the general stochastic arrival curve models. In addition, the focus of this chapter is on studying the delay and backlog performance under different scheduling disciplines where the inputs belong to gSBB. Furthermore, to demonstrate the use of results obtained, an example is given that is an application of stochastic network calculus to measurement-based admission control (MBAC). In this example, MBAC for a flow-aware network is considered, and stochastic network calculus is applied to obtain the required performance bounds for making admission control decisions.

7.1 Introduction to gSBB

The concept of generalized stochastically bounded bursty (gSBB) traffic is a simplified version of the v.b.c. stochastic arrival curve traffic model. It was initially proposed in [140] to extend the stochastically bounded burstiness (SBB) traffic model introduced in [128]. While SBB is a simplified version of the t.a.c. stochastic arrival curve traffic model, gSBB is a simplified version of the v.b.c. stochastic arrival curve traffic model.

Definitions 7.1 and 7.2 defines SBB and gSBB, respectively.

Definition 7.1. *A process $A(t)$ is said to be stochastically bounded bursty (SBB) with upper rate ρ and bounding function f, denoted by $A \sim_{ta} \langle f, \rho t \rangle$, if there exists $f \in \bar{\mathcal{G}}$ and for all $0 \leq s \leq t$ and all $\sigma > 0$ there holds*

$$P\{A(s,t) \geq \rho \cdot (t-s) + \sigma\} \leq f(\sigma). \tag{7.1}$$

Y. Jiang, Y. Liu, *Stochastic Network Calculus*,
DOI: 10.1007/978-1-84800-127-5_7,
© Springer-Verlag London Limited 2008

Definition 7.2. *A process $A(t)$ is said to be generalized stochastically bounded bursty (gSBB) with upper rate ρ and bounding function $f \in \bar{\mathcal{F}}$, denoted by $A \sim_{vb} \langle f, \rho t \rangle$, if, for all $t \geq 0$, letting $Q(t; \rho) = \sup_{0 \leq s \leq t} \{A(s, t) - \rho \cdot (t - s)\}$, one has*

$$P\{Q(t; \rho) > \sigma\} \leq f(\sigma). \tag{7.2}$$

As introduced in Chapter 3, the SBB model can apply to Gaussian self-similar input processes, such as fractional Brownian motion, and gSBB traffic contains non-Gaussian self-similar input processes, such as α-stable self-similar processes that are not SBB in general.

As introduced in Chapter 3, many types of traffic belong to SBB. For example, SBB traffic includes the Gaussian self-similar type traffic, such as fractional Brownian motion (fBm) with Hurst parameter $1/2 < H < 1$.

Also in Chapter 3, it was shown that if a certain type of traffic is SBB, it also is gSBB. For the same an fBm example, Duffield and O'Connell proved in [34] that for fBm input process with $1/2 < H < 1$, the queue size satisfies $P\{Q(t) > x\} \leq \beta e^{-\alpha x^{\gamma}}$, where α, $\beta > 0$ and $0 < \gamma < 1$ are constants, which implies that such fBm processes also belong to gSBB.

Notice that the power function $x^{-\alpha}$ is not an element of the function class $\bar{\mathcal{G}}$. Hence, an input process with a power function, say $x^{-\alpha}$, as its bounding function is not SBB in the sense of Definition 7.1. Actually, paper [128], where SBB was initially defined, left traffic of this type as open problem for further research. On the other hand, the power function has often been used for network analysis. For example, a number of research works ([49] [50] [60] [79]) proposed to use an α-stable self-similar process to model Internet traffic. The α-stable model captures not only the self-similarity and long-range correlation but also the heavy tail property. The tail approximation of an α-stable distribution is given by $P\{X > x\} \sim K_2 x^a$, where $0 < \alpha < 2$ and $K_2 > 0$ is a constant depending on α (see [121]). In addition, Laskin et al. in [89] tried to use the so-called fractional Lévy motion (fLm) mentioned by Mandelbrot in [103] to model Internet traffic, the queue distribution of which is dominated by a power law. Moreover, many researchers have noticed that real time traffic has long-tailed characteristics that may be characterized using a power function. For example, Heyman and Lekshman [61] and Jelenkovi et al. [66] explored the long-tailed characteristic of the scene length distribution of MPEG video streams, which has the form of a power function. In these cases, the traffic is not SBB but can be shown to be gSBB.

Recall the (σ, ρ) traffic model introduced in Chapter 2. We say an input process $A(t)$ is deterministically bounded bursty (DBB) with upper rate ρ and burstiness σ, denoted by $A \sim \langle \sigma, \rho \rangle$, if, for all $0 \leq s \leq t$,

$$A(s, t) \leq \rho \cdot (t - s) + \sigma.$$

From Definition 7.2, we see that DBB is a special case of gSBB whose bounding function is given by

$$f(x) = \begin{cases} 1 & \text{if } x < \sigma, \\ 0 & \text{if } x \geq \sigma. \end{cases}$$

Roughly, the differences between bounding functions for DBB, SBB, and gSBB can be illustrated by Figure 7.1.

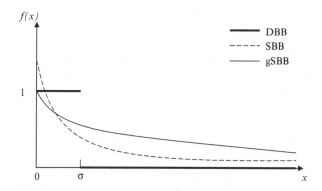

Fig. 7.1. Comparison of bounding functions for DBB, SBB, and gSBB

Based on Definition 7.2, it can be shown that many types of traffic belong to gSBB in addition to those introduced in Chapter 3. For example, Glynn and Whitt in [51] proved that when the input process $A(t)$ is stationary and satisfies a large deviation condition, if the serving rate C is greater than $E[A(t)]$, then the queue length distribution decays exponentially. Thus, this kind of traffic is gSBB with an upper rate $\rho > E[A(t)]$ and an exponential bounding function. As discussed above, Duffield and O'Connell in [34] proved that the queue length of an fBm input process is bounded by a Weibull type distribution. Hence, the fBm traffic is gSBB with a Weibull type bounding function. Furthermore, Jelenkovi in [65] proved that for a server with capacity ρ, if its traffic input $A(t)$ is long-tailed and has distribution function $F(x) = 1 - x^{-\alpha}l(x)$, where $l(x)$ is a slow variation function such as $\log x$, and ρ is larger than $E[A(t)]$, then its queue length is bounded by

$$P\{Q(t, \rho) > x\} \leq K_1 x^{-\alpha}, \tag{7.3}$$

where $K_1 > 0$ is a constant. Based on Definition 7.2, it is clear that $A(t)$ is gSBB with upper rate ρ and bounding function $K_1 x^{-\alpha}$. While the first two types of traffic can also be modeled by SBB, the last one is gSBB but not SBB.

Comparing Definition 7.2 for gSBB with Definition 7.1 for SBB, we can see that, for the same bounding function, (7.2) is tighter than (7.1). Clearly, if $A(t)$ is gSBB with upper rate ρ and bounding function $f \in \bar{\mathcal{G}}$, then $A(t)$ is SBB with the same upper rate and the same bounding function. On the

other hand, following the same discussion on the relationship between the
t.a.c. stochastic arrival curve and v.b.c. stochastic arrival curve in Chapter 3,
it can be shown that if $A(t)$ is SBB with upper rate ρ and bounding function
$f \in \bar{\mathcal{G}}$, it also is gSBB with upper rate $\rho + \epsilon$ and bounding function

$$g_\epsilon(x) = f(x) + \frac{1}{\epsilon} \int_x^\infty f(u)du \qquad (7.4)$$

for any $\epsilon > 0$.

The discussion above tells us that if a traffic source can be modeled by
SBB, it can also be modeled by gSBB (but maybe with a larger bounding
function). In addition, gSBB may be used to model traffic that does not have
a bounding function $f(x) \in \bar{\mathcal{G}}$.

7.2 Properties of gSBB

The definition of gSBB implies that it is a special case of the *v.b.c. stochastic
arrival curve* traffic model with a linear stochastic arrival curve, i.e. $\alpha(t) =
\rho \cdot t + \sigma$. Therefore, all results from earlier chapters on the v.b.c. stochastic
arrival curve also apply to gSBB.

When the server has a constant service rate, we present in the following
some interesting results. We can show that if the input process is gSBB with
upper rate ρ and bounding function $f \in \bar{\mathcal{F}}$, after passing through a work-
conserving system with constant service rate $C > \rho$, the output process is
also gSBB with the same upper rate ρ and the same bounding function f. In
fact, we have the following stronger result.

Theorem 7.3. *Consider a work-conserving system with constant service rate
C. Let $A(t)$ and $A^*(t)$ be the input and output processes of the system, respec-
tively. Assume that $A(t) \sim_{vb} \langle f, \rho t \rangle$ for some $\rho > 0$ and $f \in \bar{\mathcal{F}}$. Then, for any
$t \geq 0$, we have*

$$Q^*(t; \rho) \leq Q(t; \rho), \qquad (7.5)$$

*where $Q(t, \rho) = \sup_{0 \leq s \leq t}\{A(s,t) - \rho(t-s)\}$ and $Q^*(t, \rho) = \sup_{0 \leq s \leq t}\{A^*(s,t) -
\rho(t-s)\}$.*

Proof. Obviously, if $\rho \geq C$ we always have $Q^*(t; \rho) = 0 \leq Q(t; \rho)$. We assume
that $\rho < C$. Since $A(t) \sim_{vb} \langle f, \rho t \rangle$, by definition, we have $Q(t; \rho) < \infty$. It
is straightforward that we have $Q^*(t; \rho) < \infty$. Without loss of generality, we
assume in the following $Q^*(t; \rho) < \infty$. By definition,

$$Q^*(t; \rho) = \sup_{0 \leq s \leq t} \{A^*(s,t) - (t-s)\rho\}.$$

Then, for any given $\epsilon > 0$, there exists $s_o \leq t$ such that

$$A^*(s_o, t) - (t - s_o)\rho > Q^*(t; \rho) - \epsilon.$$

Without loss of generality, we may assume $\epsilon < (C - \rho)/2$. Since $Q^*(t; \rho)$ can actually be interpreted as the queue length at time t of a virtual system with constant service rate ρ and input A^*, we naturally have for this queue length of the virtual system

$$
\begin{aligned}
Q^*(t; \rho) &\geq A^*(s_o - 1, t) - \rho(t - s_o + 1) \\
&= A^*(s_o, t) - \rho(t - s_o) + A^*(s_o - 1, s_o) - \rho \\
&> Q^*(t; \rho) - \epsilon + A^*(s_o - 1, s_o) - \rho.
\end{aligned}
$$

From this, we get

$$
A^*(s_o - 1, s_o) < \rho + \epsilon < C.
$$

Note that the server is work-conserving with service rate C. Then the input queue length is 0 after s_o. This indicates that, after s_o, all the workload arriving up to time s_o has been transmitted already. Therefore, $A^*(s_o, t)$ is just a part of $A(s_o, t)$. Hence we have $A^*(s_o, t) \leq A(s_o, t)$. Then

$$
\begin{aligned}
Q(t; \rho) &\geq A(s_o, t) - \rho(t - s_o) \\
&\geq A^*(s_o, t) - \rho(t - s_o) > Q^*(t; \rho) - \varepsilon
\end{aligned}
$$

By the arbitrariness of ϵ we get that $Q(t; \rho) \geq Q^*(t; \rho)$. This ends the proof. $\square$

With Theorem 7.3, we immediately get the following result.

Corollary 7.4. *With the same assumption as in Theorem 7.3, if the input is gSBB (i.e., $A(t) \sim_{vb} \langle f, \rho t \rangle$) for some $\rho > 0$ and $f \in \bar{\mathcal{F}}$, then the output is also gSBB with $A^*(t) \sim_{vb} \langle f, \rho t \rangle$.*

It can be easily verified that the corollary above follows also from Theorem 5.12 in Chapter 5, where the server with constant service rate C provides a deterministic service curve $\beta(t) = Ct$.

Theorem 7.3 tells us that the outgoing stream is less bursty than the incoming stream in the sense that the up-to-date maximal cumulative burstiness is smaller. Similar results can be found in [101] and [63]. In addition, Theorem 7.3 is consistent with the results for a work-conserving constant-rate server with leak-bucket constrained input (e.g., see Lemma 1.4.2 (iii) of [18]). However, we must notice that Theorem 7.3 holds only when there is no cross traffic. We will see in the next section that if cross traffic exists, the bounding function of the outgoing traffic may become much larger.

Example 7.5. Suppose there is a stream $A_0(t)$ passing through a series of work-conserving servers with service rate $C = \rho + 1$. Use $A_i(t)$ to denote the outgoing stream from the ith server. If the stream is gSBB at the beginning with $A_0(t) \sim_{vb} \langle e^{-x}, \rho t \rangle$, we then have from Corollary 7.4 that $A_i(t) \sim_{vb} \langle e^{-x}, \rho t \rangle$ for all $i \geq 0$. If we would limit ourselves to the SBB model and always use SBB representing traffic, we could only get that the bounding function of $A_1(t)$ is given by

$$f_1(x) = e^{-x} + \int_x^\infty e^{-u} du = 2e^{-x}.$$

In general, the bounding function of $A_i(t)$ under the SBB model is

$$f_i(x) = 2^i e^{-x}.$$

If we consider $i = 10$, for $\sigma \leq 10 \ln 2 \approx 6.931$, we could not obtain any useful information from the result above, since after ten nodes we would have

$$P\{A_{10}(s,t) \geq (t-s)\rho + 10\ln 2\} \leq 2^{10} e^{-10\ln 2} = 1.$$

However, by Corollary 7.4, we have

$$\begin{aligned}
&P\{A_{10}(s,t) \geq (t-s)\rho + 10\ln 2\} \\
&\leq P\{Q_{10}(t;\rho) \geq 10\ln 2\} \\
&\leq 2e^{-10\ln 2} < 0.002.
\end{aligned}$$

From the example above, we see that besides the fact that the extent of gSBB traffic is larger than that of SBB traffic, the conservation feature of gSBB for its bounding functions is a significant advantage compared with the divergent feature for bounding functions with the SBB model.

One implication of the gSBB input-output relation is that, for a traffic stream passing through a network, if its initial SBB characteristic is known, we may first convert it to gSBB and then apply the gSBB input-output relation to analyze its network performance. As illustrated in the example above, although the converted gSBB bounding function for the stream at the first server may be larger (than its initial SBB bounding function), the resulting bounding function after the last hop from gSBB input-output relation analysis could be much smaller than what would be obtained from SBB input-output relation analysis.

7.3 Analysis on Different Scheduling Disciplines

In this section, we consider a work-conserving system shared by multiple input processes under different service disciplines. Within each source, first-in-first-out (FIFO) is assumed. Note that the discrete time model is considered. We do not distinguish the order of arrivals arriving at the same time within each source and assume that, upon service, ties are broken arbitrarily among such arrivals.

7.3.1 General Results

In this section, we do not assume any particular service discipline. For the outgoing stream of each source, we have the following result.

Theorem 7.6. *Suppose that we have N sources sharing a work-conserving system with service rate C. Assume that $A_j(t) \sim_{vb} \langle f_j, \rho_j t \rangle$, where $A_j(t)$ is the input process from source j, and $\sum_{j=1}^{N} \rho_j < C$. Let $A_j^*(t)$ be the output process of source j. Then $A_j^*(t) \sim_{vb} \langle g_j^{(1)}, \rho_j t \rangle$, where*

$$g_j^{(1)}(x) = g_j(x) + \frac{1}{\varepsilon} \int_x^\infty g_j(u)\, du$$

and

$$g_j(x) = f_1 \otimes f_2 \otimes \cdots \otimes f_N(x). \tag{7.6}$$

Proof. To derive the output burstiness of flow j, we can first derive the leftover service curve provided by the server. According to an early result on the leftover service curve, which is Corollary 5.44 in Chapter 5, we can have the following leftover weak stochastic service curve for flow j:

$$S_j \sim_{ws} \left\langle f_1 \otimes \cdots \otimes f_{j-1} \otimes f_{j+1} \cdots \otimes f_N, Ct - \sum_{k=1, k \neq j}^{N} \rho_k t \right\rangle.$$

Then, according to Theorem 5.9 in Chapter 5, we can have

$$A_j^* \sim_{ta} \left\langle f_1 \otimes f_2 \otimes \cdots \otimes f_N(x), (\rho_j t) \oslash \left(Ct - \sum_{k=1, k \neq j}^{N} \rho_k t \right) \right\rangle,$$

where

$$(\rho_j t) \oslash \left(Ct - \sum_{k=1, k \neq j}^{N} \rho_k t \right)(t) = \sup_{s \geq 0} \left\{ \rho_j(s+t) - \left(C - \sum_{k=1, k \neq j}^{N} \rho_k \right) s \right\}$$

$$= \rho_j t.$$

We hence have

$$A_j^* \sim_{ta} \langle f_1 \otimes f_2 \otimes \cdots \otimes f_N(x), \rho_j t \rangle.$$

Then, according to the relationship between the t.a.c. SAC and v.b.c. SAC, we have

$$A_j^*(t) \sim_{vb} \langle g_j^{(1)}, \rho_j t \rangle,$$

where

$$g_j^{(1)}(x) = g_j(x) + \frac{1}{\varepsilon} \int_x^\infty g_j(u)\, du$$

and

$$g_j(x) = f_1 \otimes f_2 \otimes \cdots \otimes f_N(x).$$

$\square$

For the delay, we have the following result.

Theorem 7.7. *Assume that $A(t) \sim_{vb} \langle f, \rho t \rangle$ is the input process of a work-conserving system with constant service rate $C > \rho$. Also assume, without loss of generality, $f(0) = 1$. Then the delay satisfies*

$$P\{D(t) \geq k\} \leq f((C - \rho)k). \tag{7.7}$$

Proof. Since $f(0) = 1$, Theorem 7.7 holds trivially for $k = 0$.

Consider $k \geq 1$. Let $Q(t)$ denote the queue length at time t. If for some $j < k$ we have $Q(t + j) = 0$, then we must have $D(t) \leq j < k$. Hence,

$$P\{D(t) \geq k\} \leq P\{Q(t+j) > 0; \ j = 0, 1, \cdots, k-1\}. \tag{7.8}$$

Let $Q(t; \rho) = \sup_{0 \leq s \leq t}\{A(s, t) - \rho(t - s)\}$ and $Q(t) = Q(t; C)$. When $Q(t) = Q(t; C) > 0$, we must also have $Q(t; \rho) > 0$ since $Q(t; \rho) \geq Q(t; C)$. Then, we have

$$
\begin{aligned}
Q(t; \rho) &= \sup_{0 \leq s < t} \{A(s, t) - \rho(t - s)\} \\
&\geq \sup_{0 \leq s < t} \{A(s, t) - C(t - s)\} + \inf_{0 \leq s < t} \{(C - \rho)(t - s)\} \\
&= Q(t; C) + (C - \rho).
\end{aligned}
$$

In addition, if $Q(t) > 0$ and $Q(t + 1) > 0$, we have

$$
\begin{aligned}
Q(t + 1; \rho) &= Q(t; \rho) + A(t + 1) - \rho \\
&\geq Q(t; C) + C - \rho + A(t + 1) - \rho \\
&= Q(t; C) + A(t + 1) - C + 2(C - \rho) \\
&= Q(t + 1; C) + 2(C - \rho).
\end{aligned}
$$

Inductively, if $Q(t) > 0$, $Q(t + 1) > 0$, $\cdots$, $Q(t + k - 1) > 0$, then we have

$$Q(t + k - 1; \rho) \geq Q(t + k - 1; C) + k(C - \rho). \tag{7.9}$$

Therefore, by (7.8) and (7.9),

$$
\begin{aligned}
P\{D(t) \geq k\} &\leq P\{Q(t + k - 1; \rho) > k(C - \rho)\} \\
&\leq f(k(C - \rho)).
\end{aligned}
$$

$\square$

7.3.2 First In First Out (FIFO)

In this section, we assume that the system adopts the FIFO service discipline. If, at time t, $Q(t - 1) < C$, we assume that, upon service, ties are broken arbitrarily among arrivals that arrive at t simultaneously. In this case we cannot obtain a much better result than Theorem 7.6 for output processes.

For the delay, obviously, we have

$$D(t) = \left\lceil \frac{Q(t)}{C} \right\rceil,$$

where $\lceil \cdot \rceil$ is the ceiling function denoting the smallest integer that is greater than or equal to a given number. Then $D(t) > k$ is equivalent to $Q(t) > kC$ and we have the following theorem.

Theorem 7.8. *Assume that $A(t) \sim_{vb} \langle f, \rho \rangle$, which is passing through a work-conserving system with capacity $C > \rho$ and FIFO discipline. Then, for $k \geq 1$,*

$$P\{D(t) \geq k\} \leq f\left(kC - \rho\right). \tag{7.10}$$

Proof. Since $C > \rho$, when $Q(t) > 0$ we have, as discussed in the proof of Theorem 7.7,

$$Q(t) = Q(t; C) \leq Q(t; \rho) + \rho - C.$$

Hence, for $k \geq 1$,

$$P\{D(t) \geq k\} = P\{Q(t) > (k-1)C\}$$
$$\leq P\{Q(t, \rho) > kC - \rho\} \leq f(kC - \rho).$$

□

It can be easily verified from Theorems 7.7 and 7.8 that FIFO can have better performance in terms of delay for each individual source than a general scheduler whose service discipline is unknown.

7.3.3 Strict Priority (SP)

We now consider strict priority discipline. Assume that, if $i < j$, then the source i has a higher priority than the source j, which means that source j will not be served if there exists a workload from source i waiting for serving. Within the same source, FIFO is adopted.

For the output traffic, the following result holds.

Theorem 7.9. *Suppose that we have N sources sharing a work-conserving system with service rate C, which serves according to strict priority order. Let $A_j(t)$ be the input process from source j. Assume that $A_j(t) \sim_{vb} \langle f_j, \rho_j t \rangle$, where $\sum_{j=1}^{N} \rho_j < C$. Let $A_j^*(t)$ be the output process of source j. Then $A_1^*(t) \sim_{vb} \langle f_1, \rho_1 t \rangle$ and, for $j \geq 2$, we have $A_j^*(t) \sim_{vb} \langle g_j^{(1)}, \rho_j t \rangle$, where*

$$g_j^{(1)}(x) = g_j(x) + \frac{1}{\varepsilon} \int_x^\infty g_j(u)\, du$$

and

$$\begin{cases} g_2(x) = f_1 \otimes f_2\,(x) \\ \cdots \\ g_N(x) = f_1 \otimes f_2 \otimes \cdots \otimes f_N\,(x) \end{cases} \tag{7.11}$$

with any $0 < p_{ki} < 1$ *and* $\sum_{i=1}^{k} p_{ki} + p_{kk} = 1$, $k = 2, \cdots, N$.

Proof. For $A_1(t)$, it is exactly the same as it passes through a work-conserving server with capacity $C > \rho_1$. By Theorem 7.3, we see that $A_1^*(t) \sim_{vb} \langle f_1, \rho_1 t \rangle$.

Now consider $A_2(t)$. Compared with other traffic streams, $A_1(t) + A_2(t)$ has the highest priority. Hence it is equivalent to the case where $A_1(t) + A_2(t)$ passes through a work-conserving server with capacity $C > \rho_1 + \rho_2$. By Theorem 7.6, we get that $A_2^*(t) \sim_{vb} \langle g_2^{(1)}, \rho_2 t \rangle$. By similar discussions, we can get $g_3^{(1)}, \cdots, g_N^{(1)}$. $\square$

For the delay of each source, we have the following bound.

Theorem 7.10. *Denote by $D_j(t)$ the delay of source j. With the same assumption as in Theorem 7.9, we have, for $k \geq 1$,*

$$P\{D_1(t) \geq k\} \leq f_1(kC - \rho_1) \tag{7.12}$$

and

$$P\{D_j(t) \geq k\} \leq g_j(k(C - r_j)), \tag{7.13}$$

for $j \geq 2$, where $r_j = \rho_1 + \cdots + \rho_j$ and

$$g_j(x) = f_1 \otimes f_2 \otimes \cdots \otimes f_j\,(x). \tag{7.14}$$

Proof. We can get (7.12) by Theorem 7.9. In fact, for $A_1(t)$, it is exactly the same as the case of only one input process in a work-conserving system with capacity C and FIFO. For $j \geq 2$, we apply Theorems 7.3 and 7.7 to the aggregate traffic $A_1(t) + \cdots + A_j(t)$. By the superposition property of the v.b.c. stochastic arrival curve, we know that this traffic is gSBB with upper rate $\rho_1 + \cdots + \rho_j$ and bounding function $g_j(x)$ defined by (7.14). Then, (7.13) follows from Theorem 7.7. $\square$

7.3.4 Generalized Processor Sharing (GPS)

We finally consider a work-conserving server with capacity C shared by N flows using the generalized processor sharing (GPS) service discipline [112]. Assign the ith flow a parameter $\phi_i > 0$. Similar to above, let $Q(t)$ denote the total queue length at time t and $Q_i(t)$ denote the portion of the queue that belongs to flow i. In addition, A_i^* denotes the output of flow i.

For GPS, if in the time interval $(s, t]$ $Q_i(\tau) > 0$, then, for any $s < \tau \leq t$ [112],

$$\frac{A_i^*(s,t)}{A_j^*(s,t)} \geq \frac{\phi_i}{\phi_j}, \quad j = 1, 2, \cdots, N. \tag{7.15}$$

Without loss of generality, we assume that $\sum_{i=1}^{N} \phi_i = 1$ and call ϕ_i the ith serving weight. By (7.15), we see that if traffic from source i is backlogged all the time in the interval $(s,t]$, then the available serving rate for source i is at least $\phi_i C$ for the whole time period. This implies that the server provides strict service curve $\phi_i C t$ to flow i. Then, if $\phi_j C > \rho_j$, Theorem 7.11 can be proved in the same way as Theorem 7.3. If we do not have $\phi_j C > \rho_j$, Theorem 7.6 can be applied.

Theorem 7.11. *Assume that we have N sources sharing a work-conserving system with service rate C that adopts GPS service discipline. Assign each source i a sharing weight $\phi_i > 0$ for $1 \leq i \leq N$. Assume that $A_j(t) \sim_{vb} \langle f_j, \rho_j t \rangle$, where $A_j(t)$ is the input process from source j, and $\sum_{j=1}^{N} \rho_j < C$. Let $A_j^*(t)$ be the output process of source j. Then, $A_j^*(t) \sim_{vb} \langle g_j, \rho_j t \rangle$, where if $\phi_j C > \rho_j$, $g_j(x) = f_j(x)$; otherwise, $g_j(x)$ is determined from Theorem 7.6.*

For the delay, since, under GPS, if $Q_j(t) > 0$, the amount of work waiting in queue $Q_j(t)$ will be served at a rate not less than $\phi_j C$, we can follow the same method used in proving Theorem 7.8 to obtain the following result.

Theorem 7.12. *Let $D_j(t)$ be the delay for source j. With the same assumption as in Theorem 7.11, if $\phi_j C > \rho_j$, we have, for $k \geq 1$,*

$$P\{D_j(t) \geq k\} \leq f_j(k\phi_j C - \rho_j); \tag{7.16}$$

otherwise, the delay has a probabilistic bound determined from Theorem 7.7.

Note that when some other conditions on the sources and the weight assignment are satisfied in the GPS system, we will see in Chapter 9 that improved results may be obtained for each source.

7.4 Application to Measurement-Based Admission Control

Having studied the several representative scheduling disciplines, to demonstrate the use of the results obtained, the rest of this chapter focuses on an example that applies stochastic network calculus to measurement-based admission control (MBAC). The focus is on MBAC for a flow-aware network. We will first give an introduction to MBAC. Then, a per-flow MBAC scheme will be described, which is followed by the analysis using the earlier results in this and previous chapters.

7.4.1 Introduction to MBAC

Measurement-based admission control is an important technique for providing stochastic service guarantees. MBAC does not require a priori source characterization, which in many cases may be difficult or impossible to obtain. Instead, MBAC uses measurements to capture the behavior of existing flows and uses this information together with some (possibly coarse) knowledge of the requesting flow to make an admission decision. In addition, based on online measurements, MBAC can better make use of network resources and hence achieve high network utilization.

Figure 7.2 depicts the structure of MBAC. It shows that an MBAC scheme includes three elements: (1) admission decision algorithm; (2) traffic estimator; and (3) resource estimator. The MBAC scheme keeps measuring traffic in the system and remaining system resources such as available bandwidth and buffer size. Based on the measurements, the traffic estimator estimates how much traffic is in the system and what its characteristics are; the resource estimator estimates how much resource remains.

For a specific MBAC implementation, the system in Figure 7.2 can be a single node, a domain, or an end-to-end network. If the system is a network domain, the measurement points for the traffic estimator and the resource estimator, as well as the admission decision algorithm, can be implemented at each node (which results in the node-by-node MBAC or hop-by-hop MBAC), at the ingress (which results in ingress MBAC), or at the egress (which results in egress MBAC), or at a central controller such as bandwidth broker in DiffServ (which results in centralized MBAC). If the system is the whole end-to-end network, the three elements for MBAC may be implemented at end-systems/applications, which results in endpoint MBAC. In this chapter, we focus on single-node MBAC algorithms in which the system in Figure 7.2 is the single link. Nevertheless, most discussions in this chapter can be extended to the network domain case and the end-to-end network case by viewing the network domain or the end-to-end network as a black box or single node.

When a new flow requests admission to the system, the MBAC scheme uses the admission control algorithm to decide if this flow can be admitted. This decision is based on the inputs from the traffic estimator and the resource estimator. In addition, the decision may also be based on some inputs from the requesting flow, which typically include its QoS requirement and its traffic description.

In MBAC, the MBAC scheme typically uses the a priori source characterizations only for incoming flows. For existing flows that have been in the system, it uses measurements to characterize them.

In the literature, many MBAC algorithms have been proposed and investigated [75][13][125]. While these algorithms use different analytical bases for the admission test, they commonly assume or require that [75] *(1) FIFO be used for aggregating flows; (2) statistical service guarantees be provided to the aggregate of admitted flows; and (3) each flow in the aggregate requires and*

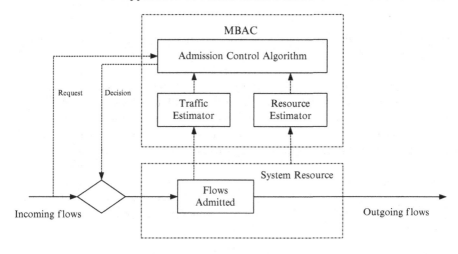

Fig. 7.2. MBAC structure

experiences the same statistical service guarantees as the aggregate. We call these algorithms *aggregate MBAC* algorithms. For analyzing such algorithms, the superposition property may be used together with the service guarantees property of stochastic network calculus to derive the target delay and backlog bounds, from which the admission decision can further be made.

While the assumptions and requirements for aggregate MBAC have made such MBAC algorithms simple, network applications are so diverse that their QoS requirements can be far from each other. In such cases, *per-flow MBAC* algorithms may be preferred [117]. In the rest of this chapter, we shall focus on a flow-aware network where flows can be identified and particularly on MBAC for the network.

7.4.2 Introduction to Flow-Aware Networking

In a flow-aware network, a flow is defined to be and identified as a set of packets related to an instance of some network application observed at a given network point with an inter-packet interval less than a certain *time-out* period. Specifically, a flow consists of packets having the same values in certain header fields. A flow is said to have ended or left when no packet with the same header field values is observed for the time-out period. There are several possible ways to identify a flow. One is to use the 5-tuple of IP addresses, protocol, and port numbers. Another is to use the flow label field in the IP header as specified by IPv6 associated with the source and/or destination addresses. Here, we simply assume each flow can be identified, but how this is done is out of the scope of this book.

Flow-aware networking is proposed as an alternative QoS architecture for the Internet [11][117]. While an IntServ network also requires flow-level identification, its per-flow service guarantees are mainly provided in the deterministic guaranteed service manner, which can cause significant underutilization of network resources (e.g., see [117]). Although IntServ has defined Controlled Load service for utilizing statistical multiplexing gain to achieve higher network utilization, the requirement of a signaling protocol and that TSpec (token bucket traffic specification) be used for specifying the traffic has imposed significant constraints on customers and limited its use [117].

A flow-aware network is designed to achieve high network utilization and provide a stochastic service guarantee without the need of using signaling or TSpec. Particularly, it achieves this by assuming that the peak rate of a flow is always smaller than a certain ratio of the service capacity [117]. Let C be the total capacity and ϕ_i the ratio. Then, this assumption implies that the cumulative amount of traffic $A_i(s, s + t)$ generated in $(s, s + t]$ by the flow satisfies

$$A_i(s, s + t) \leq \phi_i Ct, \tag{7.17}$$

where ϕ_i may be different for one flow from one flow to the other, and it can be carried by packets of the flow; e.g., in some IP header field such as the traffic specification code point field in DiffServ networks [76].

Using (7.17) as the *implicit* traffic descriptor of an incoming flow, no signaling is needed to convey explicit traffic information from the sender to the network. In addition, the service requirement of the flow may be implicitly set in the network or can be carried by some header field of the flow's first packet [76]. Under the DiffServ architecture, similar approach has been used. Particularly, the DSCP (DiffServ code point) field carried by each packet tells each node along its path the service it requires [10]. The detailed way of mapping the header field to the service requirement is out of the scope of this book.

To provide service guarantees in a flow-aware network, per-flow MBAC is important [11] [117].

7.4.3 Dynamic Priority Scheduling-Based MBAC

Admission control is highly dependent on the scheduling discipline adopted and its setting since different scheduling or service disciplines can result in different service guarantees provided to a flow. For example, Table 2.1 in Chapter 2 shows the difference in terms of rate guarantee between several widely studied scheduling disciplines. In addition, it was studied in Chapter 9 that by changing the weight assignment in a GPS scheduler, the service guarantee in terms of LRD isolation may be met.

GPS is an ideal scheduling discipline and a good candidate for providing per-flow service guarantees, its key drawback being that its implementation complexity increases quickly with the number of flows it handles. While FIFO is simple to implement, it does not distinguish between flows, and hence the service guarantees are provided to the flow aggregate.

In the rest of this section, we consider a dynamic priority scheduling (DPS) discipline based on which measurement-based admission control is performed.

In the dynamic priority scheduling discipline considered, each admitted flow has its dedicated queue. Priority scheduling is performed among admitted flows in the system. An earlier admitted flow has higher priority over all later admitted flows. This is achieved by always giving the newly admitted flow a lower priority than all existing flows. When a flow is detected as non-active for a certain time period, known as the time-out period, it is considered to have left the system and its corresponding buffer is released together with its priority. A common buffer pool is maintained in the MBAC algorithm. When an incoming flow is admitted, a certain size of buffer is allocated to the flow. The buffer size allocated is determined based on the analysis presented later.

As can be seen from the description above, although the relative priority of a flow with respect to other flows is nearly fixed, its exact priority level is dynamic over time. In particular, the level of an existing flow increases by one priority level over all existing flows admitted after it.

With this DPS discipline, by the nature of priority discipline, the experienced statistical service guarantees of an admitted flow will not be adversely affected by flows admitted after it. In fact, the experienced service guarantees of an admitted flow can become better and better due to some earlier admitted flows leaving the system. An implication of the DPS discipline is that when admission control is performed, there is no need to recheck the service guarantees provided to existing flows or to reallocate resources to the existing flows to maintain their service guarantees. This makes both the DPS discipline and the DPS-based MBAC easy to implement.

When the first packet of a new flow A_n is detected, implying an incoming flow requesting admission, the admission control algorithm admits the flow only when the criteria

$$r_n + \hat{r} \leq \phi C, \tag{7.18}$$

$$f_d(d_n) \leq \epsilon_n^d, \tag{7.19}$$

$$b_n + \hat{b} \leq M, \tag{7.20}$$

are met, where C denotes the link capacity, $\phi(< 1)$ the maximum allowed utilization level of C, M the total buffer size, $r_n(= \phi_n C)$ the (implicit upper) rate of the incoming flow, ϵ_n^d the delay requirement, and b_n the buffer size that will be allocated to the flow if it is admitted. In addition, $\hat{r}$ denotes the mean traffic rate of all existing flows in the system, which is measured, and $\hat{b}$ the total buffer size allocated to flows in the system.

In (7.18) to (7.20), (7.18) represents the admission criterion for rate or throughput, and (7.19) represents the criterion for delay. The probability that the delay D_n to be experienced by the incoming flow is greater than the required delay d_n is less than ϵ_n^d. In (7.19), the delay function $f_d(y)$, which satisfies $P\{D_n > y\} \leq f_d(y)$, will be given in the next subsection. For (7.20), b_n is the minimum buffer size with which the required loss probability is met. Specifically,

$$b_n = \min\{x : f_l(x) \leq \epsilon_n^l\}, \tag{7.21}$$

where ϵ_n^l denotes the loss requirement of the incoming flow. The loss function $f_l(x)$ in (7.21) will also be given later.

If no b_n satisfying (7.21) exists, the flow is rejected. In addition, if any one of (7.18) to (7.20) cannot be satisfied, the flow is rejected. The admission control algorithm rejects a flow by simply dropping packets from the flow, or if there is a best-effort traffic class, the flow is added to this class. It is left as the responsibility of the sender and/or receiver of the flow to react to the possible dropping, but how such a reaction is done is out of the scope of this book.

7.4.4 Analysis

Note that, in the DPS-based MBAC scheme, if an incoming flow is admitted, it will be placed at the lowest priority level as compared with all existing flows. As a result, the incoming flow will see an integrated effect from these existing flows. Particularly, we can view the existing flows as an aggregate and equivalently consider a priority server with two inputs: the aggregate and the incoming flow.

As in the previous chapters, let $A_i(t)$ be the arrival process of each flow i in the system and $A_i(s, s + t)$ the amount of traffic generated by the process in $(s, s+t]$. Suppose all flows have stationary increments; i.e., $A_i(s, s + t) =_{st} A_i(t)$ for all $s, t > 0$. Let $A(t)$ be the aggregate arrival process of all flows in the system and $A(s, s + t)$ the amount of traffic generated by the aggregate process in $(s, s + t]$.

We then have $A(t) = \sum_{i=1}^{I} A_i(t)$, where I denotes the number of flows in the system. When I becomes large, $A(t)$ tends toward Gaussian under some general assumptions. In addition, denote the amount of traffic generated by each flow in $(t-1, t]$ by $a_i(t) = A_i(t) - A_i(t-1) \equiv A_i(t-1, t)$ and the amount of traffic generated in $(t - 1, t]$ by all flows in the system $a(t) = \sum_{i=1}^{I} a_i(t)$. We then have $A(t, t + \tau) = \sum_{s=t}^{t+\tau} a_i(s)$, which also tends toward Gaussian when the time interval becomes large. For these reasons, a Gaussian process has often been used to characterize the existing traffic in MBAC (e.g., [21] [83] [1][104]). The mean and variance of a Gaussian process can be estimated from measurements [41].

For a Gaussian process, letting $\hat{r}t$ and $\hat{v}(t)$ respectively be its mean and variance, there holds for any $s, t \geq 0$

$$P\{A(s, s + t) > \rho t + \sigma\} = \Psi \left(\frac{(\rho - \hat{r})t + \sigma}{\sqrt{\hat{v}(t)}} \right), \tag{7.22}$$

where $\Psi(x) \equiv \frac{1}{2\pi} \int_x^{\infty} e^{-\frac{y^2}{2}} dy$.

Equation (7.22) implies that the Gaussian process can be considered to have a t.a.c. stochastic arrival curve. Then, all properties of the t.a.c. stochastic arrival curve can be applied to analyze Gaussian processes. In the following, an approximation is instead introduced for the analysis in this chapter.

Available results in the literature [21][83][1][104] suggest the following approximation for $\hat{Q}(t;c)$, the queue length at time t of a virtual single-server queue system with server rate $c > \hat{r}$ fed with the same traffic $A(t)$ of the Gaussian process:

$$P\{\hat{Q}(t;c) > x\} \approx \exp\left(-\inf_{s\geq 0}\frac{(x + (c - \hat{r})s)^2}{2\hat{v}(s)}\right). \tag{7.23}$$

Simulation results under various cases indicate that the approximation (7.23) may in fact be a general upper bound for $P\{\hat{Q}(t;c) > x\}$ [1], and under some general conditions, it has been proved in [21] that (7.23) is an asymptotic upper bound on $P\{\hat{Q}(t;c) > x\}$. For these reasons, we rewrite (7.23) as

$$P\{\hat{Q}(t;c) > x\}$$
$$\lessapprox \hat{f}(x) \equiv \exp\left(-\frac{(x + (c - \hat{r})s)^2}{2\hat{v}^*}\right), \tag{7.24}$$

where $\hat{v}^* \equiv \hat{v}(s^*)$ and s^* is chosen such that $\frac{(x+(c-\hat{r})s)^2}{2\hat{v}(s)}$ reaches its minimum at s^*.

For the aggregate traffic $\hat{A}(t)$ of existing flows in the MBAC system, according to the definition of a v.b.c. stochastic arrival curve in Chapter 3, we now have from (7.24) that $\hat{A}(t) \sim_{vb} \langle \hat{f}, c \cdot t \rangle$, which holds for any $c > \hat{r}$. For ease of explanation and later analysis, we let $c = \hat{r} + (1-u)C$ and consequently

$$\hat{A}(t) \sim_{vb} \left\langle \hat{f}, (\hat{r} + (1 - u)C)t \right\rangle. \tag{7.25}$$

Here, u can be interpreted as a utilization parameter that can be chosen between the actual utilization $\frac{\hat{r}+r_n}{C}$, which will result from admitting the requesting flow, and the maximum allowed utilization level α. In other words,

$$\frac{\hat{r} + r_n}{C} \leq u \leq \alpha. \tag{7.26}$$

The remainder of this section presents analytical support for determining $f_d(y)$ in (7.19) and $f_l(x)$ in (7.21) using stochastic network calculus results. Particularly, as discussed above, we view the system as a priority server with two priority levels: while existing aggregate traffic is at the high priority level, the requesting flow is at the low priority level. Then, from Theorem 5.42 and the v.b.c. stochastic arrival curve characterization of existing traffic in (7.25), we have the following result.

Corollary 7.13. *Consider a constant-rate priority server with two inputs. Suppose the total service rate is C and the input at the high priority level has $\hat{A}(t) \sim_{vb} \left\langle \hat{f}, (\hat{r} + (1 - u)C)t \right\rangle$. Then the server provides to the flow at the low priority level a weak stochastic service curve $S \sim_{ws} \langle g(x), \beta(t) \rangle$ with $\beta(t) = (uC - \hat{r})t; g(x) = \hat{f}(x)$.*

Applying Corollary 7.13 to Theorems 5.1 and 5.4, we obtain the following corollary.

Corollary 7.14. *Under the same condition as in Corollary 7.13, if the input flow at the low priority level has* $A_n(t) \sim_{vb} \langle f_n, r_n \cdot t \rangle$, *then its backlog* $B_n(t)$ *and delay* $D_n(t)$ *in the system satisfy*

$$P(B_n(t) > x) \le f_l(x),$$
$$P(D_n(t) > y) \le f_d(y),$$

where

$$f_l(x) = f_n \otimes \hat{f}(x), \tag{7.27}$$

$$f_d(y) = f_n \otimes \hat{f}\left((uC - \hat{r})y\right). \tag{7.28}$$

Here, we have assumed that the aggregate traffic of existing flows in the system is approximated using Gaussian and (7.24). In addition, we have adopted the implicit traffic descriptor (7.17) for the incoming flow as used in [117], which implies $A_n \sim \langle 0, \phi_n C \rangle$. Applying these to (7.27) and (7.28), we can further get

$$f_l(x) = exp\left(-\frac{x^2}{2\tilde{v}_x^*}\right), \tag{7.29}$$

$$f_d(y) = exp\left(-\frac{(uC - \hat{r})^2 y^2}{2\tilde{v}_y^*}\right), \tag{7.30}$$

where $\tilde{v}_x^* \equiv \tilde{v}(s_x^*)$ and s_x^* is chosen such that $\frac{(x+(c-\hat{r})s)^2}{2\tilde{v}(s)}$ reaches its minimum at $s = s_x^*$; $\tilde{v}_y^* \equiv \tilde{v}(s_y^*)$ and s_y^* is chosen such that $\frac{((uC-\hat{r})y+(c-\hat{r})s)^2}{2\tilde{v}(s)}$ reaches its minimum at s_y^*.

Here while in Corollaries 7.13 and 7.14, we have considered only two priority levels, here the result can be easily extended to more levels, as shown in Section 7.3. In such cases, it is easy to verify from the proof that we can view $\tilde{A}(t)$ and $\tilde{A}^*(t)$ respectively as the aggregate input and output of all flows that are not at the lowest priority level and consequently get the proposition proved. In addition, for any flow at a certain priority level, we can view $\tilde{A}(t)$ and $\tilde{A}^*(t)$ respectively as the aggregate input and output of all flows having higher priority than this flow and consequently prove that the server provides to the flow a weak stochastic service curve as in Corollary 7.13.

Note that Corollaries 7.13 and 7.14 are general in the sense that they hold as long as the two input flows have v.b.c. stochastic arrival curves. In Chapter 3, we saw that many types of traffic can be modeled by a v.b.c. stochastic arrival curve. Hence, although Gaussian approximation has been used in this chapter for its popularity and reasonably good performance as investigated by other researchers (e.g., see [21] [86]), the v.b.c. stochastic arrival curve allows us to use other approximations for existing aggregate traffic instead. In other words, other approximations for existing traffic and other descriptors for the incoming flow can also be used with Corollaries 7.13 and 7.14. Under these cases, by applying the corresponding $\hat{f}$ and f_n to Corollaries 7.13 and 7.14, the required $f_d(y)$ and $f_l(x)$ can be derived and applied to (7.19) and (7.21) for making an admission decision.

Also note that, u can be selected between $\frac{\hat{r}+r_n}{C}$ and ϕ. Roughly, given $\hat{f}(x)$ by (7.24), a smaller u results in a tighter $f_l(x)$ and a tighter $f_d(y)$. Because of this, by selecting u properly, higher utilization may be achieved.

7.5 Summary and Bibliographic Comments

In this chapter we have introduced the concept of generalized stochastically bounded bursty (gSBB) traffic, which was initially defined by Yin, Jiang et al. in [140]. The v.b.c. stochastic arrival curve traffic model is indeed based on and a generalization of gSBB. Because of this, all properties and results for the v.b.c. stochastic arrival curve traffic model also apply to the gSBB model. In addition, this chapter has discussed some interesting properties of gSBB, particularly the input-output relation of a constant- rate system with gSBB input.

The focus of this chapter was on studying a system shared by a number of gSBB sources using different scheduling disciplines. The output characterization and the bounding probability for delay under these disciplines were analyzed. These results can also be easily extended to the v.b.c. stochastic arrival curve traffic model.

To demonstrate the use of stochastic network calculus results, we studied measurement-based admission control for a flow-aware network. A simple per-flow MBAC scheme was introduced to provide stochastic service guarantees in the network. This scheme uses dynamic priority to schedule flows in the system, where a newly admitted flow is always given lower priority than existing flows. The admission decision is based on traffic measurements of existing flows together with service requirements of the incoming flow. With this DPS-based MBAC, per-flow stochastic service guarantees can be provided. The admission control is based on delay and loss analysis using results from the previous chapters. An attractive feature of the MBAC scheme studied is that the guaranteed stochastic service to an admitted flow is not adversely affected by flows admitted after it. In fact, as expected, the experienced service guarantees of an admitted flow become better and better due to some earlier admitted flows leaving the system. An implication of the DPS-based MBAC algorithm is that when admission control is performed, there is no need to recheck the service guarantees provided to existing flows or to reallocate resources to the existing flows to maintain their service guarantees.

The concept of gSBB was initially defined by Yin, Jiang et al. in [140]. Analyzing scheduling disciplines with gSBB inputs can be found from [77] by Jiang et al. Many MBAC schemes have been proposed, and several reviews of them can be found in the literature (e.g., [125] [107] [75] and references therein). The flow-aware networking architecture was initially introduced in [11] [117]. Discussion and proposals for avoiding signaling in per-flow measurement-based admission control can be found in [117] [75] and [76]. The MBAC scheme based on dynamic priority was introduced in [72] by Jiang et al. where the analysis was based on stochastic network calculus.

Problems

7.1. Consider the system described in Example 7.5, and find the nodes from which the bounds derived under the SBB model is greater than that derived under the gSBB model.

7.2. Consider a constant-rate server with capacity C providing service to a flow that can be characterized by a Gaussian process with mean $\hat{r}t$ and variance $\hat{v}(t)$. Derive the delay distribution using Theorem 7.7.

7.3. Consider a constant-rate server with capacity C providing service in a FIFO manner to a flow that can be characterized by a Gaussian process with mean $\hat{r}t$ and variance $\hat{v}(t)$. Derive the delay distribution using Theorem 7.7 and 7.8.

7.4. Consider a constant-rate server with capacity C providing service in a FIFO manner to a flow that can be characterized by a Gaussian process with mean $\hat{r}t$ and variance $\hat{v}(t)$. Derive the delay distribution using results from Chapter 5 and compare the results with those from Problems 7.2 and 7.3.

7.5. Prove Theorem 7.11.

7.6. Prove Theorem 7.12.

7.7. Prove Corollary 7.13.

7.8. Prove Corollary 7.14.

7.9. Based on the relationship between SBB and gSBB, or the t.a.c. stochastic arrival curve and v.b.c. stochastic arrival curve, the gSBB characterization of the Gaussian process can be obtained. Apply it to obtain the required bounding functions f_l and f_d for the DPS-based MBAC scheme. Then, compare them with the corresponding results in Section 7.4.3.

8

Traffic Conformance Study

In this chapter, we will apply stochastic network calculus to a traffic conformance study.

To achieve a certain level of quality of service (QoS) assurance, a network will have service level agreements (SLAs) with its users and neighboring domains, which, in general, describe the QoS level that the service provider is committed to provide and the specification of traffic that users or neighboring domains are allowed to send for the subscribed QoS level. For example, in a Differentiated Services network [10], all incoming flows must conform to a certain pre-determined SLA and the conformance is measured by a policer at the ingress router of the network. Based on the SLA, the network will provide a certain level of QoS to the conformant part of these flows. Since flows may interact with each other and compete for resources at each node of a network, an interesting and important question arises as to whether a flow is still conformant to its original traffic specification after crossing the network.

This chapter considers conformance deterioration for both individual flows and aggregates of flows. In some situations, an individual flow needs to negotiate SLAs with networks along its end-to-end path. In this case, the per-flow conformance deterioration along its end-to-end path is considered. Another case is also considered where the individual user only needs to establish an SLA with the first access network, and the access network will negotiate a bulk SLA with its next intermediate network for the corresponding aggregate of flows. For example, several users may subscribe to the same level of service, each has its individual SLA with the first access network, and traffic from these users is aggregated in the same class. When such an aggregate exits the first network and enters the next network, the aggregate will be checked for its conformance based on the bulk SLA between these two domains.

In this chapter, we study analytically the extent to which a flow and an aggregate of flows become non-conformant in two typical network scenarios. In particular, we investigate conformance deterioration in a per-flow scheduling network where network servers guarantee a certain level of service to each flow and in an aggregate scheduling network where network servers provide a

Y. Jiang, Y. Liu, *Stochastic Network Calculus*,
DOI: 10.1007/978-1-84800-127-5_8,
© Springer-Verlag London Limited 2008

certain level of service to each aggregation of flows to support scalable QoS provisioning. Based on a relationship between the conformance deterioration and stochastic burstiness increase that will be established in this chapter and results from the previous chapters, analytical bounds on conformance deterioration probability are presented for both the per-flow and the per-aggregate cases.

8.1 Network Model

Consider a network as shown in Figure 8.1. In this network, every incoming flow under consideration is shaped by a token bucket shaper at an ingress router, whose token generation rate and bucket size are set based on some pre-determined SLA. At the corresponding egress router a token bucket meter with the same parameters as the ingress shaper checks the conformance of its outgoing traffic. If the burstiness of the input flow increases and consequently some packets of the flow do not conform to the token bucket meter at the egress, they will be marked as OUT of profile. This chapter is concerned with the conformance deterioration probability, which is defined as the ratio of the number of OUT packets to that of received packets recorded in the token bucket meter at the egress router. The two network scenarios under investigation are per-flow scheduling networks, where network servers guarantee a certain level of service to each flow, and aggregate scheduling networks, where network servers provide a certain level of service to each aggregation of flows.

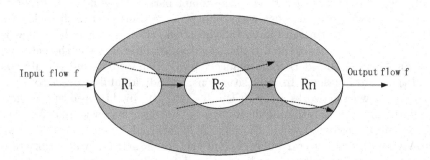

Fig. 8.1. Network model

The burstiness increase for a flow after crossing a certain network element was first studied by Cruz [28][29] in a deterministic framework. Reference [28] obtained the burstiness of an output flow given the burstiness of the input flow. Some recent works [92][22] studied the worst-case burstiness increase under aggregate scheduling. However, these deterministic bounds on worst-case burstiness increase cannot be used to obtain the conformance deterioration probability since the conformance deterioration probability is a stochastic metric. Hence, the stochastic burstiness increase needs to be investigated in order to determine the conformance deterioration probability. To study the stochastic burstiness increase of an input flow after crossing a network, the initial stochastic characterization of the flow before being shaped by the token bucket is needed. The m.b.c stochastic arrival curve concept described in previous chapters is used to model an input traffic process before it enters the network. Here, it is assumed that the bounding functions for all input flows of interest are known or can be easily obtained. The deterministic service curve, stochastic service curve, and stochastic strict service curve concepts as explained in previous chapters are used to model servers in this chapter.

8.1.1 Conformance Deterioration and Stochastic Burstiness Increase

To analytically calculate the bound of the conformance deterioration probability for a flow checked by a token bucket meter, the same flow is fed to a virtual server with a constant service rate that is the same as the token generation rate of the token bucket meter. This section will establish the relationship between conformance deterioration probability and stochastic burstiness increase measured in the virtual server fed with the same input flow. The following theorem shows that the probability that a packet is marked as OUT by the token bucket meter is bounded by the probability that the queue length in the virtual server exceeds the bucket depth of the token bucket meter.

Theorem 8.1 (Relationship between Non-conformance and Stochastic Burstiness). *Consider a flow fed into a token bucket meter and a virtual initially empty constant-rate server, respectively. The token bucket has parameters (ρ, σ_{th}), where ρ is the token generation rate and σ_{th} is the bucket depth. The constant-rate server has service rate ρ. Then, $P_{nonconf}(t) \leq P_{W(t;r)>\sigma_{th}} \leq P_{M(t;r)>\sigma_{th}}$ where $P_{nonconf}(t)$ denotes the probability that one packet is found to be OUT, $W(t;r) \equiv \sup_{0 \leq s \leq t}\{A(s,t) - r(t - s)\}$, which is the queue length at the constant-rate server, $P_{W(t;r)>\sigma_{th}}$ is the probability that the queue length $W(t;r)$ in the constant rate server exceeds σ_{th}, $M(t;r) \equiv \sup_{0 \leq s \leq t} \sup_{0 \leq u \leq s}[A(u,s) - r(s - u)]$, which is the maximum up-to-date backlog at time t for the constant-rate server, and $P_{M(t;r)>\sigma_{th}}$ is the probability that the maximum up-to-date backlog $M(t)$ exceeds σ_{th}.*

Proof. Consider the case where one packet arriving at time t has been found non-conformant by the token bucket. Then, there exists some $s < t$ for which the amount of traffic arrival during $[s, t)$ satisfies:

$$A(s, t) > \rho(t - s) + \sigma_{th}.$$

Therefore,

$$P_{nonconf}(t) \leq P\{A(s,t) > \rho(t-s) + \sigma_{th}\}$$
$$= P\{A(s,t) - \rho(t-s) > \sigma_{th}\}$$
$$\leq P\left\{\sup_{0 \leq s^* \leq t} \{A(s^*,t) - \rho(t-s^*)\} > \sigma_{th}\right\}$$
$$= P_{W(t;r) > \sigma_{th}}$$
$$\leq P\left\{\sup_{0 \leq s \leq t} \sup_{0 \leq s^* \leq s} \{A(s^*,s) - \rho(s-s^*)\} > \sigma_{th}\right\}$$
$$= P_{M(t;r) > \sigma_{th}}.$$

This completes the proof. $\square$

With Theorem 8.1, it is clear that to obtain the bound for the conformance deterioration probability, one approach is to derive the queue length distribution of the output flow in the corresponding virtual server. Since the queue length distribution in the virtual server is characterized by a bounding function in the m.b.c. stochastic arrival curve definition, the bounding function is used here to characterize the stochastic burstiness for the flow of interested. Therefore, the bounding function of the output flow at the egress of a network is needed given the initial bounding function of the input flow at the ingress.

8.1.2 Property of Token Bucket Shaper

Since the token bucket shaper is the first network element passed by an incoming flow to the network, the following theorems provide insights into the output burstiness of the token bucket shaper, which will be used for subsequent analysis of conformance deterioration analysis.

Theorem 8.2 (Property of Token Bucket Shaper). *Consider a shaping system with token bucket shaper (ρ, σ). Let $A(t)$ and $A^*(t)$ be the input process and output process of the system, respectively. Assume that $A(t) \sim_{mb} \langle f, \rho \rangle$. Then, for any $t \geq 0$,*

$$A^*(t) \sim_{mb} \langle g, \rho \rangle, \tag{8.1}$$

where

$$g(x) = \begin{cases} f(x) & \text{if } x \leq \sigma, \\ 0 & \text{if } x > \sigma. \end{cases} \tag{8.2}$$

Proof. Using a method similar to the proof of Theorem 5 in [140],

$$M^*(t;\rho) \leq M(t;\rho),$$

where $M(t;\rho)$ and $M^*(t;\rho)$ denote the maximum up-to-date queue length in the virtual constant server for the input process and output process, respectively. In addition, the output traffic is constrained by the token bucket regulator; i.e., $A^*(s,t) \leq \rho(t-s) + \sigma$. Hence,

$$M^*(t; \rho) = \sup_{0 \leq s \leq t} \sup_{0 \leq u \leq s} \{A^*(s, u) - \rho(u - s)\} \leq \sigma,$$

which implies that, for any $x > \sigma$, $P\{M^*(t; \rho) \geq x\} = 0$. This, together with the above, ends the proof. □

8.2 Conformance Study of Per-Flow Scheduling Network

This section studies conformance deterioration of a flow after crossing a per-flow scheduling network. To study the end-to-end conformance deterioration, the single-node case is considered first and then the results are extended to the multi-node case.

8.2.1 Single-Node Case

Theorem 5.21 in Chapter 5 derived the stochastic burstiness of the output flow after crossing a node that offers a stochastic service curve to the input flow with an m.b.c. stochastic arrival curve. Then, based on the relationship between stochastic burstiness and non-conformance derived in Theorem 8.1, one can immediately obtain the following theorem on the non-conformance probability of a flow after crossing a node that offers a service curve to the input flow.

Theorem 8.3 (Single-Node Non-conformance Probability Bound).
Assume that a node offers a deterministic service curve β to its input. Let $A(t)$ be the input process of the node. Assume that $A(t) \sim_{mb} \langle f, r \rangle$. The output flow is checked for its conformance by a token bucket meter with token generation rate r and token bucket depth σ_{th}. Let $P_{nonconf}(t)$ denote the probability that one packet is found to be OUT. Thus,

$$P_{nonconf}(t) \leq f(\sigma_{th} - \alpha \oslash \beta(0)), \tag{8.3}$$

where $\alpha(t) = rt$ and $\alpha \oslash \beta(0) = \sup_{s \geq 0}\{\alpha(s) - \beta(s)\}$.

Reference [53] presents another general server model, which is the guaranteed rate (GR) server model. It has been proven that many well-known schedulers belong to GR (e.g., see [68] and references therein), as mentioned earlier in Chapter 2. The behavior of a GR server is determined by two parameters: a rate R and an error term E. In [92], it was proven that a GR node has a rate-latency service curve $\beta(t)$: $\beta(t) = R(t - E - \frac{L_{\max,i}}{R})^+$, where $L_{\max,i}$ is the maximum packet size of the input flow. Therefore, the following corollary can be derived directly by using the service curve of a GR scheduler to analyze the stochastic burstiness increase of a flow after it passes through the GR scheduler.

Corollary 8.4 (Non-conformance Probability Bound under a GR Node). *Consider a GR node with rate R and error term E. Let $A(t)$ be the input process of the node. Assume that $A(t) \sim_{mb} \langle f, \rho \rangle$. The output flow is checked for its conformance by a token bucket meter with token generation rate ρ and token bucket depth σ_{th}. Let $P_{nonconf}(t)$ denote the probability that one packet is found to be OUT. Given $\rho \leq R$, for any $t > 0$,*

$$P_{nonconf}(t) \leq f\left(\sigma_{th} - \rho\left(E + \frac{L_{\max,i}}{R}\right)\right), \tag{8.4}$$

where $L_{\max,i}$ is the maximum packet size of the flow under consideration.

Remark. For a WFQ scheduler, the error term is $E = \frac{L_{\max}}{C}$, where C is its total capacity and the $L_{\max}$ is the maximum packet size among all flows in the same server. Hence, it has a rate-latency service curve $\beta(t) = R\left(t - E - \frac{L_{\max,i}}{R}\right)^{+}$. According to the corollary above under WFQ, the output traffic burstiness bounding function for an input flow with bounding function $f(x)$ will be $g(x) = f(x - \alpha \oslash \beta(0)) = f\left(x - \rho\left(\frac{L_{\max}}{C} + \frac{L_{\max,i}}{R}\right)\right)$. From this bounding function, it can be seen that, even for a WFQ scheduler that can provide service isolation among different service classes, if the packet size $L_{\max}$ of inter-class traffic is large enough compared with the packet size $L_{\max,i}$ of the flow under consideration, the effect of inter-class traffic on conformance deterioration of the flow considered cannot be ignored.

8.2.2 Multi-node Case

This section studies the conformance deterioration of a flow crossing a network of nodes in tandem. Suppose that there are a total of N nodes and each node i provides a service curve β_i to the flow. Then, according to the concatenation property of a deterministic service curve as shown in Chapter 2, the network provides to the flow a concatenated deterministic service curve to the flow that is given by

$$\beta_{net} = \beta_1 \otimes \beta_2 \cdots \otimes \beta_N. \tag{8.5}$$

With this concatenated deterministic service curve and Theorem 8.1, the following result is immediately obtained.

Theorem 8.5 (Multi-node Non-conformance Probability Bound). *Consider a flow crossing a path with N nodes in tandem, and each node i provides deterministic service curve β_i to the flow. Let $A(t)$ be the input process of the flow and $A(t) \sim_{mb} \langle f, r \rangle$. The output flow is checked for its conformance by a token bucket meter with token generation rate r and token bucket depth σ_{th}. Then, the non-conformance probability $P_{nonconf}(t)$ at the egress is bounded by*

$$P_{nonconf}(t) \leq f\left(\sigma_{th} - \alpha \oslash \beta_{net}(0)\right), \tag{8.6}$$

where $\alpha(t) = rt$ and $\beta_{net} = \beta_1 \otimes \beta_2 \cdots \otimes \beta_N$.

By using Theorem 8.2, the m.b.c. bounding function can be obtained for the input traffic after passing through the token bucket shaper at the ingress of the network. Then, the end-to-end non-conformance probability of the output flow at the egress of the network can be further obtained by applying Theorem 8.5.

8.3 Conformance Study of Aggregate Scheduling Network

To provide scalable support of QoS in a network, one method is to let each node in the network provide service to aggregates of flows. By doing this, the core node does not need to maintain per-flow state information. In such a network, each node performs aggregate scheduling instead of per-flow scheduling. This section first conducts conformance analysis for each flow within the aggregate under aggregate scheduling and then analyzes conformance deterioration for each aggregate.

8.3.1 Per-Flow in Single-Node Case

Following the same approach as in Section 8.2, this section studies the conformance deterioration by analyzing the stochastic burstiness increase of input flows, for which the per-flow service received by a flow within the aggregate is required. From Theorem 2.27 in Chapter 2, we have the following results. For a node serving two flows f and h, if the node guarantees a deterministic service curve β to the aggregate of the two flows and flow h has an arrival curve α^h, then the node offers to the flow f a deterministic service curve $\beta^f = \left(\beta - \alpha^h\right)^+$.

Based on this per-flow service curve, one can obtain a result on the per-flow stochastic burstiness increase under aggregate scheduling by applying this leftover deterministic service curve to results in Chapter 5. Note that the per-flow service curve used in this approach is a deterministic service curve that is derived under the assumption that all the input flows are deterministically bounded. In addition, the resulting bound on conformance deterioration is the worst-case bound. Since the traffic model used in this chapter is a stochastically bounded traffic model, it would be possible to get a more accurate characterization of the per-flow service in a stochastic form, which enables tighter bounds to be obtained in conformance analysis.

Theorem 8.6 (Per-Flow Stochastic Burstiness Bound under Deterministic Per-Flow Service Curve). *Consider a node providing a deterministic service curve β to two flows f and h, that are FIFO-aggregated. Let $A_i(t)$ and $A_i^*(t)$ be the flow i $(i = f, h)$ input process and output process of the node, respectively. Suppose that $A_f(t) \sim_{mb} \langle f^f, r^f \rangle$ and $A_h(t)$ is token bucket bounded by (r^h, σ^h). Then,*

$$A_f^*(t) \sim_{mb} \left\langle [g^f]_1, r^f \right\rangle \tag{8.7}$$

with

$$g^f(x) = f^f\left(x - \alpha^f \oslash \beta^f(0)\right), \tag{8.8}$$

where $\alpha^f(t) = r^f t$, $\beta^f = \left(\beta - \alpha^h\right)^+$.

Remark. Based on Theorem 8.6 on the per-flow stochastic burstiness and Theorem 8.1, the following result on the non-conformance probability bound is immediately obtained.

Theorem 8.7 (Per-Flow Non-conformance Bound under Deterministic Per-Flow Service Curve). *Consider a node providing a deterministic service curve β to two flows f and h that are FIFO-aggregated. Let $A_i(t)$ be the flow i ($i = f, h$) input process of the node. Suppose that $A_f(t) \sim_{mb} \left\langle f^f, r^f \right\rangle$ and $A_h(t)$ is token bucket bounded by (r^h, σ^h). The output flow is checked for its conformance by a token bucket meter with token generation rate r^f and token bucket depth σ_{th}. Let $P_{nonconf}(t)$ denote the probability that one packet is found to be OUT. Then,*

$$P_{nonconf}(t) = f^f\left(\sigma_{th} - \alpha^f \oslash \beta^f(0)\right), \tag{8.9}$$

where $\alpha^f(t) = r^f t$, $\beta^f = \left(\beta - \alpha^h\right)^+$.

Remark. The service curve used in this theorem is the worst-case leftover deterministic service curve within an aggregate under aggregate scheduling. However, if the cross traffic aggregated in same aggregate is stochastically bounded, one can have a tighter and more accurate characterization of the per-flow service received by a flow under aggregate scheduling, which is derived in Chapters 5 and 6. For this, we need to derive the stochastic leftover service curve, then derive the burstiness increase for the input processes, and then derive the non-conformance probabilities for these input processes after passing a server under aggregate scheduling.

Lemma 8.8 (Stochastic Per-Flow Service Curve under Aggregate Scheduling for General Case). *Consider a server fed with a flow A that is the aggregation of two constituent flows A_f and A_h. Suppose the server provides a deterministic service curve β to the aggregate flow A. If flow A_h has an m.b.c. stochastic arrival curve $A_h \sim_{mb} \left\langle f^h, r^h \right\rangle$ and $\beta^f \in \mathcal{F}$, then the server guarantees to flow A_f a stochastic service curve $S_f \sim_{sc} \left\langle f^h, \beta^f \right\rangle$, where*

$$\beta^f(t) = \beta(t) - r^h(t), \tag{8.10}$$
$$g^f(x) = f^h(x). \tag{8.11}$$

Proof. Theorem 5.42 in Chapter 5 obtained the following result on the per-flow stochastic service for a system with a stochastic service curve and m.b.c.

stochastic arrival curve. Then, flow f receives a per-flow stochastic service curve $\left(f^f, \beta^f\right)$ from the node with

$$\beta^f(t) = \beta(t) - r^h(t),$$
$$f^f(x) = f^h \otimes 0(x) = f^h(x).$$

$\square$

Lemma 8.8 shows that a deterministic server under aggregate scheduling can be considered a stochastic service providing a per-flow stochastic service curve to its input flows. Based on this per-flow stochastic service curve, we can derive the burstiness increase for these input processes.

Theorem 8.9 (Per-Flow Stochastic Burstiness Bound under Stochastic Per-Flow Service Curve for General Case). *Consider a node providing a deterministic service curve β to two flows f and h that are FIFO-aggregated. Let $A_i(t)$ and $A_i^*(t)$ be the flow i $(i = f, h)$ input process and output process of the node, respectively. Suppose that $A_h(t) \sim_{mb} \left\langle f^h, r^h \right\rangle$ and $A_f(t) \sim_{mb} \left\langle f^f, r^f \right\rangle$. Then, we have $A_f^*(t) \sim_{mb} \left\langle f^{f*}, r^{f*} \right\rangle$ with*

$$f^{f*}(x) = f^f \otimes f^h(x), \tag{8.12}$$
$$r^{f*}(t) = r^f(t) \oslash \left(\beta(t) - r^h(t)\right). \tag{8.13}$$

Proof. Based on the per-flow stochastic service derived in Lemma 8.8, the stochastic burstiness increase of a flow under aggregate scheduling can be derived according to Theorem 5.21 in Chapter 5. In this case, for any $t \geq 0$,

$$A_f^*(t) \sim_{mb} \left\langle f^{f*}, r^{f*} \right\rangle$$

with

$$r^{f*}(t) = r^f(t) \oslash \left(\beta(t) - r^h(t)\right),$$
$$f^{f*}(x) = f^f \otimes f^h(x).$$

$\square$

Note that the result above is derived under the case where it is not known whether the two input processes are independent or not. If the server can be modeled by a stochastic strict service curve and the service process is independent of the two independent input processes, we can have the following tighter results for the per-flow stochastic burstiness bound.

Lemma 8.10 (Stochastic Leftover Service Curve under Aggregate Scheduling for Independent Case). *Consider a server fed with a flow A that is the aggregation of two constituent independent flows A_f and A_h. Suppose the server provides a deterministic strict service curve β to the aggregate flow A. If flow A_h has the m.b.c. stochastic arrival curve $A_h \sim_{mb} \left\langle f^h, r^h \right\rangle$ and*

$\beta^f \in \mathcal{F}$, then flow f receives a stochastic strict service curve β with impairment process $I = A_h(t) - A_h(t - s)$. Then, the server guarantees to flow A_f stochastic service curve $S_f \sim_{sc} \langle f^h, \beta^f \rangle$, where

$$\beta^f(t) = \beta(t) - r^h(t), \tag{8.14}$$
$$g^f(x) = f^h(x). \tag{8.15}$$

Proof. According to the definition of a deterministic strict service curve, during any backlogged period $[s, t)$, we can have, for all $t \geq 0, A^*(t) \geq A(t - s) + \beta(s)$. Then

$$A_f^*(t) + A_h^*(t) \geq \beta(s) + A_f(t - s) + A_h(t - s).$$

Since $A_h^*(t) \leq A_h(t)$,

$$A_f^*(t) - A_f(t - s) \geq \beta(s) - (A_h(t) - A_h(t - s)).$$

Since $A_f^*(t - s) \leq A_f(t - s)$, we have

$$A_f^*(t) - A_f^*(t - s) \geq \beta(s) - (A_h(t) - A_h(t - s)).$$

Then, according to the definition of a stochastic strict service curve in Definition 4.11 in Chapter 4, flow f receives a *stochastic strict service curve* β with *impairment process* $I = A_h(t) - A_h(t - s)$.

In addition, we have $A_h(t) \sim_{mb} \langle f^h, r^h \rangle$. According to Lemma 8.8, the server provides a stochastic service curve $S^f \sim_{sc} \langle f^h, \beta^f \rangle$ for flow f with

$$\beta^f(t) = \beta(t) - r^h(t).$$

$\square$

Theorem 8.11 (Per-Flow Stochastic Burstiness Bound under Stochastic Per-Flow Service Curve for Independent Case).

Consider a node providing a deterministic strict service curve β to two independent flows f and h that are FIFO-aggregated. Let $A_i(t)$ and $A_i^*(t)$ be the flow i $(i = f, h)$ input process and output process of the node, respectively. Suppose that $A_h(t) \sim_{mb} \langle f^h, r^h \rangle$ and $A_f(t) \sim_{mb} \langle f^f, r^f \rangle$. Then, we have $A_f^*(t) \sim_{mb} \langle f^{f*}, r^{f*} \rangle$ with

$$r^{f*}(t) = r^f(t) \oslash (\beta(t) - r^h(t)), \tag{8.16}$$
$$f^{f*}(x) = 1 - \bar{f}^f * \bar{f}^h(x), \tag{8.17}$$

where $\bar{f}^f(x) = 1 - [f^f(x)]_1$ and $\bar{f}^h(x) = 1 - [f^h(x)]_1$.

Proof. Based on the leftover stochastic service curve obtained in Lemma 8.10, the stochastic burstiness increase of a flow under aggregate scheduling can be derived according to Theorem 6.5 in Chapter 6. In this case, for any $t \geq 0$,

$$A_f^*(t) \sim_{mb} \langle f^{f*}, r^{f*} \rangle$$

with

$$r^{f*}(t) = r^f(t) \oslash (\beta(t) - r^h(t)),$$
$$f^{f*}(x) = 1 - \bar{f}^f * \bar{f}^h(x),$$

where $\bar{f}^f(x) = 1 - [f^f(x)]_1$ and $\bar{f}^h(x) = 1 - [f^h(x)]_1$. $\square$

With Theorem 8.1, the following results on non-conformance probability bound follow from Theorems 8.9 and 8.11.

Theorem 8.12 (Per-Flow Non-conformance Probability Bound under Aggregation for General Case). *Consider a node providing a service curve β to two flows f and h that are FIFO-aggregated. Let $A(t)$ be the input process of the node. Suppose that $A_h(t) \sim_{mb} \langle f^h, r^h \rangle$ and $A_f(t) \sim_{mb} \langle f^f, r^f \rangle$. The output of flow f is checked for its conformance by a token bucket meter with token generation rate r^f and token bucket depth σ_{th}. Let $P_{nonconf}(t)$ denote the probability that one packet is found to be OUT. Then*

$$P_{nonconf}(t) \leq f^f \otimes f^h \left(\sigma_{th} - \alpha^f \oslash \beta^f(0) \right), \tag{8.18}$$

where $\alpha^f(s) = r^f s$, $\alpha^f \oslash \beta^f(0) = \sup_{s \geq 0} \{\alpha^f(s) - \beta^f(s)\}$, and $\beta^f(s) = \beta(s) - r^h s$.

Theorem 8.13 (Per-Flow Non-conformance Probability Bound under Aggregation for Independent Case). *Consider a node providing a service curve β to two flows f and h that are FIFO-aggregated. Let $A(t)$ be the input process of the node. Suppose that $A_h(t) \sim_{mb} \langle f^h, r^h \rangle$ and $A_f(t) \sim_{mb} \langle f^f, r^f \rangle$. The output of flow f is checked for its conformance by a token bucket meter with token generation rate r^f and token bucket depth σ_{th}. Let $P_{nonconf}(t)$ denote the probability that one packet is found to be OUT. If the flows f and h are independent of each other, then*

$$P_{nonconf}(t) \leq 1 - \bar{f}^f * \bar{f}^h \left(\sigma_{th} - \alpha^f \oslash \beta^f(0) \right), \tag{8.19}$$

where $\alpha^f(t) = r^f t$, $\alpha^f \oslash \beta^f(0) = \sup_{s \geq 0} \{\alpha^f(s) - \beta^f(s)\}$, $\beta^f(s) = \beta(s) - r^h s$, $\bar{f}^f(\sigma) = 1 - [f^f(\sigma)]_1$, and $\bar{f}^h(\sigma) = 1 - [f^h(\sigma)]_1$.

Remark. When the per-flow non-conformance probability in the first server is analyzed, Theorem 8.13 can be used since the two flows are independent of each other. However, when they exit the first server, the result derived for the general case in Theorem 8.12 needs to be used to analyze the non-conformance probability in subsequent servers since they will no longer be independent of one another when they exit the server.

8.3.2 Per-Flow in Multi-node Case

As shown earlier, a series of stochastic service curves and stochastic strict service curves in tandem can be concatenated as a network stochastic service curve. Combining these results with the results derived above on the non-conformance probability bounds for the single-node case, we can have the following results on multi-node non-conformance probability bounds for the general case and independent case, respectively.

Theorem 8.14 (Multi-node Non-conformance Probability Bound for General Case). *Consider a flow f crossing a path with N nodes in tandem, and each node i provides a service curve β^i to the flows f and h_i, which are FIFO-aggregated. Suppose that $A_{h_i}(t) \sim_{mb} \langle f^{h_i}, r^{h_i} \rangle$ and $A_f(t) \sim_{mb} \langle f^f, r^f \rangle$. The output flow from the system is checked for its conformance by a token bucket meter with token generation rate r and token bucket depth σ_{th}. Then, the non-conformance probability $P_{nonconf}(t)$ is bounded by*

$$P_{nonconf}(t)$$
$$\leq f^f \otimes f^{h_1} \otimes \cdots \otimes f^{h_N} \left(\sigma - \alpha^f \oslash \left(\beta^{f_1} \otimes \cdots \otimes \beta^{f_N} \right)(0) \right), \qquad (8.20)$$

where $\alpha^f(t) \equiv r^f t$, and $\beta^{f_i}(t) = \beta^i(t) - r^{h_i}(t)$, $i = 1, \cdots, N$.

For a special case where all cross flows along the end-to-end path is independent with the flow of interested, a tighter bound can be obtained in the same way as Theorem 8.13.

Theorem 8.15 (Multi-Node Non-Conformance Probability Bound for Independent Case). *Consider a flow f crossing a path with N nodes in tandem and the i-th node providing a service curve β^i to two flows f and h_i that are FIFO-aggregated. Suppose that $A_{h_i}(t) \sim_{mb} \langle f^{h_i}, r^{h_i} \rangle$ and $A_f(t) \sim_{mb} \langle f^f, r^f \rangle$. The output flow f from the system is checked for its conformance by a token bucket meter with token generation rate r and token bucket depth σ_{th}. Then the non-conformance probability $P_{nonconf}(t)$ of flow f is bounded by*

$$P_{nonconf}(t) \leq 1 - \bar{f}^f * \bar{f}^{h_1} * \cdots * \bar{f}^{h_N} \left(\sigma - \alpha^f \oslash \left(\beta^{f_1} \otimes \cdots \otimes \beta^{f_N} \right)(0) \right), \quad (8.21)$$

where $\bar{f}^f(t) = 1 - \left[f^f(t) \right]_1$, $\bar{f}^{h_i} = 1 - \left[f^{h_i} \right]_1$, $\alpha^f(t) \equiv r^f t$, and $\beta^{f_i}(t) = \beta^i(t) - r^{h_i}(t)$, $i = 1, \cdots, N$.

The results presented in this section provide an approach for analyzing conformance deterioration of a flow after crossing an aggregate scheduling network. In particular, as illustrated in Figure 8.2, the procedures are as follows.

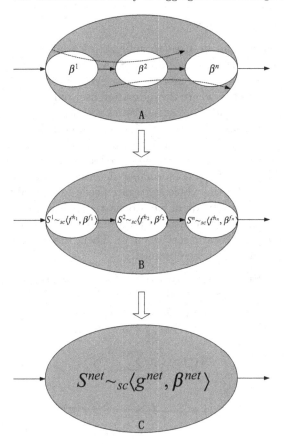

Fig. 8.2. Aggregate scheduling in multi-node case

Procedures to obtain the end-to-end non-conformance probability bound:

1. Determine the initial bounding functions f^f for the stochastic burstiness of flow f under consideration with rate r^f and each cross-flow in the same aggregate at each hop along the end-to-end path with rate r^{h_i}.

2. Determine the bounding functions for the stochastic burstiness of flow f after passing through a token bucket shaper according to Theorem 8.2.

3. Convert each aggregate scheduling server (providing a service curve to the aggregate) to a per-flow scheduling server (providing a stochastic service curve to the flow) according to Theorems 8.8 or 8.10 for general case or independent case, respectively.

4. Obtain the end-to-end non-conformance probability bound according to Theorems 8.14 or 8.15 for the general case or independent case, respectively.

8.3.3 Per-Aggregate Case

All the results above can be used to analyze the conformance deterioration of an individual flow when it negotiates SLAs with networks along its end-to-end path. However, there is another service configuration mentioned in the beginning of this chapter, where the individual user only establishes SLA with its first access network and the access network will negotiate a bulk SLA for its corresponding aggregate of flows with its next intermediate network. When such an aggregate exits the first network and enters the next network, the aggregate will be checked for its conformance based on the bulk SLA between these two domains. To study conformance deterioration in this scenario, the stochastic burstiness for the whole aggregate needs to be analyzed. According the superposition property of m.b.c stochastic arrival curve, an aggregate of flows with the m.b.c. stochastic arrival curves can be considered as one flow with an m.b.c. stochastic service curve. Then, the following result for an aggregate with N flows can be obtained.

Theorem 8.16 (Stochastic Burstiness for an Aggregate). *Consider an aggregate that consists of N flows with input process $A_i(t)$, $(i = 1, \ldots, N)$. Assume that, for each flow i, $A_i(t) \sim_{mb} \langle f_i, r_i \rangle$. Let $A(t) = \sum_{i=1}^{N} A_i(t)$ be the input process of the aggregate. Then, for any $t \geq 0$,*

$$A(t) \sim \left\langle g, \sum_{i=1}^{i=N} r_i \right\rangle, \tag{8.22}$$

where

$$g(\sigma) = f_1 \otimes f_2 \otimes \cdots \otimes f_N(\sigma), \tag{8.23}$$

If all the flows in the aggregate are independent of each other,

$$g(\sigma) = 1 - \bar{f}_1 * \bar{f}_2 * \cdots * \bar{f}_N(\sigma) \tag{8.24}$$

where $\bar{f}_i(\sigma) = 1 - [f_i(\sigma)]_1$ for $i = 1, 2 \cdots N$.

Similarly, with the result above and Theorem 8.1, one can obtain a non-conformance probability bound for the aggregate of flows.

Corollary 8.17 (Non-conformance Probability Bound for an Aggregate). *Consider an aggregate that consists of N flows with input process $A_i(t)$, $(i = 1, \ldots, N)$. Assume, for each flow i, $A_i(t) \sim_{mb} \langle f_i, r_i \rangle$. The aggregate is checked for its conformance by a token bucket meter with token generation rate $\sum_{i=1}^{i=N} r_i$ and token bucket depth σ_{th}. Then, the non-conformance probability $P_{nonconf}(t)$ is bounded by*

$$P_{nonconf}(t) \leq f_1 \otimes f_2 \cdots \otimes f_N(\sigma_{th}). \tag{8.25}$$

If all the flows in the aggregate are independent of each other,

$$P_{nonconf}(t) \leq 1 - \bar{f}_1 * \bar{f}_2 \cdots * \bar{f}_N(\sigma_{th}), \tag{8.26}$$

where $f_i(\sigma) = 1 - \bar{f}_i(\sigma)$, for $i = 1, 2 \cdots N$.

8.4 Simulation Results

In this section, the analytical results are verified with simulations using ns-2 [106]. Figure 8.3 shows the network topology used in simulation, which was also used in [57], where traffic is sent from source S_i to destination D_i. There are two classes of traffic competing for resources at each node, which is a GR server implementing the WFQ scheduler. Traffic from sources S_{2i+1}, $i = 0, 1, 2$, belongs to class 1 and traffic from sources $S_{2i}, i = 1, 2$, belongs to class 2 at each node. Before entering the network, traffic from each source S_{2i+1} is shaped by a token bucket shaper to conform to a certain specification. The conformance deterioration of flow F_1 from S_1 to D_1 is investigated. The conformance of flow F_1 is checked at the output port R_3 to D_1 of node R_3 using a token bucket meter. For simplicity, Poisson sources are used for flows in traffic class 1 from S_{2i+1} to D_{2i+1}, and exponential ON/OFF sources are used for flows in traffic class 2 from S_{2i} to D_{2i} in the experiments. The theoretical results on the conformance deterioration probability for the Poisson input flow are verified. In [35], it has been shown that the queue length distribution of a Poisson traffic input with mean arrival rate λ in a constant-rate server with server rate ρ satisfies

$$\Pr(B(\infty) > x) = 1 - \left(1 - \frac{\lambda}{\rho}\right) \sum_{n=0}^{x} \frac{[\frac{\lambda}{\rho}(n - x)]^n}{n!} e^{-\frac{\lambda}{\rho}(n-x)}. \qquad (8.27)$$

Clearly, by definition, Poisson traffic has a v.b.c. stochastic arrival curve whose bounding function is given by (8.27). Since the Poisson process is i.i.d., according to (3.38), Poisson traffic also has an m.b.c. stochastic arrival curve with the same bounding function given by (8.27). Therefore, the non-conformance probability bound of a Poisson traffic flow after crossing the network can be obtained by applying this bounding function to the results derived in Sections 8.2 and 8.3.

8.4.1 Per-Flow Scheduling Network in Single-Node Case

The first experiment considers the single-node case. In this case, there are only $S_1, S_2, R_1, R_2, D_1, D_2$ in the simulated network shown in Figure 8.3. Server R_1 guarantees per-flow service to flow F_1 from S_1 to D_1 since there is no other cross traffic in traffic class 1 for flow F_1. This scenario investigates the stochastic burstiness increase of flow F_1 after it passes one WFQ node R_1. Poisson source S_1 generates flow F_1 at an average rate of 45 pkts/sec. The size of each packet from flow F_1 is fixed at 128 bytes. Therefore, the average sending rate of flow F_1 is 45 kbps. For the flow F_2 from S_2 to D_2 in traffic class 2, an ON/OFF source is used that has an average sending rate of 50 kbps and packet size 5 times that of flow F_1. Only the flow F_1 is shaped by a token bucket shaper, whose token generation rate is 50 kbps and bucket depth is 15 tokens. The token size in all experiments is 128 bytes. The access

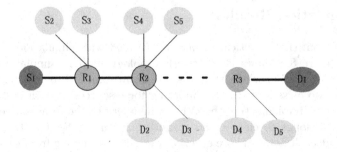

Fig. 8.3. Network topology used in simulation

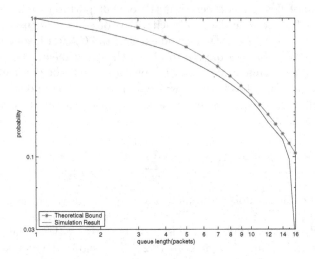

Fig. 8.4. Queue length tail distribution after crossing a single node in a per-flow scheduling network

link capacity of link S_1 to R_1 is 10 Mbps. The network core link capacity of R_1 to R_2 is 200 kbps and the weight ratio between class 1 and class 2 is 1 : 1 for the WFQ node in the core network. Flow F_1 belongs to class 1 and F_2 belongs to class 2. The link capacity of the last hop is 50 kbps. The last hop R_2 to D_1 for F_1 is a constant-rate server, since there is no other traffic sharing this link, that has the same rate as the token generation rate of the token bucket shaper. The queuing length distribution at this hop is the virtual queuing length distribution for flow F_1, which is used to measure the stochastic burstiness of the output traffic.

Figure 8.4 shows the simulated queue length tail distribution of flow F_1 at the last hop, where the theoretical bound is obtained by substituting x with $x - \rho \left(T + \frac{L_{max,1}}{R} \right)$ in (8.27) according to Corollary 8.4. For a WFQ scheduler

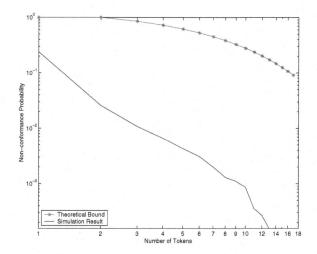

Fig. 8.5. Non-conformance probability after crossing a single node in a per-flow scheduling network

here, $T = \frac{L\max}{C}$, where C is its total capacity and $L_{\max}$ is the maximum packet size among all flows in the same server. $L_{\max,1}$ is the maximum packet size for F_1 and R is the reserved rate for F_1. The unit for the queue length is a packet that has the same size as the packets from flow F_1. As can be seen from the figure, although flow F_1 becomes more bursty after passing through node R_1 since its virtual queue length exceeds the token bucket depth 15, its burstiness increase remains bounded by the theoretical result.

Next, the result for the non-conformance probability bound is verified. Figure 8.5 shows the simulated non-conformance probability and its theoretical bound. For this, a token bucket meter with the same token generation rate (50 kbps) as the token bucket shaper is placed at the last hop of flow F_1 to check its conformance. The same experiment settings described above were adopted, except that the bucket depth of the token bucket shaper at the ingress and the token bucket meter at the last hop were changed in order to investigate the effect on the non-conformance probability of flow F_1. Note that the token bucket shaper at the ingress node and the token bucket meter at the last hop have the same parameters in all experiments in order to check conformance for the considered flow F_1. To obtain the non-conformance probability bound, the following procedures are used:

1. Determine the initial bounding function for the input flow F_1 with rate $r = 50$ kbps by using Equation (8.27).

2. Determine the bounding functions for the stochastic burstiness of the flow under consideration after passing through a token bucket shaper according to Theorem 8.2.

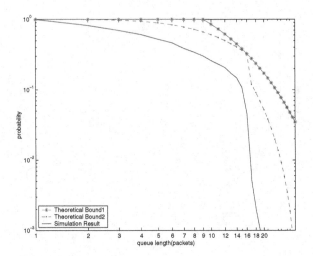

Fig. 8.6. Queue length tail distribution after crossing a single node in an aggregate scheduling network

3. Obtain the non-conformance probability bound for different token bucket depths σ_{th} by using the inequality (8.4) in Corollary 8.4.

Figure 8.5 shows the simulated non-conformance probability and its theoretical bound.

8.4.2 Aggregate Scheduling Network in Single-Node Case

The second experiment considers the single node case in an aggregate scheduling network. In this experiment, all other settings are exactly the same as in the first experiment except that a cross flow F_3 from S_3 to D_3 with the same source setting (including token bucket shaping) as flow F_1 enters the network and competes for resources with flows F_1 and F_2 at the WFQ node R_1. F_1 and F_3 are aggregated in the same class (class 1) to verify the analytical results on the aggregate scheduling network. Flow F_2 belongs to class 2.

Figure 8.6 shows the simulated queue length distribution of flow F_1 at its last hop. The theoretical bound 2 is obtained by Theorem 8.11, in which the stochastic service curve is derived from Lemma 8.10. The theoretical bound 1 in Figure 8.6 is derived from Theorem 8.6. Figure 8.6 shows that the theoretical bound 2 is tighter than the theoretical bound 1. This results from the fact that Theorem 8.11 makes use of the stochastic service curve offered to flow F_1 by the WFQ node under aggregate scheduling, which can be derived from Lemma 8.10. In contrast, Theorem 8.6 uses the worst-case service curve offered to the flow by the node under aggregate scheduling, which was derived based on results from Theorem 2.27.

Next, the result for the non-conformance probability bound is verified with the same experiment settings described above except that the bucket depth of

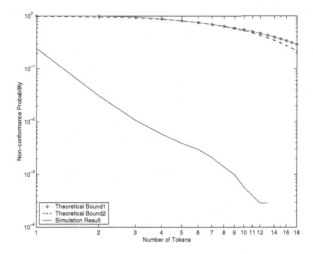

Fig. 8.7. Non-conformance probability after crossing a single node in an aggregate scheduling network

the token bucket shaper at the ingress node and the token bucket meter at the last hop are changed in order to investigate the effect on the non-conformance probability of flow F_1. For the same reason as mentioned above, Figure 8.7 shows that the theoretical non-conformance probability bound 2 is also tighter than the theoretical non-conformance probability bound 1.

8.4.3 Aggregate Scheduling Network in Multi-node Case

In the third experiment, the simulated network topology is exactly the same as that shown in Figure 8.3. Traffic from sources S_{2i+1}, $i = 0, 1, 2$, belongs to class 1 and traffic from sources S_{2i}, $i = 1, 2$, belongs to class 2 in each node. All other settings are the same as in the experiments discussed above except that Poisson sources S_{2i+1} generate flow F_{2i+1} at an average rate of 45 pkts/sec and exponential ON/OFF flows F_{2i} from S_{2i} to D_{2i} have an average sending rate of 50 kbps and packet size five times that of flow F_{2i+1}. The stochastic burstiness increase of flow F_1 is explored to verify the analytical results on aggregate scheduling in the multi-node case.

Figure 8.8 shows that after passing through two WFQ nodes, flow 1 becomes more bursty since the simulated result shows that, at its last hop, the queue length, which implies burstiness, can be larger than 15, the depth of the token bucket shaper. Nevertheless, the simulation results are bounded by the theoretical bound 1 derived from Theorem 8.6 and theoretical bound 2 derived from Theorem 8.11 by applying (8.27) to these two theorems. For the same reason as explained in the second experiment above, theoretical bound 2 is shown to be tighter than theoretical bound 1, as expected.

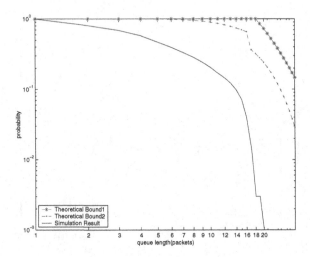

Fig. 8.8. Queue length tail distribution after crossing multi-nodes in an aggregate scheduling network

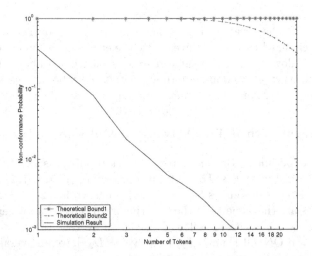

Fig. 8.9. Non-conformance probability after crossing multi-nodes in an aggregate scheduling network

The result on the non-conformance probability bound is also verified with the same experiment settings, except that the bucket depth of the token bucket shaper at the ingress node and the token bucket meter at the last hop are changed in order to investigate the effect on the non-conformance probability of flow F_1. To obtain the non-conformance probability bound, the following procedures are used:

1. Determine the initial bounding functions for the stochastic burstiness of F_1 with rate 50 kbps and each cross-flow with rate $r^{h_i} = 50$ kbps according to (8.27).

2. Determine the bounding functions for the stochastic burstiness of F_1 after passing through a token bucket shaper according to Theorem 8.2.

3. Convert each aggregate scheduling server (providing a service curve to the aggregate) to a per-flow scheduling server (providing a stochastic service curve to the flow) according to Lemma 8.10.

4. Obtain the end-to-end non-conformance probability bound for different token bucket depths σ_{th} by using the inequality (8.21) in Theorem 8.15.

Figure 8.9 shows the non-conformance probability of flow F_1 after passing through two WFQ nodes and the corresponding theoretical bounds. It is shown that the theoretical bound 1 derived from Theorem 8.6 is close to 1, which is overly conservative. The reason is that Theorem 8.6 uses the worst-case deterministic per-flow service curve and each server will make the original burstiness bounding function of flow F_1 shift to the right by some constant amount according to Theorem 8.6 and then the bound will be 1 in the range between 0 and the accumulation of the constant amount. Therefore, if the accumulation of the constant amount due to shifting is greater than the token bucket depth, the non-conformance deterioration probability bound derived from Theorem 8.6 will be close to 1, which is overly conservative and indeed useless as a bound. On the other hand, since the theoretical bound 2 derived from Theorem 8.11 makes use of the stochastic service curve instead of the worse case deterministic service curve, the bound is tighter than the theoretical bound 1.

8.5 Summary and Bibliographic Comments

In this chapter, we have analytically studied the conformance deterioration problem in networks with service level agreements. We first established the relationship between conformance deterioration and the stochastic burstiness increase of a flow. Then, based on the analysis in previous chapters, the stochastic characterization of the flow was utilized to analyze the stochastic burstiness increase in a per-flow scheduling network and an aggregate scheduling network.

To investigate the stochastic per-flow burstiness increase for individual flows in the aggregate scheduling network, we also investigated the stochastic behavior of a server providing deterministic service to the aggregate of flows.

As discussed in Chapters 5 and 6, an aggregate scheduling server providing a service curve to an aggregate can be regarded as a per-flow scheduling server providing a stochastic service curve to each individual flow in the aggregate. This has helped improve the bound on conformance deterioration. Furthermore, we have applied the concatenation property for analysis of stochastic burstiness increase. These results are not only useful for the analysis of the situation presented in this chapter but also shed some light on conformance analysis in aggregate scheduling networks with other general topologies.

As shown by the simulation results in Section 8.4, there is still some room for improvement on the non-conformance probability bound. The non-conformance probability bound may be improved by further research. Note that Figures 8.4, 8.6, and 8.8 show that the theoretical bounds on the queue length tail distribution of output flows in the virtual queuing system are close to the simulation results. However, the non-conformance probability checked by the token bucket meter is bounded by the probability that the queue length of the output flow in the virtual queuing system exceeds the token bucket depth, as shown in Theorem 8.1. Therefore, the major cause for the looseness of the non-conformance bounds is the difference between the non-conformance probability and the probability that the queue length in the virtual queuing system exceeds a certain threshold. Further study on the differences between the token bucket meter and the virtual queuing system may lead to a much tighter non-conformance probability bound.

The content of this chapter is mainly based on [99] by Liu, Tham and Jiang. The problem of conformance deterioration was initially investigated by Guerin and Pla [57] through extensive simulations. They studied the conformance deterioration caused by interactions among flows aggregated in the same traffic class. Both per-flow and per-aggregate conformance deterioration were investigated in [57]. The authors observed through simulations the impact of link load, number of cross flows and number of hops traversed by the flow on conformance deterioration. However, [57] does not provide any analytical study on what is the extent to which a flow becomes non-conformant after crossing a network.

Besides [57], there are several other works addressing related issues that use different methods. The work in [56] investigated the distortion of a constant bit rate (CBR) flow when it is aggregated with other flows after crossing several network elements. The work in [120] extended the results in [56] to consider the same issue with variable packet sizes. Another related work is [97], which studied conformance deterioration in a single-node case, a radio access network under the UMTS framework.

Problems

8.1. Prove Theorem 8.6.

8.2. Consider a system with the same setting as the example shown in Section 8.4.1 except that each flow has the same $m.b.c.$ stochastic arrival curve, $\langle e^{-0.25t}, 50\text{kbps}\rangle$. Find the non-conformance probability for F_1.

8.3. Consider a system with the same setting as the example shown in Section 8.4.2 except that each flow has the same $m.b.c.$ stochastic arrival curve, $\langle e^{-0.25t}, 50\text{kbps}\rangle$. Find the non-conformance probability for F_1.

8.4. Consider a system with the same setting as the example shown in Section 8.4.3 except that each flow has the same $m.b.c.$ stochastic arrival curve, $\langle e^{-0.25t}, 50\text{kbps}\rangle$. Find the non-conformance probability for F_1.

8.5. For the system shown in Problem 8.2, if there is an impairment process I for the server, assume $I \sim_{mb} \langle e^{-0.25t}, 50\text{kbps}\rangle$. Find the non-conformance probability for F_1.

8.6. For the system shown in Problem 8.3, if there is an impairment process I for the server, assume $I \sim_{mb} \langle e^{-0.25t}, 50\text{kbps}\rangle$. Find the non-conformance probability for F_1.

8.7. For the system shown in Problem 8.4, if there is an impairment process I for each server, assume $I \sim_{mb} \langle e^{-0.25t}, 50\text{kbps}\rangle$. Find the non-conformance probability for F_1.

8.8. Under the same condition as in Theorem 8.12 except that β is a strict service curve and there is an impairment process $I \sim_{mb} \langle f_i, \alpha_i \rangle$ for the server, find the non-conformance probability for flow f.

8.9. Under the same condition as in Theorem 8.13 except that β is a strict service curve and there is an independent impairment process $I \sim_{mb} \langle f_i, \alpha_i \rangle$ for the server, find the non-conformance probability for flow f.

9

LRD Isolation in Generalized Processor Sharing

This chapter introduces the application of stochastic network calculus to analysis of queuing processes in generalized processor sharing (GPS) and packet-based GPS (PGPS) systems with long-range dependent (LRD) traffic inputs.

The GPS discipline is a widely studied non-FIFO scheduling discipline [84], due to its attractive characteristics. One is that each backlogged session is guaranteed a minimum service rate in GPS. This ensures that the misbehavior of other flows has a limited effect on an individual session, and provides the foundation of isolation between sessions. Achieving isolation further enables GPS to guarantee differentiated QoS for individual sessions. Another attractive characteristic of GPS is that it is work-conserving and any excess service rate can be redistributed among backlogged flows. The second characteristic enables GPS to obtain a statistical multiplexing gain between input flows. Because of these two characteristics, GPS is deemed an ideal scheduling discipline that meets the following two requirements. One is to provide isolation between flows, where isolation means that the queuing process behaves no worse than its single server queue (SSQ) process with a comparable service rate. This guarantees that the scheduling discipline is able to protect an individual flow against misbehavior from other flows. The other is to realize a statistical multiplexing gain. This suggests that a flow can utilize excess service rate allocated to other flows. When GPS is extended to packet-switched networks, it is usually referred to as weighted fair queuing (WFQ)[33] or packet-based GPS (PGPS) [113].

Long-range dependent (LRD) traffic is an important class of traffic in modern-day networks because long-range dependency is exhibited in many types of networks and network traffic, such as Ethernet [94], WWW [27], compressed video traffic [9, 62], and TCP traffic [48]. Since LRD traffic has burstiness extending over various timescales, a Weibull bound rather than a conventional exponential bound is usually associated with LRD traffic's single-server queue process [55].

By applying the results from previous chapters, this chapter studies the queuing behavior of a single-server system, where the GPS discipline is

Y. Jiang, Y. Liu, *Stochastic Network Calculus*,
DOI: 10.1007/978-1-84800-127-5_9,
© Springer-Verlag London Limited 2008

adopted and the inputs are LRD flows. In particular, we derive two bounds for individual queuing processes in the GPS system. Complimenting the analysis on GPS in Section 7.3.4, these bounds provide valuable insights into the isolation between multiple GPS sessions. More specifically, it is shown that the index parameter in the upper bound of one LRD flow, in addition to the decay rate and the asymptotic constant, may be affected by other LRD flows. In addition, a necessary and sufficient condition for a flow being guaranteed to be *LRD-isolated* from other flows is derived. Based on this condition, a technique that can be used to quickly check if a flow can be guaranteed to be LRD-isolated from other flows with a given GPS service weight assignment is introduced. When some flows have already been assigned contract weights according to some service level agreement (SLA) that cannot be changed, the introduced technique can also be used to determine the minimum contract weight to be assigned to the flow in order for it to be guaranteed to be LRD-isolated from other flows.

9.1 Introduction

In this section, we briefly review the fundamental knowledge on the GPS scheduling discipline and the queue length distribution of LRD traffic. Their relations with that arrival curve and service curve are also shown to facilitate the analysis based on results from the earlier chapters.

9.1.1 GPS Fundamentals

Generalized processor sharing (GPS) is a scheduling discipline defined under the assumption that sources are described by fluid models [143]. Consider a GPS server with rate γ serving N sessions. Let each session i be assigned a weight parameter that is a fixed real-valued positive number ϕ_i. The set $\{\phi_1, \phi_2, ..., \phi_N\}$ thus represents the GPS assignment. Each session is assumed to have its dedicated queue. The N sessions share the server in the following way [113], as also introduced in Section 7.3.4:

- It is work-conserving; i.e., as long as there are packets backlogged in any of the GPS queues, the server is never idle.
- The excess service rate, if any, is redistributed among the backlogged sessions in proportion to their weight parameters.
- Let $S_k(s, t)$ denote the amount of traffic served in the time interval $[s, t]$ for session k. If session i is backlogged in the system during the entire interval $[s, t]$ (i.e., there is always traffic queued for session i), then

$$\frac{S_i(s, t)}{S_j(s, t)} \geq \frac{\phi_i}{\phi_j}, \quad j = 1, 2, ..., N. \tag{9.1}$$

From (9.1), it is clear that when session i is backlogged, it is guaranteed a backlog clearing rate (or equivalently a guaranteed service rate) of at least

$$\gamma_i = \frac{\phi_i}{\sum_{j=1}^{N} \phi_j} \gamma. \tag{9.2}$$

As shown in Table 2.1 in Chapter 2, it is easy to verify that the GPS server provides to flow i a deterministic strict service curve $\beta_i(t) = \frac{\phi_i}{\sum_{j=1}^{N} \phi_j} \gamma t$.

Let the arrival process for a stationary GPS session i be $A_i(t)$ with long-term average rate λ_i. Assume $\sum_{i=1}^{N} \lambda_i < \gamma$.

In order to characterize the effect of backlogs from a set of sessions, the concept of the so-called *feasible ordering* [143] of the sessions will be frequently referred to hereafter and is defined based on their arrival rates and GPS service weight parameters as follows [113].

Definition 9.1. *For a given set of input traffic flows in a GPS system whose long-term average rate is λ_i, an ordering is called a feasible ordering among the sessions with respect to $\{\lambda_1, \lambda_2, ..., \lambda_N\}$ and GPS service weight parameters $\{\phi_1, \phi_2, ..., \phi_N\}$ if*

$$\lambda_i < \varphi_i \left(\gamma - \sum_{j=1}^{i-1} \lambda_j \right), \quad 1 \leq i \leq N, \tag{9.3}$$

where $\varphi_i = \frac{\phi_i}{\sum_{j=i}^{N} \phi_j}$ is a constant associated with weight parameters and by convention, $\sum_{j=1}^{i-1} \lambda_j = 0$ when $i = 1$.

Note that one of the results of feasible ordering is that for a given set of input traffic flows in a GPS server with $\sum_{i=1}^{N} \lambda_i < \gamma$ there always exists at least one feasible ordering that satisfies (9.3) after being relabeled (e.g., see [143]).

Also note that the right-hand side of (9.3) can be considered as the service rate available to flow i. It is clear, by definition, that those flows ordered earlier than flow i will affect the service rate available to flow i. However, they will not affect the index parameter of the queuing process of a heavier-tailed LRD flow i, as will be explained later in more detail.

9.1.2 LRD Traffic Characterization

LRD traffic is often characterized by heavy traffic bursts that extend over a wide range of timescales [114] [132]. The LRD traffic backlog, buffered within a singe-server queue (SSQ), often possesses a tail distribution that decays slower than that of traditional (e.g., Poisson) traffic. More specifically, the queue length distribution of traditional traffic obeys a certain exponential form. For the case of LRD traffic, the Weibull distribution has been used to characterize the slower decaying SSQ distribution [9] [37] [116].

The queue length distribution, which is Weibull bounded (WB), is defined as follows [109].

Definition 9.2. *A stochastic SSQ process, denoted by $W^{SSQ,\gamma}(t)$, where γ is the service rate of the queue, is WB(C, η, υ) with parameters $C(> 0)$ denoting the asymptotic constant, $\eta(> 0)$ denoting the decay rate, and $(0 <)\upsilon(\leq 1)$ denoting the index parameter, if it satisfies*

$$P\{W^{SSQ,\gamma}(t) > w\} < Ce^{-\eta w^{\upsilon}} \tag{9.4}$$

for all $w \geq 0$ and all $t \geq 0$.

In Definition 9.2, the quantity $P\{W^{SSQ,\gamma}(t) > w\}$ essentially represents the probability that the backlog of the SSQ with service rate γ will exceed a certain queue size w. In other words, $P\{W^{SSQ,\gamma}(t) > w\}$ represents the queue length distribution of the SSQ. In addition, the decay rate η increases with γ because when the service rate increases, the likelihood that the queue length exceeds w will decrease. Also, the index parameter υ can be further expressed in terms of the Hurst parameter H, which is commonly used to characterize the degree of long-range dependence [9] [37] [116] and, more specifically, $\upsilon = 2(1 - H)$, where $0.5 \leq H < 1$. A traffic process with $H = 0.5$ corresponds to conventional traffic with a queue length distribution that decays exponentially. A larger H, or a smaller υ, corresponds to heavier-tailed LRD traffic.

The definition of WB shows that it is indeed a special case of a gSBB or v.b.c. stochastic arrival curve with bounding function $Ce^{-\eta w^{\upsilon}}$. Therefore, WB has all properties of a gSBB and v.b.c. stochastic arrival curve.

9.1.3 LRD Isolation of Flows

In Definition 9.2, the index parameter is what differentiates an LRD flow from a short-range dependent (SRD) flow. Although the decay rate and constant parameters also define the queuing process, these parameters form the exponential bound parameters commonly associated with an SRD flow. Hence their presence, by definition, is for the purpose of describing the SRD property of the flow.

The index parameter, found in the Weibull bound formula, was introduced to bound flows exhibiting LRD behavior that cannot be suitably bounded by just the constant parameter and the decay rate. Hence, the LRD property of a flow, by definition, is primarily due to its index parameter. Accordingly, we introduce the following notion of *LRD isolation*.

Definition 9.3. *A flow, when multiplexed with other flows in a queue system, is said to be LRD-isolated (from other flows) in that queue system if its resulting queue process has the same or larger index parameter (i.e., less heavy tailed) as the index parameter associated with its SSQ process with service rate equivalent to that guaranteed in the queue system.*

This notion of "LRD isolation" is different from the conventional understanding of *flow isolation*. In flow isolation, the major concern is the flow's service rate, and *a flow is said to be isolated from other flows if this flow is not adversely affected by these flows* [88]. Based on this, an LRD flow is flow isolated if and only if its queue process is not adversely affected after it is multiplexed and served with other flows in the GPS server.

It can be shown that flow isolation is guaranteed for a flow in a GPS server if the flow can be ordered first in a feasible ordering. The reason is that under this case, the flow is always guaranteed a service rate greater than its long term average rate based on (9.3), which is not affected by other flows. In addition, Lemma 9.11 will show that the flow's queue process in the GPS system is not adversely affected (with respect to its SSQ process) by other flows. However, if the flow cannot be ordered first in any feasible ordering, the guaranteed service rate to the flow may depend on the arrival rates of some other flows. In other words, it may vary over time and hence the queue process of the flow in the GPS system could be affected adversely.[1] As a result, if a flow cannot be ordered first in any feasible ordering, the flow may or may not be guaranteed to be flow isolated from other flows. However, a flow can still be guaranteed to be LRD-isolated (from heavier-tailed flows) even if some lighter-tailed flows have to be ordered before this flow in *all* feasible orderings, as will be discussed later in this section. Clearly, flow isolation implies LRD isolation but not vice versa. Since the index parameter is the most important measure of the LRD property (heaviness or lightness of the tail) of a flow, the notion of LRD isolation as defined above is useful when studying LRD flows.

9.2 Analysis of LRD Traffic

9.2.1 Single Arrival Process

In this subsection, we establish the relationship between a WB SSQ and a Weibull bounded burstiness (WBB) arrival process. We begin by defining the burstiness constraint qualifier that describes the arrival process of LRD traffic as follows.

Similar to the notation in Definition 9.2, let C denote the asymptotic constant, υ the index parameter, μ the decay rate[2], and ρ the long-term "upper rate" of the arrival process, which will be further elaborated in Lemma 9.5.

Definition 9.4. *A traffic arrival process $A(t)$ is WBB(ρ, C, μ, υ) with parameters ρ, C, μ, and υ if it satisfies*

$$P\{A(s,t) > \rho(t-s) + w\} < Ce^{-\mu w^{\upsilon}} \tag{9.5}$$

---

[1] Note that, when $\lambda_i = \phi_i \gamma$, flow i cannot be ordered first according to (9.3), although it is flow-isolated.

[2] Not to be confused with the symbol η, which denotes the decay rate of a WB SSQ process.

for all $w \geq 0$ and all $0 \leq s \leq t$.

Here again, $A(s,t)$ is the amount of arrival traffic accumulated in time interval $[s,t]$. In addition, the decay rate μ will increase with ρ, just as η will increase with γ in a WB SSQ process (see Definition 9.2).

It can be seen that WBB is a special case of a t.a.c. stochastic arrival curve with bounding function $Ce^{-\mu w^v}$. Therefore, WBB has all properties of a t.a.c. stochastic arrival curve. Additionally, WBB has interesting properties useful to the objectives of this chapter, which are presented below.

Lemma 9.5. *An arrival process $A(t)$ that is WBB(ρ, C, μ, v) possesses the property that its parameter ρ is always larger than or equal to its long-term average rate*

$$\rho \geq \lim_{t-s\to\infty} \frac{E[\int_s^t A(u)du]}{t-s}. \tag{9.6}$$

Proof. First, we have

$$
\begin{aligned}
E&\left[\int_s^t A(u)\,du\right] \\
&= \int_0^\infty \Pr\left\{\int_s^t A(u)\,du > x\right\} dx \\
&= \int_0^{\rho(t-s)} \Pr\left\{\int_s^t A(u)\,du > x\right\} dx \\
&\quad + \int_0^\infty \Pr\left\{\int_s^t A(u)\,du > \rho(t-s) + x\right\} dx \\
&< \rho(t-s) + \int_0^\infty Ce^{-\mu x^v}\,dx.
\end{aligned}
$$

Second, as long as $v > 0$, we have

$$\lim_{t-s\to\infty} \frac{\int_0^\infty Ce^{-\mu x^v}\,dx}{t-s} = \lim_{t\to\infty} \frac{\int_0^t Ce^{-\mu x^v}\,dx}{t} = \lim_{t\to\infty} Ce^{-\mu t^v} = 0.$$

Therefore,

$$\rho \geq \lim_{t-s\to\infty} \frac{E[\int_s^t A(u)du]}{t-s}.$$

□

The long-term upper rate ρ is useful for the purpose of bounding the entire ensemble of sample time observations that constitute the stochastic arrival process $A(t)$. In particular, let $A_n(t)$ be the nth sample observation of $A(t)$ in $[s,t]$, and let $\lambda_n = \lim_{t-s\to\infty} \frac{\int_s^t A(n,u)du}{t-s}$ be the corresponding average arrival rate for this sample. If we were to repeat the observation of $A(t)$ infinitely many times using different start times, so that n approaches infinity, then we would have a corresponding list of average arrival rates $\lambda_1, \lambda_2, ..., \lambda_{n \to \infty}$. This long term upper rate ρ ranges between the lower limit $E[\lambda_n]$ and the higher limit $\rho_{max} = \max[\lambda_1, \lambda_2, ..., \lambda_{n \to \infty}]$. For a conservative (loose) WBB bound on $A(t)$, one may set ρ to the higher limit ρ_{max}. However, notice that the long-term upper rate, defined in (9.5), is applied continuously even if the arrival process is inactive. Therefore, a lower value of ρ, where $\rho_{max} \geq \rho \geq E[\lambda_n]$, may suffice to produce a tighter WBB bound on $A(t)$. To summarize, the use of the long-term upper rate ρ in (9.5) is essential for a general stochastic process that may not be stationary (i.e., $\lambda_1 \neq \lambda_2 \neq ... \neq \lambda_{n \to \infty}$). However, in practical arrival processes, stationarity is an implicit property for a flow that has some fixed arrival rate λ. This means that if this flow is presented to the queue at different start times, the same average rate λ applies. Hence, for the case of practical flows, $\lambda_1 = \lambda_2 = ... = \lambda_{n \to \infty} = \lambda$ and therefore $\rho = \lambda$. Although many of the later derivations following this definition are still based on ρ, readers should be aware that for practical considerations ρ ought to be replaced by λ since practical arrival processes are by default implicitly stationary in property. In fact, in the consideration of the GPS and PGPS discipline in Sections 9.3, 9.4, and 9.5, we consider λ instead of ρ. Finally, it is also noted that, besides ρ, the WBB expression in (9.5) also contains other parameters, such as the decay rate μ, the index v, and the asymptotic constant C. These parameters can similarly be modified to obtain either loose or tight WBB bounds.

Following the relationship between the t.a.c. stochastic arrival curve and v.b.c. stochastic arrival curve, the following theorem establishes the relationship between a WBB arrival process and a WB SSQ process.

Theorem 9.6. *Consider a work-conserving SSQ that transmits at rate γ. Suppose the queue is fed with a single arrival process $A(t)$, and let $W^{SSQ,\gamma}(t)$ be the workload stored in the queue at time t. Then:*

(i)   *If $W^{SSQ,\gamma}(t)$ is WB, then $A(t)$ is WBB with long-term upper rate $\rho = \gamma$.*
(ii)   *If $A(t)$ is WBB with long-term upper rate $\rho = \gamma - \varepsilon$ for some $\varepsilon > 0$, then $W^{SSQ,\gamma}(t)$ is WB.*

Although LRD traffic is usually described in terms of some WB SSQ process, it is still insufficient to proceed on to GPS analysis since in GPS we are concerned with multiple arrival processes rather than a single arrival process. If there is no burstiness constraint on a single arrival process, there is not much that can be deduced about the stability of a GPS server that is serving a number of these arrival processes. With the introduction of Theorem 9.6, we can now proceed further since it is now known that any LRD arrival process resulting in a WB SSQ process must satisfy the WBB constraint with some long-term upper rate ρ. This means that for a GPS server serving a number of LRD sources, as long as the sum of the long-term upper rates of these LRD sources does not exceed the service capacity of the GPS server, the GPS queue will be stable and further analysis can proceed.

9.2.2 Aggregate Process

In this subsection, several bounds on the aggregate WB SSQ process are presented, based on the superposition property of the v.b.c. stochastic arrival curve. These bounds will later be used frequently for the analysis of GPS and PGPS.

Lemma 9.7. *Let $W_1(t)$ be WB(C_1, η_1, v_1) and $W_2(t)$ be WB(C_2, η_2, v_2). The two processes can either be dependent or independent. Then, $W_1(t) + W_2(t)$ is WB $((C_1 + C_2 + C^*), \eta, v)$, satisfying*

$$P\{W_1(t) + W_2(t) > w\} < (C_1 + C_2 + C^*)e^{-\eta w^v}, \qquad (9.7)$$

where $\eta = \frac{1}{\frac{1}{\eta_1} + \frac{1}{\eta_2}}$, $v = \min(v_1, v_2)$, and $C^* = (C_1 + C_2)\left[e^{-\eta\left(w_0^{v_{max}} - w_0^v\right)} - 1\right]$.

Proof. According to the superposition property of the v.b.c. stochastic arrival curve, we have

$$P\{W_1(t) + W_2(t) > w\} < C_1 e^{-\eta_1 w^{v_1}} \otimes C_2 e^{-\eta_2 w^{v_2}}$$
$$< C_1 e^{-\eta_1 p w^{v_1}} + C_2 e^{-\eta_2(1-p)w^{v_2}}, \text{ for any } 0 \le p \le 1.$$

We choose p such that $\eta_1 p = \eta_2(1-p)$, i.e., $p = \frac{\eta_2}{\eta_1 + \eta_2}$. Defining $\eta = \frac{\eta_1 \eta_2}{\eta_1 + \eta_2}$ and $v = \min(v_1, v_2)$, we obtain

$$P\{W_1(t) + W_2(t) > w\} < C_1 e^{-\eta w^{v_1}} + C_2 e^{-\eta w^{v_2}}.$$

If $0 < w < 1$, then we have

$$P\{W_1(t) + W_2(t) > w\} < (C_1 + C_2) e^{-\eta w^{v_{max}}}, \qquad (9.8)$$

where $v_{max} = \max[v_1, v_2]$.

If $w \ge 1$, then we have

$$P\{W_1(t) + W_2(t) > w\} < (C_1 + C_2) e^{-\eta w^v}, \qquad (9.9)$$

where $v = \min[v_1, v_2]$.

It is noted that both (9.8) and (9.9) have the Weibull bound form except with different index parameters. Next, we try to combine (9.8) and (9.9) so the same index parameter, namely v rather than v_{max}, can also be used for the case where $0 < w < 1$. First, we notice that the bound using the index v_{max} in (9.8) is always larger than the bound using the index in (9.9) for the range $0 < w < 1$. Once $w > 1$, the bound in $0 < w < 1$ is always larger than the bound in (9.8). At $w = 0$ and $w = 1$, the bounds in (9.8) and (9.9) have exactly the same values. Hence, in order to extend (9.9), which uses the index v, to provide a bound for the same case where $0 < w < 1$, we can always add an additional asymptotic constant factor C^* to raise the bound of (9.9). This additional asymptotic constant C can be easily obtained, as it is related to the maximum displacement between (9.8) and (9.9) when $0 < w < 1$. More specifically, let

$$f(w) = (C_1 + C_2) e^{-\eta w^{v_{max}}} - (C_1 + C_2) e^{-\eta w^v}.$$

Notice that $f(w)$ is zero at $w = 0$ and $w = 1$, and $f(w) > 0$ only for $0 < w < 1$, where both $e^{-\eta w^{v_{max}}}$ and $e^{-\eta w^v}$ monotonically decrease with w. Therefore, there exists a unique maximum point of $f(w)$ for $w \in (0,1)$. Let w_0 maximize $f(w)$ for $0 < w < 1$. Specifically, w_0 is the solution to the following non-algebraic equation:

$$\frac{e^{-\eta w^{v_{max}}}}{w^{v_{max}}} v_{max} = \frac{e^{-\eta w^v}}{w^v} v.$$

Hence the additional asymptotic constant C^* is given by

$$\begin{aligned}
C^* &= f(w_0) e^{-\eta w_0^v} \\
&= (C_1 + C_2) \left[e^{-\eta w_0^{v_{max}}} - e^{-\eta w_0^v} \right] e^{-\eta w_0^v} \\
&= (C_1 + C_2) \left[e^{-\eta \left(w_0^{v_{max}} - w_0^v \right)} - 1 \right].
\end{aligned}$$

Therefore, we have

$$P\{W_1(t) + W_2(t) > w\} < (C_1 + C_2 + C^*) e^{-\eta w^v},$$

where $w \geq 0$.   □

Lemma 9.7 can be applied step-by-step to obtain the following theorem for the case involving multiple WB processes.

Theorem 9.8. *Let $W_i(t)$, $1 \leq i \leq N$ be N WB processes with parameters (C_i, η_i, v_i), respectively. These processes can either be dependent or independent. Then, $W_1(t) + W_2(t) + \cdots + W_N(t)$ is $WB((\sum_{i=1}^{N} C_i + C^*), \eta, v)$, satisfying*

$$Pr\left\{ \sum_{i=1}^{N} W_i(t) > w \right\} < \left(\sum_{i=1}^{N} C_i + C^* \right) e^{-\eta w^v}, \qquad (9.10)$$

where $\eta = \frac{1}{\sum_{i=1}^{N} \frac{1}{\eta_i}}$, $v = \min(v_1, v_2, ..., v_N)$, and C^* is a constant as given in Lemma 9.7.

Given Lemma 9.7, the proof of Theorem 9.8 is straightforward and hence omitted. For N WB queuing processes with the same LRD degree (i.e., the same v), $v = \min(v_1, v_2, ..., v_N)$ is the tightest lower bound on the index parameter. But, for N WB queuing processes with different LRD degrees, it is a loose bound because the index parameter of multiplexed LRD flows is in general heavier tailed than the individual flows due to multiplexing gain.

Similar to the study on the independent case of two gSBB processes, in the case where $W_1(t)$ and $W_2(t)$ are two independent processes, Lemma 9.9 and Theorem 9.10 present alternate bounds to those obtained in Lemma 9.7 and Theorem 9.8, respectively. The alternate bounds are useful since in certain cases they are tighter.

Lemma 9.9. *Let $W_1(t)$ and $W_2(t)$ be two independent processes $WB(C_1, \eta_1, v_1)$ and $WB(C_2, \eta_2, v_2)$, respectively. If $\eta_2 \le \eta_1$ and $v_2 \le v_1$, then for $\forall w > 2$, $W_1(t) + W_2(t)$ has an upper bound of the form*

$$P\{W_1(t) + W_2(t) > w\} < C_2^{WB}(w)e^{-\eta w^v}, \qquad (9.11)$$

where $\eta = \min\{\eta_1, \eta_2\} = \eta_2$, $v = \min\{v_1, v_2\} = v_2$, and

$$C_2^{WB}(w) = C_2 h(C_1) + C_1,$$

where $h(C_1) = 1 + C_1 v \eta(e^\eta - 1) + C_1 w^v \eta$.

Note that the η in Lemma 9.7 is $\frac{\eta_1 \eta_2}{\eta_1 + \eta_2}$, which is always less than or equal to $\min(\eta_1, \eta_2)$, which is the η in (9.11). Hence Lemma 9.9 yields a larger (thus better) decay rate. In fact, if $\eta_2 \approx \eta_1$, then η in Lemma 9.9 is almost twice the value of η in Lemma 9.7. However, the asymptotic constant in Lemma 9.9 increases with w, which is a trade-off. For a heavy-tailed arrival process where $v \to 0$ so that, for practical and finite values of w, $w^v \to 1$ and thus $C_2^{WB}(w)$ approaches a constant, the penalty for using Lemma 9.9 is insignificant. Conversely, if η_2 differs significantly from η_1 (i.e., $\eta_2 \ll \eta_1$), then $\eta \to \min(\eta_1, \eta_2)$, making Lemma 9.7 more attractive.

Table 9.1 summarizes the preferences (in terms of which lemma to use to obtain the bound) assuming that in all the scenarios the queue size of interest is larger than or equal to 2.

Table 9.1. Preference for Lemma 9.7 or Lemma 9.9 in different scenarios

Scenario	Preference
$\eta_2 \approx \eta_1$ and v_2 is small	Lemma 9.9
$\eta_2 \ll \eta_1$ and v_2 is large	Lemma 9.7
All other cases	Either is ok

Similar to the way in which Lemma 9.7 is extended to Theorem 9.8, we now extend Lemma 9.9 to Theorem 9.10, whose proof can be obtained by recursively applying Lemma 9.9.

Theorem 9.10. *Let $W_i(t)$, $1 \le i \le N$, be N independent WB processes with parameters (C_i, η_i, v_i). If the queuing processes can be rearranged such that*

the Nth queuing process has the property that $\eta_N \leq \eta_j$ and $\upsilon_N \leq \upsilon_j$ for $1 \leq j \leq N - 1$, then, for $\forall w > 2$, $W_1(t) + W_2(t) + \cdots + W_N(t)$ has an upper bound of the form

$$P\left\{\sum_{i=1}^{N} W_i(t) > w\right\} < C_N^{WB}(w)e^{-\eta w^{\upsilon}}, \qquad (9.12)$$

where $\eta = \min\{\eta_1, \eta_2, ..., \eta_N\} = \eta_N$, $\upsilon = \min\{\upsilon_1, \upsilon_2, ..., \upsilon_N\} = \upsilon_N$ and

$$C_N^{WB}(w) = \sum_{j=1}^{N}\left[C_j \prod_{l=1}^{j-1} h(C_l)\right], \qquad (9.13)$$

where $h(C_l) = 1 + C_l \upsilon \eta(e^{\eta} - 1) + C_l w^{\upsilon}\eta$, and by convention $\prod_{l=1}^{j-1} h(C_l) = 1$ when $j = 1$.

9.3 Sample Path Behavior of LRD Traffic in a GPS System

Recall from Theorem 9.6 that any LRD traffic input whose queue length distribution is characterized by a WB distribution has an arrival process that satisfies the WBB constraint with some long-term upper rate ρ. Hereafter, we consider N stationary flows that maintain the same long-term average rate λ_i, $i = 1, 2, ..., N$, irrespective of the start time of the flow. As mentioned earlier (in the discussion after Lemma 9.5), the long-term upper rate ρ reduces to the more familiar λ.

9.3.1 GPS Decomposition

Let A_i denote a sample path (or a single realization) of the random arrival process $A_i(t)$ and $Q_i^{GPS,\gamma}$ denote the corresponding sample path of the GPS queue backlog due to the sample arrival process A_i. To obtain relevant bounds on $Q_i^{GPS,\gamma}$, we use a method similar to that in [143] to decompose the GPS system into N fictitious WB single server queues (SSQs), denoted by $\delta_i^{SSQ,\gamma_i}(t)$, with individual rates γ_1, γ_2, ..., γ_N, where $\gamma_i > \lambda_i$, $\sum_{i=1}^{N} \gamma_i \leq \gamma$, and $\gamma_i \leq \varphi_i(\gamma - \sum_{j=1}^{i-1} \gamma_j)$. Now, the reason for considering the N fictitious WB SSQs is that their bounds are easier to obtain and would surely bound $Q_i^{GPS,\gamma}$ as well. This is because the N fictitious WB SSQs do not consider multiplexing gain, while the $Q_i^{GPS,\gamma}$ queue process does.

Without loss of generality, let 1, 2,..., N be a feasible ordering of the fictitious processes with respect to γ_i's. From Lemma 3 of [143], Lemma 9.11 can be derived.

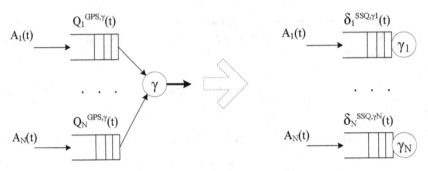

Fig. 9.1. Decomposing a GPS system into N fictitious SSQs

Lemma 9.11. *For any t,*

$$Q_i^{GPS,\gamma}(t) \le \varphi_i \sum_{j=1}^{i-1} \delta_j^{SSQ,\gamma_j}(t) + \delta_i^{SSQ,\gamma_i}(t), \tag{9.14}$$

where each δ_i^{SSQ,γ_i} SSQ process is independent.

Lemma 9.11 provides an upper bound on the queue length $Q_i^{GPS,\gamma}(t)$ of an individual session in the GPS system in terms of the queue length $\delta_i^{SSQ,\gamma_i}(t)$ in the fictitious system. It is clear from Lemma 9.11 that to bound the distribution of $Q_i^{GPS,\gamma}(t)$, it suffices to bound the following aggregate of fictitious queue length processes:

$$\varphi_i \delta_1^{SSQ,\gamma_1}(t) + \varphi_i \delta_2^{SSQ,\gamma_2}(t) + ... + \varphi_i \delta_{i-1}^{SSQ,\gamma_{i-1}}(t) + \delta_i^{SSQ,\gamma_i}(t) \tag{9.15}$$

In what follows, we will provide two bounds on (9.15), i.e., the right-hand side of (9.14).

9.3.2 A General Bound

For N individual LRD flows sharing a GPS server on the condition of queue stability (i.e., $\sum_{i=1}^{N} \lambda_i < \gamma$) and under the assumption that 1, 2,... N is a feasible ordering with respect to ϕ_i and λ_i, $\lambda_i < \gamma_i$ for $i = 1, 2, ..., N$, we present a GPS bound in Theorem 9.12 that is based on Theorem 9.8.

Theorem 9.12. *Each individual queue length distribution in the GPS system has an upper bound as follows:*

$$P\{Q_i^{GPS,\gamma}(t) > q\} < C_i^{GPS} e^{-\eta_i^{GPS} q^{v_i^{GPS}}}, \tag{9.16}$$

where

$$v_i^{GPS} = \min_{1 \le j \le i} \{v_j\}, \tag{9.17}$$

$$\eta_i^{GPS} = \frac{1}{\sum_{j=1}^{i} \frac{1}{\bar{\eta}_j}}, \tag{9.18}$$

$$C_i^{GPS} = \left(\sum_{j=1}^{i} C_j + C^* \right) e^{-\eta_i^{GPS}}, \tag{9.19}$$

and, in the above,

$$\bar{\eta}_j = \begin{cases} \frac{\eta_j}{\varphi_i^{\upsilon_j}} & 1 \le j < i \\ \eta_i & j = i \end{cases}$$

and C^* can be obtained similarly as in Theorem 9.8.

Proof. First, because all the input flows are LRD flows, we have

$$P\{\delta_j^{SSQ,\gamma_j}(t) > q\} < C_j e^{-\eta_j q^{\upsilon_j}}, \quad j = 1, 2, ..., N. \tag{9.20}$$

Secondly letting

$$\delta_{j,eqv}^{SSQ,\gamma_j}(t) = \varphi_i \delta_j^{SSQ,\gamma_j}(t), \, j < i, \tag{9.21}$$

we have

$$P\{\delta_{j,eqv}^{SSQ,\gamma_j}(t) > q\} = Pr\{\delta_j^{SSQ,\gamma_j}(t) > \frac{q}{\varphi_i}\} < C_j e^{-\bar{\eta}_j q^{\upsilon_j}}, \tag{9.22}$$

for $1 \le j < i$, where $\bar{\eta}_j = \frac{\eta_j}{\varphi_i^{\upsilon_j}}$. Finally, since (9.15) can now be written as

$$\delta_{1,eqv}^{SSQ,\gamma_1}(t) + \delta_{2,eqv}^{SSQ,\gamma_2}(t) + ... + \delta_{i-1,eqv}^{SSQ,\gamma_{i-1}}(t) + \delta_i^{SSQ,\gamma_i}(t), \tag{9.23}$$

by combining (9.20), (9.22) and Lemma 9.11, one can easily verify the result in (9.16) based on Theorem 9.8. □

Theorem 9.12 gives a general upper bound on queue length distribution in a GPS system. It is important to note that the GPS upper bound on flow i is not affected by the flows that are ordered after flow i (because they do not factor in the upper bound expression for flow i). It is affected only by flows 1 to $i - 1$, but the impact on the bound is *negligible* as long as flow i is heavier-tailed (i.e., has a smaller index parameter v_i) than any of the flows 1 through $i - 1$. In fact, the index parameter in the bound for flow i is not affected at all as long as flows 1 to $i - 1$ are lighter tailed than flow i.

9.3.3 An Alternate Bound

In Theorem 9.13, an alternate upper bound on individual session queue length in GPS with LRD traffic is provided based on Theorem 9.10. Such a bound may be better than the bound previously given in Theorem 9.12 but can only be applied under the condition that for any given i there exists a $1 \le k \le i$ such that both $\bar{\eta}_k$ and v_k are minimal in addition to the conditions stated for Theorem 9.12.

Theorem 9.13. *If there exists a $1 \le k \le i$ such that $\bar{\eta}_k = \min_{1 \le j \le i}\{\bar{\eta}_j\}$ and $v_k = \min_{1 \le j \le i}\{v_j\}$, then for $\forall q > 2$, the upper bound for individual session queue length is*

$$P\{Q_i^{GPS,\gamma}(t) > q\} < C_i^{GPS}(q)e^{\eta_i^{GPS}}q^{v_i^{GPS}}, \tag{9.24}$$

where

$$v_i^{GPS} = \min_{1 \le j \le i}(v_j) = v_k, \tag{9.25}$$

$$\eta_i^{GPS} = \min_{1 \le j \le i}(\bar{\eta}_j) = \bar{\eta}_k, \tag{9.26}$$

$$C_i^{GPS}(q) = C_k \prod_{l=1,l \ne k}^{i} h_i^{GPS}(C_l) +$$

$$\sum_{j=1,j \ne k}^{i} \left[C_j \prod_{l=1,l \ne k}^{j-1} h_i^{GPS}(C_l) \right], \tag{9.27}$$

with $h_i^{GPS}(C_l) = 1 + C_l v_i^{GPS} \eta_i^{GPS}(e^{\eta_i^{GPS}} - 1) + C_l w^{v_i^{GPS}} \eta_i^{GPS}$, and by convention $\prod_{l=1,l \ne k}^{j-1} h_i^{GPS}(C_l) = 1$ when $j = 1$.

Proof. Without loss of generality, assume that $k < i$. The aggregate process in (9.23) can be rewritten such that the *kth* process with the minimum decay rate as well as with the minimum index parameter appears last in the sequence as follows:

$$\delta_{1,eqv}^{SSQ,\gamma_1}(t) + \delta_{2,eqv}^{SSQ,\gamma_2}(t) + \ldots + \delta_{k-1,eqv}^{SSQ,\gamma_{k-1}}(t)$$

$$+\delta_{k+1,eqv}^{SSQ,\gamma_{k+1}}(t) + \ldots + \delta_i^{SSQ,\gamma_i}(t) + \delta_{k,eqv}^{SSQ,\gamma_k}(t). \tag{9.28}$$

Hence, by applying Theorem 9.10, Theorem 9.13 can be easily verified.   □

Theorem 9.13 provides an upper bound on an actual session i's backlog $Q_i^{GPS,\gamma}(t)$ in the GPS system when there exists a very heavy-tailed LRD flow with the smallest index parameter (as well as the smallest decay rate). One implication of Theorem 9.13, similar to Theorem 9.12, is that it is desirable to order the flows that are heavier-tailed as close to the end of a feasible ordering as possible, again since the index parameter in the upper bound for the individual queue length of flow i will not be affected if and only if the flows 1 through $i - 1$ are all lighter-tailed than flow i.

9.4 Technique to Check and Ensure LRD Isolation

Recall from the discussion immediately following Definition 9.1 that in a stable GPS system where $\sum_{j=1}^{N} \lambda_j < \gamma$, there exists at least one feasible ordering for a given weight assignment. Before we discuss LRD isolation, it is useful to revisit the concept of flow isolation with Lemma 9.14.

Lemma 9.14. *In a stable GPS system, if flow i satisfies the condition:*

$$\lambda_i < \gamma \frac{\phi_i}{\sum_{j=1}^{N} \phi_j}, \tag{9.29}$$

then the flow is flow-isolated.

Proof. The proof is straightforward since the right-hand side of (9.29) is the minimum guaranteed rate. Yet, we still provide the required proof for this lemma since several intermediate results of this proof will be used later to prove newer results pertaining to LRD isolation. Relabel flow i as flow 1 and all other $N - 1$ flows to be flows 2 to N. Note that flow 1 now satisfies (9.3), and hence all we need to show is that the remaining $N-1$ flows can be feasibly ordered after flow 1. To this end, consider a new GPS system with service rate $\gamma' = \gamma - \lambda_1$. Since $\gamma' > \sum_{j=2}^{N} \lambda_j$, the new GPS system is also stable, and hence there always exists a feasible ordering such that (after relabeling the flows 2 to N) we have for any flow $2 \leq i \leq N$

$$\lambda_i < \frac{\phi_i}{\sum_{j=i}^{N} \phi_j} \left(\gamma' - \sum_{j=2}^{i-1} \lambda_j \right)$$

$$= \frac{\phi_i}{\sum_{j=i}^{N} \phi_j} \left(\gamma - \sum_{j=1}^{i-1} \lambda_j \right). \tag{9.30}$$

Note that the equations above becomes the same as (9.3), which means that if flow 1 is ordered first, the remaining $N - 1$ flows can also be ordered to yield a feasible ordering. Therefore, flow 1 is flow-isolated. $\square$

It should be noted that (9.29) is only a sufficient condition for flow isolation, not a necessary condition. In fact, it is a sufficient condition to guarantee a flow to be flow-isolated. However, as mentioned earlier, a flow can still be isolated even if it cannot be "guaranteed" to be flow-isolated, or even if it does not satisfy (9.29).

Based on Lemma 9.14, an obvious method to guarantee the flow isolation of every flow is to assign the weight of every flow according to (9.29) such that every flow i can be ordered in the first place in a feasible ordering. As mentioned earlier, being able to order a flow first in any feasible ordering is the most applicable condition to guarantee a flow to be flow-isolated for, say, admission control purposes. That, however, is not necessary to guarantee just LRD isolation of a flow, which is less strict than flow isolation, as will be discussed later.

9.4.1 Limitations of Existing Methods

In this subsection, we discuss the shortcomings of the existing methods for assigning weights to achieve flow isolation and testing whether a flow can be flow-isolated for a given weight assignment.

A GPS system may support the following three types (or service classes) of flows. A Type 1 flow requires a higher QoS than that provided by flow isolation, so it requires a contract weight that is much larger than $\frac{\lambda_i}{\gamma} \sum_{j=1}^{N} \phi_j$; A Type 2 flow requires flow isolation and thus needs a contract weight that is a little larger than $\frac{\lambda_i}{\gamma} \sum_{j=1}^{N} \phi_j$. A Type 3 flow only requires LRD isolation (but not flow isolation) and thus can have a contract weight less than $\frac{\lambda_i}{\gamma} \sum_{j=1}^{N} \phi_j$. Note that the contract weight cannot be changed as long as the service level agreement (SLA) is in effect. On the other hand, a (lightly loaded) GPS system may assign a flow an *extra* weight (if available) to provide the flow with better service, and such extra weights can be adjusted (e.g., transferred to other flows) by the GPS system.

The method of assigning weights based on (9.29) has a limited applicability in supporting Types 1 and 2 but is not applicable to Type 3 flows. From users or applications' viewpoint, having Type 3 flows is useful because certain applications may require a less strict performance guarantee than that given by flow isolation, and such flows can be admitted into a GPS system and with less costs to the users or applications. In addition, from the GPS system's viewpoint, supporting Type 3 flows allows it to admit more flows than otherwise possible, thus increasing its utilization and potential revenues.

For example (hereafter referred to as Example 1), consider a GPS system with $\gamma = 16$ and five flows numbered 1 through 5 in descending order of their index parameters whose $\lambda_i = i$ where, $1 \leq i \leq 5$. Assume that the total weight is $\sum_{j=1}^{5} \phi_j = 16$, and in addition flows 1 and 2 have been assigned contract weights of $\phi_1 = 1.1$ and $\phi_2 = 4$, respectively. Since the remaining weight for flows 3, 4 and 5 is 10.9 but the sum of their arrival rates is 12, it is clear that (9.29) cannot be used to assign the weights to all three remaining flows to guarantee their flow isolation.

In general, due to the existence of Type 1 flows (e.g., flow 2 in Example 1), flow isolation may not always be achievable by every flow, and accordingly the existing approach based on (9.29) may not be useful. Note that, even if flow i does not satisfy (9.29), it may still be LRD isolated. In Example 1, one can assign 2.6 to flow 3 to ensure its LRD isolation (which can be verified using the technique to be proposed later), even though such a weight violates (9.29).

As another example (hereafter called Example 2) showing the deficiency of the existing approaches, assume that the weight assignment for the same five flows as in Example 1 is now $\{1.1, 2.1, 1, 4, 7.8\}$. It is clear that (9.29) cannot be used to test if flows 3 and 4 (both of which violate (9.29)) are LRD-isolated or not. In addition, (9.3) in Definition 9.1 is not effective either. More specifically, in order to use it to test whether flow 4 can be guaranteed to be LRD isolated or not, a naive approach will test if the ordering of 1, 2, 3, 4, 5 is feasible, and because it is not, it will have to examine the ordering of 1, 3, 2, 4, 5 and then the ordering of 2, 3, 1, 4, 5 and so on. In the worst case, to test if flow i can be guaranteed to be LRD-isolated or not, all possible orderings involving j lighter-tailed flows, where $0 \leq j \leq (i-1)$, have to be tested. Thus, the (worst-case) time complexity of the testing process is $O(i!)$. When the number of flows is large, such an approach is clearly infeasible.

9.4.2 Necessary and Sufficient Condition

We now determine, for a given flow i, not only the set of lighter-tailed flows, denoted by f_i, that can be ordered before flow i in a feasible ordering, but also the minimum contract weight to ensure the LRD isolation of flow i. To this end, we first initialize f_i to be empty. Then, if there exists a flow k where $1 \leq k < i$ that satisfies

$$\frac{\lambda_k}{\phi_k} < \frac{\gamma - \sum_{j \in f_i} \lambda_j}{\sum_{j=1}^{N} \phi_j - \sum_{j \in f_i} \phi_j}, \qquad (9.31)$$

we add flow k to f_i and update the right-hand side of (9.31), which will be denoted by $R(f_i)$. We repeat the process above until no such flow k exists and denote the resulting set by F_i and accordingly the final value of $R(f_i)$ by $R(F_i)$. Note that this process of obtaining F_i has the worst-case time complexity of $O(i^2)$.

One can easily verify that when a flow k that satisfies (9.31) is added to f_i, the resulting $R(f_i)$ increases; i.e., $R(f_i) < R(f_i \cup k) \leq R(F_i)$ if $f_i \subseteq F_i$. Conversely, if we were to add a flow k' that does not satisfy (9.31) to f_i, then $R(f_i \cup k') \leq R(f_i)$. In other words, $R(F_i)$ is the maximum value that flow i can obtain from all flows that are lighter-tailed than flow i. This observation is important for proving the following theorem, which provides a both necessary and sufficient condition for the LRD isolation guarantee of flow i.

Theorem 9.15. *Suppose there are N flows in a GPS system that are numbered in the descending order of their index parameters as $1, 2, ..., N$, and their contract weights are $\phi_1, \phi_2, ..., \phi_N$, respectively. Then flow i is guaranteed to be LRD-isolated from other flows if and only if*

$$\frac{\lambda_i}{\phi_i} < \frac{\gamma - \sum_{j \in F_i} \lambda_j}{\sum_{j=1}^{N} \phi_j - \sum_{j \in F_i} \phi_j} = R(F_i). \qquad (9.32)$$

Proof. (i) To show that (9.32) is a sufficient condition, we note that flow i also satisfies (9.31), just as any flow $k < i$ in F_i does. Accordingly, if we let $F_i' = F_i \cup \{i\}$ and note that when f_i is empty $R(f_i) = \frac{\gamma}{\sum_{j=1}^{N} \phi_j}$, we have the following (based on the observation drawn preceding the theorem):

$$\frac{\gamma - \sum_{j \in F_i'} \lambda_j}{\sum_{j=1}^{N} \phi_j - \sum_{j \in F_i'} \phi_j} > \frac{\gamma - \sum_{j \in F_i} \lambda_j}{\sum_{j=1}^{N} \phi_j - \sum_{j \in F_i} \phi_j} > \frac{\gamma}{\sum_{j=1}^{N} \phi_j}.$$

Accordingly, we can easily conclude that

$$\frac{\sum_{j \in F_i'} \lambda_j}{\sum_{j \in F_i'} \phi_j} < \frac{\gamma}{\sum_{j=1}^{N} \phi_j}.$$

The above means that if we treat the flows in F_i' as one *big* flow with arrival rate $\sum_{j \in F_i'} \lambda_j$ and weight $\sum_{j \in F_i'} \phi$, it satisfies (9.29). Hence, according to Lemma 5.1, there exists a feasible ordering with this *big* flow ordered first. In other words, flow i can be feasibly ordered before any heavier-tailed flow. Note that the exact ordering of the flows within F_i will not affect the LRD isolation of flow i. In fact, the flows in F_i can be feasibly ordered according to the order in which they are added to F_i in (9.31), with flow i being ordered right after them.

(ii) We now prove that (9.32) is necessary by contradiction. Suppose (9.32) does not hold for flow i but there still exists a feasible ordering with flow i ordered before any heavier-tailed flows. Denote the set of all the (lighter-tailed) flows that are feasibly ordered before flow i by F_i^* (which may be empty). According to (9.3), we should have:

$$\frac{\lambda_i}{\phi_i} < \frac{\gamma - \sum_{j \in F_i^*} \lambda_j}{\sum_{j=1}^{N} \phi_j - \sum_{j \in F_i^*} \phi_j} = R(F_i^*).$$

However, since F_i^* contains zero or more flows in F_i and zero or more flows not in F_i, we have $R(F_i^*) \le R(F_i)$ based on the discussion preceding the theorem; or in other words,

$$\frac{\lambda_i}{\phi_i} < R(F_i^*) \le R(F_i),$$

which contradicts the assumption that (9.32) does not hold for flow i.   □

Note that if a flow satisfies (9.29), it will satisfy (9.31) but not vice versa. With (9.32), whether a flow is guaranteed to be LRD isolated or not depends only on the weights assigned to the flows in F_i, and flow i itself. In Example 1, one can easily verify that $F_3 = \{1, 2\}$ and $R(F_3) = (16 - 3)/(16 - 5.1) = 1.19$. Hence, if $\phi_3 = 2.6$, flow 3 satisfies (9.32) and thus is guaranteed to be LRD-isolated. On the other hand, in previous Example 2 (where the weight assignment for five flows is $\{1.1, 2.1, 1, 4, 7.8\}$), one can easily verify that since $F_3 = F_4 = \{1, 2\}$ and $R(F_3) = R(F_4) = 13/12.8$, (9.32) cannot be satisfied by flow 3, and thus flow 3 is not guaranteed to be LRD-isolated. On the other hand, flow 4 satisfies (9.32) and thus is guaranteed to be LRD-isolated.

9.4.3 Weight Adjustment and Assignment

Theorem 9.15 is also useful for weight assignment and adjustment in order to guarantee a flow's LRD isolation. More specifically, the observation drawn preceding the theorem (i.e., $R(F_i)$ is maximum with respect to flow i) serves as the base for determining a minimal ϕ_i to guarantee the LRD isolation of flow i.

For instance, consider again Example 2, but now assume that only the weights assigned to flows 1, 2, and 4 are contract weights (i.e., non-adjustable). If we want to ensure LRD isolation of flow 3, we must increase ϕ_3 to above 13/12.8. Such an increase can be accomplished if ϕ_5 has an *extra* weight of 2 that can be transferred to flow 3 (and, as a result, ϕ_5 is reduced to 5.8 from 7.8).

The technique above to adjust the weight of a single flow to ensure its LRD isolation can certainly be extended to ensure LRD isolation of more than one flow provided that there are extra weights in the GPS system that can be adjusted or transferred. As a slightly different example from those above (which we call Example 3), consider five flows numbered in descending order of their index parameters whose arrival rates are more or less randomly distributed as $\{2, 4, 5, 1, 3\}$. Suppose that $\gamma = 17$ (which is sufficient to make the system stable) and the total weight is a constant 17. In addition, suppose that flow 2 (which is a Type 1 flow) has been assigned a contract weight of 7 (and thus the method based on (9.29) cannot be used for weight assignment to guarantee flow isolation of all the other flows, as discussed earlier). If all four other flows are Type 3 flows that only require LRD isolation, we can use Theorem 9.15 to assign contract weights to them to guarantee their LRD isolation as follows (note that one can easily verify that flow 2 can be ordered first in any feasible ordering, so it is already flow-isolated).

For the first flow, from Theorem 9.15, we need to have $\phi_1 > \lambda_1 = 2$, so we set $\phi_1 = 2.1$ (theoretically speaking, we can set $\phi_1 = 2 + \epsilon$, where $\epsilon > 0$ can have a very small value). For flow 3, we first obtain $F_3 = \{1, 2\}$, and then from (9.32) we have

$$\phi_3 > \lambda_3 \frac{\sum_1^5 \phi - \phi_1 - \phi_2}{\gamma - \lambda_1 - \lambda_2}$$

$$= 5 \cdot \frac{17 - 2.1 - 7}{17 - 2 - 4} = 3.59.$$

Accordingly, we set $\phi_3 = 3.6$ to flow 3. Similarly, we set $\phi_4 = 0.72$ and $\phi_5 = 0^3$. The extra weight available in the system is $17 - 2.1 - 7 - 3.6 - 0.72 = 1.58$, which may be distributed among the five flows in an arbitrary manner.

To further illustrate the usefulness of the proposed technique, let us consider the following corollary of Theorem 9.15 that may be used in the case of online admission control.

Corollary 9.16. *If a flow i is provided a contract weight ϕ_i that guarantees it to be either flow-isolated or just LRD-isolated, it will be guaranteed to be flow-isolated or just LRD-isolated after a new flow j is admitted as long as the system remains stable.*

Proof. Note that, in the corollary, flow j cannot take away any existing contract weights already assigned to the other flows, so its contract weight

---

[3] Note that, with $\phi_5 = 0$, flow 5 gets best-effort service.

can only come from the extra weight available in the system before it was admitted.

If flow i is guaranteed to be flow-isolated before flow j is admitted, flow i must satisfy (9.29). Hence, flow i is guaranteed to be flow-isolated after flow j is admitted.

Now assume flow i was only guaranteed to be LRD-isolated but not guaranteed to be flow-isolated before flow j was admitted. Under this assumption, there existed a feasible ordering in which the set of flows ordered in front of flow i, F_i, are all lighter-tailed than flow i. Now treat $F_i \cup \{i\}$ as one big flow F_i'. Just as shown in Part (i) of the proof for Theorem 9.15, this big flow F_i' satisfies (9.29) and thus can be ordered in the first place in a feasible ordering. Thus, flow i is still guaranteed to be LRD-isolated.   □

Let us continue Example 3 by assuming that the online admission control receives a request for a new flow (flow 6). Suppose that its arrival rate is $\lambda_6 = 1$, and its index parameter is in between those of flows 2 and 3. To ensure its LRD isolation, we first obtain $F_6 = \{1, 2\}$ and then conclude that we need a contract $\phi_6 > 0.718$. Since we have an extra weight of 1.58, we can assign $\phi_6 = 0.72$ and redistribute the remaining extra weight $1.58 - 0.72 = 0.86$ among all six flows.

Note that, from Corollary 9.16, admitting flow 6 as done in the case above will not affect either the flow isolation or LRD isolation of any flows, or in other words, their guaranteed (contracted) performance. There are, however, cases where a heavy-tailed flow has been assigned a weight more than its arrival rate, and hence the remaining weight is not enough to ensure the LRD isolation of the newly arrived flow. An example is that for the same set of five flows described in Example 3, but this time flow 4 instead of flow 2 is a Type 1 flow that requires a contract weight of 5. To ensure each of the four other flows are LRD-isolated, we need the assignment $\{2.1, 4.1, 5.1, 5, 0\}$, which leaves an extra weight of only 0.7. Hence, when flow 6 arrives, it needs $\phi_6 > 1$ to ensure its LRD isolation. In such a case, the system may decide not to admit flow 6 or admit it without ensuring its LRD isolation.

9.5 Sample Path Behavior of LRD Traffic in a PGPS System

The results obtained for the GPS system are now extended to the PGPS system. While the GPS discipline assumes that the input traffic behaves like a fluid such that multiple sessions can be served bit by bit, the packet-based GPS (PGPS) is a more practical discipline in that only one packet at a time may be served. In other words, a PGPS server considers the arrival of a packet only after its last bit has been received. To manage this difference, the PGPS server is often taken to consist of two parts, a regulator and a PGPS core that is a GPS scheduler (see Chapter 4 in [112]), as illustrated in Figure 9.2.

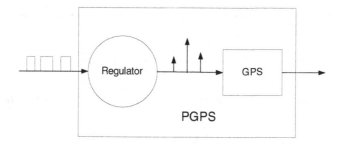

Fig. 9.2. PGPS server

Partially complete (or partially arrived) packets are queued in the regulator, which passes only complete (or arrived) packets to the PGPS core. The output of this regulator, which is the input to the PGPS core, is a series of impulses whose heights represent the sizes of the packets.

Let A_i be the session i input traffic to the PGPS server, which is also the input to the regulator, $A_{i,reg}$ be the output traffic from the regulator, which is the input traffic to the PGPS core, and finally $A(s,t)$ be the total amount of traffic that arrived in time interval $[s,t]$.

It is not difficult to verify that the queuing process of $A_{i,reg}(s,t)$ is also bounded by the queuing process of $A_i(s,t)$ with an extra length L; i.e., $Q_i^{PGPS}(s,t) \leq Q_i^{GPS}(s,t) + L$, where L is the maximum length of all arrived packets (e.g. see Corollary 1 in [113]). From the queuing process Q_i of A_i, which is WB(C, η, v), we obtain the queuing process Q_i^{PGPS} of $A_{i,reg}$,

$$
\begin{aligned}
P\{Q_i^{PGPS}(s,t) > q\} &\leq P\{Q_i^{GPS}(s,t) + L > q\} \\
&= P\{Q_i^{GPS}(s,t) > q - L\} \\
&< C_i e^{-\eta_i (q-L)^{v_i}} \\
&\leq C_i e^{\eta_i L^{v_i}} e^{-\eta_i q^{v_i}},
\end{aligned} \tag{9.33}
$$

which is WB($Ce^{\eta L^{v_i}}, \eta, v$). In other words, the two GPS upper bounds derived in Theorems 9.12 and 9.13 in the previous section can be extended to the PGPS domain via a simple transformation of the asymptotic constant $C_i \rightarrow C_i e^{\eta_i L^{v_i}}$ provided that the queue length or backlog is large enough to exceed the maximum packet length L; i.e., $q > L$. Note that this assumption ($q > L$) is reasonable because in practice the buffer size B is much larger than L (i.e., $B \gg L$) and, in addition, since the main concern is whether the backlog is about to exceed B, the values of q that are of interest should be close to B and thus larger than L.

For completeness, we now present Theorems 9.17 and 9.18 which are derived from Theorems 9.12 and 9.13 respectively via the use of the simple transformation $C_i \rightarrow C_i e^{\eta_i L^{v_i}}$ as follows.

Theorem 9.17. *Let $Q_i^{PGPS,\gamma}$, $1 \leq i \leq N$ represent the ith queuing process of the PGPS system with N LRD arrival processes. Then, at any time t, for* *any queue length $q > L$, where L is the maximum packet length of all the N sessions, we have*

$$P\left\{Q_i^{PGPS,\gamma} > q\right\} < C_i^{PGPS} e^{-\eta_i^{GPS} q \upsilon_i^{GPS}}, \tag{9.34}$$

where υ_i^{GPS}, and η_i^{GPS} have already been defined in (9.17) and (9.18), and

$$C_i^{PGPS} = \left(\sum_{j=1}^{i} C_j e^{\bar{\eta}_j L^{\upsilon_j}} + C^*\right),$$

where C^* can be obtained similarly as in Theorem 9.8.

Theorem 9.18. *Under the same assumptions used for Theorem 9.13 except that the server is now a PGPS server, at any time t, for any $q > L > 2$, where L is the maximum packet length of all the N sessions*

$$Pr\{Q_i^{PGPS,\gamma} > q\} < C_i^{PGPS}(q) e^{-\eta_i^{GPS} q \upsilon_i^{GPS}}, \tag{9.35}$$

where υ_i^{GPS}, and η_i^{GPS} have already been defined in (9.25) and (9.18), and

$$C_i^{PGPS}(q) = C_k e^{\bar{\eta}_k L^{\upsilon_k}} \prod_{l=1, l \neq k}^{i} h_i^{GPS}(C_l e^{\eta_l L^{\upsilon_l}})$$

$$+ \sum_{j=1, j \neq k}^{i} \left[C_j e^{\bar{\eta}_j L^{\upsilon_j}} \prod_{l=1, l \neq k}^{j-1} h_i^{GPS}(C_l e^{\eta_l L^{\upsilon_l}})\right]$$

with

$$h_i^{GPS}(C_l e^{\eta_l L^{\upsilon_l}}) = (1 + C_l e^{\bar{\eta}_l L^{\upsilon_l}} \upsilon_i^{GPS} \eta_i^{GPS}(e^{\eta_i^{GPS}} - 1)$$

$$+ C_l e^{\bar{\eta}_l L^{\upsilon_l}} q^{\upsilon_i^{GPS}} \eta_i^{GPS})$$

and, by convention, $\prod_{l=1, l \neq k}^{j-1} h_i^{GPS}(C_l e^{\eta_l L^{\upsilon_l}}) = 1$ when $j = 1$.

Note that the bounds above shed light on the LRD isolation among LRD sources sharing a PGPS server. To illustrate this, consider a simple case of two independent LRD sources with a feasible ordering of 1, 2. From Theorem 9.12, the source that appears first in the feasible ordering is always guaranteed to be LRD-isolated. Therefore, the queuing process that is of interest is the last queuing process in the feasible ordering, i.e., $Q_2^{PGPS,\gamma}$. By applying Theorems 9.17 and 9.18, three possible sets of bounds can be obtained as follows:
(i) If $\eta_1 \leq \eta_2$ and $\upsilon_1 \leq \upsilon_2$ then from Theorem 9.18 we have

$$P\{Q_2^{PGPS,\gamma} > q\} < C_{2'}^{PGPS}(q) e^{-\eta_1 q^{\upsilon_1}}, \tag{9.36}$$

where

$$C_{2'}^{PGPS}(q) = C_1 e^{\eta_1 L^{\upsilon_1}} h(C_2 e^{\eta_2 L^{\upsilon_2}}) + C_2 e^{\eta_2 L^{\upsilon_2}}.$$

(ii) Otherwise, $\eta_2 \leq \eta_1$ and $\upsilon_2 \leq \upsilon_1$, then from Theorem 9.18

$$P\{Q_2^{PGPS,\gamma} > q\} < C_2^{PGPS}(q)e^{-\eta_2 q^{\upsilon_2}}, \tag{9.37}$$

where

$$C_2^{PGPS}(q) = C_2 e^{\eta_2 L^{\upsilon_2}} h(C_1 e^{\eta_1 L^{\upsilon_1}}) + C_1 e^{\eta_1 L^{\upsilon_1}}.$$

(iii) In general, regardless of the relationship between η_1 and η_2 and that between υ_1 and υ_2, from Theorem 9.17, we have

$$P\{Q_2^{PGPS,\gamma} > q\} < (C_1 e^{\eta_1 L^{\upsilon_1}} + C_2 e^{\eta_2 L^{\upsilon_2}}) \times$$
$$e^{-\eta(q_0^{\upsilon_{max}} - q_0^{\upsilon})} e^{-\eta q^{\upsilon}}, \tag{9.38}$$

where

$$\eta = \frac{\eta_1 \eta_2}{\eta_1 + \eta_2} \quad and \quad \upsilon = \min\{\upsilon_1, \upsilon_2\}.$$

The index parameter (as well as the decay rate parameter) of the three bounds shown in (9.36)–(9.38) indicates the influence of source 1 on source 2. In the first case, the bound on $Q_2^{PGPS,\gamma}$ decays slower, and in fact it adopts the same index parameter as that in the bound on the heavier-tailed queuing process δ_1^{SSQ,γ_1}. This means that source 2 is not guaranteed to be LRD-isolated from source 1. In the second case, source 2 is not much affected by source 1 since the bound on $Q_2^{PGPS,\gamma}$ adopts the same index parameter as the bound on δ_2^{SSQ,γ_2}. Finally, in the third case, which is useful when neither of the first two cases is applicable, the bound on $Q_2^{PGPS,\gamma}$ decays slower than both the bound on δ_1^{SSQ,γ_1} and the bound on δ_2^{SSQ,γ_2}.

9.6 Summary and Bibliographic Comments

In this chapter, by applying the relationship between the t.a.c. stochastic arrival curve and v.b.c. stochastic arrival curve, we have established the relationship between a Weibull bounded burstiness (WBB) arrival process and a Weibull bounded (WB) queuing process, which brings more validity to the analysis of the upper bounds on the queuing process with long-range dependent (LRD) traffic inputs.

In addition, this chapter develops several upper bounds on the queue length distribution of the generalized processor sharing (GPS) scheduling discipline with LRD traffic inputs. The GPS bounds have also been extended to a packet-based GPS (PGPS) system. These explicit bounds contribute additional results to stochastic network calculus. In addition, they show that the long range dependency and queue length distribution of an LRD source in a GPS system will in general not be adversely affected despite the presence of other admitted sources as long as it can be feasibly ordered before other heavier tailed flows.

The content of this chapter is mainly based on [141] by Yu, Thng, Jiang, and Qiao. Also in [141], some numerical results on a PGPS system with LRD input flows are given to demonstrate the usefulness of the bounds. There is a vast body of literature on GPS and PGPS. Some closely related works include [131] [139] [143]. While in [131] the focus is on deterministic constraint inputs, an upper bound is developed for the individual session queue length when the input traffic is short-range dependent and particularly has exponentially bounded burstiness (EBB) [138]. The notion of flow isolation can be found in [88] and the notion of LRD isolation was initially introduced by Yu, Thng, Jiang and Qiao in [141].

Problems

9.1. It is said that (9.29) is only a sufficient condition for flow isolation but not a necessary condition. Give an example scenario where flow is isolated but the condition (9.29) is not satisfied.

9.2. Prove Lemma 9.9.

9.3. Prove Lemma 9.11.

9.4. Prove Theorem 9.17.

9.5. Prove Theorem 9.18.

9.6. For Example 2 where the weight assignment for five flows is {1.1, 2.1, 1, 4, 7.8}, assume that only weights assigned to flows 1, 2, and 3 are contract weights. Find how to adjust the weight to ensure LRD isolation for flow 4.

9.7. In Example 2, let the weight assignment for five flows be {1.3, 0.9, 1.2, 3.8, 7.6}. Find which flows are guaranteed to be flow-isolated and which flows are guaranteed to be LRD-isolated.

A

Open Research Challenges

In this book, stochastic network calculus has been introduced, which is a fundamental theory and framework for performance evaluation of computer networks with focus on stochastic service guarantee analysis. The results presented in the book provide important tools and approaches for understanding the behavior of complex computer networks.

Central to stochastic network calculus are the traffic models and server models that are the focus of Chapters 3 and 4. In Chapters 5 and 6, the following five basic properties were proved under the general case and the independent case, making tractable service guarantee analysis of feedforward stochastic networks possible:

- Service Guarantees – Stochastic backlog and delay guarantees can be derived.
- Output Characterization – The output of a flow from a server can be represented using the same traffic model.
- Concatenation Property – The concatenation of servers can be represented using the same server model.
- Leftover Service – The service received by a flow in an aggregate can be represented using the same server model.
- Superposition Property – The superposition of flows can be represented using the same traffic model.

In addition, in Chapter 7, the analysis was extended to consider different scheduling disciplines and admission control, both of which are critical elements in providing QoS guarantees. In Chapters 8 and 9, traffic conformance and LRD isolation, new QoS measures in addition to delay and backlog, were introduced and studied.

However, there are many changes in the context of or closely related to stochastic network calculus that are critical but still open and require further research. In the following sections, we discuss some of them.

A.1 Applicability Condition Study of Stochastic Network Calculus

As discussed in this book, a key issue of stochastic network calculus is to find proper traffic and server models. Like traditional queuing theory, which has been a successful analytical tool for telephone networks, where the traffic model is represented by a stochastic arrival process and the server model by a stochastic service process, stochastic network calculus is also based on some properly defined traffic models and server models. Different from traditional queuing theory, the traffic models and server models defined for network calculus often rely on the cumulative arrival process and cumulative service process. Under deterministic network calculus, the idea of using an envelope to upper-bound the cumulative arrival process is largely credited to Cruz [28][29], and the idea of using an envelope to lower-bound the cumulative service process is from many researchers (e.g., [18][92][54][129][112]). The traffic envelope is now commonly called the arrival curve and the service envelope is called the service curve in the context of deterministic network calculus. Equipped with these two definitions, many results have been proved for deterministic network calculus (e.g., [28][29][18][92][71]) that have played important roles in the provision of deterministic service guarantees for the Internet [124][40].

Inspired by the definitions of (deterministic) arrival curve and (deterministic) service curve, researchers have extended and generalized these two definitions to the stochastic setting, as discussed earlier in this book. To date, several definitions of stochastic arrival curve that generalize the (deterministic) arrival curve, and several definitions of stochastic service curve that generalize the (deterministic) service curve are available. Surprisingly, the most direct generalizations (e.g., in [24][127][93]), which are special cases of the t.a.c. stochastic arrival curve or weak stochastic service curve discussed in this book, have limited use without additional constraints on the traffic and server models [69][24] [127][93]. In Chapters 3–6, it was discussed that, in order to get the desired results easily, stronger definitions for the stochastic arrival curve and stochastic service curve are needed. Particularly, by revealing the implicit principles of (deterministic) arrival curve and service curve, this book introduces some new definitions for the stochastic arrival curve and stochastic service curve, respectively. With these new definitions, the five basic properties for stochastic network calculus can be proved under both the general case and independent case and are essential to the success of stochastic network calculus and already found in its deterministic counterpart [18][92].

It is shown in Chapter 5 that, without additional conditions, only some combination of a stochastic arrival curve and stochastic service curve can directly provide the five basic properties essential to network analysis. Nevertheless, with additional conditions enforced on the traffic models and/or the server models, other combinations of traffic models and server models may also support the five basic properties. Here several questions immediately arise: What are the additional constraints that make one combination applicable to service guarantee analysis, and what are the implications of these constraints for the analysis and results?

Therefore, the following issues need to be investigated:

- A deep investigation on the applicability conditions of the current traffic and server models for stochastic network calculus.
- A thorough comparison of the conditions on the issue above and their corresponding results, which will provide guidance in choosing the right traffic and server models to obtain optimal results under the stochastic network calculus framework.
- Mapping of existing traffic models and server models in the literature to stochastic arrival curves and stochastic service curves, respectively, so that people who are using these models can grasp and apply stochastic network calculus more easily.
- New traffic models and/or server models that better suit the needs of network analysis.

A.2 Advanced Properties

While the five basic properties make tractable service guarantee analysis of feedforward stochastic networks possible, they are not sufficient in analyze more complex network scenarios for which advanced properties of stochastic network calculus are needed.

- **Feedback Analysis** Feedback is often found in complex computer networks. There are two types of feedback. One is that some output traffic is fed back to the input and becomes part of the input traffic to the network. Another is that some network information such as the output traffic information is used to control the input traffic. For example, the conventional queuing networks with loops may be considered to have the first type of feedback. The Internet Transmission Control Protocol (TCP), which uses window congestion control, relies on the second type of feedback.

  While there are many results for networks with loops, the analysis of congestion control loops has proven to be challenging. To date, simple models exist mainly for the TCP throughput; e.g., [105] [111]. These throughput equations play a crucial role for the design of new network mechanisms and constitute the basis, for example, for the TCP-friendly rate control protocol [46] or the alternative best-effort service [64] for time-critical applications.

  In the context of network calculus, the five basic properties for network analysis introduced and studied in this book are not sufficient for feedback analysis. It is hence critical to formulate feedback analysis in the context of network calculus. Particularly, while the concept of feedback is closely related to control theory, this relation needs to be extended under a different algebra, the min-plus algebra [6] that constitutes the basis of network calculus. In the context of deterministic network calculus, results for the first type of feedback and a fundamental control-theoretic model of window congestion control have been developed (see e.g,. [17] [2] [18] [92] [7], and [82]). However, in the context of stochastic network calculus, there has been little progress on feedback analysis. Since many networks are only capable of providing stochastic services and stochastic service guarantees can better exploit the statistical multiplexing gain and improve the network utilization, studying feedback under and for stochastic network calculus becomes even more important.

- **Multi-access Analysis** In some networks, users share the same communication link using multiple access mechanisms for media access control (MAC). While some of these networks look very simple in structure, their analysis is indeed hard. Existing analysis mainly considers cases where the network is saturated. In addition, it assumes simple and possibly unrealistic traffic or service models. The analysis is based on conventional queuing theory. We believe network calculus provides a new tool that can ease multi-access analysis. However, little progress or effort on this has been found in the network calculus literature. Since wireless networks, where MAC is the fundamental issue, are becoming more and more popular. Multi-access analysis, we believe, is a critical research issue for network calculus that deserves more attention.

- **Data Scaling** In some networks, a flow may be split and/or scale into new flows to be routed to possibly different destinations. One example network scenario is scalable video streaming, where several video streams are generated from the same original stream. These streams may have different quality levels and data rates to suit different users' needs and/or to adapt to network conditions. In such cases, it is essential to study the data scaling property and routing property. While some results are available for deterministic networks [18][45], their stochastic counterparts are still missing for stochastic network calculus.

- **Loss Analysis** Existing studies on stochastic service guarantees have mainly focused on the delay, throughput, and backlog. Very often, results obtained from the backlog analysis are used directly to approximately describe the loss. However, this approximation in general gives loose bounds. It is hence of great interest to study the loss behavior directly and improve the results under the theory of stochastic network calculus. Under deterministic network calculus, there has been some effort to design a composable service model with loss [4], which could be a useful reference for analyzing loss under stochastic network calculus.

- **Dynamic Case Analysis** In this book, most traffic and server models have been defined such that stationary increments are often implicitly assumed. However, traffic processes and service processes may be dynamic and/or non-stationary. Under deterministic network calculus, some effort has been made to address networks with dynamic servers [19]. For stochastic network calculus, interestingly, by extending the various stochastic arrival curve and stochastic service curve models to dynamic case in the same way as used in [19] to extend the arrival curve and service curve to dynamic, almost all results in this book can be easily extended and obtain their corresponding counterparts in the dynamic setting. However, in this case, all the resulting bounding functions will generally be dynamic and time-dependent. Since many results of stochastic network calculus rely on bounding functions, it would hence be interesting to investigate properties of dynamic and possibly non-stationary processes and explore them to provide the desired service guarantees.

In fact, a network often behaves differently over time. For example, due to the bursty nature of traffic sources in the network, the traffic load at one time can be much different from the load at another time with different statistical properties. Such differences over time in network loads and other network conditions have great impact on the analytical results. It hence becomes even more important to perform dynamic and possibly non-stationary case analysis under stochastic network calculus.

- **Time-Domain Modeling and Analysis** In deterministic network calculus, two widely used server models, latency rate (LR) [129] and guaranteed rate (GR) [53], have been proved to be equivalent (see, e.g., [68]). The service curve model for deterministic network calculus can be considered to be generalized from the LR model. Essentially, LR models the service process using the amount of service delivered by the server in some special time period. However, under GR, the service is captured by comparing it with a virtual time function in the time domain. An appealing property of time-domain modeling is that the time-domain model can be easily extended to analyze networks with flow aggregation for deterministic service guarantees [26][71]. However, it is unclear if a stochastic version of the virtual time function can be found and how the corresponding analysis can be performed.

For the research challenges identified above, there are very few results in the network calculus literature. To the best of our knowledge, available results are mainly under the deterministic network calculus framework, as cited above. For stochastic network calculus, all these challenges remain open. One possible reason for this is that the five basic properties were proved only very recently, and the five basic properties are a basis and prerequisite for resolving these open problems.

A.3 Network Information Theory for the Internet

Even though information theory has been very successful in other fields of communications, it is not so for computer communication networks. Two principal reasons have been identified for this failure [38]. One is that information theory has historically focused on the stand-alone point-to-point source-channel-destination model of communication, ignoring the bursty nature of real sources in the network case. Another is that information theory has concentrated on the asymptotic limits of the trade-off between accuracy and rate of communication, ignoring the role of delay, which is a fundamental network quantity.

Recently, there has been attempts to try to bring together information theory and computer communication networks [38][39][136][137][59][102]. However, the studies so far are still being conducted in the restricted framework, with most interest in the capacity or throughput limits in noisy single-channel systems or noisy networks, particularly wireless networks, and with little consideration of the bursty nature and the delay sensitivity of sources in computer communication networks. As a consequence, the literature on network information theory having the goal of transmitting as much data as possible with required service guarantees in computer communication networks remains painfully blank [38][39].

That there is no network information theory that considers source burstiness and delay requirements is indeed not surprising, because of the slow progress in developing a theory for network service guarantee analysis. Without such a theory, it is unknown what kind of service guarantees a network can provide, let alone researching how to achieve the capacity and/or throughput limits in the network requiring service guarantees.

Therefore, it is important to develop results toward a network information theory for the Internet that takes into account the bursty nature and the delay and loss requirements of sources. In this direction, we can analyze the capacity limits of networks with service guarantee requirements and design network approaches to explore and/or achieve network capacity limits, which include scheduling disciplines, buffer management approaches, admission control algorithms, and routing protocols.

References

1. R. Addie, P. Mannersalo, and I. Norros. Most probable paths and performance formulae for buffers with Gaussian input traffic. *European Trans. on Telecommun.*, 13(3):183–196, 2002.

2. R. Agrawal, R. L. Cruz, C. Okino, and R. Rajan. Performance bounds for flow control protocols. *IEEE/ACM Trans. Networking*, 7(3):310–323, June 1999.

3. C. W. Anderson. Extreme value theory for a class of discrete distributions with applications to some stochastic processes. *J. Appl. Prob.*, 7:99–113, 1970.

4. S. Ayyorgun and R. L. Cruz. A composable service model with loss and a scheduling algorithm. In *Proceedings of IEEE INFOCOM'04*, 3:1950–1961, 2004.

5. S. Ayyorgun and W. Feng. A systematic approach for providing end-to-end probabilistic QoS guarantees. In *Proceeding of IEEE ICCCN'04*, 11(13): 115–122, 2004.

6. F. Baccelli, G. Cohen, G. J. Olsder, and J.-P. Quadrat. *Synchronization and Linearity: An Algebra for Discrete Event Systems*. Wiley, New York, 1992.

7. F. Baccelli and D. Hong. TCP is max-plus linear and what it tells us on its throughput. *ACM SIGCOMM Comput. Commun. Rev.*, 30:219–230, 2000.

8. J. C. R. Bennett, K. Benson, A. Charny, W. F. Courtney, and J.-Y. Le Boudec. Delay jitter bounds and packet scale rate guarantee for Expedited Forwarding. *IEEE/ACM Trans. Networking*, 10(4):529–540, August 2002.

9. J. Beran, R. Sherman, M. Taqqu, and W. Willinger. Long-range dependence in variable-bit-rate video traffic. *IEEE Trans. Commun.*, 43:1566–1579, 1995.

10. S. Blake and et al. An architecture for Differentiated Services. *IETF RFC 2475*, December 1998.

11. T. Bonald, S. Oueslati-Boulahia, and J. Roberts. IP traffic and QoS control: The need for a flow-aware architecture. In *World Telecommunication Congress*, 2002.

12. R. Braden, D. Clark, and S. Shenker. Integrated services in the Internet architecture: An overview. *IETF RFC 1633*, 1994.

13. L. Breslau, S. Jamin, and S. Shenker. Comments on the performance of measurement-based admission control algorithms. In *INFOCOM 2000*, 3: 1233–1242, 2000.

14. A. Burchard, J. Liebeherr, and S. D. Patek. A calculus for end-to-end statistical service guarantees. Technical report, CS-2001-19, University of Virginia, 2002.

15. C. S. Chang. Stability, queue length, and delay of deterministic and stochastic queueing networks. *IEEE Trans. Autom. Control*, 39(5):913–931, May 1994.

16. C.-S. Chang. On the exponentiality of stochastic linear systems under the max-plus algebra. *IEEE Trans. Autom. Control*, 41(8):1182–1188, August 1996.

17. C. S. Chang. On deterministic traffic regulation and service guarantees: A systematic approach by filtering. *IEEE Trans. Inf. Theory*, 44:1097–1110, 1998.

18. C.-S. Chang. *Performance Guarantees in Communication Networks*. Springer-Verlag, New York, 2000.

19. C.-S. Chang, R. L. Cruz, J.-Y. Le Boudec, and P. Thiran. A min, + system theory for constrained traffic regulation and dynamic service guarantees. *IEEE/ACM Trans. Networking*, 10(6):805–817, December 2002.

20. A. Charny and J.-Y. Le Boudec. Delay bounds in a network with aggregate scheduling. In *Proceedings of the First International Workshop of Quality of Future Internet Services (QOFIS'2000)*, Lecture Notes In Computer Science, 1922:1–13, 2000.

21. J. Cheo and N. B. Shroff. A central-limit-theorem-based approach for analyzing queue behavior in high-speed networks. *IEEE/ACM Trans. Networking*, 6(5):659–671, October, 1998.

22. V. Cholvi, J. Echague, and J.-Y. Le Boudec. Worst case burstiness increase due to FIFO multiplexing. *Performance Evaluation*, 49(1-4):491–506, September 2002.

23. S. Chong and S.-Q. Li. Probabilistic burstiness-curve-based connection control for real-time multimedia services in ATM networks. *IEEE J. Select. Areas Commun.*, 15(6):1072–1086, August. 1997.

24. F. Ciucu, A. Burchard, and J. Liebeherr. A network service curve approach for the stochastic analysis of networks. *ACM SIGMETRICS Performance Evaluation Review*, 33(1):279–290, June, 2005.

25. F. Ciucu, A. Burchard, and J. Liebeherr. Scaling properties of statistical end-to-end bounds in the network calculus. *IEEE Trans. Inf. Theory*, 52(6): 2300–2312, June 2006.

26. J. A. Cobb. Preserving quality of service guarantees in spite of flow aggregation. *IEEE/ACM Trans. Networking*, 10(1):43–53, February. 2002.

27. M. Crovella and A. Bestavros. Self-similarity in World Wide Web traffic: Evidence and possible causes. *IEEE/ACM Trans. Networking*, 5(6):835–846, December, 1997.

28. R. L. Cruz. A calculus for network delay, part I: Network elements in isolation. *IEEE Trans. Inf. Theory*, 37(1):114–131, January 1991.

29. R. L. Cruz. A calculus for network delay, part II: Network analysis. *IEEE Trans. Inf. Theory*, 37(1):132–141, January 1991.

30. R. L. Cruz. Quality of service guarantees in virtual circuit switched networks. *IEEE J. Select. Areas Commun.*, 13(6):1048–1056, Aug. 1995.

31. R. L. Cruz. Quality of service management in integrated services networks. In *Proceedings of the 1st Semi-Annual Research Review, CWC, UCSD*, June 1996.

32. R. L. Cruz and C. Okino. Service guarantees for window flow control. In *34th Allerton Conference of Communication, Control and Computing. Monticello, IL*, 1996.

33. A. Demers, S. Keshav, and S. Shenker. Analysis and simulation of a fair queueing algorithm. *Internet. Res. and Exper.*, 1:3–26, 1990.

34. N. Duffield and N. O'Connell. Large deviations and overflow probabilities for the general single server queue, with applications. *Math. Proc. Cambridge Philos. Soc.*, 118:363–374, 1995.

35. J. W. Robert (editor). *COST 224: Performance Evaluation and Design of Multiservice Networks.* Commission of European Communities, 1991.

36. A. Elwalid and D. Mitra. Effective bandwidth of general Markovian traffic sources and admission control of high speed networks. *IEEE/ACM Trans. Networking*, 1(3):329–343, June 1993.

37. A. Elwalid, D. Mitra, and R. Wentworth. Design of generalized processor sharing schedulers which statistically multiplex heterogeneous QoS classes. In *Proceedings of INFOCOM*, 3:1220–1230, 1999.

38. A. Ephremides and B. Hajek. Information theory and communication networks: An unconsummated union. *IEEE Trans. on Inf. Theory*, 44(6): 2416–2434, October, 1998.

39. A. Ephremides and B. Hajek. Introduction to the special issue on networking and information theory. *Joint Special Issue IEEE Trans. on Inf. Theory and IEEE/ACM Trans. on Networking*, 52(6):2285–2286, June. 2006.

40. B. D. et al. An expedited forwarding PHB. *IETF RFC 3246*, 2002.

41. D. Y. Eun and N. B. Shroff. A measurement-analytic approach for QoS estimation in a network based on the dominant time scale. *IEEE/ACM Trans. Networking*, 11(2):222–235, April, 2003.

42. D. Ferrari. Client requirements for real-time communication services. *IEEE Commun. Mag.*, 28(11):65–72, Nov. 1990.

43. D. Ferrari. Multimedia network protocols: Where are we? *Multimedia Syst.*, 4:299–304, 1996.

44. M. Fidler. An end-to-end probabilistic network calculus with moment generating functions. In *Proceedings of IWQoS*, 261–270, 2006.

45. M. Fidler and J. B. Schmitt. On the way to a distributed systems calculus: An end-to-end network calculus with data scaling. *ACM SIGMETRICS Performance Evaluation Review*, 34(1):287–298, 2006.

46. S. Floyd, M. Handley, J. Padhye, and J. Widmer. Equation-based congestion control for unicast applications. *ACM SIGCOMM Comput. Commun. Rev.*, 30:43–56, 2000.

47. T. Fry. *Probability and its Engineering Uses*, D. Van Nostrand Company, Inc., New York, 1928.

48. Y. G. G. He and J. Hou. A case for exploiting self-similarity of network traffic in TCP congestion control. In *Proceedings of IEEE International Conference on Network Protocols*, 12(15):34–43, 2002.

49. J. Gallardo, D. Makrakis, and L. Orozco-Barbosa. Use of α−stable self-similar stochastic processes for modeling traffic in broadband networks. *Performance Evaluation*, 40:71–98, 2000.

50. R. Garroppo, S. Giordano, S. Porcarelli, and G. Procissi. Testing α−stable processes in modeling broadband teletraffic. In *Proceedings of IEEE ICC'00*, 3:1615–1619, 2000.

51. P. Glynn and W. Whitt. Logarithmic asymptotics for steady-state tail probabilities in a single-server queue. *J. Appl. Prob.*, 31A:131–159, 1994.

52. P. Goyal, S. S. Lam, and H. M. Vin. Determining end-to-end delay bounds in heterogeneous networks. In *Proceeds of the Workshop on Network and Operating System Support for Digital Audio and Video (NOSSDAV'95)*, 287–298, 1995.

53. P. Goyal, S. S. Lam, and H. M. Vin. Determining end-to-end delay bounds in heterogeneous networks. *Springer Multimedia Sys.*, 5:157–163, 1997.

54. P. Goyal and H. M. Vin. Generalized guaranteed rate scheduling algorithms: A framework. *IEEE/ACM Trans. Networking*, 5(4):561–571, August 1997.

55. A. Greenberg and N. Madras. How fair is fair queuing? *J. of ACM*, 39(3): 568–598, 1992.

56. M. Grossglauser and S. Keshav. On CBR service. In *Proceedings of IEEE INFOCOM'96*, 1(1):129–137, 1996.

57. R. A. Guerin and V. Pla. Aggregation and conformance in differentiated services networks: A case study. *ACM Comput. Commun. Rev.*, 31(1):21C32, January 2001.

58. A. Gulyas, F. Nemeth, and J. J. Biro. A time adaptive stochastic network calculus for long-run network analysis. Technical report, Budapest University of Technology and Economics, March 2008.

59. P. Gupta and P. R. Kumar. The capacity of wireless networks. *IEEE Trans. Inf. Theory*, 49(8):1877–1894, March 2001.

60. F. Harmantzis, D. Hatzinakos, and I. Katzela. Tail probabilities for the multiplexing of fractional α−stable broadband traffic. In *Proceedings of the IEEE ICC'01*, 9:2665–2669, 2001.

61. D. Heyman and T. Lakshman. Source models for VBR broadcast-video traffic. *IEEE J. Select. Areas Commun.*, 4:40–48, 1996.

62. D. Heyman and T. Lakshman. What are the implications of long- range dependence for vbr-video traffic engineering. *IEEE/ACM Trans. Networking*, 4(3):301–317, June, 1996.

63. A. Hordijk, Z. Liu, and D.Towsley. Smoothing effect of the superposition of homogeneous sources in tandem networks. *J. Appl. Prob.*, 37(3):900–913, 2000.

64. P. Hurley, J.-Y. Le Boudec, P. Thiran, and M. Kara. ABE: Providing a low-delay service within best effort. *IEEE Network*, 15:60–69, 2001.

65. P. Jelenkovi. Long-tailed loss rate in a single server queue. In *Proceedings of IEEE INFOCOM'98*, 1462–1469, 1998.

66. P. Jelenkovi, A. Lazar, and N. Semret. The effect of multiple time scales and subexponentially of mpeg video streams on queuing behavior. *IEEE J. Select. Areas Commun.*, 15:1006–1010, 1997.

67. Y. Jiang. Delay bounds for a network of Guaranteed Rate servers with FIFO aggregation. *Comput. Networks*, 40(6):683–694, December 2002.

68. Y. Jiang. Relationship between guaranteed rate server and latency rate server. *Computer Networks*, 43(3):307–315, 2003.

69. Y. Jiang. A basic stochastic network calculus. In *Proceedings of ACM SIGCOMM 2006*, 123–134, 2006.

70. Y. Jiang. Delay bound and packet scale rate guarantee for some expedited forwarding networks. *Comput. Networks*, 50:15–28, 2006.

71. Y. Jiang. Per-domain packet scale rate guarantee for expedited forwarding. *IEEE/ACM Trans. Networking*, 14:630–643, June, 2006.

72. Y. Jiang, P. Emstad, A. Nevin, V. Nicola, and M. Fidler. Measurement-based admission control for a flow-aware network. In *Proceedings of EuroNGI 1st Conference on Next Generation Internet Networks - Traffic Engineering*, 318–325, 2005.

73. Y. Jiang and P. J. Emstad. Analysis of stochastic service guarantees in communication networks: A server model. In *Proceedings of the 13th International Workshop on Quality of Service (IWQoS)*, 2005.

74. Y. Jiang and P. J. Emstad. Analysis of stochastic service guarantees in communication networks: A traffic model. In *Proceedings of the 19th International Teletraffic Congress (ITC19)*, August 2005.

75. Y. Jiang, P. J. Emstad, V. Nicola, and A. Nevin. Measurement-based admission control: A revisit. In *17th Nordic Teletraffic Seminar*, 2004.

76. Y. Jiang, A. Nevin, and P. J. Emstad. Implicit admission control for a differentiated services network. In *Proc. EuroNGI 2nd Conference on Next Generation Internet Design and Engineering (NGI06)*, 2006.

77. Y. Jiang, Q. Yin, Y. Liu, and S. Jiang. Fundamental calculus on generalized stochastically bounded bursty traffic for communication networks. preprint. Submitted for publication, January 2008.

78. A. Karasaridis and D. Hatzinakos. A non-Gaussian self-similar process for broadband heavy traffic modeling. In *Proceedings of IEEE Globecom'98*, 5:2995–3000, 1998.

79. A. Karasaridis and D. Hatzinakos. Network heavy traffic modeling using $\alpha-$stable self-similar processes. *IEEE Trans. Commun.*, 49(7):1203–1214, July 2001.

80. F. Kelly. Notes on effective bandwidths. In *Stochastic Networks: Theory and Applications, Royal Statistical Society Lecture Notes Series, 4. Oxford*, 1996.

81. G. Kesidis, J. Walrand, and C. Chang. Effective bandwidths for multiclass markov fluids and other ATM sources. *IEEE/ACM Trans. Networking*, 1(4):424–428, 1993.

82. H. Kim and J. C. Hou. Network calculus based simulation for TCP congestion control: Theorems, implementation, evaluation. In *Proceedings of IEEE INFOCOM*, 4:2844–2855, 2004.

83. H. S. Kim and N. B. Shroff. Loss probability calculations and asymptotic analysis for finite buffer multiplexers. *IEEE/ACM Trans. Networking*, 9(6):755–768, December 2001.

84. L. Kleinrock. *Queueing Systems, Volume 1: Theory*. Wiley, New York, 1975.

85. E. W. Knightly. Second moment resource allocation in multi-service networks. *ACM SIGMETRICS Performance Evaluation Review*, 25(1):181–191, 1997.

86. E. W. Knightly and N. B. Shroff. Admission control for statistical QoS: Theory and practice. *IEEE Network*, 13(2):20–29, 1999.

87. J. Kurose. On computing per-session performance bounds in high-speed multi-hop computer networks. In *ACM SIGMETRICS'92*, 128–129, Newport, 1992.

88. J. F. Kurose and K. W. Ross. *Computer Networking: A Top-Down Approach Featuring the Internet*. Addison-Wesley, MA, 2000.

89. N. Laskin, I. Lambadaris, F. Harmantzis, and M. Devetsikiotis. Fractional lvy motion and its application to network traffic modeling. *Comput. Networks*, 40(3):363–375, 2002.

90. J.-Y. Le Boudec. Application of network calculus to guaranteed service networks. *IEEE Trans. Inf. Theory*, 44(3):1087–1096, May 1998.

91. J.-Y. Le Boudec and A. Charny. Packet scale rate guarantee for non-FIFO nodes. *IEEE/ACM Trans. Networking*, 11(5):810–820, January 2003.

92. J.-Y. Le Boudec and P. Thiran. *Network Calculus: A Theory of Deterministic Queueing Systems for the Internet*. Springer-Verlag, New York, 2001.

93. K. Lee. Performance bounds in communication networks with variable-rate links. *ACM SIGCOMM Computer Communication Review*, 25(4):126–136, 1995.

94. W. Leland, M. Taqqu, W. Willinger, and D. Wilson. On the self-similar nature of ethernet traffic (extended version). *IEEE/ACM Trans. Networking*, 2(1): 1–15, 1994.

95. C. Li, A. Burchard, and J. Liebeherr. A network calculus with effective bandwidth. Technical report, CS-2003-20, University of Virginia, November 2003.

96. C. Li, A. Burchard, and J. Liebeherr. A network calculus with effective bandwidth. *IEEE/ACM Trans. Networking*, 15(6):1442–1453, December 2007.

97. F. Y. Li and N. Stol. A study on traffic shaping, policing and conformance deterioration for QoS contracted networks. In *Proceedings of IEEE Globecom'02*, 2:1497–1501, 2002.

98. Y. Liu, C.-K. Tham, and Y. Jiang. A stochastic network calculus (revised). Technical report, ECE-CCN-0301, National University of Singapore, November 2004.

99. Y. Liu, C.-K. Tham, and Y. Jiang. Conformance analysis in networks with service level agreements. *Comput. Networks*, 47:885–906, 2005.

100. Y. Liu, C.-K. Tham, and Y. Jiang. A calculus for stochastic QoS analysis. *Performance Evaluation*, 64(6):547–572, July, 2007.

101. Z. Liu and D. Towsley. Burst reduction properties of rate-control throttles: downstream queue behavior. *IEEE/ACM Trans. Networking*, 3(1):82–90, February, 1995.

102. J. Luo and A. Ephremides. On the throughput, capacity, and stability regions of random multiple access. *IEEE Trans. Inf. Theory*, 52(6):2593–2607, June 2006.

103. B. Mandelbrot and J. V. Ness. Fractional Brownian motions, fractional noise and applications. *SIAM Rev.*, 10:422–437, 1968.

104. P. Mannersalo and I. Norros. A most probable path approach to queueing systems with general Gaussian input. *Comput. Networks*, 40(3):399–412, 2002.

105. M. Mathis, J. Semke, and J. Mahdavi. The macroscopic behavior of the TCP congestion avoidance algorithm. *ACM SIGCOMM Comput. Commun. Rev.*, 27:67–82, 1997.

106. S. McCanne and S. Floyd. ns2 — the network simulator. Available from http://www.isi.edu/nsnam/ns/.

107. A. W. Moore. Measurement-based management of network resources. PhD thesis, University of Cambridge, April 2002.

108. A. Muller and D. Stoyan. *Comparison Methods for Stochastic Models and Risks*. Wiley, New York, 2002.

109. I. Norros. A storage model with self-similar input. *Queueing Syst.*, 16:387–396, 1994.

110. C. M. Okino. A framework for performance guarantees in communication networks. PhD thesis, University of California, San Diego, 1998.

111. J. Padhye, V. Firoiu, D. Towsley, and R. Kurose. Modeling TCP throughput: A simple model and its empirical validation. *ACM SIGCOMM Comput. Commun. Rev.*, 28:303–314, 1998.

112. A. K. Parekh and R. G. Gallager. A generalized processor sharing approach to flow control in intergrated services networks: The single-node case. *IEEE/ACM Trans. Networking*, 1(3):344–357, June 1993.

113. A. K. Parekh and R. G. Gallager. A generalized processor sharing approach to flow control in intergrated services networks: The multiple-node case. *IEEE/ACM Trans. Networking*, 2(2):137–150, April 1994.

114. V. Paxson and A. Floyd. Wide area traffic: The failure of Poisson modeling. *IEEE/ACM Trans. Networking*, 3(3):226–244, June, 1995.

115. J. Qiu and E. W. Knightly. Inter-class resource sharing using statistical service envelopes. In *IEEE INFOCOM'99*, 3:1404–1411, 1999.

116. N. Rananand. Upper-bounds for tail probability of a queue with long-range dependent input. In *Proceedings of IEEE ICC*, 3:1466–1472, 1998.

117. J. W. Roberts. Internet traffic, QoS and pricing. In *Proceedings of IEEE*, September 2004.

118. S. Ross. *Stochastic Processes*. 2nd edition, Wiley, New York, 1996.

119. J. S. Sadowsky and W. Szpankowski. Maximum queue length and waiting time revisited: Multiserver $G/G/c$ queue. *Prob. Eng. and Inf. Sci.*, 6:157–170, 1992.

120. J. Sahni, P. Goyal, and H. M. Vin. Scheduling cbr flows: FIFO or per-flow queuing? In *Proceedings of NOSSDAV99*, 1999.

121. G. Samorodnitsky and M. Taqqu. *Stable Non-Gaussian Random Processes: Stochastic Models with Infinite Variance*. Chapman and Hall, London, 1994.

122. H. Sariowan. A service curve approach to performance guarantees in integrated-service networks. PhD thesis, University of California, San Diego, 1996.

123. R. F. Serfozo. Extreme values of queue lengths in $M/G/1$ and $GI/M/1$ systems. *Math. Oper. Res.*, 13(2):349–357, May 1988.

124. S. Shenker, C. Partridge, and R. Guerin. Specification of guaranteed quality of service. *IETF RFC 1633*, 1997.

125. K. Shiomoto, N. Yamanaka, and T. Takahashi. Overview of measurement-based connection admission control methods in ATM networks. *IEEE Commun. Surv.*, 1999.

126. S. Shreedhar and G. Varghese. Efficient fair queueing using deficit round robin. *IEEE/ACM Trans. Networking*, 4(3):375–385, June 1996.

127. D. Starobinski and M. Sidi. Stochastically bounded burstiness for communication networks. In *Proceedings of IEEE INFOCOM'99*, 36–42, 1999.

128. D. Starobinski and M. Sidi. Stochastically bounded burstiness for communication networks. *IEEE Trans. Inf. Theory*, 46(1):206–212, January 2000.

129. D. Stiliadis and A. Varma. Latency rate servers: A general model for analysis of traffic scheduling algorithms. *IEEE/ACM Trans. Networking*, 6(5):611–624, October 1998.

130. D. Stoyan. *Comparison Methods for Queues and Other Stochastic Models*. Wiley, New York, 1983.

131. J. Turner. New directions in communications. *IEEE Commun. Mag.*, 42(1): 50–57, 1986.

132. W. Willinger, M. Taqqu, W. Leland, and D. Wilson. Self-similarity in high-speed packet traffic: Analysis and modeling of ethernet traffic measurements. *Stat. Sci.*, 10:67–85, 1995.

133. D. Wu and R. Negt. Effective capacity: A wireless link model for support of quality of service. *IEEE Trans. Wireless Commun.*, 2(4):630–643, July 2003.

134. H. Xiao and Y. Jiang. Analysis of multi-server round robin scheduling disciplines. *IEICE Trans. Commun.*, E87-B:3593–3602, 2004.

135. G. G. Xie and S. Lam. Delay guarantee of Virtual Clock server. *IEEE/ACM Trans. Networking*, 3(6):683–689, December 1995.

136. L.-L. Xie and P. R. Kumar. A network information theory for wireless communication: Scaling laws and optimal operation. *IEEE Trans. Inf. Theory*, 50(5):748–767, May 2004.

137. L.-L. Xie and P. R. Kumar. On the path-loss attenuation regime for positive cost and linear scaling of transport capacity in wireless networks. *Joint Special Issue IEEE Trans. Inf. Theory and IEEE/ACM Trans. Networking*, 52(6):2313–2328, June. 2006.

138. O. Yaron and M. Sidi. Performance and stability of communication network via robust exponential bounds. *IEEE/ACM Trans. Networking*, 1(3):372–385, June 1993.

139. O. Yaron and M. Sidi. Generalized processor sharing networks with exponentially bounded burstiness arrivals. In *Proceedings of INFOCOM*, 628–634, 1994.

140. Q. Yin, Y. Jiang, S. Jiang, and P. Y. Kong. Analysis on generalized stochastically bounded bursty traffic for communication networks. In *Proc. IEEE LCN'02*, 141–149, 2002.

141. X. Yu, I. L.-J. Thng, Y. Jiang, and C. Qiao. Queueing processes in GPS and PGPS with LRD traffic inputs. *IEEE/ACM Trans. Networking*, 13(3):676–689, June, 2005.

142. L. Zhang. Virtual Clock: A new traffic control algorithm for packet switching networks. *ACM SIGCOMM Computer Communication Review*, 20(4):19–29, September, 1990.

143. Z. Zhang, D. Towsley, and J. Kursose. Statistical analysis of the generalized processor sharing scheduling discipline. *IEEE J. Select. Areas Commun.*, 13(6):1071–1080, August, 1995.

Index